A FRAMEWORK FOR K-12 SCIENCE EDUCATION

Practices, Crosscutting Concepts, and Core Ideas

Committee on a Conceptual Framework for New K-12 Science Education Standards

Board on Science Education

Division of Behavioral and Social Sciences and Education

NATIONAL RESEARCH COUNCIL
OF THE NATIONAL ACADEMIES

THE NATIONAL ACADEMIES PRESS
Washington, D.C.
www.nap.edu

THE NATIONAL ACADEMIES PRESS   500 Fifth Street, N.W.   Washington, DC   20001

NOTICE: The project that is the subject of this report was approved by the Governing Board of the National Research Council, whose members are drawn from the councils of the National Academy of Sciences, the National Academy of Engineering, and the Institute of Medicine. The members of the committee responsible for the report were chosen for their special competences and with regard for appropriate balance.

This study was supported by grant numbers D09121.R01 and D09121.R02 between the National Academy of Sciences and the Carnegie Corporation of New York. Any opinions, findings, conclusions, or recommendations expressed in this publication are those of the authors and do not necessarily reflect the views of the Carnegie Corporation of New York.

Library of Congress Cataloging-in-Publication Data

National Research Council (U.S.). Committee on a Conceptual Framework for New K-12 Science Education Standards.
  A framework for K-12 science education : practices, crosscutting concepts, and core ideas / Committee on a Conceptual Framework for New K-12 Science Education Standards, Board on Science Education, Division of Behavioral and Social Sciences and Education, National Research Council of the National Academies.
      pages cm
  Includes bibliographical references and index.
  ISBN 978-0-309-21742-2 (pbk.) — ISBN 978-0-309-21442-1 (pdf) (print) 1. Science—Study and teaching—Standards—United States. I. Title.
  LB1585.3.N38 2012
  507.1—dc23

                        2012007051

Additional copies of this report are available from the National Academies Press, 500 Fifth Street, N.W., Lockbox 285, Washington, DC 20055; (800) 624-6242 or (202) 334-3313 (in the Washington metropolitan area); Internet, http://www.nap.edu.

Copyright 2012 by the National Academy of Sciences. All rights reserved.

Printed in the United States of America

Suggested citation: National Research Council. (2012). *A Framework for K-12 Science Education: Practices, Crosscutting Concepts, and Core Ideas.* Committee on a Conceptual Framework for New K-12 Science Education Standards. Board on Science Education, Division of Behavioral and Social Sciences and Education. Washington, DC: The National Academies Press.

THE NATIONAL ACADEMIES
Advisers to the Nation on Science, Engineering, and Medicine

The **National Academy of Sciences** is a private, nonprofit, self-perpetuating society of distinguished scholars engaged in scientific and engineering research, dedicated to the furtherance of science and technology and to their use for the general welfare. Upon the authority of the charter granted to it by the Congress in 1863, the Academy has a mandate that requires it to advise the federal government on scientific and technical matters. Dr. Ralph J. Cicerone is president of the National Academy of Sciences.

The **National Academy of Engineering** was established in 1964, under the charter of the National Academy of Sciences, as a parallel organization of outstanding engineers. It is autonomous in its administration and in the selection of its members, sharing with the National Academy of Sciences the responsibility for advising the federal government. The National Academy of Engineering also sponsors engineering programs aimed at meeting national needs, encourages education and research, and recognizes the superior achievements of engineers. Dr. Charles M. Vest is president of the National Academy of Engineering.

The **Institute of Medicine** was established in 1970 by the National Academy of Sciences to secure the services of eminent members of appropriate professions in the examination of policy matters pertaining to the health of the public. The Institute acts under the responsibility given to the National Academy of Sciences by its congressional charter to be an adviser to the federal government and, upon its own initiative, to identify issues of medical care, research, and education. Dr. Harvey V. Fineberg is president of the Institute of Medicine.

The **National Research Council** was organized by the National Academy of Sciences in 1916 to associate the broad community of science and technology with the Academy's purposes of furthering knowledge and advising the federal government. Functioning in accordance with general policies determined by the Academy, the Council has become the principal operating agency of both the National Academy of Sciences and the National Academy of Engineering in providing services to the government, the public, and the scientific and engineering communities. The Council is administered jointly by both Academies and the Institute of Medicine. Dr. Ralph J. Cicerone and Dr. Charles M. Vest are chair and vice chair, respectively, of the National Research Council.

www.national-academies.org

COMMITTEE ON A CONCEPTUAL FRAMEWORK FOR NEW K-12 SCIENCE EDUCATION STANDARDS

HELEN R. QUINN (*Chair*), Stanford Linear Accelerator Center, Stanford University
WYATT W. ANDERSON, Department of Genetics, University of Georgia, Athens
TANYA ATWATER, Department of Earth Science, University of California, Santa Barbara
PHILIP BELL, Learning Sciences, University of Washington, Seattle
THOMAS B. CORCORAN, Teachers College, Columbia University
RODOLFO DIRZO, Department of Biology, Stanford University
PHILLIP A. GRIFFITHS, Institute for Advanced Study, Princeton, New Jersey
DUDLEY R. HERSCHBACH, Department of Chemistry and Chemical Biology, Harvard University
LINDA P.B. KATEHI, Office of the Chancellor, University of California, Davis
JOHN C. MATHER, NASA Goddard Space Flight Center, Greenbelt, Maryland
BRETT D. MOULDING, Utah Partnership for Effective Science Teaching and Learning, Ogden
JONATHAN OSBORNE, School of Education, Stanford University
JAMES W. PELLEGRINO, Department of Psychology and Learning Sciences Research Institute, University of Illinois at Chicago
STEPHEN L. PRUITT, Office of the State Superintendent of Schools, Georgia Department of Education (until June 2010)
BRIAN REISER, School of Education and Social Policy, Northwestern University
REBECCA R. RICHARDS-KORTUM, Department of Bioengineering, Rice University
WALTER G. SECADA, School of Education, University of Miami
DEBORAH C. SMITH, Department of Curriculum and Instruction, Pennsylvania State University

HEIDI A. SCHWEINGRUBER, *Study Co-director*
THOMAS E. KELLER, *Study Co-director*
MICHAEL A. FEDER, *Senior Program Officer* (until February 2011)
MARTIN STORKSDIECK, *Board Director*
KELLY A. DUNCAN, *Senior Program Assistant* (until October 2010)
REBECCA KRONE, *Program Associate*
STEVEN MARCUS, *Editorial Consultant*

BOARD ON SCIENCE EDUCATION

HELEN R. QUINN (*Chair*), Stanford Linear Accelerator Center, Stanford University
PHILIP BELL, Learning Sciences, University of Washington, Seattle
GEORGE BOGGS, American Association of Community Colleges (retired), Washington, DC
WILLIAM B. BONVILLIAN, Washington, DC, Office, Massachusetts Institute of Technology
JOSEPH FRANCISCO, Department of Chemistry, Purdue University
ADAM GAMORAN, Center for Education Research, University of Wisconsin–Madison
JERRY P. GOLLUB, Natural Sciences and Physics Departments, Haverford College
MARGARET A. HONEY, New York Hall of Science, New York
JANET HUSTLER, Partnership for Student Success in Science (PS³), Synopsys, Inc., Mountain View, California
SUSAN KIEFFER, Department of Geology, University of Illinois, Urbana
BRETT D. MOULDING, Utah Partnership for Effective Science Teaching and Learning, Ogden
CARLO PARRAVANO, Merck Institute for Science Education, Rahway, New Jersey
SUSAN R. SINGER, Department of Biology, Carleton College
WILLIAM B. WOOD, Department of Cellular and Developmental Biology, University of Colorado, Boulder

MARTIN STORKSDIECK, *Director*
HEIDI A. SCHWEINGRUBER, *Deputy Director*
MICHAEL A. FEDER, *Senior Program Officer* (until February 2011)
MARGARET L. HILTON, *Senior Program Officer*
THOMAS E. KELLER, *Senior Program Officer*
NATALIE NIELSEN, *Senior Program Officer*
SHERRIE FORREST, *Associate Program Officer*
REBECCA KRONE, *Program Associate*
ANTHONY BROWN, *Senior Program Assistant*
KELLY DUNCAN, *Senior Program Assistant* (until October 2010)

CONTENTS

FOREWORD

A *Framework for K-12 Science Education* represents the first step in a process to create new standards in K-12 science education. This project capitalizes on a major opportunity that exists at this moment—a large number of states are adopting common standards in mathematics and English/language arts and thus are poised to consider adoption of common standards in K-12 science education. The impetus for this project grew from the recognition that, although the existing national documents on science content for grades K-12 (developed in the early to mid-1990s) were an important step in strengthening science education, there is much room for improvement. Not only has science progressed, but the education community has learned important lessons from 10 years of implementing standards-based education, and there is a new and growing body of research on learning and teaching in science that can inform a revision of the standards and revitalize science education.

In this context, the Carnegie Corporation of New York, together with the Institute for Advanced Study, established a commission that issued a report entitled *The Opportunity Equation,* calling for a common set of standards in science to be developed. The Carnegie Corporation has taken a leadership role to ensure that the development of common science standards proceeds and is of the highest quality by funding a two-step process: first, the development of this framework by the National Research Council (NRC) and, second, the development of a next generation of science standards based on the framework led by Achieve, Inc. We are grateful for the financial support of the Carnegie Corporation for this project and for their vision in establishing the partnership and two-step process for developing the new standards.

This framework builds on the strong foundation of previous studies that sought to identify and describe the major ideas for K-12 science education. These include *Science for All Americans* and *Benchmarks for Science Literacy* (1993), developed by the American Association for the Advancement of Science (AAAS), and the *National Science Education Standards* (1996), developed by the NRC. The framework is also informed by more recent work of two of our partner organizations: the AAAS (in Project 2061 especially) and the National Science Teachers Association (particularly the 2009 Anchors project). Achieve, Inc., our third partner is this endeavor, will lead the development of next-generation standards for science education based on the framework presented in this report with the aspiration that many states will choose to adopt them. We look forward to working with these organizations in the dissemination and implementation of the vision of science and engineering education that the framework embodies.

The framework highlights the power of integrating understanding the ideas of science with engagement in the practices of science and is designed to build students' proficiency and appreciation for science over multiple years of school. Of particular note is the prominent place given to the ideas and practices of engineering.

As presidents of the National Academy of Sciences and National Academy of Engineering, we are pleased to convey this report to interested readers. We believe that the education of the children of this nation is a vital national concern. The understanding of, and interest in, science and engineering that its citizens bring to bear in their personal and civic decision making is critical to good decisions about the nation's future. The percentage of students who are motivated by their school and out-of-school experiences to pursue careers in these fields is currently too low for the nation's needs. Moreover, an ever-larger number of jobs require skills in these areas, along with those in language arts and mathematics.

We thank the committee and the many consultants and NRC staff members who contributed to this effort, as well as the thousands who took the time to comment on the draft that was made public in July 2010. That input contributed substantially to the quality of this final report.

Ralph J. Cicerone, *President*, National Academy of Sciences
Charles M. Vest, *President*, National Academy of Engineering

ACKNOWLEDGMENTS

Together with the rest of the committee, I thank the many individuals and organizations who assisted us in our work, without whom this study could not have been completed. We begin by acknowledging the generous support of the Carnegie Corporation of New York, and particularly Andrés Henriquez, for his attention to and patience with this project.

Next we recognize the importance of the partnership we developed with Achieve, Inc., the American Association for the Advancement of Science, and the National Science Teachers Association, and we are pleased to be continuing this partnership. Each organization brought its unique perspective to our many partner meetings, which led to a stronger report and better communication with the myriad communities with an interest in K-12 science education. Each of these partners has an important role to play as the implementation of ideas in the framework develops.

This report would not have been possible without the work of many individuals, teams, and organizations, and we hope we acknowledge them all here. The four design teams (listed in Appendix D) were critical in the development of the framework and providing the committee with insightful and creative models for organizing the core ideas. We are deeply indebted to them and especially to the four team leaders: Rodger Bybee, Joseph Krajcik, Cary Sneider, and Michael Wysession. These team leaders worked closely with the committee until the final stages of the project, tirelessly revising drafts of their work, discussing the research, debating possible approaches, and consistently going above and beyond their initial commitments. The work would have been impossible without them.

The committee also called on many individual experts in a variety of capacities. Some served as presenters, others provided detailed reviews of the draft framework released in July 2010, still others worked closely with groups of committee members to refine portions of the report, and a select few filled all three roles. We acknowledge Valerie Akerson, Indiana University; Charles "Andy" Anderson, Michigan State University; Angela Calabrese Barton, Michigan State University; Anita Bernhardt, Department of Education, Maine; Nancy Brickhouse, University of Delaware; Ravit Golan Duncan, Rutgers University; Daniel Edelson, National Geographic Society; Jacob Foster, Massachusetts Department of Elementary and Secondary Education; Adam Gamoran, University of Wisconsin–Madison; David Hammer, University of Maryland, College Park; David Heil, David Heil & Associates; Leslie Herrenkohl, University of Washington; Frank Keil, Yale University; Rich Lehrer, Vanderbilt University; Kathy Metz, University of California, Berkeley; Jacqueline Miller, Education Development Center; Alberto Rodriguez, San Diego State University; Aaron Rogat, Columbia University; Jo Ellen Roseman, American Association for the Advancement of Science; Leona Schauble, Vanderbilt University; Eugenie Scott, National Center for Science Education; Susan Singer, Carleton College; Jean Slattery, Achieve, Inc.; Carol Smith, University of Massachusetts at Boston; Maria Varelas, University of Illinois at Chicago; Beth Warren, TERC; Iris Weiss, Horizon Research, Inc.; and Marianne Wiser, Clark University.

The committee also benefited from the extensive feedback on the draft released during the public comment period in summer 2010. We thank the large number of individuals who sent thoughtful comments as well as the many stakeholder groups and their leaders who were generous in recording and sending us discussion group feedback (see Appendix A). The committee found this feedback invaluable in revising the report, and we think it has greatly improved the quality of the final document.

We are also deeply grateful to the many individuals at the National Research Council (NRC) who assisted the committee. The success of a large project such as the framework involves the efforts of countless staff members who work behind the scenes. We acknowledge the support and commitment of the project co-directors, Heidi Schweingruber, whose dedication to this work was demonstrated time and again at every stage of the work, and Tom Keller, who likewise played many critical roles in the process. We are grateful for the extensive, thoughtful, and cheerfully supportive work of additional staff of the Board on Science Education (BOSE) who rose to the urgency of the task time and time again—Kelly

Duncan, Rebecca Krone, Michael Feder, Natalie Nielsen, Sherrie Forrest, Mengfei Huang (a Mirzayan fellow with BOSE), and Martin Storksdieck. Matthew Von Hendy provided valuable research assistance.

We also thank Kirsten Sampson Snyder, who shepherded the report through the NRC review process; Christine McShane, who edited the draft report; and Yvonne Wise for processing the report through final production. We were also aided by the editorial skills of Steve Marcus; the work of the staff of the National Academies Press, including Virginia Bryant, Rachel Marcus, and Stephen Mautner; and Doug Sprunger in the DBASSE communications office. We owe a special debt of thanks to Sara Frueh, who worked closely with project staff on communications and press issues and attended many meetings of the four partners to discuss communication and dissemination strategy.

Prior to the public comment period, the draft underwent a condensed version of an NRC internal review. We thank the following individuals for their review of the draft report: Richard A. Duschl, College of Education, Pennsylvania State University; W.G. Ernst, Department of Geological and Environmental Sciences, Stanford University; Kim A. Kastens, Lamont-Doherty Earth Observatory, Columbia University; and Elizabeth K. Stage, Lawrence Hall of Science, University of California, Berkeley. The initial review was overseen by Lauress (Laurie) L. Wise, Human Resources Research Organization (HumRRO), Monterey, CA; and Jerry P. Gollub, Physics Department, Haverford College.

A revised draft of this report was reviewed by individuals chosen for their diverse perspective and technical expertise, in accordance with procedures approved by the NRC's Report Review Committee. The purpose of this independent review is to provide candid and critical comments that will assist the institution in making its published report as sound as possible and to ensure that the report meets institutional standards for objectivity, evidence, and responsiveness to the study charge. The review comments and draft manuscript remain confidential to protect the integrity of the deliberative process.

We thank the following individuals for their review of this report: Cristina Amon, dean, Faculty of Applied Science and Engineering, alumni chair professor of bioengineering, Department of Mechanical and Industrial Engineering, University of Toronto; William B. Bridges, Carl F. Braun professor of engineering, emeritus, California Institute of Technology; Marye Anne Fox, chancellor, Office of the Chancellor, University of California, San Diego; Kenji Hakuta, School of Education, Stanford University; John M. Hayes, scientist emeritus, Woods Hole Oceanographic Institution; John R. Jungck, Department of Biology,

Beloit College; Ron Latanision, corporate vice president, Exponent, Natick, MA; Richard Lehrer, Department of Teaching and Learning, Peabody College of Vanderbilt University; Michael E. Martinez, Department of Education, University of California, Irvine; Jennifer O'Day, principal research scientist, Education Program, American Institutes for Research, Sacramento, CA; Carlo Parravano, executive director, Merck Institute for Science Education, Rahway, NJ; R. Bruce Partridge, Department of Astronomy, Haverford College; Roy D. Pea, School of Education, Stanford University; Jana Rowland, science education director, Office of Standards and Curriculum, Oklahoma State Department of Education; Philip Rubin, chief executive officer, Haskins Laboratories, New Haven, CT; Wilfried Schmid, Mathematics Department, Harvard University; H. Eugene Stanley, university professor, and professor of physics, chemistry, physiology, and biomedical engineering, Department of Physics, Boston University; Suzanne M. Wilson, chair, Department of Teacher Education, Michigan State University; William B. Wood, distinguished professor, emeritus, Department of Biology, University of Colorado, Boulder; Yu Xie, Otis Dudley Duncan distinguished university professor of sociology, Population Studies Center, University of Michigan; and Clarice M. Yentsch, adjunct research scientist, Oceanographic Center, Nova Southeastern University.

Although the reviewers listed above have provided constructive comments and suggestions, they are not asked to endorse the conclusions or recommendations, nor did they see the final draft of the report before its release. Lorraine McDonnell and Jerry P. Gollub oversaw the review of this report. Appointed by the NRC, they were responsible for making certain that an independent examination of this report was carried out in accordance with institutional procedures and that all review comments were carefully considered. Responsibility for the final content of this report rests entirely with the authoring committee and the institution.

Finally, I would like to add my personal thanks, in particular to Heidi Schweingruber, without whose wise advice and support I could not have done my part of the job, and to my colleagues on the committee for their enthusiasm, hard work, and collaborative spirit in writing this report. They attended six meetings of two or more days in length, freely provided their comments, engaged in spirited discussion, read and commented on numerous drafts, and worked at a furious pace.

Helen R. Quinn, *Chair*
Committee on a Conceptual Framework for New K-12 Science Education Standards

SUMMARY

Science, engineering, and technology permeate nearly every facet of modern life, and they also hold the key to meeting many of humanity's most pressing current and future challenges. Yet too few U.S. workers have strong backgrounds in these fields, and many people lack even fundamental knowledge of them. This national trend has created a widespread call for a new approach to K-12 science education in the United States.

The Committee on a Conceptual Framework for New K-12 Science Education Standards was charged with developing a framework that articulates a broad set of expectations for students in science. The overarching goal of our framework for K-12 science education is to ensure that by the end of 12th grade, *all* students have some appreciation of the beauty and wonder of science; possess sufficient knowledge of science and engineering to engage in public discussions on related issues; are careful consumers of scientific and technological information related to their everyday lives; are able to continue to learn about science outside school; and have the skills to enter careers of their choice, including (but not limited to) careers in science, engineering, and technology.

Currently, K-12 science education in the United States fails to achieve these outcomes, in part because it is not organized systematically across multiple years of school, emphasizes discrete facts with a focus on breadth over depth, and does not provide students with engaging opportunities to experience how science is actually done. The framework is designed to directly address and overcome these weaknesses.

The framework is based on a rich and growing body of research on teaching and learning in science, as well as on nearly two decades of efforts to define foundational knowledge and skills for K-12 science and engineering. From this work, the committee concludes that K-12 science and engineering education should focus on a limited number of disciplinary core ideas and crosscutting concepts, be designed so that students continually build on and revise their knowledge and abilities over multiple years, and support the integration of such knowledge and abilities with the practices needed to engage in scientific inquiry and engineering design.

The committee recommends that science education in grades K-12 be built around three major dimensions (see Box S-1 for details of each dimension). These dimensions are

- Scientific and engineering practices
- Crosscutting concepts that unify the study of science and engineering through their common application across fields
- Core ideas in four disciplinary areas: physical sciences; life sciences; earth and space sciences; and engineering, technology, and applications of science

To support students' meaningful learning in science and engineering, all three dimensions need to be integrated into standards, curriculum, instruction, and assessment. Engineering and technology are featured alongside the natural sciences (physical sciences, life sciences, and earth and space sciences) for two critical reasons: (1) to reflect the importance of understanding the human-built world and (2) to recognize the value of better integrating the teaching and learning of science, engineering, and technology.

The broad set of expectations for students articulated in the framework is intended to guide the development of new standards that in turn guide revisions to science-related curriculum, instruction, assessment, and professional development for educators. A coherent and consistent approach throughout grades K-12 is key to realizing the vision for science and engineering education embodied in the framework: that students, over multiple years of school, actively engage in science and engineering practices and apply crosscutting concepts to deepen their understanding of each field's disciplinary core ideas.

The framework represents the first step in a process that should inform state-level decisions and provide a research-grounded basis for improving science teaching and learning across the country. It is intended to guide standards developers, curriculum designers, assessment developers, state and district science

THE THREE DIMENSIONS OF THE FRAMEWORK

1 Scientific and Engineering Practices
1. Asking questions (for science) and defining problems (for engineering)
2. Developing and using models
3. Planning and carrying out investigations
4. Analyzing and interpreting data
5. Using mathematics and computational thinking
6. Constructing explanations (for science) and designing solutions (for engineering)
7. Engaging in argument from evidence
8. Obtaining, evaluating, and communicating information

2 Crosscutting Concepts
1. Patterns
2. Cause and effect: Mechanism and explanation
3. Scale, proportion, and quantity
4. Systems and system models
5. Energy and matter: Flows, cycles, and conservation
6. Structure and function
7. Stability and change

3 Disciplinary Core Ideas
Physical Sciences
PS1: Matter and its interactions
PS2: Motion and stability: Forces and interactions
PS3: Energy
PS4: Waves and their applications in technologies for information transfer

Life Sciences
LS1: From molecules to organisms: Structures and processes
LS2: Ecosystems: Interactions, energy, and dynamics
LS3: Heredity: Inheritance and variation of traits
LS4: Biological evolution: Unity and diversity

Earth and Space Sciences
ESS1: Earth's place in the universe
ESS2: Earth's systems
ESS3: Earth and human activity

Engineering, Technology, and Applications of Science
ETS1: Engineering design
ETS2: Links among engineering, technology, science, and society

administrators, professionals responsible for science teacher education, and science educators working in informal settings.

The report also identifies the challenges inherent in aligning the components of K-12 science education with this new vision for science and engineering education, provides recommendations for standards development, and lays out a research agenda that would generate the insights needed to update the framework and inform new standards in the future. The committee emphasizes that greater improvements in K-12 science and engineering education will be made when all components of the system—from standards and assessments, to support for new and established teachers, to providing sufficient time for learning science—are aligned with the framework's vision.

PART I

A VISION FOR K-12 SCIENCE EDUCATION

1

A NEW CONCEPTUAL FRAMEWORK

Science and engineering—significant parts of human culture that represent some of the pinnacles of human achievement—are not only major intellectual enterprises but also can improve people's lives in fundamental ways. Although the intrinsic beauty of science and a fascination with how the world works have driven exploration and discovery for centuries, many of the challenges that face humanity now and in the future—related, for example, to the environment, energy, and health—require social, political, and economic solutions that must be informed deeply by knowledge of the underlying science and engineering.

Many recent calls for improvements in K-12 science education have focused on the need for science and engineering professionals to keep the United States competitive in the international arena. Although there is little doubt that this need is genuine, a compelling case can also be made that understanding science and engineering, now more than ever, is essential for every American citizen. Science, engineering, and the technologies they influence permeate every aspect of modern life. Indeed, some knowledge of science and engineering is required to engage with the major public policy issues of today as well as to make informed everyday decisions, such as selecting among alternative medical treatments or determining how to invest public funds for water supply options. In addition, understanding science and the extraordinary insights it has produced can be meaningful and relevant on a personal level, opening new worlds to explore and offering lifelong opportunities for enriching people's lives. In these contexts, learning science is important for everyone, even those who eventually choose careers in fields other than science or engineering.

The conceptual framework presented in this report of the Committee on a Conceptual Framework for New K-12 Science Education Standards articulates the committee's vision of the scope and nature of the education in science, engineering, and technology needed for the 21st century. It is intended as a guide to the next step, which is the process of developing standards for all students. Thus it describes the major practices, crosscutting concepts, and disciplinary core ideas that all students should be familiar with by the end of high school, and it provides an outline of how these practices, concepts, and ideas should be developed across the grade levels. Engineering and technology are featured alongside the physical sciences, life sciences, and earth and space sciences for two critical reasons: to reflect the importance of understanding the human-built world and to recognize the value of better integrating the teaching and learning of science, engineering, and technology.

By framework we mean a broad description of the content and sequence of learning expected of all students by the completion of high school—but not at the level of detail of grade-by-grade standards or, at the high school level, course descriptions and standards. Instead, as this document lays out, the framework is intended as a guide to standards developers as well as for curriculum designers, assessment developers, state and district science administrators, professionals responsible for science teacher education, and science educators working in informal settings.

There are two primary reasons why a new framework is needed at this time. One is that it has been 15 or more years since the last comparable effort at the national scale, and new understandings both in science and in teaching and learning science have developed over that time. The second is the opportunity provided by a movement of multiple states to adopt common standards in mathematics and in language arts, which has prompted interest in comparable documents for science. This framework is the first part of a two-stage process to produce a next-generation set of science standards for voluntary adoption by states. The second step—the development of a set of standards based on this framework—is a state-led effort coordinated by Achieve, Inc., involving multiple opportunities for input from the states' science educators, including teachers, and the public.

A VISION FOR K-12 EDUCATION IN THE SCIENCES AND ENGINEERING

The framework is designed to help realize a vision for education in the sciences and engineering in which students, over multiple years of school, actively engage in scientific and engineering practices and apply crosscutting concepts to deepen

their understanding of the core ideas in these fields. The learning experiences provided for students should engage them with fundamental questions about the world and with how scientists have investigated and found answers to those questions. Throughout grades K-12, students should have the opportunity to carry out scientific investigations and engineering design projects related to the disciplinary core ideas.

By the end of the 12th grade, students should have gained sufficient knowledge of the practices, crosscutting concepts, and core ideas of science and engineering to engage in public discussions on science-related issues, to be critical consumers of scientific information related to their everyday lives, and to continue to learn about science throughout their lives. They should come to appreciate that science and the current scientific understanding of the world are the result of many hundreds of years of creative human endeavor. It is especially important to note that the above goals are for all students, not just those who pursue careers in science, engineering, or technology or those who continue on to higher education.

We anticipate that the insights gained and interests provoked from studying and engaging in the practices of science and engineering during their K-12 schooling should help students see how science and engineering are instrumental in addressing major challenges that confront society today, such as generating sufficient energy, preventing and treating diseases, maintaining supplies of clean water and food, and solving the problems of global environmental change. In addition, although not all students will choose to pursue careers in science, engineering, or technology, we hope that a science education based on the framework will motivate and inspire a greater number of people—and a better representation

> The framework is designed to help realize a vision for education in the sciences and engineering in which students, over multiple years of school, actively engage in scientific and engineering practices and apply crosscutting concepts to deepen their understanding of the core ideas in these fields.

of the broad diversity of the American population—to follow these paths than is the case today.

The committee's vision takes into account two major goals for K-12 science education: (1) educating all students in science and engineering and (2) providing the foundational knowledge for those who will become the scientists, engineers, technologists, and technicians of the future. The framework principally concerns itself with the first task—what all students should know in preparation for their individual lives and for their roles as citizens in this technology-rich and scientifically complex world. Course options, including Advanced Placement (AP) or honors courses, should be provided that allow for greater breadth or depth in the science topics that students pursue, not only in the usual disciplines taught as natural sciences in the K-12 context but also in allied subjects, such as psychology, computer science, and economics. It is the committee's conviction that such an education, done well, will excite many more young people about science-related subjects and generate a desire to pursue science- or engineering-based careers.

Achieving the Vision

The framework is motivated in part by a growing national consensus around the need for greater coherence—that is, a sense of unity—in K-12 science education. Too often, standards are long lists of detailed and disconnected facts, reinforcing the criticism that science curricula in the United States tend to be "a mile wide and an inch deep" [1]. Not only is such an approach alienating to young people, but it can also leave them with just fragments of knowledge and little sense of the creative achievements of science, its inherent logic and consistency, and its universality. Moreover, that approach neglects the need for students to develop an understanding of the practices of science and engineering, which is as important to understanding science as knowledge of its content.

The framework endeavors to move science education toward a more coherent vision in three ways. First, it is built on the notion of learning as a developmental progression. It is designed to help children continually build on and revise their knowledge and abilities, starting from their curiosity about what they see around them and their initial conceptions about how the world works. The goal is to guide their knowledge toward a more scientifically based and coherent view of the sciences and engineering, as well as of the ways in which they are pursued and their results can be used.

Second, the framework focuses on a limited number of core ideas in science and engineering both within and across the disciplines. The committee made this choice in order to avoid shallow coverage of a large number of topics and to allow more time for teachers and students to explore each idea in greater depth. Reduction of the sheer sum of details to be mastered is intended to give time for students to engage in scientific investigations and argumentation and to achieve depth of understanding of the core ideas presented. Delimiting what is to be learned about each core idea within each grade band also helps clarify what is most important to spend time on and avoid the proliferation of detail to be learned with no conceptual grounding.

Third, the framework emphasizes that learning about science and engineering involves integration of the knowledge of scientific explanations (i.e., content knowledge) and the practices needed to engage in scientific inquiry and engineering design. Thus the framework seeks to illustrate how knowledge and practice must be intertwined in designing learning experiences in K-12 science education.

Limitations of This Framework

The terms "science," "engineering," and "technology" are often lumped together as a single phrase, both in this report and in education policy circles. But it is important to define what is meant by each of these terms in this report—and why.

In the K-12 context, science is generally taken to mean the traditional natural sciences: physics, chemistry, biology, and (more recently) earth, space, and environmental sciences. In this document, we include core ideas for these disciplinary areas, but not for all areas of science, as discussed further below. This limitation matches our charge and the need of schools for a next generation of standards in these areas. Engineering and technology are included as they relate to the applications of science, and in so doing they offer students a path to strengthen their understanding of the role of sciences. We use the term engineering in a very broad sense to mean any engagement in a systematic practice of design to achieve solutions to particular human problems. Likewise, we broadly use the term technology to include all types of human-made systems and processes—not in the limited sense often used in schools that equates technology with modern computational and communications devices. Technologies result when engineers apply their understanding of the natural world and of human behavior to design ways to satisfy human needs and wants. This is not to say that science necessarily precedes technology; throughout history, advances in scientific understanding often have been driven by engineers' questions as they work to design new or improved machines or systems.

Engineering and technology, defined in these broad ways, are included in the framework for several reasons. First, the committee thinks it is important for students to explore the practical use of science, given that a singular focus on the core ideas of the disciplines would tend to shortchange the importance of applications. Second, at least at the K-8 level, these topics typically do not appear elsewhere in the curriculum and thus are neglected if not included in science instruction. Finally, engineering and technology provide a context in which students can test their own developing scientific knowledge and apply it to practical problems; doing so enhances their understanding of science—and, for many, their interest in science—as they recognize the interplay among science, engineering, and technology. We are convinced that engagement in the practices of engineering design is as much a part of learning science as engagement in the practices of science [2].

It is important to note, however, that the framework is not intended to define course structure, particularly at the high school level. Many high schools already have courses designated as technology, design, or even engineering that go beyond the limited introduction to these topics specified in the framework. These courses are often taught by teachers who have specialized expertise and do not consider themselves to be science teachers. The committee takes no position on such courses—nor, in fact, on any particular set of course sequence options for students at the high school level. We simply maintain that some introduction to engineering practice, the application of science, and the interrelationship of science, engineering, and technology is integral to the learning of science for all students.

The committee's vision takes into account two major goals for K-12 science education: (1) educating all students in science and engineering and (2) providing the foundational knowledge for those who will become the scientists, engineers, technologists, and technicians of the future.

More generally, this framework should not be interpreted as limiting advanced courses that go beyond the material included here—all students at the high school level should have opportunities for advanced study in areas of interest to them, and it is hoped that, for many, this will include further study of specific science disciplines in honors or AP courses. Such course options may include topics, such as neurobiology, and even disciplines, such as economics, that are not included in this framework.

Social, Behavioral, and Economic Sciences

Although some aspects of the behavioral sciences are incorporated in the framework as part of life sciences, the social, behavioral, and economic sciences are not fully addressed. The committee did not identify a separate set of core ideas for these fields for several reasons.

First, the original charge to the committee did not include these disciplines. Second, social, behavioral, and economic sciences include a diverse array of fields (sociology, economics, political science, anthropology, all of the branches of psychology) with different methods, theories, relationships to other disciplines of science, and representation in the K-12 curriculum. Although some are currently represented in grades K-12, many are not or appear only in courses offered at the high school level.

Third, the committee based the framework on existing documents that outline the major ideas for K-12 science education, including the *National Science Education Standards (NSES)* [3], the *Benchmarks for Science Literacy* [4] and the accompanying *Atlas* [5], the *Science Framework for the 2009 National Assessment of Educational Progress (NAEP)* [6], and the *Science College Board Standards for College Success* [7]. Most of these documents do not cover all of the fields that are part of the social, behavioral, and economic sciences comprehensively, and some omit them entirely.

Fourth, understanding how to integrate the social, behavioral, and economic sciences into standards, given how subjects are currently organized in the K-12 system, is especially complex. These fields have typically not been included as part of the science curriculum and, as noted above, are not represented systematically in some of the major national-level documents that identify core concepts for K-12 science. Also, many of the topics related to the social, behavioral, and economic sciences are incorporated into curricula or courses identified as social studies and may be taught from a humanities perspective. In fact, the National Council for the Social Studies has a set of National Curriculum Standards for Social Studies that includes standards in such areas as psychology, sociology, geography, anthropology, political science, and economics [8].

The limited treatment of these fields in this report's framework should not, however, be interpreted to mean that the social, behavioral, and economic sciences should be omitted from the K-12 curriculum. On the contrary, the committee strongly believes that these important disciplines need their own framework for defining core concepts to be learned at the K-12 level and that learning (the development of understanding of content and practices) in the physical, life, earth, and space sciences and engineering should be strongly linked with parallel learning in the social, behavioral, and economic sciences. Any such framework must also address important and challenging issues of school and curriculum organization around the domain of social sciences and social studies.

Our committee has neither the charge nor the expertise to undertake that important work. Thus, although we have included references to some of the social, behavioral, and economic issues connected to the sciences that are the focus of our own framework (see, for example, Core Idea 2 in engineering, technology, and applications of science), we do not consider these references to define the entirety of what students should learn or discuss about social, behavioral, and economic sciences.

In a separate effort, the National Research Council (NRC) has plans to convene a workshop to begin exploring a definition of what core ideas in the social, behavioral, and economic sciences would be appropriate to teach at the K-12 level and at what grade levels to introduce them. As noted above, there are many quite distinct realms of study covered by the terms. Given the multiplicity and variety of disciplines involved, only a few of which are currently addressed in any way in K-12 classrooms, there is much work to be done to address the role of these sciences in the development of an informed 21st-century citizen. It is clear, however, to the authors of this report that these sciences, although different in focus, do have much in common with the subject areas included here, so that much of what this report discusses in defining scientific and engineering practices and crosscutting concepts has application across this broader realm of science.

Computer Science and Statistics

Computer science and statistics are other areas of science that are not addressed here, even though they have a valid presence in K-12 education. Statistics is basically a subdiscipline of mathematical sciences, and it is addressed to some extent in the common core mathematics standards. Computer science, too, can be seen as a branch of the mathematical sciences, as well as having some elements of engineering. But, again, because this area of the curriculum has a history and a teaching corps that are generally distinct from those of the sciences, the committee has not taken this domain as part of our charge. Once again, this omission should not be interpreted to mean that computer science or statistics should be excluded from the K-12 curriculum. There are aspects of computational and statistical thinking that must be understood and applied in learning about the sciences, and we identify these aspects, along with mathematical thinking, in our discussion of science practices in Chapter 3.

ABOUT THIS REPORT

The Committee on a Conceptual Framework for New K-12 Science Education Standards was established by the NRC to undertake the study on which this report is based. Composed of 18 members reflecting a diversity of perspectives and a broad range of expertise, the committee includes professionals in the natural sciences, mathematics, engineering, cognitive and developmental psychology, the learning sciences, education policy and implementation, research on learning science in the classroom, and the practice of teaching science.

The committee's charge was to develop a conceptual framework that would specify core ideas in the life sciences, physical sciences, earth and space sciences, and engineering and technology, as well as crosscutting concepts and practices, around which standards should be developed. The committee was also charged with articulating how these disciplinary ideas and crosscutting concepts intersect for at least three grade levels and to develop guidance for implementation (see Box 1-1).

Scope and Approach

The committee carried out the charge through an iterative process of amassing information, deliberating on it, identifying gaps, gathering further information to fill these gaps, and holding further discussions. In our search for particulars, we held three public fact-finding meetings, reviewed published reports and unpublished research, and commissioned experts to prepare and present papers. At our fourth meeting, we deliberated on the form and structure of the framework and on the content of the report's supporting chapters, to prepare a draft framework for public release in July 2010. During the fifth and sixth meetings, we considered the feedback received from the public and developed a plan for revising the draft framework based on this input (see below for further details).

BOX 1-1

COMMITTEE CHARGE

An ad hoc committee will develop and define a framework to guide the development of science education standards. In conducting the study and preparing its report, the committee will draw on current research on science learning as well as research and evaluation evidence related to standards-based education reform. This will include existing efforts to specify central ideas for science education, including the *National Science Education Standards*, AAAS Benchmarks, the 2009 NAEP Framework, and the redesign of the AP courses by the College Board.

The conceptual framework developed by the committee will identify and articulate the core ideas in science around which standards should be developed by considering core ideas in the disciplines of science (life sciences, physical sciences, earth and space sciences, and applied sciences) as well as crosscutting ideas such as mathematization,* causal reasoning, evaluating and using evidence, argumentation, and model development. The committee will illustrate with concrete examples how crosscutting ideas may play out in the context of select core disciplinary ideas and articulate expectations for students' learning of these ideas for at least three key grade levels. In parallel, the committee will develop a research and development plan to inform future revisions of the standards. Specifically in its consensus report, the committee will

- identify a small set of core ideas in each of the major science disciplines, as well as those ideas that cut across disciplines, using a set of criteria developed by the committee
- develop guidance on implementation of the framework
- articulate how these disciplinary ideas and crosscutting ideas intersect for at least three grade levels
- create examples of performance expectations
- discuss implications of various goals for science education (e.g., general science literacy, college preparation, and workforce readiness) on the priority of core ideas and articulation of leaning expectations
- develop a research and development plan to inform future revisions of the standards

---

*Mathematization is a technical term that means representing relationships in the natural world using mathematics.

The nature of the charge—to identify the scientific and engineering ideas and practices that are most important for all students in grades K-12 to learn—means that the committee ultimately had to rely heavily on its own expertise and collective judgments. To the extent possible, however, we used research-based evidence and past efforts to inform these judgments. Our approach combined evidence on the learning and teaching of science and engineering with a detailed examination of previous science standards documents. It is important to note that even where formal research is limited, the report is based on the collective experience of the science education and science education research communities. All the practices suggested have been explored in classrooms, as have the crosscutting concepts (though perhaps under other names such as "unifying themes").

Design Teams

The committee's work was significantly advanced by the contributions of four design teams, which were contracted by the NRC to prepare materials that described the core ideas in the natural sciences and engineering and outlined how these ideas could be developed across grades K-12. Each team had a designated leader who provided guidance and interacted frequently with the committee. The materials developed by the teams form the foundation for the core disciplinary ideas and grade band endpoints described in this report (Chapters 5-8). A list of the design team participants appears in Appendix D.

The design teams were asked to begin their work by considering the ideas and practices described in the *NSES* [3], *AAAS Benchmarks* [4], *Science Framework for the 2009 NAEP* [6], and *Science College Board Standards for College Success* [7] as well as the relevant research on learning and teaching in science. The teams prepared drafts and presented them to the committee during the closed portions of our first three meetings. Between meetings, the teams revised their drafts in response to committee comments. Following the release of the July 2010 draft (see the next section), the leaders of the design teams continued to interact with committee members as they planned the revisions of the draft framework. No members of the design teams participated in the discussions during which the committee reached consensus on the content of the final draft.

> The framework and subsequent standards will not lead to improvements in K-12 science education unless the other components of the system—curriculum, instruction, professional development, and assessment—change so that they are aligned with the framework's vision.

The committee recognized early in the process that obtaining feedback from a broad range of stakeholders and experts would be crucial to the success of the framework. For this reason, we obtained permission from the NRC to release a draft version of the framework for public comment.

The draft version was prepared, underwent an expedited NRC review, and was released in early July 2010. It was then posted online for a period of three weeks, during which time individuals could submit comments through an online survey. In addition, NRC staff contacted over 40 organizations in science, engineering, and education, notifying them of the public comment period and asking them to hold focus groups to gather feedback from members or to at least notify their members of the opportunity to comment online. The NRC also worked closely with the National Science Teachers Association, the American Association for the Advancement of Science, Achieve, Inc., and the Council of State Science Supervisors both to facilitate the public input process and to organize focus groups. Finally, the committee asked nine experts to provide detailed feedback on the public draft.

During the 3-week public comment period, the committee received extensive input from both individuals and groups: a total of more than 2,000 people responded to the online survey. More than 30 focus groups were held around the country, with 15-40 participants in each group. The committee also received letters from key individuals and organizations. A list of the organizations that participated in the focus groups or submitted letters is included in Appendix A.

NRC staff, together with the committee chair, reviewed all of the input and developed summaries that identified the major issues raised and outlined possible revisions to the draft framework. Committee members reviewed these summaries and also had the opportunity to review the public feedback in detail. Based on discussions at the fifth and sixth meetings, the committee made substantial revisions to the framework based on the feedback. A summary of the major issues raised in the public feedback and the revisions the committee made is included in Appendix A.

Structure of the Report

The first nine chapters of this report outline the principles underlying the framework, describe the core ideas and practices for K-12 education in the natural sciences and engineering, and provide examples of how these ideas and practices should be integrated into any standards.

The remaining four chapters of the report address issues related to designing and implementing standards and strengthening the research base that should inform them. Chapter 10 articulates the issues related to curriculum, instruction, and assessment. Chapter 11 discusses important considerations related to equity and diversity. Chapter 12 provides guidance for standards developers as they work to apply the framework. Finally, Chapter 13 outlines the research agenda that would allow a systematic implementation of the framework and related standards. The chapter also specifies the kinds of research needed for future iterations of the standards to be better grounded in evidence.

NEXT STEPS

The National Governors Association and the Council of Chief State School Officers have developed "Common Core State Standards" in mathematics and language arts, and 43 states and the District of Columbia have adopted these standards as of early 2011. The anticipation of a similar effort for science standards was a prime motivator for this NRC study and the resulting framework described in this report.

To maintain the momentum, the Carnegie Corporation commissioned the nonpartisan and nonprofit educational reform organization Achieve, Inc., to lead states in developing new science standards based on the NRC framework in this report. There is no prior commitment from multiple states to adopt such standards, so the process will be different from the Common Core process used for mathematics and language arts. But it is expected that Achieve will form partnerships with a number of states in undertaking this work and will offer multiple opportunities for public comment.

As our report was being completed, Achieve's work on science standards was already under way, starting with an analysis of international science benchmarking in high-performing countries that is expected to inform the standards development process. We understand that Achieve has also begun some preliminary planning for that process based on the draft framework that was circulated for public comment in summer 2010. The relevance of such work should deepen once the revised framework in this report, on which Achieve's standards will be based, is released. It should be noted, however, that our study and the framework described in this report are independent of the work of Achieve.

The framework and any standards that will be based on it make explicit the goals around which a science education system should be organized [9]. The committee recognizes, however, that the framework and subsequent standards will not lead to improvements in K-12 science education unless the other components of the system—curriculum, instruction, professional development, and assessment—change so that they are aligned with the framework's vision. Thus the framework and standards are necessary but not sufficient to support the desired improvements. In Chapter 10, we address some of the challenges inherent in achieving such alignment.

REFERENCES

1. Schmidt, W.H., McKnight, C.C., and Raizen, S. (1997). *A Splintered Vision: An Investigation of U.S. Science and Mathematics Education.* U.S. National Research Center for the Third International Mathematics and Science Study. Boston, MA: Kluwer Academic.

2. National Academy of Engineering and National Research Council. (2009). *Engineering in K-12 Education: Understanding the Status and Improving the Prospect.* Committee on K-12 Engineering Education. L. Katehi, G. Pearson, and M. Feder (Eds.). National Academy of Engineering. Board on Science Education, Center for Education, Division of Behavioral and Social Sciences and Education. Washington, DC: The National Academies Press.

3. National Research Council. (1996). *National Science Education Standards.* National Committee for Science Education Standards and Assessment. Washington, DC: National Academy Press.

4. American Association for the Advancement of Science. (1993). *Benchmarks for Science Literacy.* Project 2061. New York: Oxford University Press. Available: http://www.project2061.org/publications/bsl/online/index.php?txtRef=http%3A%2F%2Fwww%2Eproject2061%2Eorg%2Fpublications%2Fbsl%2Fdefault%2Ehtm%3FtxtRef%3D%26txtURIOld%3D%252Ftools%252Fbsl%252Fdefault%2Ehtm&txtURIOld=%2Fpublications%2Fbsl%2Fonline%2Fbolintro%2Ehtm [June 2011].

5. American Association for the Advancement of Science. (2007). *Atlas of Science Literacy, Volumes 1 and 2.* Project 2061. Washington, DC: Author.

6. National Assessment of Educational Progress. (2009). *Science Framework for the 2009 National Assessment of Educational Progress.* Washington, DC: U.S. Government Printing Office. Developed for the National Assessment Governing Board. Available: http://www.nagb.org/publications/frameworks/science-09.pdf [June 2011].

7. College Board. (2009). *Science College Board Standards for College Success.* Available: http://professionals.collegeboard.com/profdownload/cbscs-science-standards-2009.pdf [June 2011].

8. National Council for the Social Studies. (2010). *National Curriculum Standards for Social Studies: A Framework for Teaching, Learning, and Assessment.* Silver Spring, MD: Author.

9. National Research Council. (2006). *Systems for State Science Assessment.* M.R. Wilson and M.W. Bertenthal (Eds.). Committee on Test Design for K-12 Science Achievement. Board on Testing and Assessment, Center for Education. Division of Behavioral and Social Sciences and Education. Washington, DC: The National Academies Press.

GUIDING ASSUMPTIONS AND ORGANIZATION OF THE FRAMEWORK

The conceptual framework presented in this report is based on a large and growing body of research on teaching and learning science. Much of this research base has been synthesized in other National Research Council (NRC) reports. Research on how children learn science and the implications for science instruction in grades K-8 was central to *Taking Science to School* [1], *America's Lab Report* [2] examined the role of laboratory experiences in high school science instruction, and *Learning Science in Informal Environments* [3] focused on the role of science learning experiences outside school. Complementing these publications, *Systems for State Science Assessment* [4] studied large-scale assessments of science learning, and *Engineering in K-12 Education* [5] looked into the knowledge and skills needed to introduce students to engineering in grades K-12. All of these NRC reports have been essential input to the development of the framework.

The framework also builds on two other prior works on standards: *Benchmarks for Science Literacy* published by the American Association for the Advancement of Science (AAAS) [6] and the NRC's *National Science Education Standards (NSES)* [7]. In addition, the committee examined more recent efforts, including the *Science Framework for the 2009 National Assessment of Educational Progress* [8], *Science College Board Standards for College Success* [9], the National Science Teachers Association's (NSTA's) Science Anchors project [10], and a variety of state and international science standards and curriculum specifications.

PRINCIPLES OF THE FRAMEWORK

Several guiding principles, drawn from what is known about the nature of learning science, underlie both the structure and the content of the framework. These principles include young children's capacity to learn science, a focus on core ideas, the development of true understanding over time, the consideration both of knowledge and practice, the linkage of science education to students' interests and experiences, and the promotion of equity.

Children Are Born Investigators

The research summarized in *Taking Science to School* [1] revealed that children entering kindergarten have surprisingly sophisticated ways of thinking about the world, based in part on their direct experiences with the physical environment,

such as watching objects fall or collide and observing plants and animals [11-16]. They also learn about the world through everyday activities, such as talking with their families, pursuing hobbies, watching television, and playing with friends [3]. As children try to understand and influence the world around them, they develop ideas about their role in that world and how it works [17-19]. In fact, the capacity of young children—from all backgrounds and socioeconomic levels—to reason in sophisticated ways is much greater than has long been assumed [1]. Although they may lack deep knowledge and extensive experience, they often engage in a wide range of subtle and complex reasoning about the world [20-23].

Thus, before they even enter school, children have developed their own ideas about the physical, biological, and social worlds and how they work. By listening to and taking these ideas seriously, educators can build on what children already know and can do. Such initial ideas may be more or less cohesive and sometimes may be incorrect. However, some of children's early intuitions about the world can be used as a foundation to build remarkable understanding, even in the earliest grades. Indeed, both building on and refining prior conceptions (which can include misconceptions) are important in teaching science at any grade level. The implication of these findings for the framework is that building progressively more sophisticated explanations of natural phenomena is central throughout grades K-5, as opposed to focusing only on description in the early grades and leaving explanation to the later grades. Similarly, students can engage in scientific and engineering practices beginning in the early grades.

Focusing on Core Ideas and Practices

The framework focuses on a limited set of core ideas in order to avoid the coverage of multiple disconnected topics—the oft-mentioned mile wide and inch deep. This focus allows for deep exploration of important concepts, as well as time for students to develop meaningful understanding, to actually practice science and engineering, and to reflect on their nature. It also results in a science education that extends in a more coherent way across grades K-12.

The core ideas also can provide an organizational structure for the acquisition of new knowledge. Understanding the core ideas and engaging in the scientific and engineering practices helps to prepare students for broader understanding, and deeper levels of scientific and engineering investigation, later on—in high school, college, and beyond. One rationale for organizing content around core ideas comes from studies comparing experts and novices in any field. Experts understand the core principles and theoretical constructs of their field, and they use them to make sense of new information or tackle novel problems. Novices, in contrast, tend to hold disconnected and even contradictory bits of knowledge as isolated facts and struggle to find a way to organize and integrate them [24]. The assumption, then, is that helping students learn the core ideas through engaging in scientific and engineering practices will enable them to become less like novices and more like experts.

Importantly, this approach will also help students build the capacity to develop more flexible and coherent—that is, wide-ranging—understanding of science. Research on learning shows that supporting development of this kind of understanding is challenging, but it is aided by explicit instructional support that stresses connections across different activities and learning experiences.

> █ Building progressively more sophisticated explanations of natural phenomena is central throughout grades K-5, as opposed to focusing only on description in the early grades and leaving explanation to the later grades. █

Understanding Develops Over Time

To develop a thorough understanding of scientific explanations of the world, students need sustained opportunities to work with and develop the underlying ideas and to appreciate those ideas' interconnections over a period of years rather than weeks or months [1]. This sense of development has been conceptualized in the idea of learning progressions [1, 25, 26]. If mastery of a core idea in a science discipline is the ultimate educational destination, then well-designed learning progressions provide a map of the routes that can be taken to reach that destination. Such progressions describe both how students' understanding of the idea matures over time and the instructional supports and experiences that are needed for them to make progress. Learning progressions may extend all the way from preschool to 12th grade and beyond—indeed, people can continue learning about scientific core ideas their entire lives. Because learning progressions extend over multiple years, they can prompt educators to consider how topics are presented at each grade level so that they build on prior understanding and can support increasingly sophisticated learning. Hence, core ideas and their related learning progressions are key organizing principles for the design of the framework.

Science and Engineering Require Both Knowledge and Practice

Science is not just a body of knowledge that reflects current understanding of the world; it is also a set of practices used to establish, extend, and refine that knowledge. Both elements—knowledge and practice—are essential.

In science, knowledge, based on evidence from many investigations, is integrated into highly developed and well-tested theories that can explain bodies of data and predict outcomes of further investigations. Although the practices used to develop scientific theories (as well as the form that those theories take) differ from one domain of science to another, all sciences share certain common features at the core of their inquiry-based and problem-solving approaches. Chief among these features is a commitment to data and evidence as the foundation for developing claims. The argumentation and analysis that relate evidence and theory are also essential features of science; scientists need to be able to examine, review, and evaluate their own knowledge and ideas and critique those of others. Argumentation and analysis include appraisal of data quality, modeling of theories, development of new testable questions from those models, and modification of theories and models as evidence indicates they are needed.

Finally, science is fundamentally a social enterprise, and scientific knowledge advances through collaboration and in the context of a social system with well-developed norms. Individual scientists may do much of their work independently or they may collaborate closely with colleagues. Thus, new ideas can be the product of one mind or many working together. However, the theories, models, instruments, and methods for collecting and displaying data, as well as the norms for building arguments from evidence, are developed collectively in a vast network of scientists working together over extended periods. As they carry out their research, scientists talk frequently with their colleagues, both formally and informally. They exchange emails, engage in discussions at conferences, share research techniques and analytical procedures, and present and respond to ideas via publication in journals and books. In short, scientists constitute a community whose members work together to build a body of evidence and devise and test theories. In addition, this community and its culture exist in the larger social and economic context of their place and time and are influenced by events, needs, and norms from outside science, as well as by the interests and desires of scientists.

Similarly, engineering involves both knowledge and a set of practices. The major goal of engineering is to solve problems that arise from a specific human need or desire. To do this, engineers rely on their knowledge of science and mathematics as well as their understanding of the engineering design process. Defining and solving the problem, that is, specifying what is needed and designing a solution for it, are the parts of engineering on which we focus in this framework, both because they provide students a place to practice the application of their understanding of science and because the design process is an important way for K-12 students to develop an understanding of engineering as

▮ Science is not just a body of knowledge that reflects current understanding of the world; it is also a set of practices used to establish, extend, and refine that knowledge. ▮

a discipline and as a possible career path. The work of engineers, like the work of scientists, involves both individual and cooperative effort; and it requires specialized knowledge. Hence, we include both engineering practices and engineering core ideas in this framework.

Connecting to Students' Interests and Experiences

A rich science education has the potential to capture students' sense of wonder about the world and to spark their desire to continue learning about science throughout their lives. Research suggests that personal interest, experience, and enthusiasm—critical to children's learning of science at school or in other settings—may also be linked to later educational and career choices [27-30]. Thus, in order for students to develop a sustained attraction to science and for them to appreciate the many ways in which it is pertinent to their daily lives, classroom learning experiences in science need to connect with their own interests and experiences.

As a strategy for building on prior interest, the disciplinary core ideas identified here are described not only with an eye toward the knowledge that students bring with them to school but also toward the kinds of questions they are likely to pose themselves at different ages. Such questions as "Where do we come from?," "Why is the sky blue?," and "What is the smallest piece of matter?" are fundamental hooks that engage young people. Framing a curriculum around such sets of questions helps to communicate relevance and salience to this audience.

Promoting Equity

Equity in science education requires that all students are provided with equitable opportunities to learn science and become engaged in science and engineering practices; with access to quality space, equipment, and teachers to support and motivate that learning and engagement; and adequate time spent on science. In addition, the issue of connecting to students' interests and experiences is particularly important for broadening participation in science. There is increasing recognition that the diverse customs and orientations that members of different cultural communities bring both to formal and to informal science learning contexts are assets on which to build—both for the benefit of the student and ultimately of science itself. For example, researchers have documented that children reared in rural agricultural communities, who experience intense and regular interactions with plants and animals, develop more sophisticated understanding of ecology and biological species than do urban and suburban children of the same age [31-33].

Others have identified connections between children's culturally based storytelling and their engagement in argumentation and science inquiry, and some of these researchers have also documented pedagogical means of using such connections to support students' science learning and promote educational equity [34].

The research demonstrates the importance of embracing diversity as a means of enhancing learning about science and the world, especially as society in the United States becomes progressively more diverse with respect to language, ethnicity, and race.

The goal of educational equity is one of the reasons to have rigorous standards that apply to all students. Not only should all students be expected to attain these standards, but also work is needed to ensure that all are provided with high-quality opportunities to engage in significant science and engineering learning.

STRUCTURE OF THE FRAMEWORK

Based on the guiding principles outlined above, we have created a framework—comprised of three dimensions—that broadly outlines the knowledge and practices of the sciences and engineering that all students should learn by the end of high school:

- Dimension 1 describes scientific and engineering practices.
- Dimension 2 describes crosscutting concepts—that is, those having applicability across science disciplines.
- Dimension 3 describes core ideas in the science disciplines and of the relationships among science, engineering, and technology.

The three dimensions of the framework, which constitute the major conclusions of this report, are presented in separate chapters. However, in order to facilitate students' learning, the dimensions must be woven together in standards, curricula, instruction, and assessments. When they explore particular disciplinary ideas from Dimension 3, students will do so by engaging in practices articulated in Dimension 1 and should be helped to make connections to the crosscutting concepts in Dimension 2.

Dimension 1: Practices

Dimension 1 describes (a) the major practices that scientists employ as they investigate and build models and theories about the world and (b) a key set of engineering practices that engineers use as they design and build systems. We use the term "practices" instead of a term such as "skills" to emphasize that engaging in scientific investigation requires not only skill but also knowledge that is specific to each practice.

Similarly, because the term "inquiry," extensively referred to in previous standards documents, has been interpreted over time in many different ways throughout the science education community, part of our intent in articulating the practices in Dimension 1 is to better specify what is meant by inquiry in science and the range of cognitive, social, and physical practices that it requires. As in all inquiry-based approaches to science teaching, our expectation is that students will themselves engage in the practices and not merely learn about them secondhand. Students cannot comprehend scientific practices, nor fully appreciate the nature of scientific knowledge itself, without directly experiencing those practices for themselves.

Dimension 2: Crosscutting Concepts

The crosscutting concepts have application across all domains of science. As such, they provide one way of linking across the domains in Dimension 3. These crosscutting concepts are not unique to this report. They echo many of the unifying concepts and processes in the *National Science Education Standards* [7], the common themes in the *Benchmarks for Science Literacy* [6], and the unifying concepts in the *Science College Board Standards for College Success* [9]. The framework's structure also reflects discussions related to the NSTA Science Anchors project, which emphasized the need to consider not only disciplinary content but also the ideas and practices that cut across the science disciplines.

Dimension 3: Disciplinary Core Ideas

The continuing expansion of scientific knowledge makes it impossible to teach all the ideas related to a given discipline in exhaustive detail during the K-12 years.

But given the cornucopia of information available today virtually at a touch—people live, after all, in an information age—an important role of science education is not to teach "all the facts" but rather to prepare students with sufficient core knowledge so that they can later acquire additional information on their own. An education focused on a limited set of ideas and practices in science and engineering should enable students to evaluate and select reliable sources of scientific information and allow them to continue their development well beyond their K-12 school years as science learners, users of scientific knowledge, and perhaps also as producers of such knowledge.

With these ends in mind, the committee developed its small set of core ideas in science and engineering by applying the criteria listed below. Although not every core idea will satisfy every one of the criteria, to be regarded as core, each idea must meet at least two of them (though preferably three or all four).

Specifically, a core idea for K-12 science instruction should

1. Have broad importance across multiple sciences or engineering disciplines or be a key organizing principle of a single discipline.
2. Provide a key tool for understanding or investigating more complex ideas and solving problems.
3. Relate to the interests and life experiences of students or be connected to societal or personal concerns that require scientific or technological knowledge.
4. Be teachable and learnable over multiple grades at increasing levels of depth and sophistication. That is, the idea can be made accessible to younger students but is broad enough to sustain continued investigation over years.

In organizing Dimension 3, we grouped disciplinary ideas into four major domains: the physical sciences; the life sciences; the earth and space sciences; and engineering, technology, and applications of science. At the same time, true to Dimension 2, we acknowledge the multiple connections among domains. Indeed, more and more frequently, scientists work in interdisciplinary teams that blur traditional boundaries. As a consequence, in some instances core ideas, or elements of core ideas, appear in several disciplines (e.g., energy, human impact on the planet).

Each core idea and its components are introduced with a question designed to show some aspect of the world that this idea helps to explain. The question

> █ Just as new science enables or sometimes demands new technologies, new technologies enable new scientific investigations, allowing scientists to probe realms and handle quantities of data previously inaccessible to them. █

is followed by a description of the understanding about the idea that should be developed by the end of high school. This structure is intended to stress that posing questions about the world and seeking to answer them is fundamental to doing science.

The inclusion of core ideas related to engineering, technology, and applications of science reflects an increasing emphasis at the national level on considering connections among science, technology, engineering, and mathematics. It is also informed by a recent report from the NRC on engineering education in K-12, which highlights the linkages—which go both ways—between learning science and learning engineering. Just as new science enables or sometimes

demands new technologies, new technologies enable new scientific investigations, allowing scientists to probe realms and handle quantities of data previously inaccessible to them.

Moreover, the line between applied science and engineering is fuzzy. It is impossible to do engineering today without applying science in the process, and, in many areas of science, designing and building new experiments requires scientists to engage in some engineering practices. This interplay of science and engineering makes it appropriate to place engineering and technology as part of the science framework at the K-12 level. In this way, students can better see how science and engineering pertain to real-world problems and explore opportunities to apply their scientific knowledge to engineering design problems once this linkage is made.

Finally, our effort to identify a *small* number of core ideas may disappoint some scientists and educators who find little or nothing of their favorite science topics included in the framework. But the committee is convinced that by building a strong base of core knowledge and competencies, understood in sufficient depth to be used, students will leave school better grounded in scientific knowledge and practices—and with greater interest in further learning in science—than when instruction "covers" multiple disconnected pieces of information that are memorized and soon forgotten once the test is over.

Progressions Across K-12

The framework emphasizes developing students' proficiency in science in a coherent way across grades K-12 following the logic of learning progressions. Developing detailed learning progressions for all of the practices, concepts, and ideas that make up the three dimensions was beyond the committee's charge; however, we do provide some guidance on how students' facility with the practices, concepts, and ideas may develop over multiple grades. For the practices and cross-cutting concepts, the committee developed sketches of the possible progression for each practice or concept. These progressions do not specify grade bands because there was not enough available evidence to do so.

For the disciplinary core ideas, we provide a set of grade band endpoints for each component idea that describe the developing understanding that students should have acquired by the ends of grades 2, 5, 8, and 12, respectively. These endpoints indicate how this idea should be developed across the span of the K-12 years. In standards, curriculum, and instruction, a more complete sequence that integrates the core ideas with the practices and crosscutting concepts will be needed.

When possible, the grade band endpoints were informed by research on teaching and learning, particularly on learning progressions (see Appendix B for a list of the references the committee consulted). The committee referred to this literature to help determine students' capabilities at a particular grade band given appropriate instructional support as well as potential difficulties. However, the availability of such research is uneven across the core and component ideas of Dimension 3. For this reason, the endpoints were also informed by the committee's judgment about grade appropriateness. All in all, the endpoints provide a set of initial hypotheses about the progression of learning that can inform standards and serve as a basis for additional research.

The endpoints follow a common trend across the grades. In grades K-2, we choose ideas about phenomena that students can directly experience and investigate. In grades 3-5, we include invisible but chiefly still macroscopic entities, such as what is inside the body or Earth, with which children will have had little direct experience. When microscopic entities are introduced, no stress is placed on understanding their size—just that they are too small to see directly. However, pictures, physical models, and simulations can represent the entities and relate them to phenomena that the students can investigate and interpret. In grades 6-8, we move to atomic-level explanations of physical phenomena and cellular-level explanations of life processes and biological structures, but without detail on the inner workings of an atom or a cell. Finally, in grades 9-12 we shift to subatomic and subcellular explanations. A similar progression of scales and abstraction of models applies in addressing phenomena of large scales and deep time. We have also included some "boundary statements" that specify the level of detail students are expected to know, but standards will need to further delineate such boundaries.

The progression for practices across the grades follows a similar pattern, with grades K-2 stressing observations and explanations related to direct experiences, grades 3-5 introducing simple models that help explain observable phenomena, and a transition to more abstract and more detailed models and explanations across the grades 6-8 and 9-12. The idea behind these choices is not that young children cannot reason abstractly or imagine unseen things but that their capacity to do so in a scientific context needs to be developed with opportunities presented over time. There is ample opportunity to develop scientific thinking, argumentation, and reasoning in the context of familiar phenomena in grades K-2, and that is the experience that will best support science learning across the grades.

REFERENCES

1. National Research Council. (2007). *Taking Science to School: Learning and Teaching Science in Grades K-8*. Committee on Science Learning, Kindergarten Through Eighth Grade. R.A. Duschl, H.A. Schweingruber, and A.W. Shouse (Eds.). Board on Science Education, Center for Education. Division of Behavioral and Social Sciences and Education. Washington, DC: The National Academies Press.

2. National Research Council. (2006). *America's Lab Report: Investigations in High School Science*. Committee on High School Science Laboratories: Role and Vision, S.R. Singer, M.L. Hilton, and H.A. Schweingruber (Eds.). Board on Science Education, Center for Education. Division of Behavioral and Social Sciences and Education. Washington, DC: The National Academies Press.

3. National Research Council. (2009). *Learning Science in Informal Environments: People, Places, and Pursuits*. Committee on Learning Science in Informal Environments. P. Bell, B. Lewenstein, A.W. Shouse, and M.A. Feder (Eds.). Board on Science Education, Center for Education. Division of Behavioral and Social Sciences and Education. Washington, DC: The National Academies Press.

4. National Research Council. (2006). *Systems for State Science Assessment*. Committee on Test Design for K-12 Science Achievement. M.R. Wilson and M.W. Bertenthal (Eds.). Board on Testing and Assessment, Center for Education. Division of Behavioral and Social Sciences and Education. Washington, DC: The National Academies Press.

5. National Academy of Engineering and National Research Council. (2009). *Engineering in K-12 Education: Understanding the Status and Improving the Prospect*. Committee on K-12 Engineering Education. L. Katehi, G. Pearson, and M. Feder (Eds.). National Academy of Engineering. Board on Science Education, Center for Education. Division of Behavioral and Social Sciences and Education. Washington, DC: The National Academies Press.

6. American Association for the Advancement of Science: Project 2061. (1993). *Benchmarks for Science Literacy* Available: http://www.project2061.org/publications/bsl/online/index.php?txtRef=http%3A%2F%2Fwww%2Eproject2061%2Eorg%2Fpublications%2Fbsl%2Fdefault%2Ehtm%3FtxtRef%3D%26txtURIOld%3D%252Ftools%252Fbsl%252Fdefault%2Ehtm&txtURIOld=%2Fpublications%2Fbsl%2Fonline%2Fbolintro%2Ehtm [June 2011].

7. National Research Council. (1996). *National Science Education Standards*. National Committee for Science Education Standards and Assessment. Washington, DC: National Academy Press.

8. National Assessment of Educational Progress. (2009). *Science Framework for the 2009 National Assessment of Educational Progress.* Washington, DC: U.S. Government Printing Office. Developed for the National Assessment Governing Board. Available: http://www.nagb.org/publications/frameworks/science-09.pdf [June 2011].

9. College Board. (2009). *Science College Board Standards for College Success.* Available: http://professionals.collegeboard.com/profdownload/cbscs-science-standards-2009.pdf [June 2011].

10. National Science Teachers Association. (2009). *Science Anchors.* Arlington, VA: Author. Available http://www.nsta.org/involved/cse/scienceanchors.aspx [June 2011].

11. Baillargeon, R. (2004). How do infants learn about the physical world? *Current Directions in Psychological Science, 3,* 133-140.

12. Cohen, L.B., and Chashon, C.H. (2006). Infant cognition. In W. Damon and R.M. Lerner (Eds.), *Handbook of Child Psychology, Set, 6th Edition* (Chapter 5, vol. 2). Hoboken, NJ: Wiley.

13. Mandler, J.M. (2004). *The Foundations of Mind: Origins of Conceptual Thought.* Oxford, England: Oxford University Press.

14. Munakata, Y., Casey, B.J., and Diamond, A. (2004). Developmental cognitive neuroscience: Progress and potential. *Trends in Cognitive Science, 8,* 122-128.

15. Bullock, M., Gelman, R., and Baillargeon, R. (1982). The development of causal reasoning. In W.J. Friedman (Ed.), *The Developmental Psychology of Time.* New York: Academic Press.

16. Gelman, R., and Lucariello, J. (2002). Role of learning in cognitive development. In H. Pashler (Series Ed.) and R. Gallistel (Vol. Ed.), *Stevens' Handbook of Experimental Psychology: Learning, Motivation, and Emotion* (vol. 3, 3rd ed., pp. 395-443). Hoboken, NJ: Wiley.

17. Inagaki, K., and Hatano, G. (2002). *Young Children's Naïve Thinking About the Biological World.* New York: Psychology Press.

18. Inagaki, K., and Hatano, G. (2006). Young children's conception of the biological world. *Current Directions in Psychological Science, 15*(4), 177.

19. Keil, F.C. (2003). That's life: Coming to understand biology. *Human Development, 46,* 369-377.

20. Metz, K. (1995). Reassessment of developmental constraints on children's science instruction. *Review of Educational Research, 65,* 93-127.

21. Carey, S. (1985). *Conceptual Change in Childhood.* Cambridge, MA: MIT Press.

22. Gelman, R., and Biallargeon, R. (1983). A review of some Piagetian concepts. In J.H. Flavell and E.M. Markman (Eds.), *Handbook of Child Psychology* (vol. 3, pp. 167-230). Hoboken, NJ: Wiley.

23. Gelman, S., and Kalish, C. (2005). Conceptual development. In R.S. Siegler and D. Kuhn (Eds.), *Handbook of Child Psychology, Set, 6th Edition* (vol. 2, pp. 687-733). Hoboken, NJ: Wiley.

24. National Research Council. (1999). *How People Learn: Brain, Mind, Experience, and School.* Committee on Developments in the Science of Learning. J.D. Bransford, A.L. Brown, and R.R. Cocking (Eds.). Washington, DC: National Academy Press.

25. Consortium for Policy Research in Education. (2009). *Learning Progressions in Science: An Evidence-Based Approach to Reform.* Prepared by T. Corcoran, F. Mosher, and A. Rogat, Center on Continuous Instructional Improvement, Teachers College, Columbia University. Available: http://www.cpre.org/images/stories/cpre_pdfs/lp_science_rr63.pdf [June 2011].

26. Smith, C.L., Wiser, M., Anderson, C.W., and Krajcik, J. (2006). Implications of research on children's learning for standards and assessment: A proposed learning progression for matter and the atomic molecular theory. *Measurement, 4*(1-2), 1-98.

27. Renninger, K.A. (2000). Individual interest and its implications for understanding intrinsic motivation. In C. Sandsone and J.M. Harackiewicz (Eds.), *Intrinsic Motivation: Controversies and New Directions* (pp. 373-404). San Diego: Academic Press.

28. Renninger, K.A. (2003). Effort and Interest. In J. Guthrie (Ed.), *The Encyclopedia of Education* (2nd ed., pp. 704-707). New York: Macmillan.

29. Tai, R.H., Liu, C.Q., Maltese, A.V., and Fan, X. (2006). Planning early for careers in science. *Science, 312*(5,777), 1,143-1,144.

30. Ormerod, M.B., and Duckworth, D. (1975). *Pupils' Attitudes to Science.* Atlantic Highlands, NJ: Humanities Press.

31. Coley, J.D., Vitkin, A.Z., Seaton, C.E., and Yopchick, J.E. (2005). Effects of experience on relational inferences on children: The case of folk biology. In B.G. Bara, L. Barsalou, and M. Bucciarelli (Eds.), *Proceedings of the 27th Annual Conference of the Cognitive Science Society* (pp. 471-475). Mahwah, NJ: Lawrence Erlbaum Associates.

32. Ross, N., Medin, D., Coley, J.D., and Atran, S. (2003). Cultural and experiential differences in the development of folk biological induction. *Cognitive Development, 18*(1), 25-47.

33. Tarlowski, A. (2006). If it's an animal it has axons: Experience and culture in preschool children's reasoning about animates. *Cognitive Development, 21*(3), 249-265.

34. Hudicourt-Barnes, J. (2001). Bay odyans: Argumentation in Haitian Creole classrooms. *Hands On!, 24*(2), 7-9.

PART II

DIMENSIONS OF THE FRAMEWORK

3

Dimension 1
SCIENTIFIC AND ENGINEERING PRACTICES

From its inception, one of the principal goals of science education has been to cultivate students' scientific habits of mind, develop their capability to engage in scientific inquiry, and teach them how to reason in a scientific context [1, 2]. There has always been a tension, however, between the emphasis that should be placed on developing knowledge of the content of science and the emphasis placed on scientific practices. A narrow focus on content alone has the unfortunate consequence of leaving students with naive conceptions of the nature of scientific inquiry [3] and the impression that science is simply a body of isolated facts [4].

This chapter stresses the importance of developing students' knowledge of how science and engineering achieve their ends while also strengthening their competency with related practices. As previously noted, we use the term "practices," instead of a term such as "skills," to stress that engaging in scientific inquiry requires coordination both of knowledge and skill simultaneously.

In the chapter's three major sections, we first articulate why the learning of science and engineering practices is important for K-12 students and why these practices should reflect those of professional scientists and engineers. Second, we describe in detail eight practices we consider essential for learning science and engineering in grades K-12 (see Box 3-1). Finally, we conclude that acquiring skills in these practices supports a better understanding of how scientific knowledge is produced and how engineering solutions are developed. Such understanding will help students become more critical consumers of scientific information.

BOX 3-1

PRACTICES FOR K-12 SCIENCE CLASSROOMS

1. Asking questions (for science) and defining problems (for engineering)

2. Developing and using models

3. Planning and carrying out investigations

4. Analyzing and interpreting data

5. Using mathematics and computational thinking

6. Constructing explanations (for science) and designing solutions (for engineering)

7. Engaging in argument from evidence

8. Obtaining, evaluating, and communicating information

Throughout the discussion, we consider practices both of science and engineering. In many cases, the practices in the two fields are similar enough that they can be discussed together. In other cases, however, they are considered separately.

WHY PRACTICES?

Engaging in the practices of science helps students understand how scientific knowledge develops; such direct involvement gives them an appreciation of the wide range of approaches that are used to investigate, model, and explain the world. Engaging in the practices of engineering likewise helps students understand the work of engineers, as well as the links between engineering and science. Participation in these practices also helps students form an understanding of the crosscutting concepts and disciplinary ideas of science and engineering; moreover, it makes students' knowledge more meaningful and embeds it more deeply into their worldview.

The actual doing of science or engineering can also pique students' curiosity, capture their interest, and motivate their continued study; the insights thus gained help them recognize that the work of scientists and engineers is a creative

> The actual doing of science or engineering can pique students' curiosity, capture their interest, and motivate their continued study.

endeavor [5, 6]—one that has deeply affected the world they live in. Students may then recognize that science and engineering can contribute to meeting many of the major challenges that confront society today, such as generating sufficient energy, preventing and treating disease, maintaining supplies of fresh water and food, and addressing climate change. Any education that focuses predominantly on the detailed products of scientific labor—the facts of science—without developing an understanding of how those facts were established or that ignores the many important applications of science in the world misrepresents science and marginalizes the importance of engineering.

Understanding How Scientists Work

The idea of science as a set of practices has emerged from the work of historians, philosophers, psychologists, and sociologists over the past 60 years. This work illuminates how science is actually done, both in the short term (e.g., studies of activity in a particular laboratory or program) and historically (studies of laboratory notebooks, published texts, eyewitness accounts) [7-9]. Seeing science as a set of practices shows that theory development, reasoning, and testing are components of a larger ensemble of activities that includes networks of participants and institutions [10, 11], specialized ways of talking and writing [12], the development of models to represent systems or phenomena [13-15], the making of predictive inferences, construction of appropriate instrumentation, and testing of hypotheses by experiment or observation [16].

Our view is that this perspective is an improvement over previous approaches in several ways. First, it minimizes the tendency to reduce scientific practice to a single set of procedures, such as identifying and controlling variables, classifying entities, and identifying sources of error. This tendency overemphasizes experimental investigation at the expense of other practices, such as modeling, critique, and communication. In addition, when such procedures are taught in isolation from science content, they become the aims of instruction in and of themselves rather than a means of developing a deeper understanding of the concepts and purposes of science [17].

Second, a focus on practices (in the plural) avoids the mistaken impression that there is one distinctive approach common to all science—a single "scientific method"—or that uncertainty is a universal attribute of science. In reality, practicing scientists employ a broad spectrum of methods, and although science involves many areas of uncertainty as knowledge is developed, there are now many aspects of scientific knowledge that are so well established as to be unquestioned foundations of the culture and its technologies. It is only through engagement in the practices that students can recognize how such knowledge comes about and why some parts of scientific theory are more firmly established than others.

Third, attempts to develop the idea that science should be taught through a process of inquiry have been hampered by the lack of a commonly accepted definition of its constituent elements. Such ambiguity results in widely divergent pedagogic objectives [18]—an outcome that is counterproductive to the goal of common standards.

The focus here is on important practices, such as modeling, developing explanations, and engaging in critique and evaluation (argumentation), that have too often been underemphasized in the context of science education. In particular, we stress that critique is an essential element both for building new knowledge in general and for the learning of science in particular [19, 20]. Traditionally, K-12 science education has paid little attention to the role of critique in science. However, as all ideas in science are evaluated against alternative explanations and compared with evidence, acceptance of an explanation is ultimately an assessment of what data are reliable and relevant and a decision about which explanation is the most satisfactory. Thus knowing why the wrong answer is wrong can help secure a deeper and stronger understanding of why the right answer is right. Engaging in argumentation from evidence about an explanation supports students' understanding of the reasons and empirical evidence for that explanation, demonstrating that science is a body of knowledge rooted in evidence.

How the Practices Are Integrated into Both Inquiry and Design

One helpful way of understanding the practices of scientists and engineers is to frame them as work that is done in three spheres of activity, as shown in Figure 3-1. In one sphere, the dominant activity is investigation and empirical inquiry. In the second, the essence of work is the construction of explanations or designs using reasoning, creative thinking, and models. And in the third sphere, the ideas, such as the fit of models and explanations to evidence or the appropriateness of product designs, are analyzed, debated, and evaluated [21-23]. In all three spheres

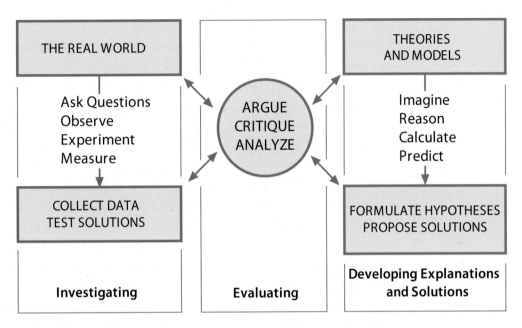

FIGURE 3-1 The three spheres of activity for scientists and engineers.

of activity, scientists and engineers try to use the best available tools to support the task at hand, which today means that modern computational technology is integral to virtually all aspects of their work.

At the left of the figure are activities related to empirical investigation. In this sphere of activity, scientists determine what needs to be measured; observe phenomena; plan experiments, programs of observation, and methods of data collection; build instruments; engage in disciplined fieldwork; and identify sources of uncertainty. For their part, engineers engage in testing that will contribute data for informing proposed designs. A civil engineer, for example, cannot design a new highway without measuring the terrain and collecting data about the nature of the soil and water flows.

The activities related to developing explanations and solutions are shown at the right of the figure. For scientists, their work in this sphere of activity is to draw from established theories and models and to propose extensions to theory or create new models. Often, they develop a model or hypothesis that leads to new questions to investigate or alternative explanations to consider. For engineers, the major practice is the production of designs. Design development also involves constructing models, for example, computer simulations of new structures or processes that may be used to test a design under a range of simulated conditions or, at a later stage, to test a physical prototype. Both scientists and engineers use their models—including sketches, diagrams, mathematical relationships, simulations, and physical models—to make predictions about the likely behavior of a system, and they then collect data to evaluate the predictions and possibly revise the models as a result.

Between and within these two spheres of activity is the practice of evaluation, represented by the middle space. Here is an iterative process that repeats at every step of the work. Critical thinking is required, whether in developing and refining an idea (an explanation or a design) or in conducting an investigation. The dominant activities in this sphere are argumentation and critique, which often lead to further experiments and observations or to changes in proposed models, explanations, or designs. Scientists and engineers use evidence-based argumentation to make the case for their ideas, whether involving new theories or designs, novel ways of collecting data, or interpretations of evidence. They and their peers then attempt to identify weaknesses and limitations in the argument, with the ultimate goal of refining and improving the explanation or design.

In reality, scientists and engineers move, fluidly and iteratively, back and forth among these three spheres of activity, and they conduct activities that might involve two or even all three of the modes at once. The function of Figure 3-1 is therefore solely to offer a scheme that helps identify the function, significance, range, and diversity of practices embedded in the work of scientists and engineers. Although admittedly a simplification, the figure does identify three overarching categories of practices and shows how they interact.

How Engineering and Science Differ

Engineering and science are similar in that both involve creative processes, and neither uses just one method. And just as scientific investigation has been defined in different ways, engineering design has been described in various ways. However, there is widespread agreement on the broad outlines of the engineering design process [24, 25].

Like scientific investigations, engineering design is both iterative and systematic. It is iterative in that each new version of the design is tested and then modified, based on what has been learned up to that point. It is systematic in that a number of characteristic steps must be undertaken. One step is identifying the problem and defining specifications and constraints. Another step is generating ideas for how to solve the problem; engineers often use research and group

sessions (e.g., "brainstorming") to come up with a range of solutions and design alternatives for further development. Yet another step is the testing of potential solutions through the building and testing of physical or mathematical models and prototypes, all of which provide valuable data that cannot be obtained in any other way. With data in hand, the engineer can analyze how well the various solutions meet the given specifications and constraints and then evaluate what is needed to improve the leading design or devise a better one.

In contrast, scientific studies may or may not be driven by any immediate practical application. On one hand, certain kinds of scientific research, such as that which led to Pasteur's fundamental contributions to the germ theory of disease, were undertaken for practical purposes and resulted in important new technologies, including vaccination for anthrax and rabies and the pasteurization of milk to prevent spoilage. On the other hand, many scientific studies, such as the search for the planets orbiting distant stars, are driven by curiosity and undertaken with the aim of answering a question about the world or understanding an

Students' opportunities to immerse themselves in these practices and to explore why they are central to science and engineering are critical to appreciating the skill of the expert and the nature of his or her enterprise.

observed pattern. For science, developing such an explanation constitutes success in and of itself, regardless of whether it has an immediate practical application; the goal of science is to develop a set of coherent and mutually consistent theoretical descriptions of the world that can provide explanations over a wide range of phenomena, For engineering, however, success is measured by the extent to which a human need or want has been addressed.

Both scientists and engineers engage in argumentation, but they do so with different goals. In engineering, the goal of argumentation is to evaluate prospective designs and then produce the most effective design for meeting the specifications and constraints. This optimization process typically involves trade-offs between competing goals, with the consequence that there is never just one "correct" solution to a design challenge. Instead, there are a number of possible solutions, and choosing among them inevitably involves personal as well as technical and cost considerations. Moreover, the continual arrival of new technologies enables new solutions.

In contrast, theories in science must meet a very different set of criteria, such as parsimony (a preference for simpler solutions) and explanatory coherence (essentially how well any new theory provides explanations of phenomena that fit with observations and allow predictions or inferences about the past to be made). Moreover, the aim of science is to find a single coherent and comprehensive theory for a range of related phenomena. Multiple competing explanations are regarded as unsatisfactory and, if possible, the contradictions they contain must be resolved through more data, which enable either the selection of the best available explanation or the development of a new and more comprehensive theory for the phenomena in question.

Although we do not expect K-12 students to be able to develop new scientific theories, we do expect that they can develop theory-based models and argue using them, in conjunction with evidence from observations, to develop explanations. Indeed, developing evidence-based models, arguments, and explanations is key to both developing and demonstrating understanding of an accepted scientific viewpoint.

■ A focus on practices (in the plural) avoids the mistaken impression that there is one distinctive approach common to all science—a single "scientific method." ■

PRACTICES FOR K-12 CLASSROOMS

The K-12 practices described in this chapter are derived from those that scientists and engineers actually engage in as part of their work. We recognize that students cannot reach the level of competence of professional scientists and engineers, any more than a novice violinist is expected to attain the abilities of a virtuoso. Yet students' opportunities to immerse themselves in these practices and to explore why they are central to science and engineering are critical to appreciating the skill of the expert and the nature of his or her enterprise.

We consider eight practices to be essential elements of the K-12 science and engineering curriculum:

1. Asking questions (for science) and defining problems (for engineering)
2. Developing and using models
3. Planning and carrying out investigations
4. Analyzing and interpreting data
5. Using mathematics and computational thinking
6. Constructing explanations (for science) and designing solutions (for engineering)
7. Engaging in argument from evidence
8. Obtaining, evaluating, and communicating information

In the eight subsections that follow, we address in turn each of these eight practices in some depth. Each discussion describes the practice, articulates the major competencies that students should have by the end of 12th grade ("Goals"), and sketches how their competence levels might progress across the preceding grades ("Progression"). These sketches are based on the committee's judgment, as there is very little research evidence as yet on the developmental trajectory of each of these practices. The overall objective is that students develop both the facility and the inclination to call on these practices, separately or in combination, as needed to support their learning and to demonstrate their understanding of science and engineering. Box 3-2 briefly contrasts the role of each practice's manifestation in science with its counterpart in engineering. In doing science or engineering, the practices are used iteratively and in combination; they should not be seen as a linear sequence of steps to be taken in the order presented.

BOX 3-2

DISTINGUISHING PRACTICES IN SCIENCE FROM THOSE IN ENGINEERING

1. Asking Questions and Defining Problems

Science begins with a question about a phenomenon, such as "Why is the sky blue?" or "What causes cancer?," and seeks to develop theories that can provide explanatory answers to such questions. A basic practice of the scientist is formulating empirically answerable questions about phenomena, establishing what is already known, and determining what questions have yet to be satisfactorily answered.

Engineering begins with a problem, need, or desire that suggests an engineering problem that needs to be solved. A societal problem such as reducing the nation's dependence on fossil fuels may engender a variety of engineering problems, such as designing more efficient transportation systems, or alternative power generation devices such as improved solar cells. Engineers ask questions to define the engineering problem, determine criteria for a successful solution, and identify constraints.

2. Developing and Using Models

Science often involves the construction and use of a wide variety of models and simulations to help develop explanations about natural phenomena. Models make it possible to go beyond observables and imagine a world not yet seen. Models enable predictions of the form "if . . . then . . . therefore" to be made in order to test hypothetical explanations.

Engineering makes use of models and simulations to analyze existing systems so as to see where flaws might occur or to test possible solutions to a new problem. Engineers also call on models of various sorts to test proposed systems and to recognize the strengths and limitations of their designs.

3. Planning and Carrying Out Investigations

Scientific investigation may be conducted in the field or the laboratory. A major practice of scientists is planning and carrying out a systematic investigation, which requires the identification of what is to be recorded and, if applicable, what are to be treated as the dependent and independent variables (control of variables). Observations and data collected from such work are used to test existing theories and explanations or to revise and develop new ones.

Engineers use investigation both to gain data essential for specifying design criteria or parameters and to test their designs. Like scientists, engineers must identify relevant variables, decide how they will be measured, and collect data for analysis. Their investigations help them to identify how effective, efficient, and durable their designs may be under a range of conditions.

4. Analyzing and Interpreting Data

Scientific investigations produce data that must be analyzed in order to derive meaning. Because data usually do not speak for themselves, scientists use a range of tools—including tabulation, graphical interpretation, visualization, and statistical analysis—to identify the significant features and patterns in the data. Sources of error are identified and the degree of certainty calculated. Modern technology makes the collection of large data sets much easier, thus providing many secondary sources for analysis.

Engineers analyze data collected in the tests of their designs and investigations; this allows them to compare different solutions and determine how well each one meets specific design criteria—that is, which design best solves the problem within the given constraints. Like scientists, engineers require a range of tools to identify the major patterns and interpret the results.

5. Using Mathematics and Computational Thinking

In **science,** mathematics and computation are fundamental tools for representing physical variables and their relationships. They are used for a range of tasks, such as constructing simulations, statistically analyzing data, and recognizing, expressing, and applying quantitative relationships. Mathematical and computational approaches enable predictions of the behavior of physical systems, along with the testing of such predictions. Moreover, statistical techniques are invaluable for assessing the significance of patterns or correlations.

In **engineering,** mathematical and computational representations of established relationships and principles are an integral part of design. For example, structural engineers create mathematically based analyses of designs to calculate whether they can stand up to the expected stresses of use and if they can be completed within acceptable budgets. Moreover, simulations of designs provide an effective test bed for the development of designs and their improvement.

BOX 3-2 continued

DISTINGUISHING PRACTICES IN SCIENCE FROM THOSE IN ENGINEERING

6. Constructing Explanations and Designing Solutions

The goal of **science** is the construction of theories that can provide explanatory accounts of features of the world. A theory becomes accepted when it has been shown to be superior to other explanations in the breadth of phenomena it accounts for and in its explanatory coherence and parsimony. Scientific explanations are explicit applications of theory to a specific situation or phenomenon, perhaps with the intermediary of a theory-based model for the system under study. The goal for students is to construct logically coherent explanations of phenomena that incorporate their current understanding of science, or a model that represents it, and are consistent with the available evidence.

Engineering design, a systematic process for solving engineering problems, is based on scientific knowledge and models of the material world. Each proposed solution results from a process of balancing competing criteria of desired functions, technological feasibility, cost, safety, esthetics, and compliance with legal requirements. There is usually no single best solution but rather a range of solutions. Which one is the optimal choice depends on the criteria used for making evaluations.

7. Engaging in Argument from Evidence

In **science,** reasoning and argument are essential for identifying the strengths and weaknesses of a line of reasoning and for finding the best explanation for a natural phenomenon. Scientists must defend their explanations, formulate evidence based on a solid foundation of data, examine their own understanding in light of the evidence and comments offered by others, and collaborate with peers in searching for the best explanation for the phenomenon being investigated.

In **engineering,** reasoning and argument are essential for finding the best possible solution to a problem. Engineers collaborate with their peers throughout the design process, with a critical stage being the selection of the most promising solution among a field of competing ideas. Engineers use systematic methods to compare alternatives, formulate evidence based on test data, make arguments from evidence to defend their conclusions, evaluate critically the ideas of others, and revise their designs in order to achieve the best solution to the problem at hand.

8. Obtaining, Evaluating, and Communicating Information

Science cannot advance if scientists are unable to communicate their findings clearly and persuasively or to learn about the findings of others. A major practice of science is thus the communication of ideas and the results of inquiry—orally, in writing, with the use of tables, diagrams, graphs, and equations, and by engaging in extended discussions with scientific peers. Science requires the ability to derive meaning from scientific texts (such as papers, the Internet, symposia, and lectures), to evaluate the scientific validity of the information thus acquired, and to integrate that information.

Engineers cannot produce new or improved technologies if the advantages of their designs are not communicated clearly and persuasively. Engineers need to be able to express their ideas, orally and in writing, with the use of tables, graphs, drawings, or models and by engaging in extended discussions with peers. Moreover, as with scientists, they need to be able to derive meaning from colleagues' texts, evaluate the information, and apply it usefully. In engineering and science alike, new technologies are now routinely available that extend the possibilities for collaboration and communication.

Practice 1   **Asking Questions and Defining Problems**

Questions are the engine that drive science and engineering.

Science asks
- What exists and what happens?
- Why does it happen?
- How does one know?

Engineering asks
- What can be done to address a particular human need or want?
- How can the need be better specified?
- What tools and technologies are available, or could be developed, for addressing this need?

Both science and engineering ask
- How does one communicate about phenomena, evidence, explanations, and design solutions?

Asking questions is essential to developing scientific habits of mind. Even for individuals who do not become scientists or engineers, the ability to ask well-defined questions is an important component of science literacy, helping to make them critical consumers of scientific knowledge.

Scientific questions arise in a variety of ways. They can be driven by curiosity about the world (e.g., Why is the sky blue?). They can be inspired by a model's or theory's predictions or by attempts to extend or refine a model or theory (e.g., How does the particle model of matter explain the incompressibility of liquids?). Or they can result from the need to provide better solutions to a problem. For example, the question of why it is impossible to siphon water above a height of 32 feet led Evangelista Torricelli (17th-century inventor of the barometer) to his discoveries about the atmosphere and the identification of a vacuum.

Questions are also important in engineering. Engineers must be able to ask probing questions in order to define an engineering problem. For example, they may ask: What is the need or desire that underlies the problem? What are the criteria (specifications) for a successful solution? What are the constraints? Other questions arise when generating possible solutions: Will this solution meet the design criteria? Can two or more ideas be combined to produce a better solution?

> **Students at any grade level should be able to ask questions of each other about the texts they read, the features of the phenomena they observe, and the conclusions they draw from their models or scientific investigations.**

What are the possible trade-offs? And more questions arise when testing solutions: Which ideas should be tested? What evidence is needed to show which idea is optimal under the given constraints?

The experience of learning science and engineering should therefore develop students' ability to ask—and indeed, encourage them to ask—well-formulated questions that can be investigated empirically. Students also need to recognize the distinction between questions that can be answered empirically and those that are answerable only in other domains of knowledge or human experience.

GOALS

By grade 12, students should be able to

- Ask questions about the natural and human-built worlds—for example: Why are there seasons? What do bees do? Why did that structure collapse? How is electric power generated?
- Distinguish a scientific question (e.g., Why do helium balloons rise?) from a nonscientific question (Which of these colored balloons is the prettiest?).
- Formulate and refine questions that can be answered empirically in a science classroom and use them to design an inquiry or construct a pragmatic solution.
- Ask probing questions that seek to identify the premises of an argument, request further elaboration, refine a research question or engineering problem, or challenge the interpretation of a data set—for example: How do you know? What evidence supports that argument?
- Note features, patterns, or contradictions in observations and ask questions about them.
- For engineering, ask questions about the need or desire to be met in order to define constraints and specifications for a solution.

PROGRESSION

Students at any grade level should be able to ask questions of each other about the texts they read, the features of the phenomena they observe, and the conclusions they draw from their models or scientific investigations. For engineering, they should ask questions to define the problem to be solved and to elicit ideas that lead to the constraints and specifications for its solution. As they progress across the grades, their questions should become more relevant, focused, and sophisticated. Facilitating such evolution will require a classroom culture that respects and values good questions, that offers students opportunities to refine their questions and questioning strategies, and that incorporates the teaching of effective questioning strategies across all grade levels. As a result, students will become increasingly proficient at posing questions that request relevant empirical evidence; that seek to refine a model, an explanation, or an engineering problem; or that challenge the premise of an argument or the suitability of a design.

Practice 2   # Developing and Using Models

Scientists construct mental and conceptual models of phenomena. Mental models are internal, personal, idiosyncratic, incomplete, unstable, and essentially functional. They serve the purpose of being a tool for thinking with, making predictions, and making sense of experience. Conceptual models, the focus of this section, are, in contrast, explicit representations that are in some ways analogous to the phenomena they represent. Conceptual models allow scientists and engineers to better visualize and understand a phenomenon under investigation or develop a possible solution to a design problem. Used in science and engineering as either structural, functional, or behavioral analogs, albeit simplified, conceptual models include diagrams, physical replicas, mathematical representations, analogies, and computer simulations. Although they do not correspond exactly to the more complicated entity being modeled, they do bring certain features into focus while minimizing or obscuring others. Because all models contain approximations and assumptions that limit the range of validity of their application and the precision of their predictive power, it is important to recognize their limitations.

Conceptual models are in some senses the external articulation of the mental models that scientists hold and are strongly interrelated with mental models. Building an understanding of models and their role in science helps students to construct and revise mental models of phenomena. Better mental models, in turn, lead to a deeper understanding of science and enhanced scientific reasoning.

Scientists use models (from here on, for the sake of simplicity, we use the term "models" to refer to conceptual models rather than mental models) to represent their current understanding of a system (or parts of a system) under study, to aid in the development of questions and explanations, and to communicate ideas

to others [13]. Some of the models used by scientists are mathematical; for example, the ideal gas law is an equation derived from the model of a gas as a set of point masses engaged in perfectly elastic collisions with each other and the walls of the container—which is a simplified model based on the atomic theory of matter. For more complex systems, mathematical representations of physical systems are used to create computer simulations, which enable scientists to predict the behavior of otherwise intractable systems—for example, the effects of increasing atmospheric levels of carbon dioxide on agriculture in different regions of the world. Models can be evaluated and refined through an iterative cycle of comparing their predictions with the real world and then adjusting them, thereby potentially yielding insights into the phenomenon being modeled.

Engineering makes use of models to analyze existing systems; this allows engineers to see where or under what conditions flaws might develop or to test possible solutions to a new problem. Engineers also use models to visualize a design and take it to a higher level of refinement, to communicate a design's features to others, and as prototypes for testing design performance. Models, particularly modern computer simulations that encode relevant physical laws and properties of materials, can be especially helpful both in realizing and testing designs for structures, such as buildings, bridges, or aircraft, that are expensive to construct and that must survive extreme conditions that occur only on rare occasions. Other types of engineering problems also benefit from use of specialized computer-based simulations in their design and testing phases. But as in science, engineers who use models must be aware of their intrinsic limitations and test them against known situations to ensure that they are reliable.

GOALS

By grade 12, students should be able to

- Construct drawings or diagrams as representations of events or systems—for example, draw a picture of an insect with labeled features, represent what happens to the water in a puddle as it is warmed by the sun, or represent a simple physical model of a real-world object and use it as the basis of an explanation or to make predictions about how the system will behave in specified circumstances.
- Represent and explain phenomena with multiple types of models—for example, represent molecules with 3-D models or with bond diagrams—and move flexibly between model types when different ones are most useful for different purposes.
- Discuss the limitations and precision of a model as the representation of a system, process, or design and suggest ways in which the model might be improved to better fit available evidence or better reflect a design's specifications. Refine a model in light of empirical evidence or criticism to improve its quality and explanatory power.
- Use (provided) computer simulations or simulations developed with simple simulation tools as a tool for understanding and investigating aspects of a system, particularly those not readily visible to the naked eye.
- Make and use a model to test a design, or aspects of a design, and to compare the effectiveness of different design solutions.

PROGRESSION

Modeling can begin in the earliest grades, with students' models progressing from concrete "pictures" and/or physical scale models (e.g., a toy car) to more abstract representations of relevant relationships in later grades, such as a diagram representing forces on a particular object in a system. Students should be asked to use diagrams, maps, and other abstract models as tools that enable them to elaborate on their own ideas or findings and present them to others [15]. Young students should be encouraged to devise pictorial and simple graphical representations of the findings of their investigations and to use these models in developing their explanations of what occurred.

More sophisticated types of models should increasingly be used across the grades, both in instruction and curriculum materials, as students progress through their science education. The quality of a student-developed model will be highly dependent on prior knowledge and skill and also on the student's understanding of the system being modeled, so students should be expected to refine their models as their understanding develops. Curricula will need to stress the role of models explicitly and provide students with modeling tools (e.g., Model-It, agent-based modeling such as NetLogo, spreadsheet models), so that students come to value this core practice and develop a level of facility in constructing and applying appropriate models.

Practice 3 — Planning and Carrying Out Investigations

Scientists and engineers investigate and observe the world with essentially two goals: (1) to systematically describe the world and (2) to develop and test theories and explanations of how the world works. In the first, careful observation and description often lead to identification of features that need to be explained or questions that need to be explored.

The second goal requires investigations to test explanatory models of the world and their predictions and whether the inferences suggested by these models are supported by data. Planning and designing such investigations require the ability to design experimental or observational inquiries that are appropriate to answering the question being asked or testing a hypothesis that has been formed. This process begins by identifying the relevant variables and considering how they might be observed, measured, and controlled (constrained by the experimental design to take particular values).

Planning for controls is an important part of the design of an investigation. In laboratory experiments, it is critical to decide which variables are to be treated as results or outputs and thus left to vary at will and which are to be treated as input conditions and hence controlled. In many cases, particularly in the case of field observations, such planning involves deciding what can be controlled and how to collect different samples of data under different conditions, even though not all conditions are under the direct control of the investigator.

Decisions must also be made about what measurements should be taken, the level of accuracy required, and the kinds of instrumentation best suited to making such measurements. As in other forms of inquiry, the key issue is one of precision—the goal is to measure the variable as accurately as possible and reduce sources of error. The investigator must therefore decide what constitutes a sufficient level of precision and what techniques can be used to reduce both random and systematic error.

GOALS

By grade 12, students should be able to

- Formulate a question that can be investigated within the scope of the classroom, school laboratory, or field with available resources and, when appropriate, frame a hypothesis (that is, a possible explanation that predicts a particular and stable outcome) based on a model or theory.
- Decide what data are to be gathered, what tools are needed to do the gathering, and how measurements will be recorded.
- Decide how much data are needed to produce reliable measurements and consider any limitations on the precision of the data.
- Plan experimental or field-research procedures, identifying relevant independent and dependent variables and, when appropriate, the need for controls.
- Consider possible confounding variables or effects and ensure that the investigation's design has controlled for them.

PROGRESSION

Students need opportunities to design investigations so that they can learn the importance of such decisions as what to measure, what to keep constant, and how to select or construct data collection instruments that are appropriate to the needs of an inquiry. They also need experiences that help them recognize that the laboratory is not the sole domain for legitimate scientific inquiry and that, for many scientists (e.g., earth scientists, ethologists, ecologists), the "laboratory" is the natural world where experiments are conducted and data are collected in the field.

In the elementary years, students' experiences should be structured to help them learn to define the features to be investigated, such as patterns that suggest causal relationships (e.g., What features of a ramp affect the speed of a given ball as it leaves the ramp?). The plan of the investigation, what trials to make and how to record information about them, then needs to be refined iteratively as students recognize from their experiences the limitations of their original plan. These investigations can be enriched and extended by linking them to engineering design projects—for example, how can students apply what they have learned about ramps to design a track that makes a ball travel a given distance, go around a loop, or stop on an uphill slope. From the earliest grades, students should have opportunities to carry out careful and systematic investigations, with appropriately supported prior experiences that develop their ability to observe and measure and to record data using appropriate tools and instruments.

Students should have opportunities to plan and carry out several different kinds of investigations during their K-12 years. At all levels, they should engage in investigations that range from those structured by the teacher—in order to expose an issue or question that they would be unlikely to explore on their own (e.g., measuring specific properties of materials)—to those that emerge from students' own

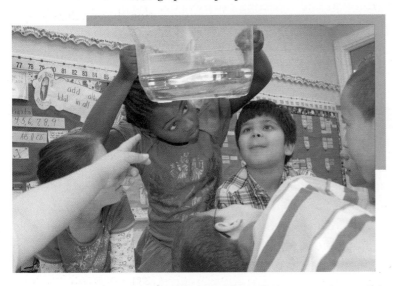

questions. As they become more sophisticated, students also should have opportunities not only to identify questions to be researched but also to decide what data are to be gathered, what variables should be controlled, what tools or instruments are needed to gather and record data in an appropriate format, and eventually to consider how to incorporate measurement error in analyzing data.

Older students should be asked to develop a hypothesis that predicts a particular and stable outcome and to explain their reasoning and justify their choice. By high school, any hypothesis should be based on a well-developed model or theory. In addition, students should be able to recognize that it is not always possible to control variables and that other methods can be used in such cases—for example, looking for correlations (with the understanding that correlations do not necessarily imply causality).

Practice 4   Analyzing and Interpreting Data

Once collected, data must be presented in a form that can reveal any patterns and relationships and that allows results to be communicated to others. Because raw data as such have little meaning, a major practice of scientists is to organize and interpret data through tabulating, graphing, or statistical analysis. Such analysis can bring out the meaning of data—and their relevance—so that they may be used as evidence.

Once collected, data must be presented in a form that can reveal any patterns and relationships and that allows results to be communicated to others.

Engineers, too, make decisions based on evidence that a given design will work; they rarely rely on trial and error. Engineers often analyze a design by creating a model or prototype and collecting extensive data on how it performs, including under extreme conditions. Analysis of this kind of data not only informs design decisions and enables the prediction or assessment of performance but also helps define or clarify problems, determine economic feasibility, evaluate alternatives, and investigate failures.

Spreadsheets and databases provide useful ways of organizing data, especially large data sets. The identification of relationships in data is aided by a range of tools, including tables, graphs, and mathematics. Tables permit major features of a large body of data to be summarized in a conveniently accessible form, graphs offer a means of visually summarizing data, and mathematics is essential for expressing relationships between different variables in the data set (see Practice 5 for further discussion of mathematics). Modern computer-based visualization tools often allow data to be displayed in varied forms and thus for learners to engage interactively with data in their analyses. In addition, standard statistical techniques can help to reduce the effect of error in relating one variable to another.

Students need opportunities to analyze large data sets and identify correlations. Increasingly, such data sets—involving temperature, pollution levels, and other scientific measurements—are available on the Internet. Moreover, information technology enables the capture of data beyond the classroom at all hours of the day. Such data sets extend the range of students' experiences and help to illuminate this important practice of analyzing and interpreting data.

GOALS

By grade 12, students should be able to

- Analyze data systematically, either to look for salient patterns or to test whether data are consistent with an initial hypothesis.
- Recognize when data are in conflict with expectations and consider what revisions in the initial model are needed.

- Use spreadsheets, databases, tables, charts, graphs, statistics, mathematics, and information and computer technology to collate, summarize, and display data and to explore relationships between variables, especially those representing input and output.
- Evaluate the strength of a conclusion that can be inferred from any data set, using appropriate grade-level mathematical and statistical techniques.
- Recognize patterns in data that suggest relationships worth investigating further. Distinguish between causal and correlational relationships.
- Collect data from physical models and analyze the performance of a design under a range of conditions.

PROGRESSION

At the elementary level, students need support to recognize the need to record observations—whether in drawings, words, or numbers—and to share them with others. As they engage in scientific inquiry more deeply, they should begin to collect categorical or numerical data for presentation in forms that facilitate interpretation, such as tables and graphs. When feasible, computers and other digital tools should be introduced as a means of enabling this practice.

In middle school, students should have opportunities to learn standard techniques for displaying, analyzing, and interpreting data; such techniques include different types of graphs, the identification of outliers in the data set, and averaging to reduce the effects of measurement error. Students should also be asked to explain why these techniques are needed.

As students progress through various science classes in high school and their investigations become more complex, they need to develop skill in additional techniques for displaying and analyzing data, such as x-y scatterplots or cross-tabulations to express the relationship between two variables. Students should be helped to recognize that they may need to explore more than one way to display their data in order to identify and present significant features. They also need opportunities to use mathematics and statistics to analyze features of data such as covariation. Also at the high school level, students should have the opportunity to use a greater diversity of samples of scientific data and to use computers or other digital tools to support this kind of analysis.

Students should be expected to use some of these same techniques in engineering as well. When they do so, it is important that they are made cognizant of the purpose of the exercise—that any data they collect and analyze are intended to help validate or improve a design or decide on an optimal solution.

Practice 5   Using Mathematics and Computational Thinking

Mathematics and computational tools are central to science and engineering. Mathematics enables the numerical representation of variables, the symbolic representation of relationships between physical entities, and the prediction of outcomes. Mathematics provides powerful models for describing and predicting such phenomena as atomic structure, gravitational forces, and quantum mechanics.

Since the mid-20th century, computational theories, information and computer technologies, and algorithms have revolutionized virtually all scientific and engineering fields. These tools and strategies allow scientists and engineers to collect and analyze large data sets, search for distinctive patterns, and identify relationships and significant features in ways that were previously impossible. They also provide powerful new techniques for employing mathematics to model complex phenomena— for example, the circulation of carbon dioxide in the atmosphere and ocean.

Mathematics and computation can be powerful tools when brought to bear in a scientific investigation. Mathematics serves pragmatic functions as a tool—both a communicative function, as one of the languages of science, and a structural function, which allows for logical deduction. Mathematics enables ideas to be expressed in a precise form and enables the identification of new ideas about the physical world. For example, the concept of the equivalence of mass and energy emerged from the mathematical analysis conducted by Einstein, based on the premises of special relativity. The contemporary understanding of electromagnetic waves emerged from Maxwell's mathematical analysis of the behavior of electric and magnetic fields. Modern theoretical physics is so heavily imbued with mathematics that it would make no sense to try to divide it into mathematical and nonmathematical parts. In much of modern science, predictions and inferences have a probabilistic nature, so understanding the mathematics of probability and of statistically derived inferences is an important part of understanding science.

Computational tools enhance the power of mathematics by enabling calculations that cannot be carried out analytically. For example, they allow the development of simulations, which combine mathematical representations of

> Increasing students' familiarity with the role of mathematics in science is central to developing a deeper understanding of how science works.

multiple underlying phenomena to model the dynamics of a complex system. Computational methods are also potent tools for visually representing data, and they can show the results of calculations or simulations in ways that allow the exploration of patterns.

Engineering, too, involves mathematical and computational skills. For example, structural engineers create mathematical models of bridge and building designs, based on physical laws, to test their performance, probe their structural limits, and assess whether they can be completed within acceptable budgets. Virtually any engineering design raises issues that require computation for their resolution.

Although there are differences in how mathematics and computational thinking are applied in science and in engineering, mathematics often brings these two fields together by enabling engineers to apply the mathematical form of scientific theories and by enabling scientists to use powerful information technologies designed by engineers. Both kinds of professionals can thereby accomplish investigations and analyses and build complex models, which might otherwise be out of the question.

Mathematics (including statistics) and computational tools are essential for data analysis, especially for large data sets. The abilities to view data from different perspectives and with different graphical representations, to test relationships between variables, and to explore the interplay of diverse external conditions all require mathematical skills that are enhanced and extended with computational skills.

GOALS

By grade 12, students should be able to

- Recognize dimensional quantities and use appropriate units in scientific applications of mathematical formulas and graphs.
- Express relationships and quantities in appropriate mathematical or algorithmic forms for scientific modeling and investigations.

- Recognize that computer simulations are built on mathematical models that incorporate underlying assumptions about the phenomena or systems being studied.
- Use simple test cases of mathematical expressions, computer programs, or simulations—that is, compare their outcomes with what is known about the real world—to see if they "make sense."
- Use grade-level-appropriate understanding of mathematics and statistics in analyzing data.

PROGRESSION

Increasing students' familiarity with the role of mathematics in science is central to developing a deeper understanding of how science works. As soon as students learn to count, they can begin using numbers to find or describe patterns in nature. At appropriate grade levels, they should learn to use such instruments as rulers, protractors, and thermometers for the measurement of variables that are best represented by a continuous numerical scale, to apply mathematics to interpolate values, and to identify features—such as maximum, minimum, range, average, and median—of simple data sets.

A significant advance comes when relationships are expressed using equalities first in words and then in algebraic symbols—for example, shifting from distance traveled equals velocity multiplied by time elapsed to $s = vt$. Students should have opportunities to explore how such symbolic representations can be used to represent data, to predict outcomes, and eventually to derive further relationships using mathematics. Students should gain experience in using computers to record measurements taken with computer-connected probes or instruments, thereby recognizing how this process allows multiple measurements to be made rapidly and recurrently. Likewise, students should gain experience in using computer programs to transform their data between various tabular and graphical forms, thereby aiding in the identification of patterns.

Students should thus be encouraged to explore the use of computers for data analysis, using simple data sets, at an early age. For example, they could use spreadsheets to record data and then perform simple and recurring calculations from those data, such as the calculation of average speed from measurements of positions at multiple times. Later work should introduce them to the use of mathematical relationships to build simple computer models, using appropriate supporting programs or information and computer technology tools. As students progress in their understanding of mathematics and computation, at every level the science classroom should be a place where these tools are progressively exploited.

Practice 6   Constructing Explanations and Designing Solutions

Because science seeks to enhance human understanding of the world, scientific theories are developed to provide explanations aimed at illuminating the nature of particular phenomena, predicting future events, or making inferences about past events. Science has developed explanatory theories, such as the germ theory of disease, the Big Bang theory of the origin of the universe, and Darwin's theory of the evolution of species. Although their role is often misunderstood—the informal use of the word "theory," after all, can mean a guess—*scientific* theories are constructs based on significant bodies of knowledge and evidence, are revised in light of new evidence, and must withstand significant scrutiny by the scientific community before they are widely accepted and applied. Theories are not mere guesses, and they are especially valued because they provide explanations for multiple instances.

In science, the term "hypothesis" is also used differently than it is in everyday language. A scientific hypothesis is neither a scientific theory nor a guess; it is a plausible explanation for an observed phenomenon that can predict what will happen in a given situation. A hypothesis is made based on existing theoretical understanding relevant to the situation and often also on a specific model for the system in question.

Scientific explanations are accounts that link scientific theory with specific observations or phenomena—for example, they explain observed relationships between variables and describe the mechanisms that support cause and effect inferences about them. Very often the theory is first represented by a specific model for the situation in question, and then a model-based explanation is developed. For example, if one understands the theory of how oxygen is obtained, transported, and utilized in the body, then a model of the circulatory system can be developed and used to explain why heart rate and breathing rate increase with exercise.

> Scientific theories are developed to provide explanations aimed at illuminating the nature of particular phenomena, predicting future events, or making inferences about past events.

Engaging students with standard scientific explanations of the world—helping them to gain an understanding of the major ideas that science has developed—is a central aspect of science education. Asking students to demonstrate their own understanding of the implications of a scientific idea by developing their own explanations of phenomena, whether based on observations they have made or models they have developed, engages them in an essential part of the process by which conceptual change can occur. Explanations in science are a natural for such pedagogical uses, given their inherent appeals to simplicity, analogy, and empirical data (which may even be in the form of a thought experiment) [26, 27]. And explanations are especially valuable for the classroom because of, rather than in spite of, the fact that there often are competing explanations offered for the same phenomenon—for example, the recent gradual rise in the mean surface temperature on Earth. Deciding on the best explanation is a matter of argument that is resolved by how well any given explanation fits with all available data, how much it simplifies what would seem to be complex, and whether it produces a sense of understanding.

Because scientists achieve their own understanding by building theories and theory-based explanations with the aid of models and representations and by drawing on data and evidence, students should also develop some facility in constructing model- or evidence-based explanations. This is an essential step in building their own understanding of phenomena, in gaining greater appreciation of the explanatory power of the scientific theories that they are learning about in class, and in acquiring greater insight into how scientists operate.

In engineering, the goal is a design rather than an explanation. The process of developing a design is iterative and systematic, as is the process of developing an explanation or a theory in science. Engineers' activities, however, have elements that are distinct from those of scientists. These elements include specifying constraints and criteria for desired qualities of the solution, developing a design plan, producing and testing models or prototypes, selecting among alternative design features to optimize the achievement of design criteria, and refining design ideas based on the performance of a prototype or simulation.

GOALS

By grade 12, students should be able to

- Construct their own explanations of phenomena using their knowledge of accepted scientific theory and linking it to models and evidence.
- Use primary or secondary scientific evidence and models to support or refute an explanatory account of a phenomenon.
- Offer causal explanations appropriate to their level of scientific knowledge.
- Identify gaps or weaknesses in explanatory accounts (their own or those of others).

In their experience of engineering, students should have the opportunity to

- Solve design problems by appropriately applying their scientific knowledge.
- Undertake design projects, engaging in all steps of the design cycle and producing a plan that meets specific design criteria.
- Construct a device or implement a design solution.
- Evaluate and critique competing design solutions based on jointly developed and agreed-on design criteria.

PROGRESSION FOR EXPLANATION

Early in their science education, students need opportunities to engage in constructing and critiquing explanations. They should be encouraged to develop explanations of what they observe when conducting their own investigations and to evaluate their own and others' explanations for consistency with the evidence. For example, observations of the owl pellets they dissect should lead them to produce an explanation of owls' eating habits based on inferences made from what they find.

As students' knowledge develops, they can begin to identify and isolate variables and incorporate the resulting observations into their explanations of phenomena. Using their measurements of how one factor does or does not affect another, they can develop causal accounts to explain what they observe. For example, in investigating the conditions under which plants grow fastest, they may notice that the plants die when kept in the dark and seek to develop an explanation for this finding. Although the explanation at this level may be as simple as "plants die in the dark because they need light in order to live and grow," it provides a basis for further questions and deeper understanding of how plants utilize light that can be developed in later grades. On the basis of comparison of their explanation with their observations, students can appreciate that an explanation such as "plants need light to grow" fails to explain why they die when no water is provided. They should be encouraged to revisit their initial ideas and produce more complete explanations that account for more of their observations.

By the middle grades, students recognize that many of the explanations of science rely on models or representations of entities that are too small to see or too large to visualize. For example, explaining why the temperature of water does not increase beyond 100°C when heated requires students to envisage water as consisting of microscopic particles and that the energy provided by heating can allow fast-moving particles to escape despite the force of attraction holding the particles together. In the later stages of their education, students should also progress to using mathematics or simulations to construct an explanation for a phenomenon.

PROGRESSION FOR DESIGN

In some ways, children are natural engineers. They spontaneously build sand castles, dollhouses, and hamster enclosures, and they use a variety of tools and materials for their own playful purposes. Thus a common elementary school activity is to challenge children to use tools and materials provided in class to solve a specific challenge, such as constructing a bridge from paper and tape and testing it until failure occurs. Children's capabilities to design structures can then be enhanced by having them pay attention to points of failure and asking them to create and test redesigns of the bridge so that it is stronger. Furthermore, design activities should not be limited just to structural engineering but should also include projects that reflect other areas of engineering, such as the need to design a traffic pattern for the school parking lot or a layout for planting a school garden box.

In middle school, it is especially beneficial to engage students in engineering design projects in which they are expected to apply what they have recently learned in science—for example, using their now-familiar concepts of ecology to solve problems related to a school garden. Middle school students should also have opportunities to plan and carry out full engineering design projects in which they define problems in terms of criteria and constraints, research the problem to deepen their relevant knowledge, generate and test possible solutions, and refine their solutions through redesign.

At the high school level, students can undertake more complex engineering design projects related to major local, national or global issues. Increased emphasis should be placed on researching the nature of the given problems, on reviewing others' proposed solutions, on weighing the strengths and weaknesses of various alternatives, and on discerning possibly unanticipated effects.

Practice 7   Engaging in Argument from Evidence

Whether they concern new theories, proposed explanations of phenomena, novel solutions to technological problems, or fresh interpretations of old data, scientists and engineers use reasoning and argumentation to make their case. In science, the production of knowledge is dependent on a process of reasoning that requires a scientist to make a justified claim about the world. In response, other scientists attempt to identify the claim's weaknesses and limitations. Their arguments can be based on deductions from premises, on inductive generalizations of existing patterns, or on inferences about the best possible explanation. Argumentation is also needed to resolve questions involving, for example, the best experimental design, the most appropriate techniques of data analysis, or the best interpretation of a given data set.

In short, science is replete with arguments that take place both informally, in lab meetings and symposia, and formally, in peer review. Historical case studies of the origin and development of a scientific idea show how a new idea is often difficult to accept and has to be argued for—archetypal examples are the Copernican idea that Earth travels around the sun and Darwin's ideas about the origin of species. Over time, ideas that survive critical examination even in the light of new data attain consensual acceptance in the community, and by this process of discourse and argument science maintains its objectivity and progress [28].

The knowledge and ability to detect "bad science" [29, 30] are requirements both for the scientist and the citizen. Scientists must make critical judgments about their own work and that of their peers, and the scientist and the citizen alike must make evaluative judgments about the validity of science-related media reports and their implications for people's own lives and society [30]. Becoming a critical consumer of science is fostered by opportunities to use critique and evaluation to judge the merits of any scientifically based argument.

In engineering, reasoning and argument are essential to finding the best possible solution to a problem. At an early design stage, competing ideas must be compared (and possibly combined) to achieve an initial design, and the choices are made through argumentation about the merits of the various ideas pertinent to the design goals. At a later stage in the design process, engineers test their potential solution, collect data, and modify their design in an iterative manner. The results of such efforts are often presented as evidence to argue about the strengths and weaknesses of a particular design. Although the forms of argumentation are similar, the criteria employed in engineering are often quite different from those of science. For example, engineers might use cost-benefit analysis, an analysis of risk, an appeal to aesthetics, or predictions about market reception to justify why one design is better than another—or why an entirely different course of action should be followed.

GOALS

By grade 12, students should be able to

- Construct a scientific argument showing how data support a claim.
- Identify possible weaknesses in scientific arguments, appropriate to the students' level of knowledge, and discuss them using reasoning and evidence.

- Identify flaws in their own arguments and modify and improve them in response to criticism.
- Recognize that the major features of scientific arguments are claims, data, and reasons and distinguish these elements in examples.
- Explain the nature of the controversy in the development of a given scientific idea, describe the debate that surrounded its inception, and indicate why one particular theory succeeded.
- Explain how claims to knowledge are judged by the scientific community today and articulate the merits and limitations of peer review and the need for independent replication of critical investigations.
- Read media reports of science or technology in a critical manner so as to identify their strengths and weaknesses.

PROGRESSION

The study of science and engineering should produce a sense of the process of argument necessary for advancing and defending a new idea or an explanation of a phenomenon and the norms for conducting such arguments. In that spirit, students should argue for the explanations they construct, defend their interpretations of the associated data, and advocate for the designs they propose. Meanwhile, they should learn how to evaluate critically the scientific arguments of others and present counterarguments. Learning to argue scientifically offers students not only an opportunity to use their scientific knowledge in justifying an explanation and in identifying the weaknesses in others' arguments but also to build their own knowledge and understanding. Constructing and critiquing arguments are both a core process of science and one that supports science education, as research suggests that interaction with others is the most cognitively effective way of learning [31-33].

Young students can begin by constructing an argument for their own interpretation of the phenomena they observe and of any data they collect. They need instructional support to go beyond simply making claims—that is, to include reasons or references to evidence and to begin to distinguish evidence from opinion. As they grow in their ability to construct scientific arguments, students can draw on a wider range of reasons or evidence, so that their arguments become more sophisticated. In addition, they should be expected to discern what aspects of the evidence are potentially significant for supporting or refuting a particular argument.

Students should begin learning to critique by asking questions about their own findings and those of others. Later, they should be expected to identify possible weaknesses in either data or an argument and explain why their criticism is justified. As they become more adept at arguing and critiquing, they should be introduced to the language needed to talk about argument, such as claim, reason, data, etc. Exploration of historical episodes in science can provide opportunities for students to identify the ideas, evidence, and arguments of professional scientists. In so doing, they should be encouraged to recognize the criteria used to judge claims for new knowledge and the formal means by which scientific ideas are evaluated today. In particular, they should see how the practice of peer review and independent verification of claimed experimental results help to maintain objectivity and trust in science.

Practice 8   Obtaining, Evaluating, and Communicating Information

Being literate in science and engineering requires the ability to read and understand their literatures [34]. Science and engineering are ways of knowing that are represented and communicated by words, diagrams, charts, graphs, images, symbols, and mathematics [35]. Reading, interpreting, and producing text* are fundamental practices of science in particular, and they constitute at least half of engineers' and scientists' total working time [36].

Even when students have developed grade-level-appropriate reading skills, reading in science is often challenging to students for three reasons. First, the jargon of science texts is essentially unfamiliar; together with their often extensive use of, for example, the passive voice and complex sentence structure, many find these texts inaccessible [37]. Second, science texts must be read so as to extract information accurately. Because the precise meaning of each word or clause may be important, such texts require a mode of reading that is quite different from reading a novel or even a newspaper. Third, science texts are multimodal [38], using a mix of words, diagrams, charts, symbols, and mathematics to communicate. Thus understanding science texts requires much more than simply knowing the meanings of technical terms.

Communicating in written or spoken form is another fundamental practice of science; it requires scientists to describe observations precisely, clarify their thinking, and justify their arguments. Because writing is one of the primary means of com-

---

*The term "text" is used here to refer to any form of communication, from printed text to video productions.

municating in the scientific community, learning how to produce scientific texts is as essential to developing an understanding of science as learning how to draw is to appreciating the skill of the visual artist. Indeed, the new *Common Core State Standards for English Language Arts & Literacy in History/Social Studies, Science, and Technical Subjects* [39] recognize that reading and writing skills are essential to science; the formal inclusion in this framework of this science practice reinforces and expands on that view. Science simply cannot advance if scientists are unable to communicate their findings clearly and persuasively. Communication occurs in a variety of formal venues, including peer-reviewed journals, books, conference presentations, and carefully constructed websites; it occurs as well through informal means, such as discussions, email messages, phone calls, and blogs. New technologies have extended communicative practices, enabling multidisciplinary collaborations across the globe that place even more emphasis on reading and writing. Increasingly, too, scientists are required to engage in dialogues with lay audiences about their work, which requires especially good communication skills.

Being a critical consumer of science and the products of engineering, whether as a lay citizen or a practicing scientist or an engineer, also requires the ability to read or view reports about science in the press or on the Internet and to recognize the salient science, identify sources of error and methodological flaws, and distinguish observations from inferences, arguments from explanations, and claims from evidence. All of these are constructs learned from engaging in a critical discourse around texts.

Engineering proceeds in a similar manner because engineers need to communicate ideas and find and exchange information—for example, about new techniques or new uses of existing tools and materials. As in science, engineering communication involves not just written and spoken language; many engineering ideas are best communicated through sketches, diagrams, graphs, models, and products. Also in wide use are handbooks, specific to particular engineering fields, that provide detailed information, often in tabular form, on how best to formulate design solutions to commonly encountered engineering tasks. Knowing how to seek and use such informational resources is an important part of the engineer's skill set.

GOALS

By grade 12, students should be able to

- Use words, tables, diagrams, and graphs (whether in hard copy or electronically), as well as mathematical expressions, to communicate their understanding or to ask questions about a system under study.

- Read scientific and engineering text, including tables, diagrams, and graphs, commensurate with their scientific knowledge and explain the key ideas being communicated.
- Recognize the major features of scientific and engineering writing and speaking and be able to produce written and illustrated text or oral presentations that communicate their own ideas and accomplishments.
- Engage in a critical reading of primary scientific literature (adapted for classroom use) or of media reports of science and discuss the validity and reliability of the data, hypotheses, and conclusions.

PROGRESSION

Any education in science and engineering needs to develop students' ability to read and produce domain-specific text. As such, every science or engineering lesson is in part a language lesson, particularly reading and producing the genres of texts that are intrinsic to science and engineering.

Students need sustained practice and support to develop the ability to extract the meaning of scientific text from books, media reports, and other forms of scientific communication because the form of this text is initially unfamiliar—expository rather than narrative, often linguistically dense, and reliant on precise logical flows. Students should be able to interpret meaning from text, to produce text in which written language and diagrams are used to express scientific ideas, and to engage in extended discussion about those ideas.

From the very start of their science education, students should be asked to engage in the communication of science, especially regarding the investigations they are conducting and the observations they are making. Careful description of observations and clear statement of ideas, with the ability to both refine a statement in response to questions and to ask questions of others to achieve clarification of what is being said begin at the earliest grades. Beginning in upper elementary and middle school, the ability to interpret written materials becomes more important. Early work on reading science texts should also include explicit instruction and practice in interpreting tables, diagrams, and charts and coordinating information conveyed by them with information in written text. Throughout their science education, students are continually introduced to new terms, and the meanings of those terms can be learned only through opportunities to use and apply them in their specific contexts. Not only must students learn technical terms but also more general academic language, such as "analyze" or "correlation," which are not part of most students' everyday vocabulary and thus need specific elaboration if they are to make sense of

From the very start of their science education, students should be asked to engage in the communication of science, especially regarding the investigations they are conducting and the observations they are making.

scientific text. It follows that to master the reading of scientific material, students need opportunities to engage with such text and to identify its major features; they cannot be expected simply to apply reading skills learned elsewhere to master this unfamiliar genre effectively.

Students should write accounts of their work, using journals to record observations, thoughts, ideas, and models. They should be encouraged to create diagrams and to represent data and observations with plots and tables, as well as with written text, in these journals. They should also begin to produce reports or posters that present their work to others. As students begin to read and write more texts, the particular genres of scientific text—a report of an investigation, an explanation with supporting argumentation, an experimental procedure—will need to be introduced and their purpose explored. Furthermore, students should have opportunities to engage in discussion about observations and explanations and to make oral presentations of their results and conclusions as well as to engage in appropriate discourse with other students by asking questions and discussing issues raised in such presentations. Because the spoken language of such discussions and presentations is as far from their everyday language as scientific text is from a novel, the development both of written and spoken scientific explanation/argumentation needs to proceed in parallel.

In high school, these practices should be further developed by providing students with more complex texts and a wider range of text materials, such as technical reports or scientific literature on the Internet. Moreover, students need opportunities to read and discuss general media reports with a critical eye and to read appropriate samples of adapted primary literature [40] to begin seeing how science is communicated by science practitioners.

In engineering, students likewise need opportunities to communicate ideas using appropriate combinations of sketches, models, and language. They should also create drawings to test concepts and communicate detailed plans; explain and critique models of various sorts, including scale models and prototypes; and present the results of simulations, not only regarding the planning and development stages but also to make compelling presentations of their ultimate solutions.

REFLECTING ON THE PRACTICES

Science has been enormously successful in extending humanity's knowledge of the world and, indeed transforming it. Understanding how science has achieved this success and the techniques that it uses is an essential part of any science education. Although there is no universal agreement about teaching the nature of science, there is a strong consensus about characteristics of the scientific enterprise that should be understood by an educated citizen [41-43]. For example, the notion that there is a single scientific method of observation, hypothesis, deduction, and conclusion—a myth perpetuated to this day by many textbooks—is fundamentally wrong [44]. Scientists do use deductive reasoning, but they also search for patterns, classify different objects, make generalizations from repeated observations, and engage in a process of making inferences as to what might be the best explanation. Thus the picture of scientific reasoning is richer, more complex, and more diverse than the image of a linear and unitary scientific method would suggest [45].

What engages *all* scientists, however, is a process of critique and argumentation. Because they examine each other's ideas and look for flaws, controversy and debate among scientists are normal occurrences, neither exceptional nor extraordinary. Moreover, science has established a formal mechanism of peer review for establishing the credibility of any individual scientist's work. The ideas that survive this process of review and criticism are the ones that become well established in the scientific community.

Our view is that the opportunity for students to learn the basic set of practices outlined in this chapter is also an opportunity to have them stand back and reflect on how these practices contribute to the accumulation of scientific knowledge. For example, students need to see that the construction of models is a major means of acquiring new understanding; that these models identify key features and are akin to a map, rather than a literal representation of reality [13]; and that the great achievement of science is a core set of explanatory theories that have wide application [46].

Understanding how science functions requires a synthesis of content knowledge, procedural knowledge, and epistemic knowledge. Procedural knowledge refers to the methods that scientists use to ensure that their findings are valid and reliable. It includes an understanding of the importance and appropriate use of controls, double-blind trials, and other procedures (such as methods to reduce error) used by science. As such, much of it is specific to the domain and can only be learned within science. Procedural knowledge has also been called "concepts of evidence" [47].

Epistemic knowledge is knowledge of the constructs and values that are intrinsic to science. Students need to understand what is meant, for example, by an observation, a hypothesis, an inference, a model, a theory, or a claim and be able to readily distinguish between them. An education in science should show that new scientific ideas are acts of imagination, commonly created these days through collaborative efforts of groups of scientists whose critiques and arguments are fundamental to establishing which ideas are worthy of pursuing further. Ideas often survive because they are coherent with what is already known, and they either explain the unexplained, explain more observations, or explain in a simpler and more elegant manner.

Science is replete with ideas that once seemed promising but have not withstood the test of time, such as the concept of the "ether" or the *vis vitalis* (the "vital force" of life). Thus any new idea is initially tentative, but over time, as it survives repeated testing, it can acquire the status of a fact—a piece of knowledge that is unquestioned and uncontested, such as the existence of atoms. Scientists use the resulting theories and the models that represent them to explain and predict causal relationships. When the theory is well tested, its predictions are reliable, permitting the application of science to technologies and a wide variety of policy decisions. In other words, science is not a miscellany of facts but a coherent body of knowledge that has been hard won and that serves as a powerful tool.

Engagement in modeling and in critical and evidence-based argumentation invites and encourages students to reflect on the status of their own knowledge and their understanding of how science works. And as they involve themselves in the practices of science and come to appreciate its basic nature, their level of sophistication in understanding how any given practice contributes to the scientific enterprise can continue to develop across all grade levels.

REFERENCES

1. Layton, D. (1973). *Science for the People: The Origins of the School Science Curriculum in England*. London, England: Allen & Unwin.

2. DeBoer, G.E. (1991). *A History of Ideas in Science Education: Implications for Practice*. New York: Teachers College Press.

3. Driver, R., Leach, J., Millar, R., and Scott, P. (1996). *Young People's Images of Science*. Buckingham, England: Open University Press.

4. Schwab, J.J. (1962). *The Teaching of Science as Enquiry*. Cambridge, MA: Harvard University Press.

5. Florman, S.C. (1976). *The Existential Pleasures of Engineering*. New York: St. Martin's Press.

6. Petroski, H. (1996). *Engineering by Design: How Engineers Get from Thought to Thing*. Cambridge, MA: Harvard University Press.

7. Collins, H., and Pinch, T. (1993). *The Golem: What Everyone Should Know About Science*. Cambridge, England: Cambridge University Press.

8. Pickering, A. (1995). *The Mangle of Practice: Time, Agency, and Science*. Chicago: University of Chicago Press.

9. Latour, B., and Woolgar, S. (1986). *Laboratory Life: The Construction of Scientific Facts*. Princeton, NJ: Princeton University Press.

10. Latour, B. (1999). *Pandora's Hope: Essays on the Reality of Science Studies*. Cambridge, MA: Harvard University Press.

11. Longino, H.E. (2002). *The Fate of Knowledge*. Princeton, NJ: Princeton University Press.

12. Bazerman, C. (1988). *Shaping Written Knowledge*. Madison: University of Wisconsin Press.

13. Nercessian, N. (2008). Model-based reasoning in scientific practice. In R.A. Duschl and R.E. Grandy (Eds.), *Teaching Scientific Inquiry: Recommendations for Research and Implementation* (pp. 57-79). Rotterdam, the Netherlands: Sense.

14. Latour, B. (1990). Visualization and cognition: Drawing things together. In M. Lynch and S. Woolgar (Eds.), *Representation in Scientific Activity* (pp. 19-68). Cambridge, MA: MIT Press.

15. Lehrer, R., and Schauble, L. (2006). Cultivating model-based reasoning in science education. In R.K. Sawyer (Ed.), *The Cambridge Handbook of the Learning Sciences* (pp. 371-187). Cambridge, England: Cambridge University Press.

16. Giere, R., Bickle, J., and Maudlin, R.F. (2006). *Understanding Scientific Reasoning*. Belmont, CA: Thomson Wadsworth.

17. Millar, R., and Driver, R. (1987). Beyond processes. *Studies in Science Education, 14*, 33-62.

18. Abd-El-Khalick, F., BouJaoude, S., Duschl, R., Lederman, N.G., Mamlok-Naaman, R., Hofstein, A., Niaz, M., Treagust, D., and Tuan, H. (2004). Inquiry in science education: International perspectives. *Science Education, 88*(3), 397-419.

19. Ford, M. (2008). Disciplinary authority and accountability in scientific practice and learning. *Science Education, 92(3)*, 404-423.

20. Berland, L.K., and Reiser, B. (2008). Making sense of argumentation and explanation. *Science Education, 93*(1), 26-55.

21. Klahr, D., and Dunbar, K. (1988). Dual space search during scientific reasoning. *Cognitive Science, 12*(1), 1-48.

22. Kind, P., Osborne, J.F., and Szu, E. (in preparation). *A Model for Scientific Reasoning*. Stanford University.

23. Schwarz, C.V., Reiser, B.J., Davis, E.A., Kenyon, L., Achér, A., Fortus, D., Shwartz, Y., Hug, B., and Krajcik, J. (2009). Developing a learning progression for scientific modeling: Making scientific modeling accessible and meaningful for learners. *Journal of Research in Science Teaching, 46*(6), 632-654.

24. National Academy of Engineering and National Research Council. (2009). *Engineering in K-12 Education: Understanding the Status and Improving the Prospects*. Committee on K-12 Engineering Education. L. Katehi, G. Pearson, and M. Feder (Eds.). Board on Science Education, Center for Education, Division of Behavioral and Social Sciences and Education. Washington, DC: The National Academies Press.

25. National Academy of Engineering. (2010). *Standards for K-12 Engineering Education?* Committee on Standards for K-12 Engineering Education. Washington, DC: The National Academies Press.

26. Ogborn, J., Kress, G., Martins, I., and Mcgillicuddy, K. (1996). *Explaining Science in the Classroom*. Buckingham, England: Open University Press.

27. Duit, R. (1991). On the role of analogies and metaphors in learning science. *Science Education, 75*(6), 649-672.

28. Longino, H. (1990). *Science as Social Knowledge*. Princeton, NJ: Princeton University Press.

29. Goldacre, B. (2008). *Bad Science*. London, England: HarperCollins.

30. Zimmerman, C., Bisanz, G.L., Bisanz, J., Klein, J.S., and Klein, P. (2001). Science at the supermarket: A comparison of what appears in the popular press, experts' advice to readers, and what students want to know. *Public Understanding of Science, 10*(1), 37-58.

31. Alexander, R.J. (2005). *Towards Dialogic Teaching: Rethinking Classroom Talk*. York, England: Dialogos.

32. Chi, M. (2009). Active-constructive-interactive: A conceptual framework for differentiating learning activities. *Topics in Cognitive Science, 1*, 73-105.

33. Resnick, L., Michaels, S., and O'Connor, C. (2010). How (well-structured) talk builds the mind. In R. Sternberg and D. Preiss (Eds.), *From Genes to Context: New Discoveries about Learning from Educational Research and Their Applications* (pp. 163-194). New York: Springer.

34. Norris, S., and Phillips, L. (2003). How literacy in its fundamental sense is central to scientific literacy. *Science Education, 87,* 224-240.

35. Lemke, J. (1998). Multiplying meaning. In J.R. Martin and R. Veel (Eds.), *Reading Science* (pp. 87-113). London, England: Routledge.

36. Tenopir, C., and King, D.W. (2004). *Communication Patterns of Engineers.* Hoboken, NJ: Wiley.

37. Martin, J.R., and Veel, R. (1998). *Reading Science.* London, England: Routledge.

38. Kress, G.R., and Van Leeuwen, T. (2001). *Multimodal Discourse: The Modes and Media of Contemporary Communication.* London, England: Hodder Arnold.

39. Council of Chief State School Officers and National Governors Association. (2010). *Common Core State Standards for English Language Arts & Literacy in History/ Social Studies, Science, and Technical Subjects.* Available: http://www.corestandards. org/assets/CCSSI_ELA%20Standards.pdf [June 2011].

40. Yarden, A. (2009). Reading scientific texts: Adapting primary literature for promoting scientific literacy. *Research in Science Education, 39*(3), 307-311.

41. Osborne, J.F., Collins, S., Ratcliffe, M., Millar, R., and Duschl, R. (2003). What "ideas about science" should be taught in school science?: A Delphi study of the "expert" community. *Journal of Research in Science Teaching, 40*(7), 692-720.

42. Mccomas, W.F., and Olson, J.K. (1998). The nature of science in international science education standards documents. In W.F. McComas (Ed.), *The Nature of Science in Science Education: Rationales and Strategies* (pp. 41-52). Dordrecht, the Netherlands: Kluwer.

43. National Research Council. (2007). *Taking Science to School: Learning and Teaching Science in Grades K-8.* Committee on Science Learning, Kindergarten Through Eighth Grade. R.A. Duschl, H.A. Schweingruber, and A.W. Shouse (Eds.). Board on Science Education, Center for Education. Division of Behavioral and Social Sciences and Education. Washington, DC: The National Academies Press.

44. Bauer, H.H. (1992). *Scientific Literacy and the Myth of the Scientific Method.* Chicago: University of Illinois Press.

45. Duschl, R.A., and Grandy, R.E. (2008). *Teaching Scientific Inquiry: Recommendations for Research and Implementation.* Rotterdam, the Netherlands: Sense.

46. Harré, R. (1984). *The Philosophies of Science: An Introductory Survey.* Oxford, England: Oxford University Press.

47. Gott, R., Duggan, S., and Roberts, R. (2008). *Concepts of Evidence and Their Role in Open-Ended Practical Investigations and Scientific Literacy.* Durham, England: Durham University.

Dimension 2
CROSSCUTTING CONCEPTS

Some important themes pervade science, mathematics, and technology and appear over and over again, whether we are looking at an ancient civilization, the human body, or a comet. They are ideas that transcend disciplinary boundaries and prove fruitful in explanation, in theory, in observation, and in design.

—American Association for the Advancement of Science [1].

In this chapter, we describe concepts that bridge disciplinary boundaries, having explanatory value throughout much of science and engineering. These crosscutting concepts were selected for their value across the sciences and in engineering. These concepts help provide students with an organizational framework for connecting knowledge from the various disciplines into a coherent and scientifically based view of the world.

Although crosscutting concepts are fundamental to an understanding of science and engineering, students have often been expected to build such knowledge without any explicit instructional support. Hence the purpose of highlighting them as Dimension 2 of the framework is to elevate their role in the development of standards, curricula, instruction, and assessments. These concepts should become common and familiar touchstones across the disciplines and grade levels. Explicit reference to the concepts, as well as their emergence in multiple disciplinary contexts, can help students develop a cumulative, coherent, and usable understanding of science and engineering.

Although we do not specify grade band endpoints for the crosscutting concepts, we do lay out a hypothetical progression for each. Like all learning in science, students' facility with addressing these concepts and related topics at any particular grade level depends on their prior experience and instruction. The research base on learning and teaching the crosscutting concepts is limited. For this reason, the progressions we describe should be treated as hypotheses that require further empirical investigation.

SEVEN CROSSCUTTING CONCEPTS OF THE FRAMEWORK

The committee identified seven crosscutting scientific and engineering concepts:

1. *Patterns.* Observed patterns of forms and events guide organization and classification, and they prompt questions about relationships and the factors that influence them.

2. *Cause and effect: Mechanism and explanation.* Events have causes, sometimes simple, sometimes multifaceted. A major activity of science is investigating and explaining causal relationships and the mechanisms by which they are mediated. Such mechanisms can then be tested across given contexts and used to predict and explain events in new contexts.

3. *Scale, proportion, and quantity.* In considering phenomena, it is critical to recognize what is relevant at different measures of size, time, and energy and to recognize how changes in scale, proportion, or quantity affect a system's structure or performance.

4. *Systems and system models.* Defining the system under study—specifying its boundaries and making explicit a model of that system—provides tools for understanding and testing ideas that are applicable throughout science and engineering.

5. *Energy and matter: Flows, cycles, and conservation.* Tracking fluxes of energy and matter into, out of, and within systems helps one understand the systems' possibilities and limitations.

6. *Structure and function.* The way in which an object or living thing is shaped and its substructure determine many of its properties and functions.

7. *Stability and change.* For natural and built systems alike, conditions of stability and determinants of rates of change or evolution of a system are critical elements of study.

This set of crosscutting concepts begins with two concepts that are fundamental to the nature of science: that observed patterns can be explained and that science investigates cause-and-effect relationships by seeking the mechanisms that underlie them.

The next concept—scale, proportion, and quantity—concerns the sizes of things and the mathematical relationships among disparate elements.

The next four concepts—systems and system models, energy and matter flows, structure and function, and stability and change—are interrelated in that the first is illuminated by the other three. Each concept also stands alone as one that occurs in virtually all areas of science and is an important consideration for engineered systems as well.

The set of crosscutting concepts defined here is similar to those that appear in other standards documents, in which they have been called "unifying concepts" or "common themes" [2-4]. Regardless of the labels or organizational schemes used in these documents, all of them stress that it is important for students to come to recognize the concepts common to so many areas of science and engineering.

Patterns

Patterns exist everywhere—in regularly occurring shapes or structures and in repeating events and relationships. For example, patterns are discernible in the symmetry of flowers and snowflakes, the cycling of the seasons, and the repeated base pairs of DNA. Noticing patterns is often a first step to organizing and asking scientific questions about why and how the patterns occur.

One major use of pattern recognition is in classification, which depends on careful observation of similarities and differences; objects can be classified into groups on the basis of similarities of visible or microscopic features or on the basis of similarities of function. Such classification is useful in codifying relationships and organizing a multitude of objects or processes into a limited number of groups. Patterns of similarity and difference and the resulting classifications may change, depending on the scale at which a phenomenon is being observed. For example, isotopes of a given element are different—they contain different numbers of neutrons—but from the perspective of chemistry they can be classified as equivalent because they have identical patterns of chemical interaction. Once patterns and variations have been noted, they lead to questions;

> **Scientists seek explanations for observed patterns and for the similarity and diversity within them. Engineers often look for and analyze patterns, too.**

scientists seek explanations for observed patterns and for the similarity and diversity within them. Engineers often look for and analyze patterns, too. For example, they may diagnose patterns of failure of a designed system under test in order to improve the design, or they may analyze patterns of daily and seasonal use of power to design a system that can meet the fluctuating needs.

The ways in which data are represented can facilitate pattern recognition and lead to the development of a mathematical representation, which can then be used as a tool in seeking an underlying explanation for what causes the pattern to occur. For example, biologists studying changes in population abundance of several different species in an ecosystem can notice the correlations between increases and decreases for different species by plotting all of them on the same graph and can eventually find a mathematical expression of the interdependences and food-web relationships that cause these patterns.

Progression

Human beings are good at recognizing patterns; indeed, young children begin to recognize patterns in their own lives well before coming to school. They observe, for example, that the sun and the moon follow different patterns of appearance in the sky. Once they are students, it is important for them to develop ways to recognize, classify, and record patterns in the phenomena they observe. For example, elementary students can describe and predict the patterns in the seasons of the year; they can observe and record patterns in the similarities and differences between parents and their offspring. Similarly, they can investigate the characteristics that allow classification of animal types (e.g., mammals, fish, insects), of plants (e.g., trees, shrubs, grasses), or of materials (e.g., wood, rock, metal, plastic).

These classifications will become more detailed and closer to scientific classifications in the upper elementary grades, when students should also begin to analyze patterns in rates of change—for example, the growth rates of plants under different conditions. By middle school, students can begin to relate patterns to the nature of microscopic and atomic-level structure—for example, they may note that chemical molecules contain particular ratios of different atoms. By high school, students should recognize that different patterns may be observed at each of the scales at which a system is studied. Thus classifications used at one scale may fail or need revision when information from smaller or larger scales is introduced (e.g., classifications based on DNA comparisons versus those based on visible characteristics).

Cause and Effect: Mechanism and Prediction

Many of the most compelling and productive questions in science are about why or how something happens. Any tentative answer, or "hypothesis," that A causes B requires a model for the chain of interactions that connect A and B. For example, the notion that diseases can be transmitted by a person's touch was initially treated with skepticism by the medical profession for lack of a plausible mechanism. Today infectious diseases are well understood as being transmitted by the passing of microscopic organisms (bacteria or viruses) between an infected person and another. A major activity of science is to uncover such causal connections, often with the hope that understanding the mechanisms will enable predictions and, in the case of infectious diseases, the design of preventive measures, treatments, and cures.

Repeating patterns in nature, or events that occur together with regularity, are clues that scientists can use to start exploring causal, or cause-and-effect, relationships, which pervade all the disciplines of science and at all scales. For example, researchers investigate cause-and-effect mechanisms in the motion of a single object, specific chemical reactions, population changes in an ecosystem or a society, and the development of holes in the polar ozone layers. Any application of science, or any engineered solution to a problem, is dependent on understanding the cause-and-effect relationships between events; the quality of the application or solution often can be improved as knowledge of the relevant relationships is improved.

Identifying cause and effect may seem straightforward in simple cases, such as a bat hitting a ball, but in complex systems causation can be difficult to tease out. It may be conditional, so that A can cause B only if some other factors are in place or within a certain numerical range. For example, seeds germinate and produce plants but only when the soil is sufficiently moist and warm. Frequently, causation can be described only in a probabilistic fashion—that is, there is some likelihood that one event will lead to another, but a specific outcome cannot be guaranteed. For example, one can predict the fraction of a collection of identical atoms that will undergo radioactive decay in a certain period but not the exact time at which a given atom decays.

One assumption of all science and engineering is that there is a limited and universal set of fundamental physical interactions that underlie all known forces and hence are a root part of any causal chain, whether in natural or designed systems. Such "universality" means that the physical laws underlying all processes are the same everywhere and at all times; they depend on gravity, electromagnetism, or weak and strong nuclear interactions. Underlying all biological processes—the inner workings of a cell or even of a brain—are particular physical and chemical processes. At the larger scale of biological systems, the universality of life manifests itself in a common genetic code.

Causation invoked to explain larger scale systems must be consistent with the implications of what is known about smaller scale processes within the system, even though new features may emerge at large scales that cannot be predicted from knowledge of smaller scales. For example, although knowledge of atoms is not sufficient to predict the genetic code, the replication of genes must be understood as a molecular-level process. Indeed, the ability to model causal processes in complex multipart systems arises from this fact; modern computational codes incorporate relevant smaller scale relationships into the model of the larger system, integrating multiple factors in a way that goes well beyond the capacity of the human brain.

In engineering, the goal is to design a system to cause a desired effect, so cause-and-effect relationships are as much a part of engineering as of science. Indeed, the process of design is a good place to help students begin to think in terms of cause and effect, because they must understand the underlying causal relationships in order to devise and explain a design that can achieve a specified objective.

One goal of instruction about cause and effect is to encourage students to see events in the world as having understandable causes, even when these causes are beyond human control. The ability to distinguish between scientific causal claims and nonscientific causal claims is also an important goal.

Progression

In the earliest grades, as students begin to look for and analyze patterns—whether in their observations of the world or in the relationships between different quantities in data (e.g., the sizes of plants over time)—they can also begin to consider what might be causing these patterns and relationships and design tests that gather more evidence to support or refute their ideas. By the upper elementary grades, students should have developed the habit of routinely asking about cause-and-effect relationships in the systems they are studying, particularly when something occurs that is, for them, unexpected. The questions "How did that happen?" or "Why did that happen?" should move toward "What mechanisms caused that to happen?" and "What conditions were critical for that to happen?"

In middle and high school, argumentation starting from students' own explanations of cause and effect can help them appreciate standard scientific theories that explain the causal mechanisms in the systems under study. Strategies for this type of instruction include asking students to argue from evidence when attributing an observed phenomenon to a specific cause. For example, students exploring why the population of a given species is shrinking will look for evidence in the ecosystem of factors that lead to food shortages, overpredation, or other factors in the habitat related to survival; they will provide an argument for how these and other observed changes affect the species of interest.

Scale, Proportion, and Quantity

In thinking scientifically about systems and processes, it is essential to recognize that they vary in size (e.g., cells, whales, galaxies), in time span (e.g., nanoseconds, hours, millennia), in the amount of energy flowing through them (e.g., lightbulbs, power grids, the sun), and in the relationships between the scales of these different quantities. The understanding of relative magnitude is only a starting point. As noted in *Benchmarks for Science Literacy*, "The large idea is that the way in which things work may change with scale. Different aspects of nature change at different rates with changes in scale, and so the relationships among them change, too" [4]. Appropriate understanding of scale relationships is critical as well to engineering—no structure could be conceived, much less constructed, without the engineer's precise sense of scale.

From a human perspective, one can separate three major scales at which to study science: (1) macroscopic scales that are directly observable—that is, what one can see, touch, feel, or manipulate; (2) scales that are too small or fast to observe directly; and (3) those that are too large or too slow. Objects at the atomic scale, for example, may be described with simple models, but the size of atoms and the number of atoms in a system involve magnitudes that are difficult to imagine. At the other extreme, science deals in scales that are equally difficult to imagine because they are so large—continents that move, for example, and galaxies in which the nearest star is 4 years away traveling at the speed of light. As size scales change, so do time scales. Thus, when considering large entities such as mountain ranges, one typically needs to consider change that occurs over long periods. Conversely, changes in a small-scale system, such as a cell, are viewed over much shorter times. However, it is important to recognize that processes that occur locally and on short time scales can have long-term and large-scale impacts as well.

In forming a concept of the very small and the very large, whether in space or time, it is important to have a sense not only of relative scale sizes but also of what concepts are meaningful at what scale. For example, the concept of solid matter is meaningless at the subatomic scale, and the concept that light takes time to travel a given distance becomes more important as one considers large distances across the universe.

Understanding scale requires some insight into measurement and an ability to think in terms of orders of magnitude—for example, to comprehend the difference between one in a hundred and a few parts per billion. At a basic level, in order to identify something as bigger or smaller than something else—and how much bigger or smaller—a student must appreciate the units used to measure it and develop a feel for quantity.

The ideas of ratio and proportionality as used in science can extend and challenge students' mathematical understanding of these concepts. To appreciate the relative magnitude of some properties or processes, it may be necessary to grasp the relationships among different types of quantities—for example, speed as the ratio of distance traveled to time taken, density as a ratio of mass to volume. This use of ratio is quite different than a ratio of numbers describing fractions of a pie. Recognition of such relationships among different quantities is a key step in forming mathematical models that interpret scientific data.

Progression

The concept of scale builds from the early grades as an essential element of understanding phenomena. Young children can begin understanding scale with objects, space, and time related to their world and with explicit scale models and maps. They may discuss relative scales—the biggest and smallest, hottest and coolest, fastest and slowest—without reference to particular units of measurement.

Typically, units of measurement are first introduced in the context of length, in which students can recognize the need for a common unit of measure—even develop their own before being introduced to standard units—through appropriately constructed experiences. Engineering design activities involving scale diagrams and models can support students in developing facility with this important concept.

Once students become familiar with measurements of length, they can expand their understanding of scale and of the need for units that express quantities of weight, time, temperature, and other variables. They can also develop an understanding of estimation across scales and contexts, which is important for making sense of data. As students become more sophisticated, the use of estimation can help them not only to develop a sense of the size and time scales relevant to various objects, systems, and processes but also to consider whether a numerical result sounds reasonable. Students acquire the ability as well to move back and forth between models at various scales, depending on the question being considered. They should develop a sense of the powers-of-10 scales and what phenomena correspond to what scale, from the size of the nucleus of an atom to the size of the galaxy and beyond.

Well-designed instruction is needed if students are to assign meaning to the types of ratios and proportional relationships they encounter in science. Thus the ability to recognize mathematical relationships between quantities should begin developing in the early grades with students' representations of counting (e.g., leaves on a branch), comparisons of amounts (e.g., of flowers on different plants), measurements (e.g., the height of a plant), and the ordering of quantities such as number, length, and weight. Students can then explore more sophisticated mathematical representations, such as the use of graphs to represent data collected. The interpretation of these graphs may be, for example, that a plant gets bigger as time passes or that the hours of daylight decrease and increase across the months.

As students deepen their understanding of algebraic thinking, they should be able to apply it to examine their scientific data to predict the effect of a change in one variable on another, for example, or to appreciate the difference between linear growth and exponential growth. As their thinking advances, so too should their ability to recognize and apply more complex mathematical and statistical relationships in science. A sense of numerical quantity is an important part of the general "numeracy" (mathematics literacy) that is needed to interpret such relationships.

Systems and System Models

As noted in the *National Science Education Standards*, "The natural and designed world is complex; it is too large and complicated to investigate and comprehend all at once. Scientists and students learn to define small portions for the convenience of investigation. The units of investigations can be referred to as 'systems.' A system is an organized group of related objects or components that form a whole. Systems can consist, for example, of organisms, machines, fundamental particles, galaxies, ideas, and numbers. Systems have boundaries, components, resources, flow, and feedback" [2].

Although any real system smaller than the entire universe interacts with and is dependent on other (external) systems, it is often useful to conceptually isolate a single system for study. To do this, scientists and engineers imagine an artificial boundary between the system in question and everything else. They then examine the system in detail while treating the effects of things outside the boundary as either forces acting on the system or flows of matter and energy across it—for

example, the gravitational force due to Earth on a book lying on a table or the carbon dioxide expelled by an organism. Consideration of flows into and out of the system is a crucial element of system design. In the laboratory or even in field research, the extent to which a system under study can be physically isolated or external conditions controlled is an important element of the design of an investigation and interpretation of results.

Often, the parts of a system are interdependent, and each one depends on or supports the functioning of the system's other parts. Yet the properties and behavior of the whole system can be very different from those of any of its parts, and large systems may have emergent properties, such as the shape of a tree, that cannot be predicted in detail from knowledge about the components and their interactions. Things viewed as subsystems at one scale may themselves be viewed as whole systems at a smaller scale. For example, the circulatory system can be seen as an entity in itself or as a subsystem of the entire human body; a molecule can be studied as a stable configuration of atoms but also as a subsystem of a cell or a gas.

An explicit model of a system under study can be a useful tool not only for gaining understanding of the system but also for conveying it to others. Models of a system can range in complexity from lists and simple sketches to detailed computer simulations or functioning prototypes.

Models can be valuable in predicting a system's behaviors or in diagnosing problems or failures in its functioning, regardless of what type of system is being examined. A good system model for use in developing scientific explanations or engineering designs must specify not only the parts, or subsystems, of the system but also how they interact with one another. It must also specify the boundary of the system being modeled, delineating what is included in the model and what is to be treated as external. In a simple mechanical system, interactions among the parts are describable in terms of forces among them that cause changes in motion or physical stresses. In more complex systems, it is not always possible or useful to consider interactions at this detailed mechanical level, yet it is equally important to ask what interactions are occurring (e.g., predator-prey relationships in an eco-system) and to recognize that they all involve transfers of energy, matter, and (in some cases) information among parts of the system.

Any model of a system incorporates assumptions and approximations; the key is to be aware of what they are and how they affect the model's reliability and precision. Predictions may be reliable but not precise or, worse, precise but not reliable; the degree of reliability and precision needed depends on the use to which the model will be put.

Progression

As science instruction progresses, so too should students' ability to analyze and model more complex systems and to use a broader variety of representations to explicate what they model. Their thinking about systems in terms of component parts and their interactions, as well as in terms of inputs, outputs, and processes, gives students a way to organize their knowledge of a system, to generate questions that can lead to enhanced understanding, to test aspects of their model of the system, and, eventually, to refine their model.

Starting in the earliest grades, students should be asked to express their thinking with drawings or diagrams and with written or oral descriptions. They should describe objects or organisms in terms of their parts and the roles those parts play in the functioning of the object or organism, and they should note relationships between the parts. Students should also be asked to create plans—for example, to draw or write a set of instructions for building something—that another child can follow. Such experiences help them develop the concept of a model of a system and realize the importance of representing one's ideas so that others can understand and use them.

As students progress, their models should move beyond simple renderings or maps and begin to incorporate and make explicit the invisible features of a system, such as interactions, energy flows, or matter transfers. Mathematical ideas, such as ratios and simple graphs, should be seen as tools for making more definitive models; eventually, students' models should incorporate a range of mathematical relationships among variables (at a level appropriate for grade-level mathematics) and some analysis of the patterns of those relationships. By high school, students should also be able to identify the assumptions and approximations that have been built into a model and discuss how they limit the precision and reliability of its predictions.

Instruction should also include discussion of the interactions *within* a system. As understanding deepens, students can move from a vague notion of interaction as one thing affecting another to more explicit realizations of a system's physical, chemical, biological, and social interactions and of their relative importance for the question at hand. Students' ideas about the interactions in a system and the explication of such interactions in their models should become more sophisticated in parallel with their understanding of the microscopic world (atoms, molecules, biological cells, microbes) and with their ability to interpret and use more complex mathematical relationships.

Modeling is also a tool that students can use in gauging their own knowledge and clarifying their questions about a system. Student-developed models may reveal problems or progress in their conceptions of the system, just as scientists' models do. Teaching students to explicitly craft and present their models in diagrams, words, and, eventually, in mathematical relationships serves three purposes. It supports them in clarifying their ideas and explanations and in considering any inherent contradictions; it allows other students the opportunity to critique and suggest revisions for the model; and it offers the teacher insights into those aspects of each student's understanding that are well founded and those that could benefit from further instructional attention. Likewise in engineering projects, developing systems thinking and system models supports critical steps in developing, sharing, testing, and refining design ideas.

Energy and Matter: Flows, Cycles, and Conservation

One of the great achievements of science is the recognition that, in any system, certain conserved quantities can change only through transfers into or out of the system. Such laws of conservation provide limits on what can occur in a system, whether human built or natural. This section focuses on two such quantities,

> The ability to examine, characterize, and model the transfers and cycles of matter and energy is a tool that students can use across virtually all areas of science and engineering.

matter and energy, whose conservation has important implications for the disciplines of science in this framework. The supply of energy and of each needed chemical element restricts a system's operation—for example, without inputs of energy (sunlight) and matter (carbon dioxide and water), a plant cannot grow. Hence, it is very informative to track the transfers of matter and energy within, into, or out of any system under study.

In many systems there also are cycles of various types. In some cases, the most readily observable cycling may be of matter—for example, water going back and forth between Earth's atmosphere and its surface and subsurface reservoirs. Any such cycle of matter also involves associated energy transfers at each stage, so to fully understand the water cycle, one must model not only how water moves between parts of the system but also the energy transfer mechanisms that are critical for that motion.

Consideration of energy and matter inputs, outputs, and flows or transfers within a system or process are equally important for engineering. A major goal in design is to maximize certain types of energy output while minimizing others, in order to minimize the energy inputs needed to achieve a desired task.

The ability to examine, characterize, and model the transfers and cycles of matter and energy is a tool that students can use across virtually all areas of science and engineering. And studying the *interactions* between matter and energy supports students in developing increasingly sophisticated conceptions of their role in any system. However, for this development to occur, there needs to be a common use of language about energy and matter across the disciplines in science instruction.

Progression

The core ideas of matter and energy and their development across the grade bands are spelled out in detail in Chapter 5. What is added in this crosscutting discussion is recognition that an understanding of these core ideas can be informative in examining systems in life science, earth and space science, and engineering contexts. Young children are likely to have difficulty studying the concept of energy in depth—everyday language surrounding energy contains many shortcuts that lead to misunderstandings. For this reason, the concept is not developed at all in K-2 and only very generally in grades 3-5. Instead, the elementary grades focus on recognition of conservation of matter and of the flow of matter into, out of, and within systems under study. The role of energy transfers in conjunction with these flows is not introduced until the middle grades and only fully developed by high school.

Clearly, incorrect beliefs—such as the perception that food or fuel is a form of energy—would lead to elementary grade students' misunderstanding of the nature of energy. Hence, although the necessity for food or fuel can be discussed, the language of energy needs to be used with care so as not to further establish such misconceptions. By middle school, a more precise idea of energy—for example, the understanding that food or fuel undergoes a chemical reaction with oxygen that releases stored energy—can emerge. The common misconceptions can be addressed with targeted instructional interventions (including student-led investigations), and appropriate terminology can be used in discussing energy across the disciplines.

Matter transfers are less fraught in this respect, but the idea of atoms is not introduced with any specificity until middle school. Thus, at the level of grades 3-5, matter flows and cycles can be tracked only in terms of the weight of the substances before and after a process occurs, such as sugar dissolving in water. Mass/weight distinctions and the idea of atoms and their conservation (except in nuclear processes) are taught in grades 6-8, with nuclear substructure and the related conservation laws for nuclear processes introduced in grades 9-12.

Structure and Function

As expressed by the National Research Council in 1996 and reiterated by the College Board in 2009, "Form and function are complementary aspects of objects, organisms, and systems in the natural and designed world. . . . Understanding of form and function applies to different levels of organization. Function can be explained in terms of form and form can be explained in terms of function" [2, 3].

The functioning of natural and built systems alike depends on the shapes and relationships of certain key parts as well as on the properties of the materials from which they are made. A sense of scale is necessary in order to know what properties and what aspects of shape or material are relevant at a particular magnitude or in investigating particular phenomena—that is, the selection of an appropriate scale depends on the question being asked. For example, the substructures of molecules are not particularly important in understanding the phenomenon of pressure, but they are relevant to understanding why the ratio between temperature and pressure at constant volume is different for different substances.

Similarly, understanding how a bicycle works is best addressed by examining the structures and their functions at the scale of, say, the frame, wheels, and pedals. However, building a lighter bicycle may require knowledge of the properties (such as rigidity and hardness) of the materials needed for specific parts of the bicycle. In that way, the builder can seek less dense materials with appropriate properties; this pursuit may lead in turn to an examination of the atomic-scale structure of candidate materials. As a result, new parts with the desired properties, possibly made of new materials, can be designed and fabricated.

Progression

Exploration of the relationship between structure and function can begin in the early grades through investigations of accessible and visible systems in the natural and human-built world. For example, children explore how shape and stability are related for a variety of structures (e.g., a bridge's diagonal brace) or purposes (e.g., different animals get their food using different parts of their bodies). As children move through the elementary grades, they progress to

understanding the relationships of structure and mechanical function (e.g., wheels and axles, gears). For upper-elementary students, the concept of matter having a substructure at a scale too small to see is related to properties of materials; for example, a model of a gas as a collection of moving particles (not further defined) may be related to observed properties of gases. Upper-elementary students can also examine more complex structures, such as subsystems of the human body, and consider the relationship of the shapes of the parts to their functions. By the middle grades, students begin to visualize, model, and apply their understanding of structure and function to more complex or less easily observable systems and processes (e.g., the structure of water and salt molecules and solubility, Earth's plate tectonics). For students in the middle grades, the concept of matter having a submicroscopic structure is related to properties of materials; for example, a model based on atoms and/or molecules and their motions may be used to explain the properties of solids, liquids, and gases or the evaporation and condensation of water.

As students develop their understanding of the relationships between structure and function, they should begin to apply this knowledge when investigating phenomena that are unfamiliar to them. They recognize that often the first step in deciphering how a system works is to examine in detail what it is made of and the shapes of its parts. In building something—say, a mechanical system—they likewise apply relationships of structure and function as critical elements of successful designs.

Stability and Change

"Much of science and mathematics has to do with understanding how change occurs in nature and in social and technological systems, and much of technology has to do with creating and controlling change," according to the American Association for the Advancement of Science. "Constancy, often in the midst of change, is also the subject of intense study in science" [4].

Stability denotes a condition in which some aspects of a system are unchanging, at least at the scale of observation. Stability means that a small disturbance will fade away—that is, the system will stay in, or return to, the stable condition. Such stability can take different forms, with the simplest being a static equilibrium, such as a ladder leaning on a wall. By contrast, a system with steady inflows and outflows (i.e., constant conditions) is said to be in dynamic equilibrium. For example, a dam may be at a constant level with steady quantities of water coming in and out. Increase the inflow, and a new equilibrium level will eventually be reached if the outflow increases as well. At extreme flows, other factors may cause *dis*equilibrium; for example, at a low-enough inflow, evaporation may cause the level of the water to continually drop. Likewise, a fluid at a constant temperature can be in a steady state with constant chemical composition even though chemical reactions that change the composition in two opposite directions are occurring within it; change the temperature and it will reach a new steady state with a different composition.

A repeating pattern of cyclic change—such as the moon orbiting Earth—can also be seen as a stable situation, even though it is clearly not static. Such a system has constant aspects, however, such as the distance from Earth to the moon, the period of its orbit, and the pattern of phases seen over time.

In designing systems for stable operation, the mechanisms of external controls and internal "feedback" loops are important design elements; feedback is important to understanding natural systems as well. A feedback loop is any mechanism in which a condition triggers some action that causes a change in that same condition, such as the temperature of a room triggering the thermostatic control that turns the room's heater on or off. Feedback can stabilize a system (negative feedback—a thermostat in a cooling room triggers heating, but only until a particular temperature range is reached) or destabilize a system (positive feedback—a fire releases heat, which triggers the burning of more fuel, which causes the fire to continue to grow).

A system can be stable on a small time scale, but on a larger time scale it may be seen to be changing. For example, when looking at a living organism over the course of an hour or a day, it may maintain stability; over longer periods, the organism grows, ages, and eventually dies. For the development of larger systems, such as the variety of living species inhabiting Earth or the formation of a galaxy, the relevant time scales may be very long indeed; such processes occur over millions or even billions of years.

When studying a system's patterns of change over time, it is also important to examine what is unchanging. Understanding the feedback mechanisms that regulate the system's stability or that drive its instability provides insight into how the system may operate under various conditions. These mechanisms are important to evaluate when comparing different design options that address a particular problem.

Any system has a range of conditions under which it can operate in a stable fashion, as well as conditions under which it cannot function. For example, a particular living organism can survive only within a certain range of temperatures, and outside that span it will die. Thus elucidating what range of conditions can lead to a system's stable operation and what changes would destabilize it (and in what ways) is an important goal.

Note that stability is always a balance of competing effects; a small change in conditions or in a single component of the system can lead to runaway changes in the system if compensatory mechanisms are absent. Nevertheless, students typically begin with an idea of equilibrium as a static situation, and they interpret a lack of change in the system as an indication that nothing is happening. Thus they need guidance to begin to appreciate that stability can be the result of multiple opposing forces; they should be taught to identify the invisible forces—to appreciate the dynamic equilibrium—in a seemingly static situation, even one as simple as a book lying on a table.

An understanding of dynamic equilibrium is crucial to understanding the major issues in any complex system—for example, population dynamics in an ecosystem or the relationship between the level of atmospheric carbon dioxide and Earth's average temperature. Dynamic equilibrium is an equally important concept for understanding the physical forces in matter. Stable matter is a system of atoms in dynamic equilibrium.

For example, the stability of the book lying on the table depends on the fact that minute distortions of the table caused by the book's downward push on the table in turn cause changes in the positions of the table's atoms. These changes then alter the forces between those atoms, which lead to changes in the upward force on the book exerted by the table. The book continues to distort the table until the table's upward force on the book exactly balances the downward pull of gravity on the book. Place a heavy enough item on the table, however, and stability is not possible; the distortions of matter within the table continue to the macroscopic scale, and it collapses under the weight. Such seemingly simple, explicit, and visible examples of how change in some factor produces changes in the system can help to establish a mental model of dynamic equilibrium useful for thinking about more complex systems.

Understanding long-term changes—for example, the evolution of the diversity of species, the surface of Earth, or the structure of the universe—requires a sense of the requisite time scales for such changes to develop. Long time scales can be difficult for students to grasp, however. Part of their understanding should grow from an appreciation of how scientists investigate the nature of these processes—through the interplay of evidence and system modeling. Student-developed models that use comparative time scales can also be helpful; for example, if the history of Earth is scaled to 1 year (instead of the absolute measures in eons), students gain a more intuitive understanding of the relative durations of periods in the planet's evolution.

Progression

Even very young children begin to explore stability (as they build objects with blocks or climb on a wall) and change (as they note their own growth or that of a plant). The role of instruction in the early grades is to help students to develop some language for these concepts and apply it appropriately across multiple examples, so that they can ask such questions as "What could I change to make this balance better?" or "How fast did the plants grow?" One of the goals of discussion of stability and change in the elementary grades should be the recognition that it can be as important to ask why something does not change as why it does.

Likewise, students should come to recognize that both the regularities of a pattern over time and its variability are issues for which explanations can be sought. Examining these questions in different contexts (e.g., a model ecosystem such as a terrarium, the local weather, a design for a bridge) broadens students' understanding that stability and change are related and that a good model for a system must be able to offer explanations for both.

In middle school, as student's understanding of matter progresses to the atomic scale, so too should their models and their explanations of stability and change. Furthermore, they can begin to appreciate more subtle or conditional situations and the need for feedback to maintain stability. At the high school level, students can model more complex systems and comprehend more subtle issues of stability or of sudden or gradual change over time. Students at this level should also recognize that much of science deals with constructing historical explanations of how things evolved to be the way they are today, which involves modeling rates of change and conditions under which the system is stable or changes gradually, as well as explanations of any sudden change.

INTERCONNECTIONS BETWEEN CROSSCUTTING CONCEPTS AND DISCIPLINARY CORE IDEAS

Students' understanding of these crosscutting concepts should be reinforced by repeated use of them in the context of instruction in the disciplinary core ideas presented in Chapters 5-8. In turn, the crosscutting concepts can provide a connective structure that supports students' understanding of sciences as disciplines and that facilitates students' comprehension of the phenomena under study in particular disciplines. Thus these crosscutting concepts should not be taught in isolation from the examples provided in the disciplinary context. Moreover, use of a common language for these concepts across disciplines will help students to recognize that the same concept is relevant across different contexts.

REFERENCES

1. American Association for the Advancement of Science. (1989). *Science for All Americans*. Project 2061. New York: Oxford University Press. Available: http://www.project2061.org/publications/sfaa/online/sfaatoc.htm [March 2011].

2. National Research Council. (1996). *National Science Education Standards*. National Committee for Science Education Standards and Assessment. Washington, DC: National Academy Press.

3. College Board. (2009). *Science College Board Standards for College Success*. Available: http://professionals.collegeboard.com/profdownload/cbscs-science-standards-2009.pdf [June 2011].

4. American Association for the Advancement of Science. (2009). *Benchmarks for Science Literacy*. Project 2061. Available: http://www.project2061.org/publications/bsl/online/index.php?txtRef=http%3A%2F%2Fwww%2Eproject2061%2Eorg%2Fpublications%2Fbsl%2Fdefault%2Ehtm%3FtxtRef%3D%26txtURIOld%3D%252Ftools%252Fbsl%252Fdefault%2Ehtm&txtURIOld=%2Fpublications%2Fbsl%2Fonline%2Fbolintro%2Ehtm [June 2011].

5

Dimension 3
DISCIPLINARY CORE IDEAS—
PHYSICAL SCIENCES

Most systems or processes depend at some level on physical and chemical subprocesses that occur within it, whether the system in question is a star, Earth's atmosphere, a river, a bicycle, the human brain, or a living cell. Large-scale systems often have emergent properties that cannot be explained on the basis of atomic-scale processes; nevertheless, to understand the physical and chemical basis of a system, one must ultimately consider the structure of matter at the atomic and subatomic scales to discover how it influences the system's larger scale structures, properties, and functions. Similarly, understanding a process at any scale requires awareness of the interactions occurring—in terms of the forces between objects, the related energy transfers, and their consequences. In this way, the physical sciences—physics and chemistry—underlie all natural and human-created phenomena, although other kinds of information transfers, such as those facilitated by the genetic code or communicated between organisms, may also be critical to understanding their behavior. An overarching goal for learning in the physical sciences, therefore, is to help students see that there are mechanisms of cause and effect in all systems and processes that can be understood through a common set of physical and chemical principles.

The committee developed four core ideas in the physical sciences—three of which parallel those identified in previous documents, including the *National Science Education Standards* and *Benchmarks for Science Literacy* [1, 2]. The three core ideas are PS1: Matter and Its Interactions, PS2: Motion and Stability: Forces and Interactions, and PS3: Energy.

We also introduce a fourth core idea: PS4: Waves and Their Applications in Technologies for Information Transfer—which introduces students to the ways in which advances in the physical sciences during the 20th century underlie all sophisticated technologies available today. This idea is included in recognition of the fact that organizing science instruction around disciplinary core ideas tends to leave out the applications of those ideas. The committee included this fourth idea to stress the interplay of physical science and technology, as well as to expand students' understanding of light and sound as mechanisms of both energy transfer (see LS3) and transfer of information between objects that are not in contact. Modern communication, information, and imaging technologies are applications of scientific understandings of light and sound and their interactions with matter. They are pervasive in our lives today and are also critical tools without which much of modern science could not be done. See Box 5-1 for a summary of these four core ideas and their components.

The first three physical science core ideas answer two fundamental questions—"What is everything made of?" and "Why do things happen?"— that are not unlike questions that students themselves might ask. These core ideas can be applied to explain and predict a wide variety of phenomena that occur in people's everyday lives, such as the evaporation of a puddle of water, the transmission of sound, the digital storage and transmission of information, the tarnishing of metals, and photosynthesis. And because such explanations and predictions rely on a basic understanding of matter and energy, students' abilities to conceive of the interactions of matter and energy are central to their science education.

The historical division between the two subjects of physics and chemistry is transcended in modern science, as the same physical principles are seen to apply from subatomic scales to the scale of the universe itself. For this reason we have chosen to present the two subjects together, thereby ensuring a more coherent approach to the core ideas across all grades. The designation of physical science courses at the high school level as either physics or chemistry is not precluded by our grouping of these disciplines; what is important is that all students are offered a course sequence that gives them the opportunity and support to learn about all these ideas and to recognize the connections between them.

BOX 5-1

CORE AND COMPONENT IDEAS IN THE PHYSICAL SCIENCES

Core Idea PS1: Matter and Its Interactions

PS1.A: Structure and Properties of Matter

PS1.B: Chemical Reactions

PS1.C: Nuclear Processes

Core Idea PS2: Motion and Stability: Forces and Interactions

PS2.A: Forces and Motion

PS2.B: Types of Interactions

PS2.C: Stability and Instability in Physical Systems

Core Idea PS3: Energy

PS3.A: Definitions of Energy

PS3.B: Conservation of Energy and Energy Transfer

PS3.C: Relationship Between Energy and Forces

PS3.D: Energy in Chemical Processes and Everyday Life

Core Idea PS4: Waves and Their Applications in Technologies for Information Transfer

PS4.A: Wave Properties

PS4.B: Electromagnetic Radiation

PS4.C: Information Technologies and Instrumentation

Core Idea PS1   Matter and Its Interactions

How can one explain the structure, properties, and interactions of matter?

The existence of atoms, now supported by evidence from modern instruments, was first postulated as a model that could explain both qualitative and quantitative observations about matter (e.g., Brownian motion, ratios of reactants and products in chemical reactions). Matter can be understood in terms of the types of atoms present and the interactions both between and within them. The states (i.e., solid, liquid, gas, or plasma), properties (e.g., hardness, conductivity), and reactions (both physical and chemical) of matter can be described and predicted based on the types, interactions, and motions of the atoms within it. Chemical reactions, which underlie so many observed phenomena in living and nonliving systems alike, conserve the number of atoms of each type but change their arrangement into molecules. Nuclear reactions involve changes in the types of atomic nuclei present and are key to the energy release from the sun and the balance of isotopes in matter.

PS1.A: STRUCTURE AND PROPERTIES OF MATTER

How do particles combine to form the variety of matter one observes?

While too small to be seen with visible light, atoms have substructures of their own. They have a small central region or nucleus—containing protons and neutrons—surrounded by a larger region containing electrons. The number of protons in the atomic nucleus (atomic number) is the defining characteristic of each element; different isotopes of the same element differ in the number of neutrons only. Despite the immense variation and number of substances, there are only some 100 different stable elements.

Each element has characteristic chemical properties. The periodic table, a systematic representation of known elements, is organized horizontally by increasing atomic number and vertically by families of elements with related chemical properties. The development of the periodic table (which occurred well before atomic substructure was understood) was a major advance, as its patterns suggested and led to the identification of additional elements with particular properties. Moreover, the table's patterns are now recognized as related to the atom's outermost electron patterns, which play an important role in explaining chemical reactivity and bond formation, and the periodic table continues to be a useful way to organize this information.

The substructure of atoms determines how they combine and rearrange to form all of the world's substances. Electrical attractions and repulsions between charged particles (i.e., atomic nuclei and electrons) in matter explain the structure of atoms and the forces between atoms that cause them to form molecules (via chemical bonds), which range in size from two to thousands of atoms (e.g., in biological molecules such as proteins). Atoms also combine due to these forces to form extended structures, such as crystals or metals. The varied properties (e.g., hardness, conductivity) of the materials one encounters, both natural and manufactured, can be understood in terms of the atomic and molecular constituents present and the forces within and between them.

Within matter, atoms and their constituents are constantly in motion. The arrangement and motion of atoms vary in characteristic ways, depending on the substance and its current state (e.g., solid, liquid). Chemical composition, temperature, and pressure affect such arrangements and motions of atoms, as well as the ways in which they interact. Under a given set of conditions, the state and some properties (e.g., density, elasticity, viscosity) are the same for different bulk quantities of a substance, whereas other properties (e.g., volume, mass) provide measures of the size of the sample at hand.

Materials can be characterized by their intensive measureable properties. Different materials with different properties are suited to different uses. The ability to image and manipulate placement of individual atoms in tiny structures allows for the design of new types of materials with particular desired functionality (e.g., plastics, nanoparticles). Moreover, the modern explanation of how particular atoms influence the properties of materials or molecules is critical to understanding the physical and chemical functioning of biological systems.

Grade Band Endpoints for PS1.A

By the end of grade 2. Different kinds of matter exist (e.g., wood, metal, water), and many of them can be either solid or liquid, depending on temperature. Matter can be described and classified by its observable properties (e.g., visual, aural, textural), by its uses, and by whether it occurs naturally or is manufactured. Different properties are suited to different purposes. A great variety of objects can be built up from a small set of pieces (e.g., blocks, construction sets). Objects or samples of a substance can be weighed, and their size can be described and measured. (Boundary: volume is introduced only for liquid measure.)

By the end of grade 5. Matter of any type can be subdivided into particles that are too small to see, but even then the matter still exists and can be detected by other means (e.g., by weighing or by its effects on other objects). For example, a model showing that gases are made from matter particles that are too small to see and are moving freely around in space can explain many observations, including the inflation and shape of a balloon; the effects of air on larger particles or objects (e.g., leaves in wind, dust suspended in air); and the appearance of visible scale water droplets in condensation, fog, and, by extension, also in clouds or the contrails of a jet. The amount (weight) of matter is conserved when it changes form, even in transitions in which it seems to vanish (e.g., sugar in solution, evaporation in a closed container). Measurements of a variety of properties (e.g., hardness, reflectivity) can be used to identify particular materials. (Boundary: At this grade level, mass and weight are not distinguished, and no attempt is made to define the unseen particles or explain the atomic-scale mechanism of evaporation and condensation.)

By the end of grade 8. All substances are made from some 100 different types of atoms, which combine with one another in various ways. Atoms form molecules that range in size from two to thousands of atoms. Pure substances are made from a single type of atom or molecule; each pure substance has characteristic physical and chemical properties (for any bulk quantity under given conditions) that can be used to identify it.

Gases and liquids are made of molecules or inert atoms that are moving about relative to each other. In a liquid, the molecules are constantly in contact with each other; in a gas, they are widely spaced except when they happen to collide. In a solid, atoms are closely spaced and vibrate in position but do not change relative locations. Solids may be formed from molecules, or they may be extended structures with repeating subunits (e.g., crystals). The changes of state that occur with variations in temperature or pressure can be described and predicted using these models of matter. (Boundary: Predictions here are qualitative, not quantitative.)

By the end of grade 12. Each atom has a charged substructure consisting of a nucleus, which is made of protons and neutrons, surrounded by electrons. The periodic table orders elements horizontally by the number of protons in the atom's nucleus and places those with similar chemical properties in columns. The repeating patterns of this table reflect patterns of outer electron states. The structure and interactions of matter at the bulk scale are determined by electrical forces within and between atoms. Stable forms of matter are those in which the electric and magnetic field energy is minimized. A stable molecule has less energy, by an amount known as the binding energy, than the same set of atoms separated; one must provide at least this energy in order to take the molecule apart.

PS1.B: CHEMICAL REACTIONS

How do substances combine or change (react) to make new substances? How does one characterize and explain these reactions and make predictions about them?

Many substances react chemically with other substances to form new substances with different properties. This change in properties results from the ways in which atoms from the original substances are combined and rearranged in the new substances. However, the total number of each type of atom is conserved (does not change) in any chemical process, and thus mass does not change either. The property of conservation can be used, along with knowledge of the chemical properties of particular elements, to describe and predict the outcomes of reactions. Changes in matter in which the molecules do not change, but their positions and their motion relative to each other do change also occur (e.g., the forming of a solution,

■ Understanding chemical reactions and the properties of elements is essential not only to the physical sciences but also is foundational knowledge for the life sciences and the earth and space sciences. ■

a change of state). Such changes are generally easier to reverse (return to original conditions) than chemical changes.

"Collision theory" provides a qualitative model for explaining the rates of chemical reactions. Higher rates occur at higher temperatures because atoms are typically moving faster and thus collisions are more frequent; also, a larger fraction of the collisions have sufficient energy to initiate the process. Although a solution or a gas may have constant chemical composition—that is, be in a steady state—chemical reactions may be occurring within it that are dynamically balanced with reactions in opposite directions proceeding at equal rates.

Any chemical process involves a change in chemical bonds and the related bond energies and thus in the total chemical binding energy. This change is matched by a difference between the total kinetic energy of the set of reactant molecules before the collision and that of the set of product molecules after the collision (conservation of energy). Some reactions release energy (e.g., burning fuel in the presence of oxygen), and others require energy input (e.g., synthesis of sugars from carbon dioxide and water).

Understanding chemical reactions and the properties of elements is essential not only to the physical sciences but also is foundational knowledge for the life sciences and the earth and space sciences. The cycling of matter and associated transfers of energy in systems, of any scale, depend on physical and chemical processes. The reactivity of hydrogen ions gives rise to many biological and geophysical phenomena. The capacity of carbon atoms to form the backbone of extended molecular structures is essential to the chemistry of life. The carbon cycle involves transfers between carbon in the atmosphere—in the form of carbon dioxide—and carbon in living matter or formerly living matter (including fossil fuels). The proportion of oxygen molecules (i.e., oxygen in the form O_2) in the atmosphere also changes in this cycle.

Grade Band Endpoints for PS1.B

By the end of grade 2. Heating or cooling a substance may cause changes that can be observed. Sometimes these changes are reversible (e.g., melting and freezing), and sometimes they are not (e.g., baking a cake, burning fuel).

By the end of grade 5. When two or more different substances are mixed, a new substance with different properties may be formed; such occurrences depend on the substances and the temperature. No matter what reaction or change in properties occurs, the total weight of the substances does not change. (Boundary: Mass and weight are not distinguished at this grade level.)

By the end of grade 8. Substances react chemically in characteristic ways. In a chemical process, the atoms that make up the original substances are regrouped into different molecules, and these new substances have different properties from those of the reactants. The total number of each type of atom is conserved, and thus the mass does not change. Some chemical reactions release energy, others store energy.

By the end of grade 12. Chemical processes, their rates, and whether or not energy is stored or released can be understood in terms of the collisions of molecules and the rearrangements of atoms into new molecules, with consequent changes in total binding energy (i.e., the sum of all bond energies in the set of molecules) that are matched by changes in kinetic energy. In many situations, a dynamic and condition-dependent balance between a reaction and the reverse reaction determines the numbers of all types of molecules present.

The fact that atoms are conserved, together with knowledge of the chemical properties of the elements involved, can be used to describe and predict chemical reactions. Chemical processes and properties of materials underlie many important biological and geophysical phenomena.

PS1.C: NUCLEAR PROCESSES

What forces hold nuclei together and mediate nuclear processes?

Phenomena involving nuclei are important to understand, as they explain the formation and abundance of the elements, radioactivity, the release of energy from the sun and other stars, and the generation of nuclear power. To explain and predict nuclear processes, two additional types of interactions—known as strong and weak nuclear interactions—must be introduced. They play a fundamental role in nuclei, although not at larger scales because their effects are very short range.

The strong nuclear interaction provides the primary force that holds nuclei together and determines nuclear binding energies. Without it, the electromagnetic forces between protons would make all nuclei other than hydrogen unstable. Nuclear processes mediated by these interactions include fusion, fission, and the radioactive decays of unstable nuclei. These processes involve changes in nuclear binding energies and masses (as described by $E = mc^2$), and typically they release much more energy per atom involved than do chemical processes.

Nuclear fusion is a process in which a collision of two small nuclei eventually results in the formation of a single more massive nucleus with greater net binding energy and hence a release of energy. It occurs only under conditions of extremely high temperature and pressure. Nuclear fusion occurring in the cores of stars provides the energy released (as light) from those stars. The Big Bang produced matter in the form of hydrogen and smaller amounts of helium and lithium. Over time, stars (including supernova explosions) have produced and dispersed all the more massive atoms, starting from primordial low-mass elements, chiefly hydrogen.

Nuclear fission is a process in which a massive nucleus splits into two or more smaller nuclei, which fly apart at high energy. The produced nuclei are often not stable and undergo subsequent radioactive decays. A common fission fragment is an alpha particle, which is just another name for a helium nucleus, given before this type of "radiation" was identified.

In addition to alpha particles, other types of radioactive decays produce other forms of radiation, originally labeled as "beta" and "gamma" particles and now recognized as electrons or positrons, and photons (i.e., high-frequency electromagnetic radiation), respectively. Because of the high-energy release in nuclear transitions, the emitted radiation (whether it be alpha, beta, or gamma type) can ionize atoms and may thereby cause damage to biological tissue.

Nuclear fission and radioactive decays limit the set of stable isotopes of elements and the size of the largest stable nucleus. Spontaneous radioactive decays follow a characteristic exponential decay law, with a specific lifetime (time scale) for each such process; the lifetimes of different nuclear decay processes range from fractions of a second to thousands of years. Some unstable but long-lived isotopes are present in rocks and minerals. Knowledge of their nuclear lifetimes allows radiometric dating to be used to determine the ages of rocks and other materials from the isotope ratios present.

In fission, fusion, and beta decay processes, atoms change type, but the total number of protons plus neutrons is conserved. Beta processes involve an additional type of interaction (the weak interaction) that can change neutrons into protons or vice versa, along with the emission or absorption of electrons or positrons and of neutrinos. Isolated neutrons decay by this process.

Grade Band Endpoints for PS1.C

By the end of grade 2. [Intentionally left blank.]

By the end of grade 5. [Intentionally left blank.]

By the end of grade 8. Nuclear fusion can result in the merging of two nuclei to form a larger one, along with the release of significantly more energy per atom than any chemical process. It occurs only under conditions of extremely high temperature and pressure. Nuclear fusion taking place in the cores of stars provides the energy released (as light) from those stars and produced all of the more massive atoms from primordial hydrogen. Thus the elements found on Earth and throughout the universe (other than hydrogen and most of helium, which are primordial) were formed in the stars or supernovas by fusion processes.

By the end of grade 12. Nuclear processes, including fusion, fission, and radioactive decays of unstable nuclei, involve changes in nuclear binding energies. The total number of neutrons plus protons does not change in any nuclear process. Strong and weak nuclear interactions determine nuclear stability and processes. Spontaneous radioactive decays follow a characteristic exponential decay law. Nuclear lifetimes allow radiometric dating to be used to determine the ages of rocks and other materials from the isotope ratios present.

Normal stars cease producing light after having converted all of the material in their cores to carbon or, for more massive stars, to iron. Elements more massive than iron are formed by fusion processes but only in the extreme conditions of supernova explosions, which explains why they are relatively rare.

Core Idea PS2   Motion and Stability: Forces and Interactions

How can one explain and predict interactions between objects and within systems of objects?

Interactions between any two objects can cause changes in one or both of them. An understanding of the forces between objects is important for describing how their motions change, as well as for predicting stability or instability in systems at any scale. All forces between objects arise from a few types of interactions: gravity, electromagnetism, and the strong and weak nuclear interactions.

PS2.A: FORCES AND MOTION

How can one predict an object's continued motion, changes in motion, or stability?

Interactions of an object with another object can be explained and predicted using the concept of forces, which can cause a change in motion of one or both of the interacting objects. An individual force acts on one particular object and is

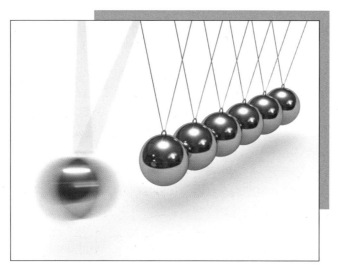

described by its strength and direction. The strengths of forces can be measured and their values compared.

What happens when a force is applied to an object depends not only on that force but also on all the other forces acting on that object. A static object typically has multiple forces acting on it, but they sum to zero. If the total (vector sum) force on an object is not zero, however, its motion will change. Sometimes forces on an object can also change its shape or orientation. For any pair of interacting objects, the force exerted by the first object on the second object is equal in strength to the force that the second object exerts on the first but in the opposite direction (Newton's third law).

At the macroscale, the motion of an object subject to forces is governed by Newton's second law of motion. Under everyday circumstances, the mathematical expression of this law in the form $F = ma$ (total force = mass times acceleration) accurately predicts changes in the motion of a single macroscopic object of a given mass due to the total force on it. But at speeds close to the speed of light, the second law is not applicable without modification. Nor does it apply to objects at the molecular, atomic, and subatomic scales, or to an object whose mass is changing at the same time as its speed.

An understanding of the forces between objects is important for describing how their motions change, as well as for predicting stability or instability in systems at any scale.

For speeds that are small compared with the speed of light, the momentum of an object is defined as its mass times its velocity. For any system of interacting objects, the total momentum within the system changes only due to transfer of momentum into or out of the system, either because of external forces acting on the system or because of matter flows. Within an isolated system of interacting objects, any change in momentum of one object is balanced by an equal and oppositely directed change in the total momentum of the other objects. Thus total momentum is a conserved quantity.

Grade Band Endpoints for PS2.A

By the end of grade 2. Objects pull or push each other when they collide or are connected. Pushes and pulls can have different strengths and directions. Pushing or pulling on an object can change the speed or direction of its motion and can start or stop it. An object sliding on a surface or sitting on a slope experiences a pull due to friction on the object due to the surface that opposes the object's motion.

By the end of grade 5. Each force acts on one particular object and has both a strength and a direction. An object at rest typically has multiple forces acting on it, but they add to give zero net force on the object. Forces that do not sum to zero can cause changes in the object's speed or direction of motion. (Boundary: Qualitative and conceptual, but not quantitative addition of forces are used at this level.) The patterns of an object's motion in various situations can be observed and measured; when past motion exhibits a regular pattern, future motion can be predicted from it. (Boundary: Technical terms, such as magnitude, velocity, momentum, and vector quantity, are not introduced at this level, but the concept that some quantities need both size and direction to be described is developed.)

By the end of grade 8. For any pair of interacting objects, the force exerted by the first object on the second object is equal in strength to the force that the second object exerts on the first but in the opposite direction (Newton's third law). The motion of an object is determined by the sum of the forces acting on it; if the total force on the object is not zero, its motion will change. The greater the mass of the object, the greater the force needed to achieve the same change in motion. For any given object, a larger force causes a larger change in motion. Forces on an object can also change its shape or orientation. All positions of objects and the directions of forces and motions must be described in an arbitrarily chosen reference frame and arbitrarily chosen units of size. In order to share information with other people, these choices must also be shared.

By the end of grade 12. Newton's second law accurately predicts changes in the motion of macroscopic objects, but it requires revision for subatomic scales or for speeds close to the speed of light. (Boundary: No details of quantum physics or relativity are included at this grade level.)

Momentum is defined for a particular frame of reference; it is the mass times the velocity of the object. In any system, total momentum is always conserved. If a system interacts with objects outside itself, the total momentum of the system can change; however, any such change is balanced by changes in the momentum of objects outside the system.

PS2.B: TYPES OF INTERACTIONS

What underlying forces explain the variety of interactions observed?

All forces between objects arise from a few types of interactions: gravity, electromagnetism, and strong and weak nuclear interactions. Collisions between objects involve forces between them that can change their motion. Any two objects in contact also exert forces on each other that are electromagnetic in origin. These forces result from deformations of the objects' substructures and the electric charges of the particles that form those substructures (e.g., a table supporting a book, friction forces).

Gravitational, electric, and magnetic forces between a pair of objects do not require that they be in contact. These forces are explained by force fields that contain energy and can transfer energy through space. These fields can be mapped by their effect on a test object (mass, charge, or magnet, respectively).

Objects with mass are sources of gravitational fields and are affected by the gravitational fields of all other objects with mass. Gravitational forces are always attractive. For two human-scale objects, these forces are too small to observe without sensitive instrumentation. Gravitational interactions are nonnegligible, however, when very massive objects are involved. Thus the gravitational force due to Earth, acting on an object near Earth's surface, pulls that object toward the planet's center. Newton's law of universal gravitation provides the mathematical model to describe and predict the effects of gravitational forces between distant objects. These long-range gravitational interactions govern the evolution and maintenance of large-scale structures in the universe (e.g., the solar system, galaxies) and the patterns of motion within them.

Electric forces and magnetic forces are different aspects of a single electromagnetic interaction. Such forces can be attractive or repulsive, depending on the relative sign of the electric charges involved, the direction of current flow, and the orientation of magnets. The forces' magnitudes depend on the magnitudes of the charges, currents, and magnetic strengths as well as on the distances between the interacting objects. All objects with electrical charge or magnetization are sources of electric or magnetic fields and can be affected by the electric or magnetic fields of other such objects. Attraction and repulsion of electric charges at the atomic scale explain the structure, properties, and transformations of matter and the contact forces between material objects (link to PS1.A and PS1.B). Coulomb's law provides the mathematical model to describe and predict the effects of electrostatic forces (relating to stationary electric charges or fields) between distant objects.

The strong and weak nuclear interactions are important inside atomic nuclei. These short-range interactions determine nuclear sizes, stability, and rates of radioactive decay (see PS1.C).

Grade Band Endpoints for PS2.B

By the end of grade 2. When objects touch or collide, they push on one another and can change motion or shape.

By the end of grade 5. Objects in contact exert forces on each other (friction, elastic pushes and pulls). Electric, magnetic, and gravitational forces between a pair of objects do not require that the objects be in contact—for example, magnets push

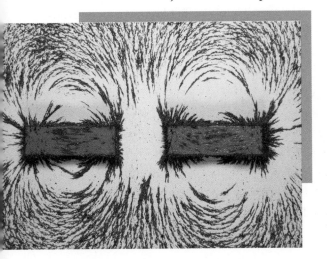

or pull at a distance. The sizes of the forces in each situation depend on the properties of the objects and their distances apart and, for forces between two magnets, on their orientation relative to each other. The gravitational force of Earth acting on an object near Earth's surface pulls that object toward the planet's center.

By the end of grade 8. Electric and magnetic (electromagnetic) forces can be attractive or repulsive, and their sizes depend on the magnitudes of the charges, currents, or magnetic strengths involved and on the distances between the interacting objects. Gravitational forces are always attractive. There is a gravitational force between any two masses, but it is very small except when one or both of the objects have large mass—for example, Earth and the sun. Long-range gravitational interactions govern the evolution and maintenance of large-scale systems in space, such as galaxies or the solar system, and determine the patterns of motion within those structures.

Forces that act at a distance (gravitational, electric, and magnetic) can be explained by force fields that extend through space and can be mapped by their effect on a test object (a ball, a charged object, or a magnet, respectively).

By the end of grade 12. Newton's law of universal gravitation and Coulomb's law provide the mathematical models to describe and predict the effects of gravitational and electrostatic forces between distant objects.

Forces at a distance are explained by fields permeating space that can transfer energy through space. Magnets or changing electric fields cause magnetic fields; electric charges or changing magnetic fields cause electric fields. Attraction and repulsion between electric charges at the atomic scale explain the structure, properties, and transformations of matter, as well as the contact forces between material objects. The strong and weak nuclear interactions are important inside atomic nuclei—for example, they determine the patterns of which nuclear isotopes are stable and what kind of decays occur for unstable ones.

PS2.C: STABILITY AND INSTABILITY IN PHYSICAL SYSTEMS

Why are some physical systems more stable than others?

Events and processes in a system typically involve multiple interactions occurring simultaneously or in sequence. The system's stability or instability and its rate of evolution depend on the balance or imbalance among these multiple effects.

A stable system is one in which the internal and external forces are such that any small change results in forces that return the system to its prior state (e.g., a weight hanging from a string). A system can be static but unstable, with any small change leading to forces that tend to increase that change (e.g., a ball at the top of a hill). A system can be changing but have a stable repeating cycle of changes, with regular patterns of change that allow predictions about the system's future (e.g., Earth orbiting the sun). And a stable system can appear to be unchanging when flows or processes within it are going on at opposite but equal rates (e.g., water in a dam at a constant height but with water flowing in that offsets the water flowing out; a person maintaining steady weight but eating food, burning calories, and excreting waste).

Stability and instability in any system depend on the balance of competing effects. A steady state of a complex system can be maintained through a set of feedback mechanisms, but changes in conditions can move the system out of its range of stability (e.g., homeostasis breaks down at too high or too low a temperature). With no energy inputs, a system starting out in an unstable state will continue to change until it reaches a stable configuration (e.g., the temperatures of hot and cold objects in contact). Viewed at a given scale, stable systems may appear static or dynamic. Conditions and properties of the objects within a system affect the rates of energy transfer and thus how fast or slowly a process occurs (e.g., heat conduction, the diffusion of particles in a fluid).

When a system has a great number of component pieces, one may not be able to predict much about its precise future. For such systems (e.g., with very many colliding molecules), one can often predict average but not detailed properties and behaviors (e.g., average temperature, motion, and rates of chemical change but not the trajectories of particular molecules).

Grade Band Endpoints for PS2.C

By the end of grade 2. Whether an object stays still or moves often depends on the effects of multiple pushes and pulls on it (e.g., multiple players trying to pull an object in different directions). It is useful to investigate what pushes and pulls keep something in place (e.g., a ball on a slope, a ladder leaning on a wall) as well as what makes something change or move.

By the end of grade 5. A system can change as it moves in one direction (e.g., a ball rolling down a hill), shifts back and forth (e.g., a swinging pendulum), or goes through cyclical patterns (e.g., day and night). Examining how the forces on and within the system change as it moves can help to explain the system's patterns of change.

A system can appear to be unchanging when processes within the system are occurring at opposite but equal rates (e.g., water behind a dam is at a constant height because water is flowing in at the same rate that water is flowing out). Changes can happen very quickly or very slowly and are sometimes hard to see (e.g., plant growth). Conditions and properties of the objects within a system affect how fast or slowly a process occurs (e.g., heat conduction rates).

By the end of grade 8. A stable system is one in which any small change results in forces that return the system to its prior state (e.g., a weight hanging from a string). A system can be static but unstable (e.g., a pencil standing on end). A system can be changing but have a stable repeating cycle of changes; such observed regular patterns allow predictions about the system's future (e.g., Earth orbiting the sun). Many systems, both natural and engineered, rely on feedback mechanisms to maintain stability, but they can function only within a limited range of conditions. With no energy inputs, a system starting out in an unstable state will continue to change until it reaches a stable configuration (e.g., sand in an hourglass).

By the end of grade 12. Systems often change in predictable ways; understanding the forces that drive the transformations and cycles within a system, as well as the forces imposed on the system from the outside, helps predict its behavior under a variety of conditions.

When a system has a great number of component pieces, one may not be able to predict much about its precise future. For such systems (e.g., with very many colliding molecules), one can often predict average but not detailed properties and behaviors (e.g., average temperature, motion, and rates of chemical change but not the trajectories or other changes of particular molecules). Systems may evolve in unpredictable ways when the outcome depends sensitively on the starting condition and the starting condition cannot be specified precisely enough to distinguish between different possible outcomes.

Core Idea PS3   Energy

How is energy transferred and conserved?

Interactions of objects can be explained and predicted using the concept of transfer of energy from one object or system of objects to another. The total energy within a defined system changes only by the transfer of energy into or out of the system.

PS3.A: DEFINITIONS OF ENERGY

What is energy?

That there is a single quantity called energy is due to the remarkable fact that a system's *total* energy is conserved. Regardless of the quantities of energy transferred between subsystems and stored in various ways within the system, the total energy of a system changes only by the amount of energy transferred into and out of the system.

At the macroscopic scale, energy manifests itself in multiple phenomena, such as motion, light, sound, electrical and magnetic fields, and thermal energy. Historically, different units were introduced for the energy present in these different phenomena, and it took some time before the relationships among them were recognized. Energy is best understood at the microscopic scale, at which it can be modeled as either motions of particles or as stored in force fields (electric, magnetic, gravitational) that mediate interactions between particles. This last concept includes electromagnetic radiation, a phenomenon in which energy stored in fields moves across space (light, radio waves) with no supporting matter medium.

Motion energy is also called kinetic energy; defined in a given reference frame, it is proportional to the mass of the moving object and grows with the square of its speed. Matter at any temperature above absolute zero contains thermal energy. Thermal energy is the random motion of particles (whether vibrations in solid matter or molecules or free motion in a gas), this energy is distributed among all the particles in a system through collisions and interactions at a distance. In contrast, a sound wave is a moving pattern of particle vibrations that transmits energy through a medium.

Electric and magnetic fields also contain energy; any change in the relative positions of charged objects (or in the positions or orientations of magnets) changes the fields between them and thus the amount of energy stored in those fields. When a particle in a molecule of solid matter vibrates, energy is continually being transformed back and forth between the energy of motion and the energy stored in the electric and magnetic fields within the matter. Matter in a stable form minimizes the stored energy in the electric and magnetic fields within it; this defines the equilibrium positions and spacing of the atomic nuclei in a molecule or an extended solid and the form of their combined electron charge distributions (e.g., chemical bonds, metals).

Energy stored in fields within a system can also be described as potential energy. For any system where the stored energy depends only on the spatial configuration of the system and not on its history, potential energy is a useful concept (e.g., a massive object above Earth's surface, a compressed or stretched spring). It is defined as a difference in energy compared to some arbitrary reference configuration of a system. For example, lifting an object increases the stored energy in the gravitational field between that object and Earth (gravitational potential energy) compared to that for the object at Earth's surface; when the object falls, the stored energy decreases and the object's kinetic energy increases. When a pendulum swings, some stored energy is transformed into kinetic energy and back again into stored energy during each swing. (In both examples energy is transferred out of the system due to collisions with air and for the pendulum also by friction in its support.) Any change in potential energy is accompanied by changes in other forms of

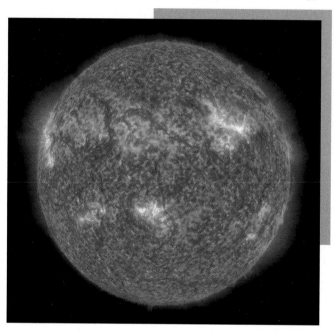

energy within the system, or by energy transfers into or out of the system.

Electromagnetic radiation (such as light and X-rays) can be modeled as a wave of changing electric and magnetic fields. At the subatomic scale (i.e., in quantum theory), many phenomena involving electromagnetic radiation (e.g., photoelectric effect) are best modeled as a stream of particles called photons. Electromagnetic radiation from the sun is a major source of energy for life on Earth.

The idea that there are different forms of energy, such as thermal energy, mechanical energy, and chemical energy, is misleading, as it implies that the nature of the energy in each of these manifestations is distinct when in fact they all are ultimately, at the atomic scale, some mixture of kinetic energy, stored energy, and radiation. It is likewise misleading to call sound or light a form of energy; they are phenomena that, among their other properties, transfer energy from place to place and between objects.

Grade Band Endpoints for PS3.A

By the end of grade 2. [Intentionally left blank.]

By the end of grade 5. The faster a given object is moving, the more energy it possesses. Energy can be moved from place to place by moving objects or through sound, light, or electric currents. (Boundary: At this grade level, no attempt is made to give a precise or complete definition of energy.)

■ At the macroscopic scale, energy manifests itself in multiple phenomena, such as motion, light, sound, electrical and magnetic fields, and thermal energy. ■

By the end of grade 8. Motion energy is properly called kinetic energy; it is proportional to the mass of the moving object and grows with the square of its speed. A system of objects may also contain stored (potential) energy, depending on their relative positions. For example, energy is stored—in gravitational interaction with Earth—when an object is raised, and energy is released when the object falls or is lowered. Energy is also stored in the electric fields between charged particles and the magnetic fields between magnets, and it changes when these objects are moved relative to one another. Stored energy is decreased in some chemical reactions and increased in others.

The term "heat" as used in everyday language refers both to thermal energy (the motion of atoms or molecules within a substance) and energy transfers by convection, conduction, and radiation (particularly infrared and light). In science, heat is used only for this second meaning; it refers to energy transferred when two objects or systems are at different temperatures. Temperature is a measure of the average kinetic energy of particles of matter. The relationship between the temperature and the total energy of a system depends on the types, states, and amounts of matter present.

By the end of grade 12. Energy is a quantitative property of a system that depends on the motion and interactions of matter and radiation within that system. That there is a single quantity called energy is due to the fact that a system's *total* energy is conserved, even as, within the system, energy is continually transferred from one object to another and between its various possible forms. At the macroscopic scale, energy manifests itself in multiple ways, such as in motion, sound, light, and thermal energy. "Mechanical energy" generally refers to some combination of motion and stored energy in an operating machine. "Chemical energy" generally is used to mean the energy that can be released or stored in chemical processes, and "electrical energy" may mean energy stored in a battery or energy transmitted by electric currents. Historically, different units and names were used for the energy present in these different phenomena, and it took some time before the relationships between them were recognized. These relationships are better understood at the microscopic scale, at which all of the different manifestations of energy can be modeled as either motions of particles or energy stored in fields (which mediate interactions between particles). This last concept includes radiation, a phenomenon in which energy stored in fields moves across space.

PS3.B: CONSERVATION OF ENERGY AND ENERGY TRANSFER

What is meant by conservation of energy?
How is energy transferred between objects or systems?

The total change of energy in any system is always equal to the total energy transferred into or out of the system. This is called conservation of energy. Energy cannot be created or destroyed, but it can be transported from one place to another and transferred between systems. Many different types of phenomena can be explained in terms of energy transfers. Mathematical expressions, which quantify changes in the forms of energy within a system and transfers of energy into or out of the system, allow the concept of conservation of energy to be used to predict and describe the behavior of a system.

When objects collide or otherwise come in contact, the motion energy of one object can be transferred to change the motion or stored energy (e.g., change in shape or temperature) of the other objects. For macroscopic objects, any such process (e.g., collisions, sliding contact) also transfers some of the energy to the surrounding air by sound or heat. For molecules, collisions can also result in energy transfers through chemical processes, which increase or decrease the total amount of stored energy within a system of atoms; the change in stored energy is always balanced by a change in total kinetic energy—that of the molecules present after the process compared with the kinetic energy of the molecules present before it.

Energy can also be transferred from place to place by electric currents. Heating is another process for transferring energy. Heat transfer occurs when two objects or systems are at different temperatures. Energy moves out of higher temperature objects and into lower temperature ones, cooling the former and heating the latter. This transfer happens in three different ways—by conduction within solids, by the flow of liquid or gas (convection), and by radiation, which can travel across space. Even when a system is isolated (such as Earth in space), energy is continually being transferred into and out of it by radiation. The processes underlying convection and conduction can be understood in terms of models of the possible motions of particles in matter.

Radiation can be emitted or absorbed by matter. When matter absorbs light or infrared radiation, the energy of that radiation is transformed to thermal motion of particles in the matter, or, for shorter wavelengths (ultraviolet, X-ray), the radiation's energy is absorbed within the atoms or molecules and may possibly ionize them by knocking out an electron.

Uncontrolled systems always evolve toward more stable states—that is, toward more uniform energy distribution within the system or between the system and its environment (e.g., water flows downhill, objects that are hotter than their surrounding environment cool down). Any object or system that can degrade with no added energy is unstable. Eventually it will change or fall apart, although in some cases it may remain in the unstable state for a long time before decaying (e.g., long-lived radioactive isotopes).

Grade-Level Endpoints for PS3.B

By the end of grade 2. Sunlight warms Earth's surface.

By the end of grade 5. Energy is present whenever there are moving objects, sound, light, or heat. When objects collide, energy can be transferred from one object to another, thereby changing their motion. In such collisions, some energy is typically also transferred to the surrounding air; as a result, the air gets heated and sound is produced.

Light also transfers energy from place to place. For example, energy radiated from the sun is transferred to Earth by light. When this light is absorbed, it warms Earth's land, air, and water and facilitates plant growth.

Energy can also be transferred from place to place by electric currents, which can then be used locally to produce motion, sound, heat, or light. The currents may have been produced to begin with by transforming the energy of motion into electrical energy (e.g., moving water driving a spinning turbine which generates electric currents).

By the end of grade 8. When the motion energy of an object changes, there is inevitably some other change in energy at the same time. For example, the friction that causes a moving object to stop also results in an increase in the thermal energy in both surfaces; eventually heat energy is transferred to the surrounding environment as the surfaces cool. Similarly, to make an object start moving or to keep it moving when friction forces transfer energy away from it,

energy must be provided from, say, chemical (e.g., burning fuel) or electrical (e.g., an electric motor and a battery) processes.

The amount of energy transfer needed to change the temperature of a matter sample by a given amount depends on the nature of the matter, the size of the sample, and the environment. Energy is transferred out of hotter regions or objects and into colder ones by the processes of conduction, convection, and radiation.

By the end of grade 12. Conservation of energy means that the total change of energy in any system is always equal to the total energy transferred into or out of the system. Energy cannot be created or destroyed, but it can be transported from one place to another and transferred between systems.

Mathematical expressions, which quantify how the stored energy in a system depends on its configuration (e.g., relative positions of charged particles, compression of a spring) and how kinetic energy depends on mass and speed, allow the concept of conservation of energy to be used to predict and describe system behavior. The availability of energy limits what can occur in any system.

Uncontrolled systems always evolve toward more stable states—that is, toward more uniform energy distribution (e.g., water flows downhill, objects hotter than their surrounding environment cool down). Any object or system that can degrade with no added energy is unstable. Eventually it will do so, but if the energy releases throughout the transition are small, the process duration can be very long (e.g., long-lived radioactive isotopes).

PS3.C RELATIONSHIP BETWEEN ENERGY AND FORCES

How are forces related to energy?

When two objects interact, each one exerts a force on the other. These forces can transfer energy between the objects. Forces between two objects at a distance are explained by force fields (gravitational, electric, or magnetic) between them. Contact forces between colliding objects can be modeled at the microscopic level as due to electromagnetic force fields between the surface particles. When two objects interacting via a force field change their relative position, the energy in the force field between them changes. For any such pair of objects the force on each object acts in the direction such that motion of that object in that direction would reduce the energy in the force field between the two objects. However, prior motion and other forces also affect the actual direction of motion.

Patterns of motion, such as a weight bobbing on a spring or a swinging pendulum, can be understood in terms of forces at each instant or in terms of transformation of energy between the motion and one or more forms of stored energy. Elastic collisions between two objects can be modeled at the macroscopic scale using conservation of energy without having to examine the detailed microscopic forces.

Grade Band Endpoints for PS3.C

By the end of grade 2. A bigger push or pull makes things go faster. Faster speeds during a collision can cause a bigger change in shape of the colliding objects.

By the end of grade 5. When objects collide, the contact forces transfer energy so as to change the objects' motions. Magnets can exert forces on other magnets or on magnetizable materials, causing energy transfer between them (e.g., leading to changes in motion) even when the objects are not touching.

By the end of grade 8. When two objects interact, each one exerts a force on the other that can cause energy to be transferred to or from the object. For example, when energy is transferred to an Earth-object system as an object is raised, the gravitational field energy of the system increases. This energy is released as the object falls; the mechanism of this release is the gravitational force. Likewise, two magnetic and electrically charged objects interacting at a distance exert forces on each other that can transfer energy between the interacting objects.

By the end of grade 12. Force fields (gravitational, electric, and magnetic) contain energy and can transmit energy across space from one object to another.

When two objects interacting through a force field change relative position, the energy stored in the force field is changed. Each force between the two interacting objects acts in the direction such that motion in that direction would reduce the energy in the force field between the objects. However, prior motion and other forces also affect the actual direction of motion.

PS3.D: ENERGY IN CHEMICAL PROCESSES AND EVERYDAY LIFE

How do food and fuel provide energy?
If energy is conserved, why do people say it is produced or used?

In ordinary language, people speak of "producing" or "using" energy. This refers to the fact that energy in concentrated form is useful for generating electricity, moving or heating objects, and producing light, whereas diffuse energy in the environment is not readily captured for practical use. Therefore, to produce energy typically means to convert some stored energy into a desired form—for example, the stored energy of water behind a dam is released as the water flows downhill and drives a turbine generator to produce electricity, which is then delivered to users through distribution systems. Food, fuel, and batteries are especially convenient energy resources because they can be moved from place to place to provide processes that release energy where needed. A system does not destroy energy when carrying out any process. However, the process cannot occur without energy being available. The energy is also not destroyed by the end of the process. Most often some or all of it has been transferred to heat the surrounding environment; in the same sense that paper is not destroyed when it is written on, it still exists but is not readily available for further use.

Naturally occurring food and fuel contain complex carbon-based molecules, chiefly derived from plant matter that has been formed by photosynthesis. The chemical reaction of these molecules with oxygen releases energy; such reactions provide energy for most animal life and for residential, commercial, and industrial activities.

Electric power generation is based on fossil fuels (i.e., coal, oil, and natural gas), nuclear fission, or renewable resources (e.g., solar, wind, tidal, geothermal, and hydro power). Transportation today chiefly depends on fossil fuels, but the use of electric and alternative fuel (e.g., hydrogen, biofuel) vehicles is increasing. All forms of electricity generation and transportation fuels have associated economic, social, and environmental costs and benefits, both short and long term. Technological advances and regulatory decisions can change the balance of those costs and benefits.

Although energy cannot be destroyed, it can be converted to less useful forms. In designing a system for energy storage, for energy distribution, or to perform some practical task (e.g., to power an airplane), it is important to design for maximum efficiency—thereby ensuring that the largest possible fraction of the energy is used for the desired purpose rather than being transferred out of the system in unwanted ways (e.g., through friction, which eventually results in heat energy transfer to the surrounding environment). Improving efficiency reduces costs, waste materials, and many unintended environmental impacts.

Grade Band Endpoints for PS3.D

By the end of grade 2. When two objects rub against each other, this interaction is called friction. Friction between two surfaces can warm of both of them (e.g., rubbing hands together). There are ways to reduce the friction between two objects.

By the end of grade 5. The expression "produce energy" typically refers to the conversion of stored energy into a desired form for practical use—for example, the stored energy of water behind a dam is released so that it flows downhill

and drives a turbine generator to produce electricity. Food and fuel also release energy when they are digested or burned. When machines or animals "use" energy (e.g., to move around), most often the energy is transferred to heat the surrounding environment.

The energy released by burning fuel or digesting food was once energy from the sun that was captured by plants in the chemical process that forms plant matter (from air and water). (Boundary: The fact that plants capture energy from sunlight is introduced at this grade level, but details of photosynthesis are not.)

It is important to be able to concentrate energy so that it is available for use where and when it is needed. For example, batteries are physically transportable energy storage devices, whereas electricity generated by power plants is transferred from place to place through distribution systems.

By the end of grade 8. The chemical reaction by which plants produce complex food molecules (sugars) requires an energy input (i.e., from sunlight) to occur. In this reaction, carbon dioxide and water combine to form carbon-based organic molecules and release oxygen. (Boundary: Further details of the photosynthesis process are not taught at this grade level.)

Both the burning of fuel and cellular digestion in plants and animals involve chemical reactions with oxygen that release stored energy. In these processes, complex molecules containing carbon react with oxygen to produce carbon dioxide and other materials.

Machines can be made more efficient, that is, require less fuel input to perform a given task, by reducing friction between their moving parts and through aerodynamic design. Friction increases energy transfer to the surrounding environment by heating the affected materials.

By the end of grade 12. Nuclear fusion processes in the center of the sun release the energy that ultimately reaches Earth as radiation. The main way in which that solar energy is captured and stored on Earth is through the complex chemical process known as photosynthesis. Solar cells are human-made devices that likewise capture the sun's energy and produce electrical energy.

A variety of multistage physical and chemical processes in living organisms, particularly within their cells, account for the transport and transfer (release or uptake) of energy needed for life functions.

All forms of electricity generation and transportation fuels have associated economic, social, and environmental costs and benefits, both short and long term.

Although energy cannot be destroyed, it can be converted to less useful forms—for example, to thermal energy in the surrounding environment. Machines are judged as efficient or inefficient based on the amount of energy input needed to perform a particular useful task. Inefficient machines are those that produce more waste heat while performing a task and thus require more energy input. It is therefore important to design for high efficiency so as to reduce costs, waste materials, and many environmental impacts.

Core Idea PS4   Waves and Their Applications in Technologies for Information Transfer

How are waves used to transfer energy and information?

Waves are a repeating pattern of motion that transfers energy from place to place without overall displacement of matter. Light and sound are wavelike phenomena. By understanding wave properties and the interactions of electromagnetic radiation with matter, scientists and engineers can design systems for transferring information across long distances, storing information, and investigating nature on many scales—some of them far beyond direct human perception.

PS4.A: WAVE PROPERTIES

What are the characteristic properties and behaviors of waves?

Whether a wave in water, a sound wave, or a light wave, all waves have some features in common. A simple wave has a repeating pattern of specific wavelength, frequency, and amplitude. The wavelength and frequency of a wave are related to one another by the speed of travel of the wave, which, for each type of wave, depends on the medium in which the wave is traveling. Waves can be combined with other waves of the same type to produce complex information-containing patterns that can be decoded at the receiving end. Waves, which transfer energy and any encoded information without the bulk motion of matter, can travel unchanged over long distances, pass through other waves undisturbed, and be detected and decoded far from where they were produced. Information can be digitized (converted into a numerical representation), sent over long distances as a series of wave pulses, and reliably stored in computer memory.

Sound is a pressure wave in air or any other material medium. The human ear and brain working together are very good at detecting and decoding patterns of information in sound (e.g., speech and music) and distinguishing them from random noise.

Resonance is a phenomenon in which waves add up in phase (i.e., matched peaks and valleys), thus growing in amplitude. Structures have particular frequencies at which they resonate when some time-varying force acting on them transfers energy to them. This phenomenon (e.g., waves in a stretched string, vibrating air in a pipe) is used in the design of all musical instruments and in the production of sound by the human voice.

When a wave passes an object that is small compared with its wavelength, the wave is not much affected; for this reason, some things are too small to see with visible light, which is a wave phenomenon with a limited range of wavelengths corresponding to each color. When a wave meets the surface between two different materials or conditions (e.g., air to water), part of the wave is reflected at that surface and another part continues on, but at a different speed. The change of speed of the wave when passing from one medium to another can cause the wave to change direction or refract. These wave properties are used in many applications (e.g., lenses, seismic probing of Earth).

Grade Band Endpoints for PS4.A

By the end of grade 2. Waves, which are regular patterns of motion, can be made in water by disturbing the surface. When waves move across the surface of deep water, the water goes up and down in place; it does not move in the direction of the wave—observe, for example, a bobbing cork or seabird—except when the water meets the beach.

Sound can make matter vibrate, and vibrating matter can make sound.

By the end of grade 5. Waves of the same type can differ in amplitude (height of the wave) and wavelength (spacing between wave peaks). Waves can add or cancel one another as they cross, depending on their relative phase (i.e., relative position of peaks and troughs of the waves), but they emerge unaffected by each other. (Boundary: The discussion at this grade level is qualitative only; it can be based on the fact that two different sounds can pass a location in different directions without getting mixed up.)

Earthquakes cause seismic waves, which are waves of motion in Earth's crust.

By the end of grade 8. A simple wave has a repeating pattern with a specific wavelength, frequency, and amplitude. A sound wave needs a medium through which it is transmitted.

Geologists use seismic waves and their reflection at interfaces between layers to probe structures deep in the planet.

By the end of grade 12. The wavelength and frequency of a wave are related to one another by the speed of travel of the wave, which depends on the type of wave and the medium through which it is passing. The reflection, refraction, and transmission of waves at an interface between two media can be modeled on the basis of these properties.

Combining waves of different frequencies can make a wide variety of patterns and thereby encode and transmit information. Information can be digitized (e.g., a picture stored as the values of an array of pixels); in this form, it can be stored reliably in computer memory and sent over long distances as a series of wave pulses.

Resonance is a phenomenon in which waves add up in phase in a structure, growing in amplitude due to energy input near the natural vibration frequency. Structures have particular frequencies at which they resonate. This phenomenon (e.g., waves in a stretched string, vibrating air in a pipe) is used in speech and in the design of all musical instruments.

PS4.B: ELECTROMAGNETIC RADIATION

What is light?
How can one explain the varied effects that involve light?
What other forms of electromagnetic radiation are there?

Electromagnetic radiation (e.g., radio, microwaves, light) can be modeled as a wave pattern of changing electric and magnetic fields or, alternatively, as particles. Each model is useful for understanding aspects of the phenomenon and its interactions with matter, and quantum theory relates the two models. Electromagnetic

By understanding wave properties and the interactions of electromagnetic radiation with matter, scientists and engineers can design systems for transferring information across long distances, storing information, and investigating nature on many scales—some of them far beyond direct human perception.

waves can be detected over a wide range of frequencies, of which the visible spectrum of colors detectable by human eyes is just a small part. Many modern technologies are based on the manipulation of electromagnetic waves.

All electromagnetic radiation travels through a vacuum at the same speed, called the speed of light. Its speed in any given medium depends on its wavelength and the properties of that medium. At the surface between two media, like any wave, light can be reflected, refracted (its path bent), or absorbed. What occurs depends on properties of the surface and the wavelength of the light. When shorter wavelength electromagnetic radiation (ultraviolet, X-rays, gamma rays) is absorbed in matter, it can ionize atoms and cause damage to living cells. However, because X-rays can travel through soft body matter for some distance but are more rapidly absorbed by denser matter, particularly bone, they are useful for medical imaging. Photovoltaic materials emit electrons when they absorb light of a high-enough frequency. This phenomenon is used in barcode scanners and "electric eye" systems, as well as in solar cells. It is best explained using a particle model of light.

Any object emits a spectrum of electromagnetic radiation that depends on its temperature. In addition, atoms of each element emit and preferentially absorb characteristic frequencies of light. These spectral lines allow identification of the presence of the element, even in microscopic quantities or for remote objects, such as a star. Nuclear transitions that emit or absorb gamma radiation also have distinctive gamma ray wavelengths, a phenomenon that can be used to identify and trace specific radioactive isotopes.

Grade Band Endpoints for PS4.B

By the end of grade 2. Objects can be seen only when light is available to illuminate them. Very hot objects give off light (e.g., a fire, the sun).

Some materials allow light to pass through them, others allow only some light through, and others block all the light and create a dark shadow on any surface beyond them (i.e., on the other side from the light source), where the light cannot reach. Mirrors and prisms can be used to redirect a light beam. (Boundary: The idea that light travels from place to place is developed through experiences with light sources, mirrors, and shadows, but no attempt is made to discuss the speed of light.)

By the end of grade 5. A great deal of light travels through space to Earth from the sun and from distant stars.

An object can be seen when light reflected from its surface enters the eyes; the color people see depends on the color of the available light sources as well as the properties of the surface. (Boundary: This phenomenon is observed, but no attempt is made to discuss what confers the color reflection and absorption properties on a surface. The stress is on understanding that light traveling from the object to the eye determines what is seen.)

Because lenses bend light beams, they can be used, singly or in combination, to provide magnified images of objects too small or too far away to be seen with the naked eye.

By the end of grade 8. When light shines on an object, it is reflected, absorbed, or transmitted through the object, depending on the object's material and the frequency (color) of the light.

The path that light travels can be traced as straight lines, except at surfaces between different transparent materials (e.g., air and water, air and glass) where the light path bends. Lenses and prisms are applications of this effect.

A wave model of light is useful for explaining brightness, color, and the frequency-dependent bending of light at a surface between media (prisms). However, because light can travel through space, it cannot be a matter wave, like sound or water waves.

By the end of grade 12. Electromagnetic radiation (e.g., radio, microwaves, light) can be modeled as a wave of changing electric and magnetic fields or as particles called photons. The wave model is useful for explaining many features of electromagnetic radiation, and the particle model explains other features. Quantum theory relates the two models. (Boundary: Quantum theory is not explained further at this grade level.)

Because a wave is not much disturbed by objects that are small compared with its wavelength, visible light cannot be used to see such objects as individual atoms. All electromagnetic radiation travels through a vacuum at the same speed, called the speed of light. Its speed in any other given medium depends on its wavelength and the properties of that medium.

When light or longer wavelength electromagnetic radiation is absorbed in matter, it is generally converted into thermal energy (heat). Shorter wavelength electromagnetic radiation (ultraviolet, X-rays, gamma rays) can ionize atoms and cause damage to living cells. Photovoltaic materials emit electrons when they absorb light of a high-enough frequency.

Atoms of each element emit and absorb characteristic frequencies of light, and nuclear transitions have distinctive gamma ray wavelengths. These characteristics allow identification of the presence of an element, even in microscopic quantities.

PS4.C: INFORMATION TECHNOLOGIES AND INSTRUMENTATION

How are instruments that transmit and detect waves used to extend human senses?

Understanding of waves and their interactions with matter has been used to design technologies and instruments that greatly extend the range of phenomena that can

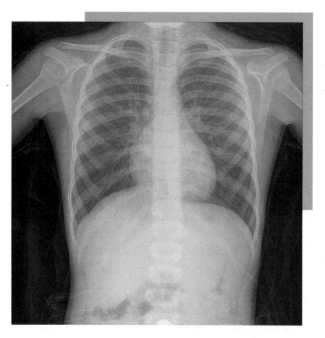

be investigated by science (e.g., telescopes, microscopes) and have many useful applications in the modern world.

Light waves, radio waves, microwaves, and infrared waves are applied to communications systems, many of which use digitized signals (i.e., sent as wave pulses) as a more reliable way to convey information. Signals that humans cannot sense directly can be detected by appropriately designed devices (e.g., telescopes, cell phones, wired or wireless computer networks). When in digitized form, information can be recorded, stored for future recovery, and transmitted over long distances without significant degradation.

Medical imaging devices collect and interpret signals from waves that can travel through the body and are affected by, and thus gather information about, structures and motion within it (e.g., ultrasound, X-rays). Sonar (based on sound pulses) can be used to measure the depth of the sea, and a system based on laser pulses can measure the distance to objects in space, because it is known how fast sound travels in water and light travels in a vacuum. The better the interaction of the wave with the medium is understood, the more detailed the information that can be extracted (e.g., medical imaging or astronomical observations at multiple frequencies).

Grade Band Endpoints for PS4.C

By the end of grade 2. People use their senses to learn about the world around them. Their eyes detect light, their ears detect sound, and they can feel vibrations by touch.

People also use a variety of devices to communicate (send and receive information) over long distances.

By the end of grade 5. Lenses can be used to make eyeglasses, telescopes, or microscopes in order to extend what can be seen. The design of such instruments is based on understanding how the path of light bends at the surface of a lens.

Digitized information (e.g., the pixels of a picture) can be stored for future recovery or transmitted over long distances without significant degradation. High-tech devices, such as computers or cell phones, can receive and decode information—convert it from digitized form to voice—and vice versa.

By the end of grade 8. Appropriately designed technologies (e.g., radio, television, cell phones, wired and wireless computer networks) make it possible to detect and interpret many types of signals that cannot be sensed directly. Designers of such devices must understand both the signal and its interactions with matter.

Many modern communication devices use digitized signals (sent as wave pulses) as a more reliable way to encode and transmit information.

By the end of grade 12. Multiple technologies based on the understanding of waves and their interactions with matter are part of everyday experiences in the modern world (e.g., medical imaging, communications, scanners) and in scientific research. They are essential tools for producing, transmitting, and capturing signals and for storing and interpreting the information contained in them.

Knowledge of quantum physics enabled the development of semiconductors, computer chips, and lasers, all of which are now essential components of modern imaging, communications, and information technologies. (Boundary: Details of quantum physics are not formally taught at this grade level.)

REFERENCES

1. National Research Council. (1996). *National Science Education Standards.* National Committee for Science Education Standards and Assessment. Washington, DC: National Academy Press.

2. American Association for the Advancement of Science. (2009). *Benchmarks for Science Literacy.* Project 2061. Available: http://www.project2061.org/publications/ bsl/online/index.php?txtRef=http%3A%2F%2Fwww%2Eproject2061%2Eorg%2 Fpublications%2Fbsl%2Fdefault%2Ehtm%3FtxtRef%3D%26txtURIOld%3D%252 Ftools%252Fbsl%252Fdefault%2Ehtm&txtURIOld=%2Fpublications%2Fbsl%2 Fonline%2Fbolintro%2Ehtm [June 2011].

6

Dimension 3
DISCIPLINARY CORE IDEAS—LIFE SCIENCES

The life sciences focus on patterns, processes, and relationships of living organisms. Life is self-contained, self-sustaining, self-replicating, and evolving, operating according to laws of the physical world, as well as genetic programming. Life scientists use observations, experiments, hypotheses, tests, models, theory, and technology to explore how life works. The study of life ranges over scales from single molecules, through organisms and ecosystems, to the entire biosphere, that is all life on Earth. It examines processes that occur on time scales from the blink of an eye to those that happen over billions of years. Living systems are interconnected and interacting. Although living organisms respond to the physical environment or geosphere, they have also fundamentally changed Earth over evolutionary time. Rapid advances in life sciences are helping to provide biological solutions to societal problems related to food, energy, health, and environment.

From viruses and bacteria to plants to fungi to animals, the diversity of the millions of life forms on Earth is astonishing. Without unifying principles, it would be difficult to make sense of the living world and apply those understandings to solving problems. A core principle of the life sciences is that all organisms are related by evolution and that evolutionary processes have led to the tremendous diversity of the biosphere. There is diversity within species as well as between species. Yet what is learned about the function of a gene or a cell or a process in one organism is relevant to other organisms because of their ecological interactions and evolutionary relatedness. Evolution and its underlying genetic mechanisms of inheritance and variability are key to understanding both the unity and the diversity of life on Earth.

The committee developed four core ideas reflecting unifying principles in life sciences. These core ideas are essential for a conceptual understanding of the life sciences and will enable students to make sense of emerging research findings. We begin at the level of organisms, delving into the many processes and structures, at scales ranging from components as small as individual atoms to organ systems that are necessary for life to be sustained. Our focus then broadens to consider organisms in their environment—how they interact with the environment's living (biotic) and physical (abiotic) features. Next the chapter considers how organisms reproduce, passing genetic information to their offspring, and how these mechanisms lead to variability and hence diversity within species. Finally, the core ideas in the life sciences culminate with the principle that evolution can explain how the diversity that is observed within species has led to the diversity of life across species through a process of descent with adaptive modification. Evolution also accounts for the remarkable similarity of the fundamental characteristics of all species.

The first core idea, LS1: From Molecules to Organisms: Structures and Processes, addresses how individual organisms are configured and how these structures function to support life, growth, behavior, and reproduction. The first core idea hinges on the unifying principle that cells are the basic unit of life.

The second core idea, LS2: Ecosystems: Interactions, Energy, and Dynamics, explores organisms' interactions with each other and their physical environment. This includes how organisms obtain resources, how they change their environment, how changing environmental factors affect organisms and ecosystems, how social interactions and group behavior play out within and between species, and how these factors all combine to determine ecosystem functioning.

The third core idea, LS3: Heredity: Inheritance and Variation of Traits across generations, focuses on the flow of genetic information between generations. This idea explains the mechanisms of genetic inheritance and describes the environmental and genetic causes of gene mutation and the alteration of gene expression.

The fourth core idea, LS4: Biological Evolution: Unity and Diversity, explores "changes in the traits of populations of organisms over time" [1] and the factors that account for species' unity and diversity alike. The section

Evolution and its underlying genetic mechanisms of inheritance and variability are key to understanding both the unity and the diversity of life on Earth.

begins with a discussion of the converging evidence for shared ancestry that has emerged from a variety of sources (e.g., comparative anatomy and embryology, molecular biology and genetics). It describes how variation of genetically determined traits in a population may give some members a reproductive advantage in a given environment. This natural selection can lead to adaptation, that is, to a distribution of traits in the population that is matched to and can change with environmental conditions. Such adaptations can eventually lead to the development of separate species in separated populations. Finally, the idea describes the factors, including human activity, that affect biodiversity in an ecosystem, and the value of biodiversity in ecosystem resilience. See Box 6-1 for a summary of these four core ideas and their components.

These four core ideas, which represent basic life sciences fields of investigation—structures and processes in organisms, ecology, heredity, and evolution—have a long history and solid foundation based on the research evidence established by many scientists working across multiple fields. The role of unifying principles in advancing modern life sciences is articulated in *The Role of Theory in Advancing 21st-Century Biology* and *A New Biology for the 21st Century* [2, 3]. In developing these core ideas, the committee also drew on the established K-12 science education literature, including *National Science Education Standards* and *Benchmarks for Science Literacy* [4, 5]. The ideas also incorporate contemporary documents, such as the *Science College Board Standards for College Success* [6], and the ideas are consistent with frameworks for national and international assessments, such as those of the National Assessment of Educational Progress (NAEP), the Programme for International Student Assessment (PISA), and the *Trends in International Mathematics and Science Study* (TIMSS) [7-9]. Furthermore, the ideas align with the core concepts for biological literacy for undergraduates to build on as described in the American Association for the Advancement of Science (AAAS) report *Vision and Change in Undergraduate Biology Education* [10].

BOX 6-1

CORE AND COMPONENT IDEAS IN THE LIFE SCIENCES

Core Idea LS1: From Molecules to Organisms: Structures and Processes

LS1.A: Structure and Function

LS1.B: Growth and Development of Organisms

LS1.C: Organization for Matter and Energy Flow in Organisms

LS1.D: Information Processing

Core Idea LS2: Ecosystems: Interactions, Energy, and Dynamics

LS2.A: Interdependent Relationships in Ecosystems

LS2.B: Cycles of Matter and Energy Transfer in Ecosystems

LS2.C: Ecosystem Dynamics, Functioning, and Resilience

LS2.D: Social Interactions and Group Behavior

Core Idea LS3: Heredity: Inheritance and Variation of Traits

LS3.A: Inheritance of Traits

LS3.B: Variation of Traits

Core Idea LS4: Biological Evolution: Unity and Diversity

LS4.A: Evidence of Common Ancestry and Diversity

LS4.B: Natural Selection

LS4.C: Adaptation

LS4.D: Biodiversity and Humans

Core Idea LS1   From Molecules to Organisms: Structures and Processes

How do organisms live, grow, respond to their environment, and reproduce?

All living organisms are made of cells. Life is the quality that distinguishes living things—composed of living cells—from nonliving objects or those that have died. While a simple definition of life can be difficult to capture, all living things—that is to say all organisms—can be characterized by common aspects of their structure and functioning. Organisms are complex, organized, and built on a hierarchical structure, with each level providing the foundation for the next, from the chemical foundation of elements and atoms, to the cells and systems of individual organisms, to species and populations living and interacting in complex ecosystems. Organisms can be made of a single cell or millions of cells working together and include animals, plants, algae, fungi, bacteria, and all other microorganisms.

Organisms respond to stimuli from their environment and actively maintain their internal environment through homeostasis. They grow and reproduce, transferring their genetic information to their offspring. While individual organisms carry the same genetic information over their lifetime, mutation and the transfer from parent to offspring produce new combinations of genes. Over generations natural selection can lead to changes in a species overall; hence, species evolve over time. To maintain all of these processes and functions, organisms require materials and energy from their environment; nearly all energy that sustains life ultimately comes from the sun.

LS1.A: STRUCTURE AND FUNCTION

How do the structures of organisms enable life's functions?

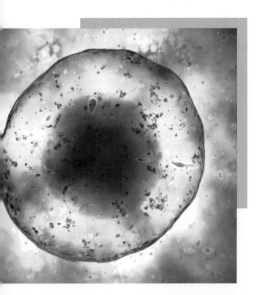

A central feature of life is that organisms grow, reproduce, and die. They have characteristic structures (anatomy and morphology), functions (molecular-scale processes to organism-level physiology), and behaviors (neurobiology and, for some animal species, psychology). Organisms and their parts are made of cells, which are the structural units of life and which themselves have molecular substructures that support their functioning. Organisms range in composition from a single cell (unicellular microorganisms) to multicellular organisms, in which different groups of large numbers of cells work together to form systems of tissues and organs (e.g., circulatory, respiratory, nervous, musculoskeletal), that are specialized for particular functions.

Special structures *within* cells are also responsible for specific cellular functions. The essential functions of a cell involve chemical reactions between many types of molecules, including water, proteins, carbohydrates, lipids, and nucleic acids. All cells contain genetic information, in the form of DNA. Genes are specific regions within the extremely large DNA molecules that form the chromosomes. Genes contain the instructions that code for the formation of molecules called proteins, which carry out most of the work of cells to perform the essential functions of life. That is, proteins provide structural components, serve as signaling devices, regulate cell activities, and determine the performance of cells through their enzymatic actions.

Grade Band Endpoints for LS1.A

By the end of grade 2. All organisms have external parts. Different animals use their body parts in different ways to see, hear, grasp objects, protect themselves, move from place to place, and seek, find, and take in food, water and air. Plants also have different parts (roots, stems, leaves, flowers, fruits) that help them survive, grow, and produce more plants.

By the end of grade 5. Plants and animals have both internal and external structures that serve various functions in growth, survival, behavior, and reproduction. (Boundary: Stress at this grade level is on understanding the macroscale systems and their function, not microscopic processes.)

By the end of grade 8. All living things are made up of cells, which is the smallest unit that can be said to be alive. An organism may consist of one single cell (unicellular) or many different numbers and types of cells (multicellular). Unicellular organisms (microorganisms), like multicellular organisms, need food, water, a way to dispose of waste, and an environment in which they can live.

Within cells, special structures are responsible for particular functions, and the cell membrane forms the boundary that controls what enters and leaves the cell. In multicellular organisms, the body is a system of multiple interacting subsystems. These subsystems are groups of cells that work together to form tissues or organs that are specialized for particular body functions. (Boundary: At this grade level, only a few major cell structures should be introduced.)

By the end of grade 12. Systems of specialized cells within organisms help them perform the essential functions of life, which involve chemical reactions that take place between different types of molecules, such as water, proteins, carbohydrates, lipids, and nucleic acids. All cells contain genetic information in the form of DNA molecules. Genes are regions in the DNA that contain the instructions that code for the formation of proteins, which carry out most of the work of cells.

Multicellular organisms have a hierarchical structural organization, in which any one system is made up of numerous parts and is itself a component of the next level. Feedback mechanisms maintain a living system's internal conditions within certain limits and mediate behaviors, allowing it to remain alive and functional even as external conditions change within some range. Outside that range (e.g., at a too high or too low external temperature, with too little food or water available), the organism cannot survive. Feedback mechanisms can encourage (through positive feedback) or discourage (negative feedback) what is going on inside the living system.

LS1.B: GROWTH AND DEVELOPMENT OF ORGANISMS

How do organisms grow and develop?

The characteristic structures, functions, and behaviors of organisms change in predictable ways as they progress from birth to old age. For example, upon reaching adulthood, organisms can reproduce and transfer their genetic information to their offspring. Animals engage in behaviors that increase their chances for reproduction, and plants may develop specialized structures and/or depend on animal behavior to accomplish reproduction.

Understanding how a single cell can give rise to a complex, multicellular organism builds on the concepts of cell division and gene expression. In multicellular organisms, cell division is an essential component of growth, development, and repair. Cell division occurs via a process called mitosis: when a cell divides in two, it passes identical genetic material to two daughter cells. Successive divisions produce many cells. Although the genetic material in each of the cells is identical, small differences in the immediate environments activate or inactivate different genes, which can cause the cells to develop slightly differently. This process of differentiation allows the body to form specialized cells that perform diverse functions, even though they are all descended from a single cell, the fertilized egg. Cell growth and differentiation are the mechanisms by which a fertilized egg develops into a complex organism. In sexual reproduction, a specialized type of cell division called meiosis occurs and results in the production of sex cells, such as gametes (sperm and eggs) or spores, which contain only one member from each chromosome pair in the parent cell.

Grade Band Endpoints for LS1.B

By the end of grade 2. Plants and animals have predictable characteristics at different stages of development. Plants and animals grow and change. Adult plants and animals can have young. In many kinds of animals, parents and the offspring themselves engage in behaviors that help the offspring to survive.

By the end of grade 5. Reproduction is essential to the continued existence of every kind of organism. Plants and animals have unique and diverse life cycles that include being born (sprouting in plants), growing, developing into adults, reproducing, and eventually dying.

By the end of grade 8. Organisms reproduce, either sexually or asexually, and transfer their genetic information to their offspring. Animals engage in characteristic behaviors that increase the odds of reproduction. Plants reproduce in a variety

of ways, sometimes depending on animal behavior and specialized features (such as attractively colored flowers) for reproduction. Plant growth can continue throughout the plant's life through production of plant matter in photosynthesis. Genetic factors as well as local conditions affect the size of the adult plant. The growth of an animal is controlled by genetic factors, food intake, and interactions with other organisms, and each species has a typical adult size range. (Boundary: Reproduction is not treated in any detail here; for more specifics about grade level, see LS3.A.)

By the end of grade 12. In multicellular organisms individual cells grow and then divide via a process called mitosis, thereby allowing the organism to grow. The organism begins as a single cell (fertilized egg) that divides successively to produce many cells, with each parent cell passing identical genetic material (two variants of each chromosome pair) to both daughter cells. As successive subdivisions of an embryo's cells occur, programmed genetic instructions and small differences in their immediate environments activate or inactivate different genes, which cause the cells to develop differently—a process called differentiation. Cellular division and differentiation produce and maintain a complex organism, composed of systems of tissues and organs that work together to meet the needs of the whole organism. In sexual reproduction, a specialized type of cell division called meiosis occurs that results in the production of sex cells, such as gametes in animals (sperm and eggs), which contain only one member from each chromosome pair in the parent cell.

LS1.C: ORGANIZATION FOR MATTER AND ENERGY FLOW IN ORGANISMS

How do organisms obtain and use the matter and energy they need to live and grow?

Sustaining life requires substantial energy and matter inputs. The complex structural organization of organisms accommodates the capture, transformation, transport, release, and elimination of the matter and energy needed to sustain them. As matter and energy flow through different organizational levels—cells, tissues, organs, organisms, populations, communities, and ecosystems—of living systems, chemical elements are recombined in different ways to form different products. The result of these chemical reactions is that energy is transferred from one system of interacting molecules to another.

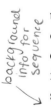

In most cases, the energy needed for life is ultimately derived from the sun through photosynthesis (although in some ecologically important cases, energy is derived from reactions involving inorganic chemicals in the absence of sunlight— e.g., chemosynthesis). Plants, algae (including phytoplankton), and other energy-fixing microorganisms use sunlight, water, and carbon dioxide to facilitate photosynthesis, which stores energy, forms plant matter, releases oxygen, and maintains plants' activities. Plants and algae—being the resource base for animals, the animals that feed on animals, and the decomposers—are energy-fixing organisms that sustain the rest of the food web.

Grade Band Endpoints for LS1.C

By the end of grade 2. All animals need food in order to live and grow. They obtain their food from plants or from other animals. Plants need water and light to live and grow.

By the end of grade 5. Animals and plants alike generally need to take in air and water, animals must take in food, and plants need light and minerals; anaerobic life, such as bacteria in the gut, functions without air. Food provides animals with the materials they need for body repair and growth and is digested to release the energy they need to maintain body warmth and for motion. Plants acquire their material for growth chiefly from air and water and process matter they have formed to maintain their internal conditions (e.g., at night).

By the end of grade 8. Plants, algae (including phytoplankton), and many micro-organisms use the energy from light to make sugars (food) from carbon dioxide from the atmosphere and water through the process of photosynthesis, which also releases oxygen. These sugars can be used immediately or stored for growth or later use. Animals obtain food from eating plants or eating other animals. Within individual organisms, food moves through a series of chemical reactions in which it is broken down and rearranged to form new molecules, to support growth, or to release energy. In most animals and plants, oxygen reacts with carbon-containing molecules (sugars) to provide energy and produce carbon dioxide; anaerobic bacteria achieve their energy needs in other chemical processes that do not require oxygen.

By the end of grade 12. The process of photosynthesis converts light energy to stored chemical energy by converting carbon dioxide plus water into sugars plus released oxygen. The sugar molecules thus formed contain carbon, hydrogen, and oxygen; their hydrocarbon backbones are used to make amino acids and other carbon-based molecules that can be assembled into larger molecules (such as proteins or DNA), used for example to form new cells. As matter and energy flow through different organizational levels of living systems, chemical elements are recombined in different ways to form different products. As a result of these chemical reactions, energy is transferred from one system of interacting molecules to another. For example, aerobic (in the presence of oxygen) cellular respiration is a chemical process in which the bonds of food molecules and oxygen molecules are broken and new compounds are formed that can transport energy to muscles. Anaerobic (without oxygen) cellular respiration follows a different and less efficient chemical pathway to provide energy in cells. Cellular respiration also releases the energy needed to maintain body temperature despite ongoing energy loss to the surrounding environment. Matter and energy are conserved in each change. This is true of all biological systems, from individual cells to ecosystems.

LS1.D: INFORMATION PROCESSING

How do organisms detect, process, and use information about the environment?

An organism's ability to sense and respond to its environment enhances its chance of surviving and reproducing. Animals have external and internal sensory receptors that detect different kinds of information, and they use internal mechanisms for processing and storing it. Each receptor can respond to different inputs (electromagnetic, mechanical, chemical), some receptors respond by transmitting impulses that travel along nerve cells. In complex organisms, most such inputs travel to the brain, which is divided into several distinct regions and circuits that serve primary roles, in particular functions such as visual perception, auditory perception, interpretation of perceptual information, guidance of motor movement, and decision making. In addition, some of the brain's circuits give rise to emotions and store memories. Brain function also involves multiple interactions between the various regions to form an integrated sense of self and the surrounding world.

Grade Band Endpoints for LS1.D

By the end of grade 2. Animals have body parts that capture and convey different kinds of information needed for growth and survival—for example, eyes for light, ears for sounds, and skin for temperature or touch. Animals respond to these inputs with behaviors that help them survive (e.g., find food, run from a predator). Plants also respond to some external inputs (e.g., turn leaves toward the sun).

By the end of grade 5. Different sense receptors are specialized for particular kinds of information, which may then be processed and integrated by an animal's brain, with some information stored as memories. Animals are able to use their perceptions and memories to guide their actions. Some responses to information are instinctive—that is, animals' brains are organized so that they do not have to think about how to respond to certain stimuli.

By the end of grade 8. Each sense receptor responds to different inputs (electromagnetic, mechanical, chemical), transmitting them as signals that travel along nerve cells to the brain. The signals are then processed in the brain, resulting in immediate behaviors or memories. Changes in the structure and functioning of many millions of interconnected nerve cells allow combined inputs to be stored as memories for long periods of time.

By the end of grade 12. In complex animals, the brain is divided into several distinct regions and circuits, each of which primarily serves dedicated functions, such as visual perception, auditory perception, interpretation of perceptual information, guidance of motor movement, and decision making about actions to take in the event of certain inputs. In addition, some circuits give rise to emotions and memories that motivate organisms to seek rewards, avoid punishments, develop fears, or form attachments to members of their own species and, in some cases, to individuals of other species (e.g., mixed herds of mammals, mixed flocks of birds). The integrated functioning of all parts of the brain is important for successful interpretation of inputs and generation of behaviors in response to them.

Core Idea LS2   Ecosystems: Interactions, Energy, and Dynamics

How and why do organisms interact with their environment and what are the effects of these interactions?

Ecosystems are complex, interactive systems that include both biological communities (biotic) and physical (abiotic) components of the environment. As with individual organisms, a hierarchal structure exists; groups of the same organisms (species) form populations, different populations interact to form communities, communities live within an ecosystem, and all of the ecosystems on Earth make up the biosphere. Organisms grow, reproduce, and perpetuate their species by obtaining necessary resources through interdependent relationships with other organisms and the physical environment. These same interactions can facilitate or restrain growth and enhance or limit the size of populations, maintaining the balance between available resources and those who consume them. These interactions can also change both biotic and abiotic characteristics of the environment. Like individual organisms, ecosystems are sustained by the continuous flow of energy, originating primarily from the sun, and the recycling of matter and nutrients within the system. Ecosystems are dynamic, experiencing shifts in population composition and abundance and changes in the physical environment over time, which ultimately affects the stability and resilience of the entire system.

LS2.A: INTERDEPENDENT RELATIONSHIPS IN ECOSYSTEMS

How do organisms interact with the living and nonliving environments to obtain matter and energy?

Ecosystems are ever changing because of the interdependence of organisms of the same or different species and the nonliving (physical) elements of the environment. Seeking matter and energy resources to sustain life, organisms in an ecosystem

interact with one another in complex feeding hierarchies of producers, consumers, and decomposers, which together represent a food web. Interactions between organisms may be predatory, competitive, or mutually beneficial. Ecosystems have carrying capacities that limit the number of organisms (within populations) they can support. Individual survival and population sizes depend on such factors as predation, disease, availability of resources, and parameters of the physical environment. Organisms rely on physical factors, such as light, temperature, water, soil, and space for shelter and reproduction. Earth's varied combinations of these factors provide the physical environments in which its ecosystems (e.g., deserts, grasslands, rain forests, and coral reefs) develop and in which the diverse species of the planet live. Within any one ecosystem, the biotic interactions between organisms (e.g., competition, predation, and various types of facilitation, such as pollination) further influence their growth, survival, and reproduction, both individually and in terms of their populations.

Grade Band Endpoints for LS2.A

By the end of grade 2. Animals depend on their surroundings to get what they need, including food, water, shelter, and a favorable temperature. Animals depend on plants or other animals for food. They use their senses to find food and water, and they use their body parts to gather, catch, eat, and chew the food. Plants depend on air, water, minerals (in the soil), and light to grow. Animals can move around, but plants cannot, and they often depend on animals for pollination or to move their seeds around. Different plants survive better in different settings because they have varied needs for water, minerals, and sunlight.

By the end of grade 5. The food of almost any kind of animal can be traced back to plants. Organisms are related in food webs in which some animals eat plants for food and other animals eat the animals that eat plants. Either way, they are "consumers." Some organisms, such as fungi and bacteria, break down dead organisms (both plants or plants parts and animals) and therefore operate as "decomposers." Decomposition eventually restores (recycles) some materials back to the soil for plants to use. Organisms can survive only in environments in which their particular needs are met. A healthy ecosystem is one in which multiple species of different types are each able to meet their needs in a relatively stable web of life. Newly introduced species can damage the balance of an ecosystem.

By the end of grade 8. Organisms and populations of organisms are dependent on their environmental interactions both with other living things and with nonliving factors. Growth of organisms and population increases are limited by access to resources. In any ecosystem, organisms and populations with similar requirements for food, water, oxygen, or other resources may compete with each other for limited resources, access to which consequently constrains their growth and reproduction. Similarly, predatory interactions may reduce the number of organisms or eliminate whole populations of organisms. Mutually beneficial interactions, in contrast, may become so interdependent that each organism requires the other for survival. Although the species involved in these competitive, predatory, and mutually beneficial interactions vary across ecosystems, the patterns of interactions of organisms with their environments, both living and nonliving, are shared.

By the end of grade 12. Ecosystems have carrying capacities, which are limits to the numbers of organisms and populations they can support. These limits result from such factors as the availability of living and nonliving resources and from such challenges as predation, competition, and disease. Organisms would have the capacity to produce populations of great size were it not for the fact that environments and resources are finite. This fundamental tension affects the abundance (number of individuals) of species in any given ecosystem.

LS2.B: CYCLES OF MATTER AND ENERGY TRANSFER IN ECOSYSTEMS

How do matter and energy move through an ecosystem?

The cycling of matter and the flow of energy within ecosystems occur through interactions among different organisms and between organisms and the physical environment. All living systems need matter and energy. Matter fuels the energy-releasing chemical reactions that provide energy for life functions and provides the material for growth and repair of tissue. Energy from light is needed for plants because the chemical reaction that produces plant matter from air and water requires an energy input to occur. Animals acquire matter from food, that is, from plants or other animals. The chemical elements that make up the molecules of organisms pass through food webs and the environment and are combined and recombined in different ways. At each level in a food web, some matter provides energy for life functions, some is stored in newly made structures, and much is discarded to the surrounding environment. Only a small fraction of the matter consumed at one level is captured by the next level up. As matter cycles and energy flows through living systems and between living systems and the physical environment, matter and energy are conserved in each change.

The carbon cycle provides an example of matter cycling and energy flow in ecosystems. Photosynthesis, digestion of plant matter, respiration, and decomposition are important components of the carbon cycle, in which carbon is exchanged between the biosphere, atmosphere, oceans, and geosphere through chemical, physical, geological, and biological processes.

Grade Band Endpoints for LS2.B

By the end of grade 2. Organisms obtain the materials they need to grow and survive from the environment. Many of these materials come from organisms and are used again by other organisms.

By the end of grade 5. Matter cycles between the air and soil and among plants, animals, and microbes as these organisms live and die. Organisms obtain gases, water, and minerals from the environment and release waste matter (gas, liquid, or solid) back into the environment.

By the end of grade 8. Food webs are models that demonstrate how matter and energy is transferred between producers (generally plants and other organisms that engage in photosynthesis), consumers, and decomposers as the three groups interact—primarily for food—within an ecosystem. Transfers of matter into and out of the physical environment occur at every level—for example, when molecules from food react with oxygen captured from the environment, the carbon dioxide and water thus produced are transferred back to the environment, and ultimately so are waste products, such as fecal material. Decomposers recycle nutrients from dead plant or animal matter back to the soil in terrestrial environments or to the water in aquatic environments. The atoms that make up the

> ▌Ecosystems are sustained by the continuous flow of energy, originating primarily from the sun, and the recycling of matter and nutrients within the system. ▌

organisms in an ecosystem are cycled repeatedly between the living and nonliving parts of the ecosystem.

By the end of grade 12. Photosynthesis and cellular respiration (including anaerobic processes) provide most of the energy for life processes. Plants or algae form the lowest level of the food web. At each link upward in a food web, only a small fraction of the matter consumed at the lower level is transferred upward, to produce growth and release energy in cellular respiration at the higher level. Given this inefficiency, there are generally fewer organisms at higher levels of a food web, and there is a limit to the number of organisms that an ecosystem can sustain.

The chemical elements that make up the molecules of organisms pass through food webs and into and out of the atmosphere and soil and are combined and recombined in different ways. At each link in an ecosystem, matter and energy are conserved; some matter reacts to release energy for life functions, some matter is stored in newly made structures, and much is discarded. Competition among species is ultimately competition for the matter and energy needed for life.

Photosynthesis and cellular respiration are important components of the carbon cycle, in which carbon is exchanged between the biosphere, atmosphere, oceans, and geosphere through chemical, physical, geological, and biological processes.

LS2.C: ECOSYSTEM DYNAMICS, FUNCTIONING, AND RESILIENCE

What happens to ecosystems when the environment changes?

Ecosystems are dynamic in nature; their characteristics fluctuate over time, depending on changes in the environment and in the populations of various species. Disruptions in the physical and biological components of an ecosystem—which can lead to shifts in the types and numbers of the ecosystem's organisms, to the maintenance or the extinction of species, to the migration of species into or out of the region, or to the formation of new species (speciation)—occur for a variety of natural reasons. Changes may derive from the fall of canopy trees in a forest, for example, or from cataclysmic events, such as volcanic eruptions. But many changes are induced by human activity, such as resource extraction, adverse land use patterns, pollution, introduction of nonnative species, and global climate change. Extinction of species or evolution of new species may occur in response to significant ecosystem disruptions.

Species in an environment develop behavioral and physiological patterns that facilitate their survival under the prevailing conditions, but these patterns may be maladapted when conditions change or new species are introduced. Ecosystems with a wide variety of species—that is, greater biodiversity—tend to be more resilient to change than those with few species.

Grade Band Endpoints for LS2.C

By the end of grade 2. The places where plants and animals live often change, sometimes slowly and sometimes rapidly. When animals and plants get too hot or too cold, they may die. If they cannot find enough food, water, or air, they may die.

By the end of grade 5. When the environment changes in ways that affect a place's physical characteristics, temperature, or availability of resources, some organisms survive and reproduce, others move to new locations, yet others move into the transformed environment, and some die.

By the end of grade 8. Ecosystems are dynamic in nature; their characteristics can vary over time. Disruptions to any physical or biological component of an ecosystem can lead to shifts in all of its populations.

Biodiversity describes the variety of species found in Earth's terrestrial and oceanic ecosystems. The completeness or integrity of an ecosystem's biodiversity is often used as a measure of its health.

By the end of grade 12. A complex set of interactions within an ecosystem can keep its numbers and types of organisms relatively constant over long periods of time under stable conditions. If a modest biological or physical disturbance to an ecosystem occurs, it may return to its more or less original status (i.e., the ecosystem is resilient), as opposed to becoming a very different ecosystem. Extreme fluctuations in conditions or the size of any population, however, can challenge the functioning of ecosystems in terms of resources and habitat availability. Moreover,

anthropogenic changes (induced by human activity) in the environment—including habitat destruction, pollution, introduction of invasive species, overexploitation, and climate change—can disrupt an ecosystem and threaten the survival of some species.

LS2.D: SOCIAL INTERACTIONS AND GROUP BEHAVIOR

How do organisms interact in groups so as to benefit individuals?

Group behaviors are found in organisms ranging from unicellular slime molds to ants to primates, including humans. Many species, with a strong drive for social affiliation, live in groups formed on the basis of genetic relatedness, physical proximity, or other recognition mechanisms (which may be species specific). Group behavior evolved because group membership can increase the chances of survival for individuals and their relatives. While some groups are stable over long periods of time, others are fluid, with members moving in and out. Groups often dissolve if their size or operation becomes counterproductive, if dominant members lose their place, or if other key members are removed from the group. Group interdependence is so strong that animals that usually live in groups suffer, behaviorally as well as physiologically, when reared in isolation, even if all of their physical needs are met.

Grade Band Endpoints for LS2.D

By the end of grade 2. Being part of a group helps animals obtain food, defend themselves, and cope with changes. Groups may serve different functions and vary dramatically in size.

By the end of grade 5. Groups can be collections of equal individuals, hierarchies with dominant members, small families, groups of single or mixed gender, or groups composed of individuals similar in age. Some groups are stable over long periods of time; others are fluid, with members moving in and out. Some groups assign specialized tasks to each member; in others, all members perform the same or a similar range of functions.

■ Group behaviors are found in organisms ranging from unicellular slime molds to ants to primates, including humans. ■

By the end of grade 8. Groups may form because of genetic relatedness, physical proximity, or other recognition mechanisms (which may be species specific). They engage in a variety of signaling behaviors to maintain the group's integrity or to warn of threats. Groups often dissolve if they no longer function to meet individuals' needs, if dominant members lose their place, or if other key members are removed from the group through death, predation, or exclusion by other members.

By the end of grade 12. Animals, including humans, having a strong drive for social affiliation with members of their own species and will suffer, behaviorally as well as physiologically, if reared in isolation, even if all of their physical needs are met. Some forms of affiliation arise from the bonds between offspring and parents. Other groups form among peers. Group behavior has evolved because membership can increase the chances of survival for individuals and their genetic relatives.

Core Idea   LS3: Heredity: Inheritance and Variation of Traits

How are characteristics of one generation passed to the next?
How can individuals of the same species and even siblings have different characteristics?

Heredity explains why offspring resemble, but are not identical to, their parents and is a unifying biological principle. Heredity refers to specific mechanisms by which characteristics or traits are passed from one generation to the next via genes. Genes encode the information for making specific proteins, which are responsible for the specific traits of an individual. Each gene can have several variants, called alleles, which code for different variants of the trait in question. Genes reside in a cell's chromosomes, each of which contains many genes. Every cell of any individual organism contains the identical set of chromosomes. When organisms reproduce, genetic information is transferred to their offspring. In species that reproduce sexually, each cell contains two variants of each chromosome, one inherited from each parent. Thus sexual reproduction gives rise to a new combination of chromosome pairs with variations between parent and offspring. Very rarely, mutations also cause variations, which may be harmful, neutral, or occasionally advantageous for an individual. Environmental as well as genetic variation and the relative dominance of each of the genes in a pair play an important role in how traits develop within an individual. Complex relationships between genes and interactions of genes with the environment determine how an organism will develop and function.

LS3.A: INHERITANCE OF TRAITS

How are the characteristics of one generation related to the previous generation?

In all organisms, the genetic instructions for forming species' characteristics are carried in the chromosomes. Each chromosome consists of a single very long DNA molecule, and each gene on the chromosome is a particular segment of that DNA. DNA molecules contain four different kinds of building blocks, called nucleotides, linked together in a sequential chain. The sequence of nucleotides spells out the information in a gene. Before a cell divides, the DNA sequence of its chromosomes is replicated and each daughter cell receives a copy. DNA controls the expression of proteins by being transcribed into a "messenger" RNA, which is translated in turn by the cellular machinery into a protein. In effect, proteins build an organism's identifiable traits. When organisms reproduce, genetic information is transferred to their offspring, with half coming from each parent in sexual reproduction. Inheritance is the key factor causing the similarity among individuals in a species population.

Grade Band Endpoints for LS3.A

By the end of grade 2. Organisms have characteristics that can be similar or different. Young animals are very much, but not exactly, like their parents and also resemble other animals of the same kind. Plants also are very much, but not exactly, like their parents and resemble other plants of the same kind.

By the end of grade 5. Many characteristics of organisms are inherited from their parents. Other characteristics result from individuals' interactions with the environment, which can range from diet to learning. Many characteristics involve both inheritance and environment.

By the end of grade 8. Genes are located in the chromosomes of cells, with each chromosome pair containing two variants of each of many distinct genes. Each

Complex relationships between genes and interactions of genes with the environment determine how an organism will develop and function.

distinct gene chiefly controls the production of a specific protein, which in turn affects the traits of the individual (e.g., human skin color results from the actions of proteins that control the production of the pigment melanin). Changes (mutations) to genes can result in changes to proteins, which can affect the structures and functions of the organism and thereby change traits.

Sexual reproduction provides for transmission of genetic information to offspring through egg and sperm cells. These cells, which contain only one chromosome of each parent's chromosome pair, unite to form a new individual (offspring). Thus offspring possess one instance of each parent's chromosome pair (forming a new chromosome pair). Variations of inherited traits between parent and offspring arise from genetic differences that result from the subset of chromosomes (and therefore genes) inherited or (more rarely) from mutations. (Boundary: The stress here is on the impact of gene transmission in reproduction, not the mechanism.)

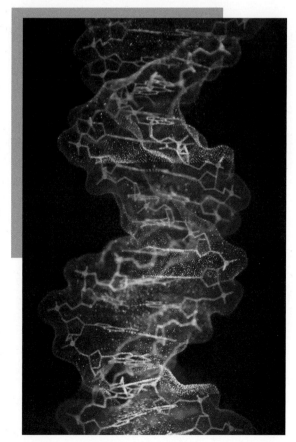

By the end of grade 12. In all organisms the genetic instructions for forming species' characteristics are carried in the chromosomes. Each chromosome consists of a single very long DNA molecule, and each gene on the chromosome is a particular segment of that DNA. The instructions for forming species' characteristics are carried in DNA. All cells in an organism have the same genetic content, but the genes used (expressed) by the cell may be regulated in different ways. Not all DNA codes for a protein; some segments of DNA are involved in regulatory or structural functions, and some have no as-yet known function.

LS3.B: VARIATION OF TRAITS

Why do individuals of the same species vary in how they look, function, and behave?

Variation among individuals of the same species can be explained by both genetic and environmental factors. Individuals within a species have similar but not identical genes. In sexual reproduction, variations in traits between parent and offspring arise from the particular set of chromosomes (and their respective multiple genes) inherited, with each parent contributing half of each chromosome pair. More rarely, such variations result from mutations, which are changes in the information that genes carry. Although genes control the general traits of any given organism, other parts of the DNA and external environmental factors can modify an individual's specific development, appearance, behavior, and likelihood of producing offspring. The set of variations of genes present, together with the interactions of genes with their environment, determines the distribution of variation of traits in a population.

Grade Band Endpoints for LS3.B

By the end of grade 2. Individuals of the same kind of plant or animal are recognizable as similar but can also vary in many ways.

By the end of grade 5. Offspring acquire a mix of traits from their biological parents. Different organisms vary in how they look and function because they have different inherited information. In each kind of organism there is variation in the traits themselves, and different kinds of organisms may have different versions of the trait. The environment also affects the traits that an organism develops—differences in where they grow or in the food they consume may cause organisms that are related to end up looking or behaving differently.

By the end of grade 8. In sexually reproducing organisms, each parent contributes half of the genes acquired (at random) by the offspring. Individuals have two of each chromosome and hence two alleles of each gene, one acquired from each parent. These versions may be identical or may differ from each other.

In addition to variations that arise from sexual reproduction, genetic information can be altered because of mutations. Though rare, mutations may result in changes to the structure and function of proteins. Some changes are beneficial, others harmful, and some neutral to the organism.

By the end of grade 12. The information passed from parents to offspring is coded in the DNA molecules that form the chromosomes. In sexual reproduction, chromosomes can sometimes swap sections during the process of meiosis (cell division), thereby creating new genetic combinations and thus more genetic variation. Although DNA replication is tightly regulated and remarkably accurate, errors do occur and result in mutations, which are also a source of genetic variation. Environmental factors can also cause mutations in genes, and viable mutations are inherited. Environmental factors also affect expression of traits, and hence affect the probability of occurrences of traits in a population. Thus the variation and distribution of traits observed depend on both genetic and environmental factors.

Core Idea LS4 Biological Evolution: Unity and Diversity

How can there be so many similarities among organisms yet so many different kinds of plants, animals, and microorganisms?
How does biodiversity affect humans?

Biological evolution explains both the unity and the diversity of species and provides a unifying principle for the history and diversity of life on Earth. Biological evolution is supported by extensive scientific evidence ranging from the fossil record to genetic relationships among species. Researchers continue to use new and different techniques, including DNA and protein sequence analyses, to test and further their understanding of evolutionary relationships. Evolution, which is continuous and ongoing, occurs when natural selection acts on the genetic variation in a population and changes the distribution of traits in that population gradually over multiple generations. Natural selection can act more rapidly after sudden changes in conditions, which can lead to the extinction of species. Through natural selection, traits that provide an individual with an advantage to best meet environmental challenges and reproduce are the ones most likely to be passed on to the next generation. Over multiple generations, this process can lead to the emergence of new species. Evolution thus explains both the similarities of genetic material across all species and the multitude of species existing in diverse conditions on Earth—its biodiversity—which humans depend on for natural resources and other benefits to sustain themselves.

LS4.A: EVIDENCE OF COMMON ANCESTRY AND DIVERSITY

What evidence shows that different species are related?

Biological evolution, the process by which all living things have evolved over many generations from shared ancestors, explains both the unity and the diversity of species. The unity is illustrated by the similarities found betwen species; which can be explained by the inheritance of similar characteristics from related ancestors. The diversity of species is also consistent with common ancestry; it is explained by the branching and diversification of lineages as populations adapted, primarily through natural selection, to local circumstances.

Evidence for common ancestry can be found in the fossil record, from comparative anatomy and embryology, from the similarities of cellular processes and structures, and from comparisons of DNA sequences between species. The understanding of evolutionary relationships has recently been greatly accelerated by using new molecular tools to study developmental biology, with researchers dissecting the genetic basis for some of the changes seen in the fossil record, as well as those that can be inferred to link living species (e.g., the armadillo) to their ancestors (e.g., glyptodonts, a kind of extinct gigantic armadillo).

Grade Band Endpoints for LS4.A

By the end of grade 2. Some kinds of plants and animals that once lived on Earth (e.g., dinosaurs) are no longer found anywhere, although others now living (e.g., lizards) resemble them in some ways.

By the end of grade 5. Fossils provide evidence about the types of organisms (both visible and microscopic) that lived long ago and also about the nature of their environments. Fossils can be compared with one another and to living organisms according to their similarities and differences.

By the end of grade 8. Fossils are mineral replacements, preserved remains, or traces of organisms that lived in the past. Thousands of layers of sedimentary rock not only provide evidence of the history of Earth itself but also of changes in organisms whose fossil remains have been found in those layers. The collection of fossils and their placement in chronological order (e.g., through the location of the sedimentary layers in which they are found or through radioactive dating) is known as the fossil record. It documents the existence, diversity, extinction, and change of many

life forms throughout the history of life on Earth. Because of the conditions necessary for their preservation, not all types of organisms that existed in the past have left fossils that can be retrieved. Anatomical similarities and differences between various organisms living today and between them and organisms in the fossil record enable the reconstruction of evolutionary history and the inference of lines of evolutionary descent. Comparison of the embryological development of different species also reveals similarities that show relationships not evident in the fully formed anatomy.

By the end of grade 12. Genetic information, like the fossil record, also provides evidence of evolution. DNA sequences vary among species, but there are many overlaps; in fact, the ongoing branching that produces multiple lines of descent can be inferred by comparing the DNA sequences of different organisms. Such information is also derivable from the similarities and differences in amino acid sequences and from anatomical and embryological evidence.

LS4.B: NATURAL SELECTION

How does genetic variation among organisms affect survival and reproduction?

Genetic variation in a species results in individuals with a range of traits. In any particular environment individuals with particular traits may be more likely than others to survive and produce offspring. This process is called natural selection and may lead to the predominance of certain inherited traits in a population and the suppression of others. Natural selection occurs only if there is variation in the genetic information within a population that is expressed in traits that lead to differences in survival and reproductive ability among individuals under specific environmental conditions. If the trait differences do not affect reproductive success, then natural selection will not favor one trait over others.

Grade Band Endpoints for LS4.B

By the end of grade 2. [Intentionally left blank.]

By the end of grade 5. Sometimes the differences in characteristics between individuals of the same species provide advantages in surviving, finding mates, and reproducing.

By the end of grade 8. Genetic variations among individuals in a population give some individuals an advantage in surviving and reproducing in their environment. This is known as natural selection. It leads to the predominance of certain traits in a population and the suppression of others. In *artificial* selection, humans have the capacity to influence certain characteristics of organisms by selective breeding. One can choose desired parental traits determined by genes, which are then passed on to offspring.

By the end of grade 12. Natural selection occurs only if there is both (1) variation in the genetic information between organisms in a population and (2) variation in the expression of that genetic information—that is, trait variation—that leads to differences in performance among individuals. The traits that positively affect survival are more likely to be reproduced and thus are more common in the population.

LS4.C: ADAPTATION

How does the environment influence populations of organisms over multiple generations?

When an environment changes, there can be subsequent shifts in its supply of resources or in the physical and biological challenges it imposes. Some individuals in a population may have morphological, physiological, or behavioral traits that provide a reproductive advantage in the face of the shifts in the environment. Natural selection provides a mechanism for species to adapt to changes in their environment. The resulting selective pressures influence the survival and reproduction of organisms over many generations and can change the distribution of traits in the population. This process is called adaptation. Adaptation can lead to organisms that are better suited for their environment because individuals with the traits adaptive to the environmental change pass those traits on to their offspring, whereas individuals with traits that are less adaptive produce fewer or no offspring. Over time, adaptation can lead to the formation of new species. In some cases, however, traits that are adaptive to the changed environment do not exist in the population and the species becomes extinct. Adaptive changes due to natural selection, as well as the net result of speciation minus extinction, have strongly contributed to the planet's biodiversity.

Adaption by natural selection is ongoing. For example it is seen in the emergence of antibiotic-resistant bacteria. Organisms like bacteria, in which multiple generations occur over shorter time spans, evolve more rapidly than those for which each generation takes multiple years.

Grade Band Endpoints for LS4.C

By the end of grade 2. Living things can survive only where their needs are met. If some places are too hot or too cold or have too little water or food, plants and animals may not be able to live there.

By the end of grade 5. Changes in an organism's habitat are sometimes beneficial to it and sometimes harmful. For any particular environment, some kinds of organisms survive well, some survive less well, and some cannot survive at all.

By the end of grade 8. Adaptation by natural selection acting over generations is one important process by which species change over time in response to changes in environmental conditions. Traits that support successful survival and reproduction in the new environment become more common; those that do not become less common. Thus, the distribution of traits in a population changes. In separated populations with different conditions, the changes can be large enough that the populations, provided they remain separated (a process called reproductive isolation), evolve to become separate species.

By the end of grade 12. Natural selection is the result of four factors: (1) the potential for a species to increase in number, (2) the genetic variation of individuals in a species due to mutation and sexual reproduction, (3) competition for an environment's limited supply of the resources that individuals need in order to survive and reproduce, and (4) the ensuing proliferation of those organisms that are better able to survive and reproduce in that environment. Natural selection leads to adaptation—that is, to a population dominated by organisms that are anatomically, behaviorally, and physiologically well suited to survive and reproduce in a specific environment. That is, the differential survival and

> **Adaptive changes due to natural selection, as well as the net result of speciation minus extinction, have strongly contributed to the planet's biodiversity.**

reproduction of organisms in a population that have an advantageous heritable trait leads to an increase in the proportion of individuals in future generations that have the trait and to a decrease in the proportion of individuals that do not. Adaptation also means that the distribution of traits in a population can change when conditions change.

Changes in the physical environment, whether naturally occurring or human induced, have thus contributed to the expansion of some species, the emergence of new distinct species as populations diverge under different conditions, and the decline—and sometimes the extinction—of some species. Species become extinct because they can no longer survive and reproduce in their altered environment. If members cannot adjust to change that is too fast or too drastic, the opportunity for the species' evolution is lost.

LS4.D: BIODIVERSITY AND HUMANS

What is biodiversity, how do humans affect it, and how does it affect humans?

Human beings are part of and depend on the natural world. Biodiversity—the multiplicity of genes, species, and ecosystems—provides humans with renewable resources, such as food, medicines, and clean water. Humans also benefit from "ecosystem services," such as climate stabilization, decomposition of wastes, and pollination that are provided by healthy (i.e., diverse and resilient) ecosystems. The resources of biological communities can be used within sustainable limits, but in many cases humans affect these ecosystems in ways—including habitat destruction, pollution of air and water, overexploitation of resources, introduction of invasive species, and climate change—that prevent the sustainable use of resources and lead to ecosystem degradation, species extinction, and the loss of valuable ecosystem services.

Grade Band Endpoints for LS4.D

By the end of grade 2. There are many different kinds of living things in any area, and they exist in different places on land and in water.

By the end of grade 5. Scientists have identified and classified many plants and animals. Populations of organisms live in a variety of habitats, and change in those habitats affects the organisms living there. Humans, like all other organisms, obtain living and nonliving resources from their environments.

By the end of grade 8. Biodiversity is the wide range of existing life forms that have adapted to the variety of conditions on Earth, from terrestrial to marine ecosystems. Biodiversity includes genetic variation within a species, in addition to species variation in different habitats and ecosystem types (e.g., forests, grasslands, wetlands). Changes in biodiversity can influence humans' resources, such as food, energy, and medicines, as well as ecosystem services that humans rely on—for example, water purification and recycling.

By the end of grade 12. Biodiversity is increased by the formation of new species (speciation) and decreased by the loss of species (extinction). Biological extinction, being irreversible, is a critical factor in reducing the planet's natural capital.

Humans depend on the living world for the resources and other benefits provided by biodiversity. But human activity is also having adverse impacts on biodiversity through overpopulation, overexploitation, habitat destruction, pollution, introduction of invasive species, and climate change. These problems have the potential to cause a major wave of biological extinctions—as many species or populations of a given species, unable to survive in changed environments, die out—and the effects may be harmful to humans and other living things. Thus sustaining biodiversity so that ecosystem functioning and productivity are maintained is essential to supporting and enhancing life on Earth. Sustaining biodiversity also aids humanity by preserving landscapes of recreational or inspirational value.

REFERENCES

1. National Academy of Sciences and Institute of Medicine. (2008). *Science, Evolution, and Creationism*. Washington, DC: The National Academies Press.

2. National Research Council. (2008). *The Role of Theory in Advancing 21st-Century Biology*. Washington, DC: The National Academies Press.

3. National Research Council. (2009). *A New Biology for the 21st Century*. Washington, DC: The National Academies Press.

4. National Research Council. (1996). *National Science Education Standards*. National Committee for Science Education Standards and Assessment. Washington, DC: National Academy Press.

5. American Association for the Advancement of Science. (2009). *Benchmarks for Science Literacy*. Project 2061. Available: http://www.project2061.org/publications/bsl/online/index.php?txtRef=http%3A%2F%2Fwww%2Eproject2061%2Eorg%2Fpublications%2Fbsl%2Fdefault%2Ehtm%3FtxtRef%3D%26txtURIOld%3D%252Ftools%252Fbsl%252Fdefault%2Ehtm&txtURIOld=%2Fpublications%2Fbsl%2Fonline%2Fbolintro%2Ehtm [June 2011].

6. College Board. (2009). *Science College Board Standards for College Success*. Available: http://professionals.collegeboard.com/profdownload/cbscs-science-standards-2009.pdf [June 2011].

7. National Assessment Governing Board. (2009). *Science Framework for the 2009 National Assessment of Educational Progress*. Washington, DC: U.S. Government Printing Office. Available: http://www.nagb.org/publications/frameworks/science-09.pdf [June 2011].

8. National Center for Education Statistics. (2009). *Program for International Student Assessment (PISA)*. Washington, DC: U.S. Department of Education. Available: http://nces.ed.gov/surveys/pisa/ [June 2011].

9. National Center for Education Statistics. (2007). *Trends in International Mathematics and Science Study (TIMSS)*. Washington, DC: U.S. Department of Education. Available: http://nces.ed.gov/timss/ [June 2011].

10. Brewer, C., and Smith, D. (Eds.). (2011). *Vision and Change in Undergraduate Biology Education*. Washington, DC: American Association for the Advancement of Science.

7

Dimension 3

DISCIPLINARY CORE IDEAS—EARTH AND SPACE SCIENCES

Earth and space sciences (ESS) investigate processes that operate on Earth and also address its place in the solar system and the galaxy. Thus ESS involve phenomena that range in scale from the unimaginably large to the invisibly small.

Earth and space sciences have much in common with the other branches of science, but they also include a unique set of scientific pursuits. Inquiries into the physical sciences (e.g., forces, energy, gravity, magnetism) were pursued in part as a means of understanding the size, age, structure, composition, and behavior of Earth, the sun, and the moon; physics and chemistry later developed as separate disciplines. The life sciences likewise are partially rooted in earth science, as Earth remains the only example of a biologically active planet, and the fossils found in the geological record of rocks are of interest to both life scientists and earth scientists. As a result, the majority of research in ESS is interdisciplinary in nature and falls under the categories of astrophysics, geophysics, geochemistry, and geobiology. However, the underlying traditional discipline of geology, involving the identification, analysis, and mapping of rocks, remains a cornerstone of ESS.

Earth consists of a set of systems—atmosphere, hydrosphere, geosphere, and biosphere—that are intricately interconnected. These systems have differing sources of energy, and matter cycles within and among them in multiple ways and on various time scales. Small changes in one part of one system can have large and sudden consequences in parts of other systems, or they can have no effect at all. Understanding the different processes that cause Earth to change over time (in a sense, how it "works") therefore requires knowledge of the multiple systems' interconnections and feedbacks. In addition, Earth is part of a broader system—the solar system—which is itself a small part of one of the many galaxies in the universe.

Because organizing ESS content is complex, given its broad scope and interdisciplinary nature, past efforts to promote earth sciences literacy have presented this content in a wide variety of ways. In this chapter, we begin at the largest spatial scales of the universe and move toward increasingly smaller scales and a more anthropocentric focus. Thus, the first core idea, ESS1: Earth's Place in the Universe, describes the universe as a whole and addresses its grand scale in both space and time. This idea includes the overall structure, composition, and history of the universe, the forces and processes by which the solar system operates, and Earth's planetary history.

The second core idea, ESS2: Earth's Systems, encompasses the processes that drive Earth's conditions and its continual evolution (i.e., change over time). It addresses the planet's large-scale structure and composition, describes its individual systems, and explains how they are interrelated. It also focuses on the mechanisms driving Earth's internal motions and on the vital role that water plays in all of the planet's systems and surface processes.

The third core idea, ESS3: Earth and Human Activity, addresses society's interactions with the planet. Connecting the ESS to the intimate scale of human life, this idea explains how Earth's processes affect people through natural resources and natural hazards, and it describes as well some of the ways in which humanity in turn affects Earth's processes. See Box 7-1 for a summary of the core and component ideas.

The committee's efforts have been strongly influenced by several recent efforts in the ESS community that have codified the essential sets of information in several fields. These projects include the *Earth Science Literacy Principles: The Big Ideas and Supporting Concepts of Earth Science* [1], *Ocean Literacy: The Essential Principles of Ocean Science K-12* [2], *Atmospheric Science Literacy:*

▌Vast amounts of new data, especially from satellites, together with modern computational models, are revealing the complexity of the interacting systems that control Earth's ever-changing surface. And many of the conclusions drawn from this science, along with some of the evidence from which they are drawn, are accessible to today's students. ▌

BOX 7-1

CORE AND COMPONENT IDEAS IN EARTH AND SPACE SCIENCES

Core Idea ESS1: Earth's Place in the Universe

ESS1.A: The Universe and Its Stars

ESS1.B: Earth and the Solar System

ESS1.C: The History of Planet Earth

Core Idea ESS2: Earth's Systems

ESS2.A: Earth Materials and Systems

ESS2.B: Plate Tectonics and Large-Scale System Interactions

ESS2.C: The Roles of Water in Earth's Surface Processes

ESS2.D: Weather and Climate

ESS2.E: Biogeology

Core Idea ESS3: Earth and Human Activity

ESS3.A: Natural Resources

ESS3.B: Natural Hazards

ESS3.C: Human Impacts on Earth Systems

ESS3.D: Global Climate Change

Essential Principles and Fundamental Concepts of Atmospheric Science [3], and *Climate Literacy: The Essential Principles of Climate Sciences* [4]. The selection of much of the framework's content was informed by these documents, thereby ensuring that the ESS core ideas we present are not only current and accurate but also relevant; they express content that the science research communities themselves recognize as being most important.

The framework includes a broader range of ideas in ESS than previous efforts related to science education standards, largely because of pertinent recent developments in ESS and the increasing societal importance of Earth-related issues. Astronomy and space exploration have prompted new ideas about how the universe works and of humans' place in it. Advances in imaging the interior of Earth have revised conceptions of how the planet formed and continues to evolve. Vast amounts of new data, especially from satellites, together with modern computational models, are revealing the complexity of the interacting systems that control Earth's ever-changing surface. And many of the conclusions drawn from this science, along with some of the evidence from which they are drawn, are accessible to today's students. Consequently, the story of Earth and the evolution of its systems, as it can be understood at the K-12 level, is much richer than what has been taught at this level in the past. Thus some of the framework's essential elements differ considerably from previous standards for K-12 science and engineering education.

The most important justification for the framework's increased emphasis on ESS is the rapidly increasing relevance of earth science to so many aspects of human society. It may seem as if natural hazards, such as earthquakes and hurricanes, have been more active in recent years, but this is primarily because the growing population of cities has heightened their impacts. The rapidly rising number of humans on the planet—doubling in number roughly every 40 years—combined with increased global industrialization, has also stressed limited planetary resources of water, arable land, plants and animals, minerals, and hydrocarbons. Only in the relatively recent past have people begun to recognize the dramatic role humans play as an essentially geological force on the surface of Earth, affecting large-scale conditions and processes.

Core Idea ESS1 Earth's Place in the Universe

What is the universe, and what is Earth's place in it?

The planet Earth is a tiny part of a vast universe that has developed over a huge expanse of time. The history of the universe, and of the structures and objects within it, can be deciphered using observations of their present condition together with knowledge of physics and chemistry. Similarly, the patterns of motion of the objects in the solar system can be described and predicted on the basis of observations and an understanding of gravity. Comprehension of these patterns can be used to explain many Earth phenomena, such as day and night, seasons, tides, and phases of the moon. Observations of other solar system objects and of Earth itself can be used to determine Earth's age and the history of large-scale changes in its surface.

ESS1.A: THE UNIVERSE AND ITS STARS

What is the universe, and what goes on in stars?

The sun is but one of a vast number of stars in the Milky Way galaxy, which is one of a vast number of galaxies in the universe.

The universe began with a period of extreme and rapid expansion known as the Big Bang, which occurred about 13.7 billion years ago. This theory is supported by the fact that it provides explanation of observations of distant galaxies receding from our own, of the measured composition of stars and nonstellar gases, and of the maps and spectra of the primordial radiation (cosmic microwave background) that still fills the universe.

Nearly all observable matter in the universe is hydrogen or helium, which formed in the first minutes after the Big Bang. Elements other than these remnants of the Big Bang continue to form within the cores of stars. Nuclear fusion within stars produces all atomic nuclei lighter than and including iron, and the process releases the energy seen as starlight. Heavier elements are produced when certain massive stars achieve a supernova stage and explode.

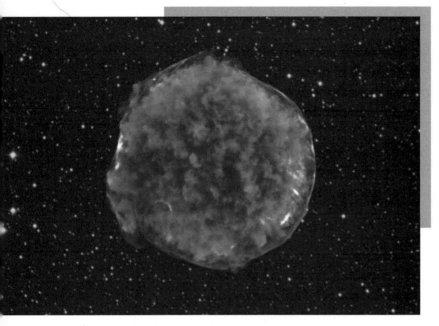

Stars' radiation of visible light and other forms of energy can be measured and studied to develop explanations about the formation, age, and composition of the universe. Stars go through a sequence of developmental stages—they are formed; evolve in size, mass, and brightness; and eventually burn out. Material from earlier stars that exploded as supernovas is recycled to form younger stars and their planetary systems. The sun is a medium-sized star about halfway through its predicted life span of about 10 billion years.

Grade Band Endpoints for ESS1.A

By the end of grade 2. Patterns of the motion of the sun, moon, and stars in the sky can be observed, described, and predicted. At night one can see the light coming from many stars with the naked eye, but telescopes make it possible to see many more and to observe them and the moon and planets in greater detail.

By the end of grade 5. The sun is a star that appears larger and brighter than other stars because it is closer. Stars range greatly in their size and distance from Earth.

By the end of grade 8. Patterns of the apparent motion of the sun, the moon, and stars in the sky can be observed, described, predicted, and explained with models. The universe began with a period of extreme and rapid expansion known as the Big Bang. Earth and its solar system are part of the Milky Way galaxy, which is one of many galaxies in the universe.

By the end of grade 12. The star called the sun is changing and will burn out over a life span of approximately 10 billion years. The sun is just one of more than 200 billion stars in the Milky Way galaxy, and the Milky Way is just one of hundreds of billions of galaxies in the universe. The study of stars' light spectra and brightness is used to identify compositional elements of stars, their movements, and their distances from Earth.

ESS1.B: EARTH AND THE SOLAR SYSTEM

What are the predictable patterns caused by Earth's movement in the solar system?

The solar system consists of the sun and a collection of objects of varying sizes and conditions—including planets and their moons—that are held in orbit around the sun by its gravitational pull on them. This system appears to have formed from a disk of dust and gas, drawn together by gravity.

Earth and the moon, sun, and planets have predictable patterns of movement. These patterns, which are explainable by gravitational forces and conservation laws, in turn explain many large-scale phenomena observed on Earth. Planetary motions around the sun can be predicted using Kepler's three empirical laws, which can be explained based on Newton's theory of gravity. These orbits may also change somewhat due to the gravitational effects from, or collisions with, other bodies. Gradual changes in the shape of Earth's orbit around the sun (over hundreds of thousands of years), together with the tilt of the planet's spin axis (or axis of rotation), have altered the intensity and distribution of sunlight falling on Earth. These phenomena cause cycles of climate change, including the relatively recent cycles of ice ages.

Gravity holds Earth in orbit around the sun, and it holds the moon in orbit around Earth. The pulls of gravity from the sun and the moon cause the patterns of ocean tides. The moon's and sun's positions relative to Earth cause lunar and solar eclipses to occur. The moon's monthly orbit around Earth, the relative positions of the sun, the moon, and the observer and the fact that it shines by reflected sunlight explain the observed phases of the moon.

Even though Earth's orbit is very nearly circular, the intensity of sunlight falling on a given location on the planet's surface changes as it orbits around the sun. Earth's spin axis is tilted relative to the plane of its orbit, and the seasons are

▌Earth and the moon, sun, and planets have predictable patterns of movement. These patterns, which are explainable by gravitational forces and conservation laws, in turn explain many large-scale phenomena observed on Earth. ▌

a result of that tilt. The intensity of sunlight striking Earth's surface is greatest at the equator. Seasonal variations in that intensity are greatest at the poles.

Grade Band Endpoints for ESS1.B

By the end of grade 2. Seasonal patterns of sunrise and sunset can be observed, described, and predicted.

By the end of grade 5. The orbits of Earth around the sun and of the moon around Earth, together with the rotation of Earth about an axis between its North and South poles, cause observable patterns. These include day and night; daily and seasonal changes in the length and direction of shadows; phases of the moon; and different positions of the sun, moon, and stars at different times of the day, month, and year.

Some objects in the solar system can be seen with the naked eye. Planets in the night sky change positions and are not always visible from Earth as they orbit the sun. Stars appear in patterns called constellations, which can be used for navigation and appear to move together across the sky because of Earth's rotation.

By the end of grade 8. The solar system consists of the sun and a collection of objects, including planets, their moons, and asteroids that are held in orbit around the sun by its gravitational pull on them. This model of the solar system can explain tides, eclipses of the sun and the moon, and the motion of the planets in the sky relative to the stars. Earth's spin axis is fixed in direction over the short term but tilted relative to its orbit around the sun. The seasons are a result of that tilt and are caused by the differential intensity of sunlight on different areas of Earth across the year.

By the end of grade 12. Kepler's laws describe common features of the motions of orbiting objects, including their elliptical paths around the sun. Orbits may change due to the gravitational effects from, or collisions with, other objects in the solar system. Cyclical changes in the shape of Earth's orbit around the sun, together with changes in the orientation of the planet's axis of rotation, both occurring over tens to hundreds of thousands of years, have altered the intensity and distribution of sunlight falling on Earth. These phenomena cause cycles of ice ages and other gradual climate changes.

ESS1.C: THE HISTORY OF PLANET EARTH

How do people reconstruct and date events in Earth's planetary history?

Earth scientists use the structure, sequence, and properties of rocks, sediments, and fossils, as well as the locations of current and past ocean basins, lakes, and rivers, to reconstruct events in Earth's planetary history. For example, rock layers show the sequence of geological events, and the presence and amount of radioactive elements in rocks make it possible to determine their ages.

Analyses of rock formations and the fossil record are used to establish relative ages. In an undisturbed column of rock, the youngest rocks are at the top, and the oldest are at the bottom. Rock layers have sometimes been rearranged by tectonic forces; rearrangements can be seen or inferred, such as from inverted sequences of fossil types. Core samples obtained from drilling reveal that the continents' rocks (some as old as 4 billion years or more) are much older than rocks on the ocean floor (less than 200 million years), where tectonic processes continually generate new rocks and destroy old ones. The rock record reveals that events on Earth can be catastrophic,  occurring over hours to years, or gradual, occurring over thousands to millions of years. Records of fossils and other rocks also show past periods of massive extinctions and extensive volcanic activity. Although active geological processes, such as plate tectonics (link to ESS2.B) and erosion, have destroyed or altered most of the very early rock record on Earth, some other objects in the solar system, such as asteroids and meteorites, have changed little over billions of years. Studying these objects can help scientists deduce the solar system's age and history, including the formation of planet Earth. Study of other planets and their moons, many of which exhibit such features as volcanism and meteor impacts similar to those found on Earth, also help illuminate aspects of Earth's history and changes.

The geological time scale organizes Earth's history into the increasingly long time intervals of eras, periods, and epochs. Major historical events include the formation of mountain chains and ocean basins, volcanic activity, the evolution and extinction of living organisms, periods of massive glaciation, and development of watersheds and rivers. Because many individual plant and animal species existed during known time periods (e.g., dinosaurs), the location of certain types of fossils in the rock record can reveal the age of the rocks and help geologists decipher the history of landforms.

Grade Band Endpoints for ESS1.C

By the end of grade 2. Some events on Earth occur in cycles, like day and night, and others have a beginning and an end, like a volcanic eruption. Some events, like an earthquake, happen very quickly; others, such as the formation of the Grand Canyon, occur very slowly, over a time period much longer than one can observe.

By the end of grade 5. Earth has changed over time. Understanding how landforms develop, are weathered (broken down into smaller pieces), and erode (get transported elsewhere) can help infer the history of the current landscape. Local, regional, and global patterns of rock formations reveal changes over time due to Earth forces, such as earthquakes. The presence and location of certain fossil types indicate the order in which rock layers were formed. Patterns of tree rings and ice cores from glaciers can help reconstruct Earth's recent climate history.

By the end of grade 8. The geological time scale interpreted from rock strata provides a way to organize Earth's history. Major historical events include the formation of mountain chains and ocean basins, the evolution and extinction of particular living organisms, volcanic eruptions, periods of massive glaciation, and development of watersheds and rivers through glaciation and water erosion. Analyses of rock strata and the fossil record provide only relative dates, not an absolute scale.

By the end of grade 12. Radioactive decay lifetimes and isotopic content in rocks provide a way of dating rock formations and thereby fixing the scale of geological time. Continental rocks, which can be older than 4 billion years, are generally much older than rocks on the ocean floor, which are less than 200 million years old. Tectonic processes continually generate new ocean seafloor at ridges and destroy old seafloor at trenches. Although active geological processes, such as plate tectonics (link to ESS2.B) and erosion, have destroyed or altered most of the very early rock record on Earth, other objects in the solar system, such as lunar rocks, asteroids, and meteorites, have changed little over billions of years. Studying these objects can provide information about Earth's formation and early history.

Core Idea ESS2 Earth's Systems

How and why is Earth constantly changing?

Earth's surface is a complex and dynamic set of interconnected systems—principally the geosphere, hydrosphere, atmosphere, and biosphere—that interact over a wide range of temporal and spatial scales. All of Earth's processes are the result of energy flowing and matter cycling within and among these systems. For example, the motion of tectonic plates is part of the cycles of convection in Earth's mantle, driven by outflowing heat and the downward pull of gravity, which result in the formation and changes of many features of Earth's land and undersea surface. Weather and climate are shaped by complex interactions involving sunlight, the ocean, the atmosphere, clouds, ice, land, and life forms. Earth's biosphere has changed the makeup of the geosphere, hydrosphere, and atmosphere over geological time; conversely, geological events and conditions have influenced the evolution of life on the planet. Water is essential to the dynamics of most earth systems, and it plays a significant role in shaping Earth's landscape.

ESS2.A: EARTH MATERIALS AND SYSTEMS

How do Earth's major systems interact?

Earth is a complex system of interacting subsystems: the geosphere, hydrosphere, atmosphere, and biosphere. The geosphere includes a hot and mostly metallic inner core; a mantle of hot, soft, solid rock; and a crust of rock, soil, and sediments. The atmosphere is the envelope of gas surrounding the planet. The hydrosphere is the ice, water vapor, and liquid water in the atmosphere, ocean, lakes, streams, soils, and groundwater. The presence of living organisms of any type defines the biosphere; life can be found in many parts of the geosphere, hydrosphere, and atmosphere. Humans are of course part of the biosphere, and human activities have important impacts on all of Earth's systems.

All Earth processes are the result of energy flowing and matter cycling within and among Earth's systems. This energy originates from the sun and from

Earth's interior. Transfers of energy and the movements of matter can cause chemical and physical changes among Earth's materials and living organisms.

Solid rocks, for example, can be formed by the cooling of molten rock, the accumulation and consolidation of sediments, or the alteration of older rocks by heat, pressure, and fluids. These processes occur under different circumstances and produce different types of rock. Physical and chemical interactions among rocks, sediments, water, air, and plants and animals produce soil. In the carbon, water, and nitrogen cycles, materials cycle between living and nonliving forms and among the atmosphere, soil, rocks, and ocean.

Weather and climate are driven by interactions of the geosphere, hydrosphere, and atmosphere, with inputs of energy from the sun. The tectonic and volcanic processes that create and build mountains and plateaus, for example, as well as the weathering and erosion processes that break down these structures and transport the products, all involve interactions among the geosphere, hydrosphere, and atmosphere. The resulting landforms and the habitats they provide affect the biosphere, which in turn modifies these habitats and affects the atmosphere, particularly through imbalances between the carbon capture and oxygen release that occur in photosynthesis, and the carbon release and oxygen capture that occur in respiration and in the burning of fossil fuels to support human activities.

Earth exchanges mass and energy with the rest of the solar system. It gains or loses energy through incoming solar radiation, thermal radiation to space, and gravitational forces exerted by the sun, moon, and planets. Earth gains mass from the impacts of meteoroids and comets and loses mass from the escape of gases into space.

Earth's systems are dynamic; they interact over a wide range of temporal and spatial scales and continually react to changing influences, including human activities. Components of Earth's systems may appear stable, change slowly over long periods of time, or change abruptly, with significant consequences for living organisms. Changes in part of one system can cause further changes to that system or to other systems, often in surprising and complex ways.

Grade Band Endpoints for ESS2.A

By the end of grade 2. Wind and water can change the shape of the land. The resulting landforms, together with the materials on the land, provide homes for living things.

By the end of grade 5. Earth's major systems are the geosphere (solid and molten rock, soil, and sediments), the hydrosphere (water and ice), the atmosphere (air), and the biosphere (living things, including humans). These systems interact in multiple ways to affect Earth's surface materials and processes. The ocean supports a variety of ecosystems and organisms, shapes landforms, and influences climate. Winds and clouds in the atmosphere interact with the landforms to determine patterns of weather. Rainfall helps shape the land and affects the types of living things found in a region. Water, ice, wind, living organisms, and gravity break rocks, soils, and sediments into smaller particles and move them around. Human activities affect Earth's systems and their interactions at its surface.

By the end of grade 8. All Earth processes are the result of energy flowing and matter cycling within and among the planet's systems. This energy is derived from the sun and Earth's hot interior. The energy that flows and matter that cycles produce chemical and physical changes in Earth's materials and living organisms. The planet's systems interact over scales that range from microscopic to global in size, and they operate over fractions of a second to billions of years. These interactions have shaped Earth's history and will determine its future.

By the end of grade 12. Earth's systems, being dynamic and interacting, cause feedback effects that can increase or decrease the original changes. A deep knowledge of how feedbacks work within and among Earth's systems is still lacking, thus limiting scientists' ability to predict some changes and their impacts.

Evidence from deep probes and seismic waves, reconstructions of historical changes in Earth's surface and its magnetic field, and an understanding of physical and chemical processes lead to a model of Earth with a hot but solid inner core, a liquid outer core, a solid mantle and crust. The top part of the mantle, along with the crust, forms structures known as tectonic plates (link to ESS2.B). Motions of the mantle and its plates occur primarily through thermal convection, which involves the cycling of matter due to the outward flow of energy from Earth's interior and the gravitational movement of denser materials toward the interior. The geological record shows that changes to global and regional climate can be caused by interactions among changes in the sun's energy output or Earth's orbit, tectonic events, ocean circulation, volcanic activity, glaciers, vegetation, and human activities. These changes can occur on a variety of time scales from sudden (e.g., volcanic ash clouds) to intermediate (ice ages) to very long-term tectonic cycles.

ESS2.B: PLATE TECTONICS AND LARGE-SCALE SYSTEM INTERACTIONS

Why do the continents move, and what causes earthquakes and volcanoes?

Plate tectonics is the unifying theory that explains the past and current movements of the rocks at Earth's surface and provides a coherent account of its geological history. This theory is supported by multiple evidence streams—for example, the consistent patterns of earthquake locations, evidence of ocean floor spreading over time given by tracking magnetic patterns in undersea rocks and coordinating them with changes to Earth's magnetic axis data, the warping of the land under loads (such as lakes and ice sheets), which show that the solid mantle's rocks can bend and even flow.

The lighter and less dense continents are embedded in heavier and denser upper-mantle rocks, and together they make up the moving tectonic plates of the lithosphere (Earth's solid outer layer, i.e., the crust and upper mantle). Tectonic plates are the top parts of giant convection cells that bring matter from the hot inner mantle up to the cool surface. These movements are driven by the release of energy (from radioactive decay of unstable isotopes within Earth's interior) and by the cooling and gravitational downward motion of the dense material of the plates after subduction (one plate being drawn under another). The plates move across Earth's surface, carrying the continents, creating and destroying ocean basins, producing earthquakes and volcanoes, and forming mountain ranges and plateaus.

Most continental and ocean floor features are the result of geological activity and earthquakes along plate boundaries. The exact patterns depend on whether

▌ Plate tectonics is the unifying theory that explains the past and current movements of the rocks at Earth's surface and provides a coherent account of its geological history. ▌

the plates are being pushed together to create mountains or deep ocean trenches, being pulled apart to form new ocean floor at mid-ocean ridges, or sliding past each other along surface faults. Most distributions of rocks within Earth's crust, including minerals, fossil fuels, and energy resources, are a direct result of the history of plate motions and collisions and the corresponding changes in the configurations of the continents and ocean basins.

This history is still being written. Continents are continually being shaped and reshaped by competing constructive and destructive geological processes. North America, for example, has gradually grown in size over the past 4 billion years through a complex set of interactions with other continents, including the addition of many new crustal segments.

Grade Band Endpoints for ESS2.B

By the end of grade 2. Rocks, soils, and sand are present in most areas where plants and animals live. There may also be rivers, streams, lakes, and ponds. Maps show where things are located. One can map the shapes and kinds of land and water in any area.

By the end of grade 5. The locations of mountain ranges, deep ocean trenches, ocean floor structures, earthquakes, and volcanoes occur in patterns. Most earthquakes and volcanoes occur in bands that are often along the boundaries between continents and oceans. Major mountain chains form inside continents or near their edges. Maps can help locate the different land and water features where people live and in other areas of Earth.

By the end of grade 8. Plate tectonics is the unifying theory that explains the past and current movements of the rocks at Earth's surface and provides a framework for understanding its geological history. Plate movements are responsible for most continental and ocean floor features and for the distribution of most rocks and minerals within Earth's crust. Maps of ancient land and water patterns, based on investigations of rocks and fossils, make clear how Earth's plates have moved great distances, collided, and spread apart.

By the end of grade 12. The radioactive decay of unstable isotopes continually generates new energy within Earth's crust and mantle providing the primary source of the heat that drives mantle convection. Plate tectonics can be viewed as the surface expression of mantle convection.

ESS2.C: THE ROLES OF WATER IN EARTH'S SURFACE PROCESSES

How do the properties and movements of water shape Earth's surface and affect its systems?

Earth is often called the water planet because of the abundance of liquid water on its surface and because water's unique combination of physical and chemical properties is central to Earth's dynamics. These properties include water's exceptional capacity to absorb, store, and release large amounts of energy as it changes state; to transmit sunlight; to expand upon freezing; to dissolve and transport many materials; and to lower the viscosities and freezing points of the material when mixed with fluid rocks in the mantle. Each of these properties plays a role in how water affects other Earth systems (e.g., ice expansion contributes to rock erosion, ocean thermal capacity contributes to moderating temperature variations).

Water is found almost everywhere on Earth, from high in the atmosphere (as water vapor and ice crystals) to low in the atmosphere (precipitation, droplets in clouds) to mountain snowcaps and glaciers (solid) to running liquid water on the land, ocean, and underground. Energy from the sun and the force of gravity drive the continual cycling of water among these reservoirs. Sunlight causes evaporation and propels oceanic and atmospheric circulation, which transports water around the globe. Gravity causes precipitation to fall from clouds and water to flow downward on the land through watersheds.

About 97 percent of Earth's water is in the ocean, and most fresh water is contained in glaciers or underground aquifers; only a tiny fraction of Earth's water is found in streams, lakes, and rivers. The relative availability of water is a major factor in distinguishing habitats for different living organisms.

Water participates both in the dissolution and formation of Earth's materials. The downward flow of water, both in liquid and solid form, shapes landscapes through the erosion, transport, and deposition of sediment. Shoreline waves in the ocean and lakes are powerful agents of erosion. Over millions of years, coastlines have moved back and forth over continents by hundreds of kilometers, largely due to the rise and fall of sea level as the climate changed (e.g., ice ages).

Grade Band Endpoints for ESS2.C

By the end of grade 2. Water is found in the ocean, rivers, lakes, and ponds. Water exists as solid ice and in liquid form. It carries soil and rocks from one place to another and determines the variety of life forms that can live in a particular location.

■ Earth is often called the water planet because of the abundance of liquid water on its surface and because water's unique combination of physical and chemical properties is central to Earth's dynamics. ■

By the end of grade 5. Water is found almost everywhere on Earth: as vapor; as fog or clouds in the atmosphere; as rain or snow falling from clouds; as ice, snow, and running water on land and in the ocean; and as groundwater beneath the surface. The downhill movement of water as it flows to the ocean shapes the appearance of the land. Nearly all of Earth's available water is in the ocean. Most fresh water is in glaciers or underground; only a tiny fraction is in streams, lakes, wetlands, and the atmosphere.

By the end of grade 8. Water continually cycles among land, ocean, and atmosphere via transpiration, evaporation, condensation and crystallization, and precipitation as well as downhill flows on land. The complex patterns of the changes

and the movement of water in the atmosphere, determined by winds, landforms, and ocean temperatures and currents, are major determinants of local weather patterns. Global movements of water and its changes in form are propelled by sunlight and gravity. Variations in density due to variations in temperature and salinity drive a global pattern of interconnected ocean currents. Water's movements—both on the land and underground—cause weathering and erosion, which change the land's surface features and create underground formations.

By the end of grade 12. The abundance of liquid water on Earth's surface and its unique combination of physical and chemical properties are central to the planet's dynamics. These properties include water's exceptional capacity to absorb, store, and release large amounts of energy; transmit sunlight; expand upon freezing; dissolve and transport materials; and lower the viscosities and melting points of rocks.

ESS2.D: WEATHER AND CLIMATE

What regulates weather and climate?

Weather, which varies from day to day and seasonally throughout the year, is the condition of the atmosphere at a given place and time. Climate is longer term and location sensitive; it is the range of a region's weather over 1 year or many years, and, because it depends on latitude and geography, it varies from place to place. Weather and climate are shaped by complex interactions involving sunlight, the ocean, the atmosphere, ice, landforms, and living things. These interactions can drive changes that occur over multiple time scales—from days, weeks, and months for weather to years, decades, centuries, and beyond—for climate.

The ocean exerts a major influence on weather and climate. It absorbs and stores large amounts of energy from the sun and releases it very slowly; in that way, the ocean moderates and stabilizes global climates. Energy is redistributed globally through ocean currents (e.g., the Gulf Stream) and also through atmospheric circulation (winds). Sunlight heats Earth's surface, which in turn heats the atmosphere. The resulting temperature patterns, together with Earth's rotation and the configuration of continents and oceans, control the large-scale patterns of atmospheric circulation. Winds gain energy and water vapor content as they cross hot ocean regions, which can lead to tropical storms.

The "greenhouse effect" keeps Earth's surface warmer than it would be otherwise. To maintain any average temperature over time, energy inputs from the sun and from radioactive decay in Earth's interior must be balanced by energy loss due to radiation from the upper atmosphere. However, what determines the temperature at which this balance occurs is a complex set of absorption, reflection, transmission, and redistribution processes in the atmosphere and oceans that determine how long energy stays trapped in these systems before being radiated away. Certain gases in the atmosphere (water vapor, carbon dioxide, methane, and nitrous oxides), which absorb and retain energy that radiates from Earth's surface, essentially insulate the planet. Without this phenomenon, Earth's surface would be too cold to be habitable. However, changes in the atmosphere, such as increases in carbon dioxide, can make regions of Earth too hot to be habitable by many species.

Climate changes, which are defined as significant and persistent changes in an area's average or extreme weather conditions, can occur if any of Earth's systems change (e.g., composition of the atmosphere, reflectivity of Earth's surface). Positive feedback loops can amplify the impacts of these effects and trigger relatively abrupt changes in the climate system; negative feedback loops tend to maintain stable climate conditions.

Some climate changes in Earth's history were rapid shifts (caused by events, such as volcanic eruptions and meteoric impacts, that suddenly put a large amount of particulate matter into the atmosphere or by abrupt changes in ocean currents);

other climate changes were gradual and longer term—due, for example, to solar output variations, shifts in the tilt of Earth's axis, or atmospheric change due to the rise of plants and other life forms that modified the atmosphere via photosynthesis. Scientists can infer these changes from geological evidence.

Natural factors that cause climate changes over human time scales (tens or hundreds of years) include variations in the sun's energy output, ocean circulation patterns, atmospheric composition, and volcanic activity. (See ESS3.D for a detailed discussion of human activities and global climate change.) When ocean currents change their flow patterns, such as during El Niño Southern Oscillation conditions, some global regions become warmer or wetter and others become colder or drier. Cumulative increases in the atmospheric concentration of carbon dioxide and other greenhouse gases, whether arising from natural sources or human industrial activity (see ESS3.D), increase the capacity of Earth to retain energy. Changes in surface or atmospheric reflectivity change the amount of energy from the sun that enters the planetary system. Icy surfaces, clouds, aerosols, and larger particles in the atmosphere, such as from volcanic ash, reflect sunlight and thereby decrease the amount of solar energy that can enter the weather/climate system. Conversely, dark surfaces (e.g., roads, most buildings) absorb sunlight and thus increase the energy entering the system.

Grade Band Endpoints for ESS2.D

By the end of grade 2. Weather is the combination of sunlight, wind, snow or rain, and temperature in a particular region at a particular time. People measure these conditions to describe and record the weather and to notice patterns over time.

By the end of grade 5. Weather is the minute-by-minute to day-by-day variation of the atmosphere's condition on a local scale. Scientists record the patterns of the weather across different times and areas so that they can make predictions about what kind of weather might happen next. Climate describes the ranges of an area's typical weather conditions and the extent to which those conditions vary over years to centuries.

By the end of grade 8. Weather and climate are influenced by interactions involving sunlight, the ocean, the atmosphere, ice, landforms, and living things. These interactions vary with latitude, altitude, and local and regional geography, all of which can affect oceanic and atmospheric flow patterns. Because these patterns are so complex, weather can be predicted only probabilistically.

The ocean exerts a major influence on weather and climate by absorbing energy from the sun, releasing it over time, and globally redistributing it through ocean currents. Greenhouse gases in the atmosphere absorb and retain the energy radiated from land and ocean surfaces, thereby regulating Earth's average surface temperature and keeping it habitable.

By the end of grade 12. The foundation for Earth's global climate system is the electromagnetic radiation from the sun as well as its reflection, absorption, storage, and redistribution among the atmosphere, ocean, and land systems and this energy's reradiation into space. Climate change can occur when certain parts of Earth's systems are altered. Geological evidence indicates that past climate changes were either sudden changes caused by alterations in the atmosphere; longer term changes (e.g., ice ages) due to variations in solar output, Earth's orbit, or the orientation of its axis; or even more gradual atmospheric changes due to plants and other organisms that captured carbon dioxide and released oxygen. The time scales of these changes varied from a few to millions of years. Changes in the atmosphere due to human activity have increased carbon dioxide concentrations and thus affect climate (link to ESS3.D).

Global climate models incorporate scientists' best knowledge of physical and chemical processes and of the interactions of relevant systems. They are tested by their ability to fit past climate variations. Current models predict that, although future regional climate changes will be complex and varied, average global temperatures will continue to rise. The outcomes predicted by global climate models strongly depend on the amounts of human-generated greenhouse gases added to the atmosphere each year and by the ways in which these gases are absorbed by the ocean and the biosphere. Hence the outcomes depend on human behaviors (link to ESS3.D) as well as on natural factors that involve complex feedbacks among Earth's systems (link to ESS2.A).

ESS2.E: BIOGEOLOGY

How do living organisms alter Earth's processes and structures?

Evolution, including the emergence and extinction of species, is a natural and ongoing process that is shaped by Earth's dynamic processes. The properties and conditions of Earth and its atmosphere affect the environments and conditions within which life emerged and evolved—for example, the range of frequencies of light that penetrate the atmosphere to Earth's surface. Organisms continually evolve to new and often more complex forms as they adapt to new environments. The evolution and proliferation of living things have changed the makeup of Earth's geosphere, hydrosphere, and atmosphere over geological time. Plants,

algae, and microorganisms produced most of the oxygen (i.e., the O_2) in the atmosphere through photosynthesis, and they enabled the formation of fossil fuels and types of sedimentary rocks. Microbes also changed the chemistry of Earth's surface, and they continue to play a critical role in nutrient cycling (e.g., of nitrogen) in most ecosystems.

Organisms ranging from bacteria to human beings are a major driver of the global carbon cycle, and they influence global climate by modifying the chemical makeup of the atmosphere. Greenhouse gases in particular are continually moved through the reservoirs represented by the ocean, land, life, and atmosphere. The abundance of carbon in the atmosphere is reduced through the ocean floor accumulation of marine sediments and the accumulation of plant biomass; atmospheric carbon is increased through such processes as deforestation and the burning of fossil fuels.

As Earth changes, life on Earth adapts and evolves to those changes, so just as life influences other Earth systems, other Earth systems influence life. Life and the planet's nonliving systems can be said to co-evolve.

Grade Band Endpoints for ESS2.E

By the end of grade 2. Plants and animals (including humans) depend on the land, water, and air to live and grow. They in turn can change their environment (e.g., the shape of land, the flow of water).

By the end of grade 5. Living things affect the physical characteristics of their regions (e.g., plants' roots hold soil in place, beaver shelters and human-built dams alter the flow of water, plants' respiration affects the air). Many types of rocks and minerals are formed from the remains of organisms or are altered by their activities.

By the end of grade 8. Evolution is shaped by Earth's varying geological conditions. Sudden changes in conditions (e.g., meteor impacts, major volcanic eruptions) have caused mass extinctions, but these changes, as well as more gradual ones, have ultimately allowed other life forms to flourish. The evolution and proliferation of living things over geological time have in turn changed the rates of weathering and erosion of land surfaces, altered the composition of Earth's soils and atmosphere, and affected the distribution of water in the hydrosphere.

By the end of grade 12. The many dynamic and delicate feedbacks between the biosphere and other Earth systems cause a continual co-evolution of Earth's surface and the life that exists on it.

Core Idea ESS3 **Earth and Human Activity**

How do Earth's surface processes and human activities affect each other?

Earth's surface processes affect and are affected by human activities. Humans depend on all of the planet's systems for a variety of resources, some of which are renewable or replaceable and some of which are not. Natural hazards and other geological events can significantly alter human populations and activities. Human activities, in turn, can contribute to the frequency and intensity of some natural hazards. Indeed, humans have become one of the most significant agents of change in Earth's surface systems. In particular, it has been shown that climate change—which could have large consequences for all of Earth's surface systems, including the biosphere—is driven not only by natural effects but also by human activities. Sustaining the biosphere will require detailed knowledge and modeling of the factors that affect climate, coupled with the responsible management of natural resources.

ESS3.A: NATURAL RESOURCES

How do humans depend on Earth's resources?

Humans depend on Earth's land, ocean, atmosphere, and biosphere for many different resources, including air, water, soil, minerals, metals, energy, plants, and animals. Some of these resources are renewable over human lifetimes, and some are nonrenewable (mineral resources and fossil fuels) or irreplaceable if lost (extinct species).

Materials important to modern technological societies are not uniformly distributed across the planet (e.g., oil in the Middle East, gold in California). Most elements exist in Earth's crust at concentrations too low to be extracted, but in some locations—where geological processes have concentrated them—extraction is economically viable. Historically, humans have populated regions that are climatically, hydrologically, and geologically advantageous for fresh water availability, food production via agriculture, commerce, and other aspects of civilization. Resource availability affects geopolitical relationships and can limit development. As the global human population increases and people's demands for better living conditions increase, resources considered readily available in the past, such as land for agriculture or drinkable water, are becoming scarcer and more valued.

All forms of resource extraction and land use have associated economic, social, environmental, and geopolitical costs and risks, as well as benefits. New technologies and regulations can change the balance of these factors—for example, scientific modeling of the long-term environmental impacts of resource use can help identify potential problems and suggest desirable changes in the patterns of use. Much energy production today comes from nonrenewable sources, such as coal and oil. However, advances in related science and technology are reducing the cost of energy from renewable resources, such as sunlight, and some regulations are favoring their use. As a result, future energy supplies are likely to come from a much wider range of sources.

Grade Band Endpoints for ESS3.A

By the end of grade 2. Living things need water, air, and resources from the land, and they try to live in places that have the things they need. Humans use natural resources for everything they do: for example, they use soil and water to grow food, wood to burn to provide heat or to build shelters, and materials such as iron or copper extracted from Earth to make cooking pans.

By the end of grade 5. All materials, energy, and fuels that humans use are derived from natural sources, and their use affects the environment in multiple ways. Some resources are renewable over time, and others are not.

By the end of grade 8. Humans depend on Earth's land, ocean, atmosphere, and biosphere for many different resources. Minerals, fresh water, and biosphere resources are limited, and many are not renewable or replaceable over human lifetimes. These resources are distributed unevenly around the planet as a result of past geological processes (link to ESS2.B). Renewable energy resources, and the technologies to exploit them, are being rapidly developed.

By the end of grade 12. Resource availability has guided the development of human society. All forms of energy production and other resource extraction have associated economic, social, environmental, and geopolitical costs and risks, as well as benefits. New technologies and regulations can change the balance of these factors.

ESS3.B: NATURAL HAZARDS

How do natural hazards affect individuals and societies?

Natural processes can cause sudden or gradual changes to Earth's systems, some of which may adversely affect humans. Through observations and knowledge of historical events, people know where certain of these hazards—such as earthquakes, tsunamis, volcanic eruptions, severe weather, floods, and coastal erosion—are likely to occur. Understanding these kinds of hazards helps us prepare for and respond to them.

Natural hazards and other geological events have shaped the course of human history, sometimes significantly altering the size of human populations or driving human migrations. ∎

While humans cannot eliminate natural hazards, they can take steps to reduce their impacts. For example, loss of life and economic costs have been greatly reduced by improving construction, developing warning systems, identifying and avoiding high-risk locations, and increasing community preparedness and response capability.

Some natural hazards are preceded by geological activities that allow for reliable predictions; others occur suddenly, with no notice, and are not yet predictable. By tracking the upward movement of magma, for example, volcanic eruptions can often be predicted with enough advance warning to allow neighboring regions to be evacuated. Earthquakes, in contrast, occur suddenly; the specific time, day, or year cannot be predicted. However, the history of earthquakes in a region and the mapping of fault lines can help forecast the likelihood of future events. Finally, satellite monitoring of weather patterns, along with measurements from land, sea, and air, usually can identify developing severe weather and lead to its reliable forecast.

Natural hazards and other geological events have shaped the course of human history, sometimes significantly altering the size of human populations or driving human migrations. Natural hazards can be local, regional, or global in origin, and even local events can have distant impacts because of the interconnectedness of human societies and Earth's systems. Human activities can contribute to the frequency and intensity of some natural hazards (e.g., flooding, forest fires), and risks from natural hazards increase as populations—and population densities—increase in vulnerable locations.

Grade Band Endpoints for ESS3.B

By the end of grade 2. Some kinds of severe weather are more likely than others in a given region. Weather scientists forecast severe weather so that communities can prepare for and respond to these events.

By the end of grade 5. A variety of hazards result from natural processes (e.g., earthquakes, tsunamis, volcanic eruptions, severe weather, floods, coastal erosion). Humans cannot eliminate natural hazards but can take steps to reduce their impacts.

By the end of grade 8. Some natural hazards, such as volcanic eruptions and severe weather, are preceded by phenomena that allow for reliable predictions. Others, such as earthquakes, occur suddenly and with no notice, and thus they are not yet predictable. However, mapping the history of natural hazards in a region, combined with an understanding of related geological forces can help forecast the locations and likelihoods of future events.

By the end of grade 12. Natural hazards and other geological events have shaped the course of human history by destroying buildings and cities, eroding land, changing the course of rivers, and reducing the amount of arable land. These events have significantly altered the sizes of human populations and have driven human migrations. Natural hazards can be local, regional, or global in origin, and their risks increase as populations grow. Human activities can contribute to the frequency and intensity of some natural hazards.

ESS3.C: HUMAN IMPACTS ON EARTH SYSTEMS

How do humans change the planet?

Recorded history, as well as chemical and geological evidence, indicates that human activities in agriculture, industry, and everyday life have had major impacts on the land, rivers, ocean, and air. Humans affect the quality, availability, and distribution of Earth's water through the modification of streams, lakes, and groundwater. Large areas of land, including such delicate ecosystems as wetlands, forests, and grasslands, are being transformed by human agriculture, mining, and the expansion of settlements and roads. Human activities now cause land erosion and soil movement annually that exceed all natural processes. Air and water pollution caused by human activities affect the condition of the atmosphere and of rivers and lakes, with damaging effects on other species and on human health. The activities of humans have significantly altered the biosphere, changing or destroying natural habitats and causing the extinction of many living species. These changes also affect the viability of agriculture or fisheries to support human populations. Land use patterns for agriculture and ocean use patterns for fishing are affected not only by changes in population and needs but also by changes in climate or local conditions (such as desertification due to overuse or depletion of fish populations by overextraction).

Thus humans have become one of the most significant agents of change in the near-surface Earth system. And because all of Earth's subsystems are interconnected, changes in one system can produce unforeseen changes in others.

The activities and advanced technologies that have built and maintained human civilizations clearly have large consequences for the sustainability of these civilizations and the ecosystems with which they interact. As the human population grows and per-capita consumption of natural resources increases to provide a greater percentage of people with more developed lifestyles and greater longevity, so do the human impacts on the planet.

Some negative effects of human activities are reversible with informed and responsible management. For example, communities are doing many things to help protect Earth's resources and environments. They are treating sewage, reducing the amount of materials they use, and reusing and recycling materials. Regulations regarding water and air pollution have greatly reduced acid rain and stream pollution, and international treaties on the use of certain refrigerant gases have halted the growth of the annual ozone hole over Antarctica. Regulation of fishing and the development of marine preserves can help restore and maintain fish populations. In addition, the development of alternative energy sources can reduce the environmental impacts otherwise caused by the use of fossil fuels.

The sustainability of human societies and of the biodiversity that supports them requires responsible management of natural resources not only to reduce existing adverse impacts but also to prevent such impacts to the extent possible. Scientists and engineers can make major contributions by developing technologies that produce less pollution and waste and that preclude ecosystem degradation.

Grade Band Endpoints for ESS3.C

By the end of grade 2. Things that people do to live comfortably can affect the world around them. But they can make choices that reduce their impacts on the land, water, air, and other living things—for example, by reducing trash through reuse and recycling.

Recorded history, as well as chemical and geological evidence, indicates that human activities in agriculture, industry, and everyday life have had major impacts on the land, rivers, ocean, and air.

By the end of grade 5. Human activities in agriculture, industry, and everyday life have had major effects on the land, vegetation, streams, ocean, air, and even outer space. But individuals and communities are doing things to help protect Earth's resources and environments. For example, they are treating sewage, reducing the amounts of materials they use, and regulating sources of pollution such as emissions from factories and power plants or the runoff from agricultural activities.

By the end of grade 8. Human activities have significantly altered the biosphere, sometimes damaging or destroying natural habitats and causing the extinction of many other species. But changes to Earth's environments can have different impacts (negative and positive) for different living things. Typically, as human populations and per-capita consumption of natural resources increase, so do the negative impacts on Earth unless the activities and technologies involved are engineered otherwise.

By the end of grade 12. The sustainability of human societies and the biodiversity that supports them requires responsible management of natural resources. Scientists and engineers can make major contributions—for example, by developing technologies that produce less pollution and waste and that preclude ecosystem degradation. When the source of an environmental problem is understood and international agreement can be reached, human activities can be regulated to mitigate global impacts (e.g., acid rain and the ozone hole near Antarctica).

ESS3.D: GLOBAL CLIMATE CHANGE

How do people model and predict the effects of human activities on Earth's climate?

Global climate change, shown to be driven by both natural phenomena and by human activities, could have large consequences for all of Earth's surface systems, including the biosphere (see ESS3.C for a general discussion of climate). Humans are now so numerous and resource dependent that their activities affect every part of the environment, from outer space and the stratosphere to the deepest ocean.

However, by using science-based predictive models, humans can anticipate long-term change more effectively than ever before and plan accordingly.

Global changes usually happen too slowly for individuals to recognize, but accumulated human knowledge, together with further scientific research, can help people learn more about these challenges and guide their responses. For example, there are historical records of weather conditions and of the times when plants bloom, animals give birth or migrate, and lakes and rivers freeze and thaw. And scientists can deduce long-past climate conditions from such sources as fossils, pollen grains found in sediments, and isotope ratios in samples of ancient materials.

Scientists build mathematical climate models that simulate the underlying physics and chemistry of the many Earth systems and their complex interactions with each other. These computational models summarize the existing evidence, are tested for their ability to match past patterns, and are then used (together with other kinds of computer models) to forecast how the future may be affected by human activities. The impacts of climate change are uneven and may affect some regions, species, or human populations more severely than others.

Climate models are important tools for predicting, for example, when and where new water supplies will be needed, when and which natural resources will become scarce, how weather patterns may change and with what consequences, whether proposed technological concepts for controlling greenhouse gases will work, and how soon people will have to leave low-lying coastal areas if sea levels continue to rise. Meanwhile, important discoveries are being made—for example, about how the biosphere is responding to the climate changes that have already occurred, how the atmosphere is responding to changes in anthropogenic greenhouse gas emissions, and how greenhouse gases move between the ocean and the atmosphere over long periods. Such information, from models and other scientific and engineering efforts, will continue to be essential to planning for humanity's—and the global climate's—future.

It is important to note that although forecasting the consequences of environmental change is crucial to society, it involves so many complex phenomena and uncertainties that predictions, particularly long-term predictions, always have uncertainties. These arise not only from uncertainties in the underlying science but also from uncertainties about behavioral, economic, and political factors that affect human activity and changes in activity in response to recognition of the problem. However, it is clear not only that human activities play a major role in climate change but also that impacts of climate change—for example, increased frequency of severe storms due to ocean warming—have begun to influence human activities. The prospect of future impacts of climate change due to further increases in atmospheric carbon is prompting consideration of how to avoid or restrict such increases.

Grade Band Endpoints for ESS3.D

By the end of grade 2. [Intentionally left blank.]

By the end of grade 5. If Earth's global mean temperature continues to rise, the lives of humans and other organisms will be affected in many different ways.

By the end of grade 8. Human activities, such as the release of greenhouse gases from burning fossil fuels, are major factors in the current rise in Earth's mean surface temperature (global warming). Reducing human vulnerability to whatever climate changes do occur depend on the understanding of climate science, engineering capabilities, and other kinds of knowledge, such as understanding of human behavior and on applying that knowledge wisely in decisions and activities.

By the end of grade 12. Global climate models are often used to understand the process of climate change because these changes are complex and can occur slowly over Earth's history. Though the magnitudes of humans' impacts are greater than they have ever been, so too are humans' abilities to model, predict, and manage current and future impacts. Through computer simulations and other studies, important discoveries are still being made about how the ocean, the atmosphere, and the biosphere interact and are modified in response to human activities, as well as to changes in human activities. Thus science and engineering will be essential both to understanding the possible impacts of global climate change and to informing decisions about how to slow its rate and consequences—for humanity as well as for the rest of the planet.

REFERENCES

1. Earth Science Literacy Initiative. (2010). *Earth Science Literacy Principles: The Big Ideas and Supporting Concepts of Earth Science*. Arlington, VA: National Science Foundation. Available: http://www.earthscienceliteracy.org/es_literacy_6may10_.pdf [June 2011].

2. National Geographic Society. (2006). *Ocean Literacy: The Essential Principles of Ocean Science K-12*. Washington, DC: Author. Available: http://www.coexploration. org/oceanliteracy/documents/OceanLitChart.pdf [June 2011].

3. University Corporation for Atmospheric Research. (2008). *Atmospheric Science Literacy: Essential Principles and Fundamental Concepts of Atmospheric Science*. Boulder, CO: Author. Available: http://eo.ucar.edu/asl/pdfs/ASLbrochureFINAL.pdf [June 2011].

4. U.S. Global Change Research Program/Climate Change Science Program. (2009). *Climate Literacy: The Essential Principles of Climate Sciences*. Washington, DC: Author. Available: http://downloads.climatescience.gov/Literacy/Climate%20 Literacy%20Booklet%20Low-Res.pdf [June 2011].

8

Dimension 3
DISCIPLINARY CORE IDEAS—
ENGINEERING, TECHNOLOGY, AND
APPLICATIONS OF SCIENCE

In Chapter 3, we assert that "any [science] education that focuses predominantly on the detailed products of scientific labor—the facts of science—without developing an understanding of how those facts were established or that ignores the many important applications of science in the world misrepresents science and marginalizes the importance of engineering." This statement has two implications for science education standards in general and for this report's framework in particular. The first is that students should learn how scientific knowledge is acquired and how scientific explanations are developed. The second is that students should learn how science is utilized, in particular through the engineering design process, and they should come to appreciate the distinctions and relationships between engineering, technology, and applications of science (ETS). These three terms are defined in Box 8-1.

Chapter 3 describes how an understanding of engineering practices can develop as they are used in the classroom to help students acquire and apply science knowledge. There is also a domain of knowledge related to these practices, and it constitutes the framework's first ETS core idea—ETS1: Engineering Design. Although there is not yet broad agreement on the full set of core ideas in engineering [1], an emerging consensus is that design is a central practice of engineering; indeed, design is the focus of the vast majority of K-12 engineering curricula currently in use. The committee is aware that engineers not only design new technologies, but they also sometimes fabricate, operate, inspect, and maintain them. However, from a teaching and learning point of view, it is the iterative cycle of design that offers the greatest potential for applying science knowledge in the

BOX 8-1

DEFINITIONS OF TECHNOLOGY, ENGINEERING, AND APPLICATIONS OF SCIENCE

Technology is any modification of the natural world made to fulfill human needs or desires [2].

Engineering is a systematic and often iterative approach to designing objects, processes, and systems to meet human needs and wants [2].

An application of science is any use of scientific knowledge for a specific purpose, whether to do more science; to design a product, process, or medical treatment; to develop a new technology; or to predict the impacts of human actions.

classroom and engaging in engineering practices. The components of this core idea include understanding how engineering problems are defined and delimited, how models can be used to develop and refine possible solutions to a design problem, and what methods can be employed to optimize a design.

The second ETS core idea calls for students to explore, as its name implies, the "Links Among Engineering, Technology, Science, and Society" (ETS2). The applications of science knowledge and practices to engineering, as well as to such areas as medicine and agriculture, have contributed to the technologies and the systems that support them that serve people today. Insights gained from scientific discovery have altered the ways in which buildings, bridges, and cities are constructed; changed the operations of factories; led to new methods of generating and distributing energy; and created new modes of travel and communication. Scientific insights have informed methods of food production, waste disposal, and the diagnosis and treatment of disease. In other words, science-based, or science-improved, designs of technologies and systems affect the ways in which people interact with each other and with the environment, and thus these designs deeply influence society.

In turn, society influences science and engineering. Societal decisions, which may be shaped by a variety of economic, political, and cultural factors, establish goals and priorities for technologies' improvement or replacement. Such decisions also set limits—in controlling the extraction of raw materials, for example, or in setting allowable emissions of pollution from mining, farming, and industry. Goals, priorities, and limits are needed for regulating new technologies, which can have deep impacts on society and the environment. The impacts may not have been anticipated when the technologies were introduced (e.g., refrigerant gases that depleted stratospheric ozone) or may build up over time to levels that require mitigation (toxic pesticides, lead in gasoline). Thus the balancing of technologies' costs, benefits, and risks is a critical element of ETS2. Box 8-2 summarizes the framework's two ETS core ideas and their components.

The fields of science and engineering are mutually supportive. New technologies expand the reach of science, allowing the study of realms previously inaccessible to investigation; scientists depend on the work of engineers to produce the instruments and computational tools they need to conduct research. Engineers in turn depend on the work of scientists to understand how different technologies work so they can be improved; scientific discoveries are exploited to create new technologies in the first place. Scientists and engineers often work together in teams, especially in new fields, such as nanotechnology or synthetic biology that blur the lines between science and engineering. Students should come to understand these interactions and at increasing levels of sophistication as they mature. Their appreciation of the interface of science, engineering, and society should give them deeper insights into local, national, and global issues.

BOX 8-2

CORE AND COMPONENT IDEAS IN ENGINEERING, TECHNOLOGY, AND APPLICATIONS OF SCIENCE

Core Idea ETS1: Engineering Design

ETS1.A: Defining and Delimiting an Engineering Problem

ETS1.B: Developing Possible Solutions

ETS1.C: Optimizing the Design Solution

Core Idea ETS2: Links Among Engineering, Technology, Science, and Society

ETS2.A: Interdependence of Science, Engineering, and Technology

ETS2.B: Influence of Engineering, Technology, and Science on Society and the Natural World

---

The 2010 National Academy of Engineering report *Standards for K-12 Engineering Education?* [1] concluded that it is not appropriate at present to develop standalone K-12 engineering standards. But the report also made it clear that engineering concepts and skills are already embedded in existing standards for science and technology education, at both the state and national levels—and the report recommended that this practice continue. In addition, it affirmed the value of teaching engineering ideas, particularly engineering design, to young students.

In line with those conclusions and recommendations, the goal of this section of the framework—and of this chapter—is not to replace current K-12 engineering and technology courses. The chapter's goal is rather to strengthen the science education provided to K-12 students by making the connections between engineering, technology, and applications of science explicit, both for standards developers and curriculum developers. In that way, we hope to ensure that all students, whatever their path through K-12 education, gain an appreciation of these connections.

Core Idea ETS1   Engineering Design

How do engineers solve problems?

The design process—engineers' basic approach to problem solving—involves many different practices. They include problem definition, model development and use, investigation, analysis and interpretation of data, application of mathematics and computational thinking, and determination of solutions. These engineering practices incorporate specialized knowledge about criteria and constraints, modeling and analysis, and optimization and trade-offs.

ETS1.A: DEFINING AND DELIMITING AN ENGINEERING PROBLEM

What is a design for?
What are the criteria and constraints of a successful solution?

The engineering design process begins with the identification of a problem to solve and the specification of clear goals, or criteria, that the final product or system must meet. Criteria, which typically reflect the needs of the expected end-user of a technology or process, address such things as how the product or system will function (what job it will perform and how), its durability, and its cost. Criteria should be quantifiable whenever possible and stated so that one can tell if a given design meets them.

Engineers must contend with a variety of limitations, or constraints, when they engage in design. Constraints, which frame the salient conditions under which the problem must be solved, may be physical, economic, legal, political, social, ethical, aesthetic, or related to time and place. In terms of quantitative measurements, constraints may include limits on cost, size, weight, or performance, for example. And although constraints place restrictions on a design, not all of them are permanent or absolute.

Grade Band End Points for ETS1.A

By the end of grade 2. A situation that people want to change or create can be approached as a problem to be solved through engineering. Such problems may have many acceptable solutions. Asking questions, making observations, and gathering information are helpful in thinking about problems. Before beginning to design a solution, it is important to clearly understand the problem.

By the end of grade 5. Possible solutions to a problem are limited by available materials and resources (constraints). The success of a designed solution is determined by considering the desired features of a solution (criteria). Different proposals for solutions can be compared on the basis of how well each one meets the specified criteria for success or how well each takes the constraints into account.

By the end of grade 8. The more precisely a design task's criteria and constraints can be defined, the more likely it is that the designed solution will be successful. Specification of constraints includes consideration of scientific principles and other relevant knowledge that are likely to limit possible solutions (e.g., familiarity with the local climate may rule out certain plants for the school garden).

By the end of grade 12. Design criteria and constraints, which typically reflect the needs of the end-user of a technology or process, address such things as the product's or system's function (what job it will perform and how), its durability, and limits on its size and cost. Criteria and constraints also include satisfying any requirements set by society, such as taking issues of risk mitigation into account, and they should be quantified to the extent possible and stated in such a way that one can tell if a given design meets them.

Humanity faces major global challenges today, such as the need for supplies of clean water and food or for energy sources that minimize pollution, which can be addressed through engineering. These global challenges also may

have manifestations in local communities. But whatever the scale, the first thing that engineers do is define the problem and specify the criteria and constraints for potential solutions.

ETS1.B: DEVELOPING POSSIBLE SOLUTIONS

What is the process for developing potential design solutions?

The creative process of developing a new design to solve a problem is a central element of engineering. This process may begin with a relatively open-ended phase during which new ideas are generated both by individuals and by group processes such as brainstorming. Before long, the process must move to the specification of solutions that meet the criteria and constraints at hand. Initial ideas may be communicated through informal sketches or diagrams, although they typically become more formalized through models. The ability to build and use physical, graphical, and mathematical models is an essential part of translating a design idea into a finished product, such as a machine, building, or any other working system. Because each area of engineering focuses on particular types of systems (e.g., mechanical, electrical, biotechnological), engineers become expert in the elements that such systems need. But whatever their fields, all engineers use models to help develop and communicate solutions to design problems.

Models allow the designer to better understand the features of a design problem, visualize elements of a possible solution, predict a design's performance, and guide the development of feasible solutions (or, if possible, the optimal solution). A physical model can be manipulated and tested for parameters of interest, such as strength, flexibility, heat conduction, fit with other components, and durability. Scale models and prototypes are particular types of physical models. Graphical models, such as sketches and drawings, permit engineers to easily share and discuss design ideas and to rapidly revise their thinking based on input from others.

Mathematical models allow engineers to estimate the effects of a change in one feature of the design (e.g., material composition, ambient temperature) on other features, or on performance as a whole, before the designed product

> Models allow the designer to better understand the features of a design problem, visualize elements of a possible solution, predict a design's performance, and guide the development of feasible solutions.

is actually built. Mathematical models are often embedded in computer-based simulations. Computer-aided design (CAD) and computer-aided manufacturing (CAM) are modeling tools commonly used in engineering.

Data from models and experiments can be analyzed to make decisions about modifying a design. The analysis may reveal performance information, such as which criteria a design meets, or predict how well the overall designed system or system component will behave under certain conditions. If analysis reveals that the predicted performance does not align with desired criteria, the design can be adjusted.

Grade Band Endpoints for ETS1.B

By the end of grade 2. Designs can be conveyed through sketches, drawings, or physical models. These representations are useful in communicating ideas for a problem's solutions to other people. To design something complicated, one may need to break the problem into parts and attend to each part separately but must then bring the parts together to test the overall plan.

By the end of grade 5. Research on a problem should be carried out—for example, through Internet searches, market research, or field observations—before beginning to design a solution. An often productive way to generate ideas is for people to work together to brainstorm, test, and refine possible solutions. Testing a solution involves investigating how well it performs under a range of likely conditions. Tests are often designed to identify failure points or difficulties, which suggest the elements of the design that need to be improved. At whatever stage, communicating with peers about proposed solutions is an important part of the design process, and shared ideas can lead to improved designs.

There are many types of models, ranging from simple physical models to computer models. They can be used to investigate how a design might work, communicate the design to others, and compare different designs.

By the end of grade 8. A solution needs to be tested, and then modified on the basis of the test results, in order to improve it. There are systematic processes for evaluating solutions with respect to how well they meet the criteria and constraints of a problem. Sometimes parts of different solutions can be combined to create a solution that is better than any of its predecessors. In any case, it is important to be able to communicate and explain solutions to others.

Models of all kinds are important for testing solutions, and computers are a valuable tool for simulating systems. Simulations are useful for predicting what would happen if various parameters of the model were changed, as well as for making improvements to the model based on peer and leader (e.g., teacher) feedback.

By the end of grade 12. Complicated problems may need to be broken down into simpler components in order to develop and test solutions. When evaluating solutions, it is important to take into account a range of constraints, including cost, safety, reliability, and aesthetics, and to consider social, cultural, and environmental impacts. Testing should lead to improvements in the design through an iterative procedure.

Both physical models and computers can be used in various ways to aid in the engineering design process. Physical models, or prototypes, are helpful in testing product ideas or the properties of different materials. Computers are useful for a variety of purposes, such as in representing a design in 3-D through CAD software; in troubleshooting to identify and describe a design problem; in running simulations to test different ways of solving a problem or to see which one is most efficient or economical; and in making a persuasive presentation to a client about how a given design will meet his or her needs.

ETS1.C: OPTIMIZING THE DESIGN SOLUTION

How can the various proposed design solutions be compared and improved?

Multiple solutions to an engineering design problem are always possible because there is more than one way to meet the criteria and satisfy the constraints. But the aim of engineering is not simply to design a solution to a problem but to design the best solution. Determining what constitutes "best," however, requires value judgments, given that one person's view of the optimal solution may differ from another's.

Optimization often requires making trade-offs among competing criteria. For example, as one criterion (such as lighter weight) is enhanced, another (such as unit cost) might be sacrificed (i.e., cost may be increased due to the higher cost of lightweight materials). In effect, one criterion is devalued or traded off for another that is deemed more important. When multiple possible design options are under consideration, with each optimized for different criteria, engineers may use a trade-off matrix to compare the overall advantages and disadvantages of the different proposed solutions.

The decision as to which criteria are critical and which ones can be traded off is a judgment based on the situation and the perceived needs of the end-user of the product or system. Because many factors—including environmental or health impacts, available technologies, and the expectations of users—change over time and vary from place to place, a design solution that is considered optimal at one time and place may appear far from optimal at other times and places. Thus different designs, each of them optimized for different conditions, are often needed.

Grade Band Endpoints for ETS1.C

By the end of grade 2. Because there is always more than one possible solution to a problem, it is useful to compare designs, test them, and discuss their strengths and weaknesses.

By the end of grade 5. Different solutions need to be tested in order to determine which of them best solves the problem, given the criteria and the constraints.

By the end of grade 8. There are systematic processes for evaluating solutions with respect to how well they meet the criteria and constraints of a problem. Comparing different designs could involve running them through the same kinds of tests and systematically recording the results to determine which design performs best. Although one design may not perform the best across all tests, identifying the characteristics of the design that performed the best in each test can provide useful information for the redesign process—that is, some of those characteristics may be incorporated into the new design. This iterative process of testing the most promising solutions and modifying what is proposed on the basis of the test results leads to greater refinement and ultimately to an optimal solution. Once such a suitable solution is determined, it is important to describe that solution, explain how it was developed, and describe the features that make it successful.

By the end of grade 12. The aim of engineering is not simply to find a solution to a problem but to design the best solution under the given constraints and criteria. Optimization can be complex, however, for a design problem with numerous desired qualities or outcomes. Criteria may need to be broken down into simpler ones that can be approached systematically, and decisions about the priority of certain criteria over others (trade-offs) may be needed. The comparison of multiple designs can be aided by a trade-off matrix. Sometimes a numerical weighting system can help evaluate a design against multiple criteria. When evaluating solutions, all relevant considerations, including cost, safety, reliability, and aesthetic, social, cultural, and environmental impacts, should be included. Testing should lead to design improvements through an iterative process, and computer simulations are one useful way of running such tests.

Core Idea ETS2   Links Among Engineering, Technology, Science, and Society

How are engineering, technology, science, and society interconnected?

New insights from science often catalyze the emergence of new technologies and their applications, which are developed using engineering design. In turn, new technologies open opportunities for new scientific investigations. Together, advances in science, engineering, and technology can have—and indeed have had—profound effects on human society, in such areas as agriculture, transportation, health care, and communication, and on the natural environment. Each system can change significantly when new technologies are introduced, with both desired effects and unexpected outcomes.

ETS2.A: INTERDEPENDENCE OF SCIENCE, ENGINEERING, AND TECHNOLOGY

What are the relationships among science, engineering, and technology?

The fields of science and engineering are mutually supportive, and scientists and engineers often work together in teams, especially in fields at the borders of science and

> Together, advances in science, engineering, and technology can have—and indeed have had—profound effects on human society.

engineering. Advances in science offer new capabilities, new materials, or new understanding of processes that can be applied through engineering to produce advances in technology. Advances in technology, in turn, provide scientists with new capabilities to probe the natural world at larger or smaller scales; to record, manage, and analyze data; and to model ever more complex systems with greater precision. In addition, engineers' efforts to develop or improve technologies often raise new questions for scientists' investigation.

Grade Band Endpoints for ETS2.A

By the end of grade 2. People encounter questions about the natural world every day. There are many types of tools produced by engineering that can be used in science to help answer these questions through observation or measurement. Observations and measurements are also used in engineering to help test and refine design ideas.

By the end of grade 5. Tools and instruments (e.g., rulers, balances, thermometers, graduated cylinders, telescopes, microscopes) are used in scientific exploration to gather data and help answer questions about the natural world. Engineering design can develop and improve such technologies. Scientific discoveries about the natural world can often lead to new and improved technologies, which are developed through the engineering design process. Knowledge of relevant scientific concepts and research findings is important in engineering.

By the end of grade 8. Engineering advances have led to important discoveries in virtually every field of science, and scientific discoveries have led to the development of entire industries and engineered systems. In order to design better technologies, new science may need to be explored (e.g., materials research prompted by desire for better batteries or solar cells, biological questions raised by medical problems). Technologies in turn extend the measurement, exploration, modeling, and computational capacity of scientific investigations.

By the end of grade 12. Science and engineering complement each other in the cycle known as research and development (R&D). Many R&D projects may involve scientists, engineers, and others with wide ranges of expertise. For example, developing a means for safely and securely disposing of nuclear waste will require the participation of engineers with specialties in nuclear engineering, transportation, construction, and safety; it is likely to require as well the contributions of scientists and other professionals from such diverse fields as physics, geology, economics, psychology, and sociology.

ETS2.B: INFLUENCE OF ENGINEERING, TECHNOLOGY, AND SCIENCE ON SOCIETY AND THE NATURAL WORLD

How do science, engineering, and the technologies that result from them affect the ways in which people live? How do they affect the natural world?

From the earliest forms of agriculture to the latest technologies, all human activity has drawn on natural resources and has had both short- and long-term consequences, positive as well as negative, for the health of both people and the natural environment. These consequences have grown stronger in recent human history. Society has changed dramatically, and human populations and longevity have increased, as advances in science and engineering have influenced the ways in which people interact with one another and with their surrounding natural environment.

Science and engineering affect diverse domains—agriculture, medicine, housing, transportation, energy production, water availability, and land use, among others. The results often entail deep impacts on society and the environment, including some that may not have been anticipated when they were introduced or that may build up over time to levels that require attention. Decisions about the use of any new technology thus involve a balancing of costs, benefits, and risks—aided, at times, by science and engineering. Mathematical modeling, for example, can help provide insight into the consequences of actions beyond the scale of place, time, or system complexity that individual human judgments can readily encompass, thereby informing both personal and societal decision making.

Human populations and longevity have increased, as advances in science and engineering have influenced the ways in which people interact with one another and with their surrounding natural environment.

Not only do science and engineering affect society, but society's decisions (whether made through market forces or political processes) influence the work of scientists and engineers. These decisions sometimes establish goals and priorities for improving or replacing technologies; at other times they set limits, such as in regulating the extraction of raw materials or in setting allowable levels of pollution from mining, farming, and industry.

Grade Band Endpoints for ETS2.B

By the end of grade 2. People depend on various technologies in their lives; human life would be very different without technology. Every human-made product is designed by applying some knowledge of the natural world and is built by using materials derived from the natural world, even when the materials are not themselves natural—for example, spoons made from refined metals. Thus, developing and using technology has impacts on the natural world.

By the end of grade 5. Over time, people's needs and wants change, as do their demands for new and improved technologies. Engineers improve existing technologies or develop new ones to increase their benefits (e.g., better artificial limbs), to decrease known risks (e.g., seatbelts in cars), and to meet societal demands (e.g., cell phones). When new technologies become available, they can bring about changes in the way people live and interact with one another.

By the end of grade 8. All human activity draws on natural resources and has both short- and long-term consequences, positive as well as negative, for the health of both people and the natural environment. The uses of technologies and any limitations on their use are driven by individual or societal needs, desires, and values; by the findings of scientific research; and by differences in such factors as climate, natural resources, and economic conditions. Thus technology use varies from region to region and over time. Technologies that are beneficial for a certain purpose may later be seen to have impacts (e.g., health-related, environmental) that were not foreseen. In such cases, new regulations on use or new technologies (to mitigate the impacts or eliminate them) may be required.

By the end of grade 12. Modern civilization depends on major technological systems, including those related to agriculture, health, water, energy, transportation, manufacturing, construction, and communications. Engineers continuously modify these technological systems by applying scientific knowledge and engineering design practices to increase benefits while decreasing costs and risks. Widespread adoption of technological innovations often depends on market forces or other societal demands, but it may also be subject to evaluation by scientists and engineers and to eventual government regulation. New technologies can have deep impacts on society and the environment, including some that were not anticipated or that may build up over time to a level that requires attention or mitigation. Analysis of costs, environmental impacts, and risks, as well as of expected benefits, is a critical aspect of decisions about technology use.

REFERENCES

1.	National Academy of Engineering. (2010). *Standards for K-12 Engineering Education?* Committee on Standards for K-12 Engineering Education. Washington, DC: The National Academies Press.

2.	National Assessment Governing Board. (2010). *Technology and Engineering Literacy Framework for the 2014 National Assessment of Educational Progress.* Available: http://www.nagb.org/publications/frameworks/prepub_naep_tel_framework_2014.pdf [April 2011].

PART III

REALIZING THE VISION

INTEGRATING THE THREE DIMENSIONS

This framework is designed to help realize a vision of science education in which students' experiences over multiple years foster progressively deeper understanding of science. Students actively engage in scientific and engineering practices in order to deepen their understanding of crosscutting concepts and disciplinary core ideas. In the preceding chapters, we detailed separately the components of the three dimensions: scientific and engineering practices, crosscutting concepts, and disciplinary core ideas. In order to achieve the vision embodied in the framework and to best support students' learning, all three dimensions need to be integrated into the system of standards, curriculum, instruction, and assessment.

WHAT INTEGRATION INVOLVES

The committee recognizes that integrating the three dimensions in a coherent way is challenging and that examples of how it can be achieved are needed. We also acknowledge that there is no single approach that defines how to integrate the three dimensions into standards, curriculum, instruction, and assessment. One can in fact envision many different ways to achieve such integration, with the main components of the framework being conveyed with a high degree of fidelity, but with different choices as to when to stress a particular practice or crosscutting idea. For these reasons, in this chapter we offer only preliminary examples of the type of integration we envision, noting that the development of standards, curriculum, instruction, and assessment that successfully integrates the three dimensions is an area ripe for research and innovation.

Because standards guide and shape curriculum, instruction, and assessment, the task of integrating the three dimensions of the framework for K-12 science education begins with the development of standards. A major task for developers will be to create standards that integrate the three dimensions. The committee suggests that this integration should occur in the standards statements themselves and in performance expectations that link to the standards.

Standards and performance expectations that are aligned to the framework must take into account that students cannot fully understand scientific and engineering ideas without engaging in the practices of inquiry and the discourses by which such ideas are developed and refined [1-3]. At the same time, they cannot learn or show competence in practices except in the context of specific content. For example, students ask questions or design investigations about particular phenomena, such as the growth of plants, the motion of objects, and the phases of the moon. Furthermore, crosscutting concepts have value because they provide students with connections and intellectual tools that are related across the differing areas of disciplinary content and can enrich their application of practices and their understanding of core ideas. For example, being aware that it is useful to analyze diverse things—such as the human body or a watershed—as systems can help students generate productive questions for further study. Thus standards and performance expectations must be designed to gather evidence of students' ability to apply the practices and their understanding of the crosscutting concepts in the contexts of specific applications in multiple disciplinary areas.

In the committee's judgment, specification of "performance expectations" is an essential component of standards. This term refers to statements that describe activities and outcomes that students are expected to achieve in order to demonstrate their ability to understand and apply the knowledge described in the disciplinary core ideas. Following the model of the College Board's *Science Standards for College Success,* we agree that "performance expectations specify what students should know, understand, and be able to do. . . . They also illustrate how students engage in science practices to develop a better understanding of the essential knowledge. These expectations support targeted instruction and assessment by providing tasks that are measurable and observable" [4].

In this chapter we provide two examples of how the three dimensions might be brought together in performance expectations. The first example is based on a component of one of the core ideas in the life sciences (see Table 9-1), the other on a component of a core idea in the physical sciences (see Table 9-2).

The three dimensions will also need to be integrated into curriculum and instruction. A detailed discussion of all the ways in which practices, crosscutting concepts, and disciplinary core ideas can be integrated into curriculum and instruction is beyond the scope of the framework. However, in addition to the examples of performance expectations presented in Tables 9-1 and 9-2, we provide a single example that shows first steps toward this kind of integration. This example, which draws on the first component of the first physical science core idea—PS1.A: Structure and Properties of Matter—shows how a disciplinary core idea can be developed using particular practices and linked to particular crosscutting concepts for each grade band. It also describes some of the ways in which students might be asked to use specific practices to demonstrate their understanding of core ideas. Finally, the example incorporates boundary statements that make explicit what is *not* expected of students at a given level. The committee recommends that boundary statements be incorporated into standards so as to provide guidance for curriculum developers and designers of instruction. Such boundaries serve two purposes: (1) to delimit what level of detail is appropriate and (2) to indicate what knowledge related to a core idea may be too challenging for all students to master by the end of the grade band. However, any boundaries introduced here or in the specification of performance expectations will need to be subjected to further research and revisited over time, as more is learned about what level of expectation is appropriate in the context of curricula and instruction of the type envisaged in this framework.

It is important to note that this example is not intended as a complete description of instruction but only as a sketch of some experiences that can support learning of the core idea component. It illustrates how the practices both help students learn and provide a means by which they can demonstrate their understanding.

TWO ILLUSTRATIONS OF PERFORMANCE EXPECTATIONS

Two examples in this section illustrate how the three dimensions can be integrated into performance expectations. Table 9-1 presents the first example, which is based on a component—Organization for Matter and Energy Flow in Organisms (LS1.C)—of the first core idea in the life sciences. Table 9-2 presents the second example, which is based on a component—Structure and Properties of Matter (PS1.A)—of the first core idea in the physical sciences.

TABLE 9-1 Sample Performance Expectations in the Life Sciences

LS1. C: ORGANIZATION FOR MATTER AND ENERGY FLOW IN ORGANISMS		
	By the End of Grade 2	**By the End of Grade 5**
Tasks	Classify animals into two groups based on what they eat, and give three or more different examples of animals in each group.	Explain how animals use food and provide examples and evidence that support each type of use.
Criteria	Students should identify at least two of the three groups of animals (plant eaters, those that eat other animals, and those that eat both plants and other animals). The animals offered as examples should be correctly grouped. Students should be asked to offer evidence that supports the claim that these animals belong in the groups they have placed them in and asked to also consider and include animals from classes they have neglected (e.g., birds or fish, if they interpret animal to mean mammal).	A full explanation should be supported by diagrams and argument from evidence. It should include and support the claims that food provides materials for building body tissue and that it is the fuel used to produce energy for driving life processes. An example of building materials should include reference to growth and repair. Evidence for growth and repair should include use of some of food's weight in the process of adding body weight or tissue. An example of use of energy should include internal motion (e.g., heartbeat), external motion (self-propulsion, breathing), or maintenance of body temperature. Evidence for energy use should refer to the need for energy transfer in performing the activity. (At this level, detail is not expected on how food is actually used to provide energy.)

By the End of Grade 8	By the End of Grade 12
Construct an explanation for why the air a human breathes out contains a lower proportion of oxygen than the air he or she breathed in. The explanation should address where in the body the oxygen was used, how it was used, and how it was transported there.	Construct a model that describes the aerobic chemical processes that enable human cells to obtain and transfer energy to meet their needs.
A full explanation should contain a claim that oxygen's use in all cells of the body is part of the chemical reaction that releases energy from food. The claim should be supported with reasoning about (1) the role of oxygen in chemical reactions' release of energy and (2) how the oxygen and food are transported to the cells through the body's respiratory and circulatory systems.	The model should include diagrams and text to indicate that various compounds derived from food—including sugars and fats—react with oxygen and release energy either for the cells' immediate needs or to drive other chemical changes. It should include the example of producing adenosine triphosphate (ATP) from adenosine diphosphate (ADP) and indicate that this process increases stored energy. It should show that subsequent conversions between ATP and ADP release stored energy, for example, to cause contraction of muscles.

TABLE 9-1 Continued

LS1. C: ORGANIZATION FOR MATTER AND ENERGY FLOW IN ORGANISMS

	By the End of Grade 2	By the End of Grade 5	
Disciplinary Ideas	All animals need food in order to live and grow. They can get their food from plants or from other animals.	All living organisms require energy. Animals and plants alike generally need to take in air and water, animals must take in food, and plants need light and minerals; anaerobic life, such as bacteria in the gut, functions without air. Food provides animals with the materials they need for body repair and growth and is digested to release the energy they need to maintain body warmth and for motion.	
Practices	Presenting information (e.g., orally, visually by sorting pictures of animals into groups, or by writing labels or simple sentences that describe why animals are in different groups). Argument from evidence: supporting placement of animals in group.	Argumentation: Supporting claims with evidence.	
Crosscutting Concepts	Patterns: Grouping of animals by similarity of what they eat.	Patterns, similarity, and diversity: Living organisms have similar needs but diverse ways of obtaining food. Matter conservation.	

By the End of Grade 8	By the End of Grade 12
Through the process of photosynthesis, plants, algae (including phytoplankton), and many microorganisms use the energy from light to make sugars (food) from carbon dioxide from the atmosphere and water. This process also releases oxygen gas. These sugars can be used immediately or stored for growth or later use. Animals obtain food from eating plants or eating other animals. Within individual organisms, food moves through a series of chemical reactions in which it is broken down and rearranged to form new molecules, to support growth or to release energy. In animals and plants oxygen reacts with carbon-containing molecules (sugars) to provide energy and produce waste carbon dioxide; anaerobic bacteria achieve their energy needs in other chemical processes that do not need oxygen.	The process of photosynthesis converts light energy to stored chemical energy by converting carbon dioxide and water into sugars plus released oxygen. The sugar molecules thus formed contain carbon, hydrogen, and oxygen, and they are used to make amino acids and other carbon-based molecules that can be assembled into the larger molecules (such as proteins or DNA) needed to form new cells. As matter and energy flow through different organizational levels of living systems, chemical elements are recombined in different ways to form different products. As a result of these chemical reactions, energy is transferred from one system of interacting molecules to another. For example, aerobic cellular respiration is a chemical process whereby the bonds of food molecules and oxygen molecules are broken and new compounds are formed that can transport energy to muscles. Anaerobic cellular respiration follows a different and less efficient chemical pathway to provide energy in cells. Cellular respiration also releases the energy needed to maintain body temperature despite ongoing energy loss to the surrounding environment. Matter and energy are conserved in each change. This is true of all biological systems, from individuals to ecosystems.
Constructing explanations. Argument (supporting proposed explanation with arguments from evidence).	Modeling Presenting information (using labeled diagrams and text to present and explicate a model that describes and elucidates the process in question).
Cause and effect: Oxygen is needed for the chemical reaction that releases energy from food. Matter cycles and conservation; energy flows and conservation. Systems: Roles of respiratory and circulatory systems.	Systems: Organisms have systems for processes at the cellular level that are used to carry out the functions needed for life. Matter cycles and conservation; energy flows and conservation.

TABLE 9-2 Sample Performance Expectations in the Physical Sciences

PS1.A: STRUCTURE AND PROPERTIES OF MATTER

	By the End of Grade 2	By the End of Grade 5	
Tasks	Students support claims as to whether something is a solid or a liquid by providing descriptive evidence. Note: It is inappropriate at this grade level to use a material, such as sand, that is made of visible scale particles but flows as the test material for this question. Test examples should be readily classifiable.	Students provide strategies for collecting evidence as to whether matter still exists when it is not visible.	
Criteria	Descriptive evidence that a material is a solid would include the object's definite shape; for a liquid it would be that the material takes the shape of the container or that the material flows to the lowest part of the container.	Design includes ways to measure weight with and without an invisible material (gas or solute) present. For example, weighing the same container with different amounts of air, such as an inflated and deflated balloon or basketball; or weighing pure water and sugar before and after the sugar is dissolved in the water. (At this level, detail is not expected on how food is actually used to provide energy.)	

By the End of Grade 8	By the End of Grade 12
Students create atomic and molecular models to explain the differences between the solid, liquid, and gaseous states of a substance.	Students first develop models that describe a neutral atom and a negative or positive ion. They then use these models to describe the similarities and differences between the atoms of neighboring elements in the periodic table (side by side or one above the other).
The model should show that atoms/molecules in a solid (1) are close together, (2) are limited in motion but vibrate in place, and (3) cannot move past or around each other and thus are fixed in relative position. The model should also show that atoms/molecules in a liquid (1) are about as close together as in a solid, (2) are always disordered, (3) have greater freedom to move than in a solid, and (4) can slide past one another and move with a range of speeds. Finally, the model should show that atoms/molecules in a gas (1) are much farther away from each other than in solid or liquid form, (2) are always disordered, (3) move freely with a range of speeds, and (4) sometimes collide with each other or the container's walls and bounce off.	The models should show that the atom consists of an inner core called the nucleus, which consists of protons and neutrons; that the number of protons in the nucleus is the atomic number and determines the element; that the nucleus is much smaller in size than the atom; that the outer part of the atom contains electrons; that in a neutral atom, the number of electrons matches the number of protons (because protons and electrons have an opposite electric charge); and that ions have an additional or a "missing" electron.

Different isotopes of a given element have different numbers of neutrons, but in all stable cases the number of neutrons is not very different from the number of protons. |

TABLE 9-2 Continued

PS1.A: STRUCTURE AND PROPERTIES OF MATTER

	By the End of Grade 2	By the End of Grade 5
Criteria continued		
Disciplinary Ideas	Different kinds of matter exist (e.g., wood, metal, water). Solids and liquids have different properties, which can be used to sort them. Some substances can be either solid or liquid, depending on the temperature. Substances can be observed, weighed, and measured in other ways.	Matter of any type can be subdivided into particles (tiny pieces) that are too small to see, but even then the matter still exists and can be detected by other means (such as through its effects on other objects). Gases are matter in which the gas particles are moving freely around in space and can be detected by their impacts on surfaces (e.g., of a balloon) or on larger and visible objects (wind blowing leaves, dust suspended in air). The amount (weight) of matter is conserved when it changes form, even in transitions in which it seems to vanish (e.g., sugar in solution).

By the End of Grade 8	By the End of Grade 12
	The electrons occupy a set of "layered" states, with a given number allowed in each of the first few layers. (Details of orbitals and reasons behind the counting of states are not expected.) The "outermost" position of the electrons corresponds to the least strongly bound electrons. The filling level of the outermost layer can be used to explain chemical properties and the types of ions most readily formed.

Atoms side by side in the periodic table are close to each other in mass and differ by one in their numbers of protons. They have different chemical properties.

Atoms above or below the other in the periodic table have similar chemical properties but differ significantly in mass and atomic number. |
| Gases and liquids are made of molecules or inert atoms that are moving about relative to each other. In a liquid, the molecules are constantly in contact with others; in a gas they are widely spaced except when they happen to collide. In a solid, atoms are closely spaced and may vibrate in position but do not change relative locations. Solids may be formed from molecules or may be extended structures with repeating subunits (e.g., crystals, metals). The changes of state that occur with changes of temperature or pressure can be described and predicted using these three models (solid, liquid, or gas) of matter. (Predictions here are qualitative, not quantitative.) | Each atom has a charged substructure consisting of a nucleus (made from protons and neutrons) surrounded by electrons. The periodic table orders elements by the number of protons in the atom's nucleus and places those with similar chemical properties in columns. The repeating patterns of this table reflect patterns of outer electron states. |

TABLE 9-2 **Continued**

PS1.A: STRUCTURE AND PROPERTIES OF MATTER			
	By the End of Grade 2	**By the End of Grade 5**	
Practices	Argumentation (e.g., using criteria for solids and liquids to make the case that a substance is one or the other).	Designing investigations.	
Crosscutting Concepts	Patterns (a great diversity of solid and liquid materials exist, but certain features are similar for all solids and all liquids).	Matter cycles and conservation.	

The performance expectations shown in these tables describe what students are expected to know and how they should be able to use these two scientific ideas. In each table, the first two rows describe the tasks that students are expected to perform and the criteria by which their performance will be evaluated. The last three rows in the tables show the disciplinary ideas, practices, and crosscutting concepts that are to be brought together in performing the tasks. Examples are shown for four grade levels (2, 5, 8, and 12) to illustrate how the performance expectations should increase in sophistication during 12+ years of instruction. Across such a span, with appropriate learning experiences, students' conceptual knowledge increases in depth and sophistication, as does the nature of the practices. Thus performance expectations at the higher grades should reflect deeper understanding, more highly developed practices, and more complex reasoning.

Note that what we describe in Tables 9-1 and 9-2 is just an initial illustration of the performance expectations for each grade band. When standards are developed that are based on the framework, they will need to include performance expectations that cover all of the disciplinary core ideas, integrate practices, and link to crosscutting concepts when appropriate. For any given aspect of content knowledge, multiple practices and crosscutting concepts could be matched to that content to yield additional appropriate performance expectations. Assessments

By the End of Grade 8	By the End of Grade 12
Modeling Developing evidence-based explanations.	Modeling
Cause and effect: Changing the temperature causes changes in the motion of particles of matter. Systems and system models: Students model substances as systems composed of particles.	Structure and function: Atoms have structures that determine the chemical behavior of the element and the properties of substances. Patterns, similarity, and diversity: The periodic table can be used to see the patterns of chemical behavior based on patterns of atomic structure.

should thus use a broad set of performance expectations across the multiple items. In addition, the criteria used to judge the quality of a given performance outcome need to specify the features of the practice (e.g., a description, model, evidence-based explanation) that are relevant for the specific content and grade band.

As discussed in Chapter 4, the expectations regarding how the practices develop over the grade bands reflect an increasing competence in the use of information and the assembly of models, descriptions, explanations, and arguments. For some further examples of performance expectations that link content and practice similarly and that are appropriate for formulating both classroom-based and large-scale assessments of whether students have mastered particular standards, we refer the reader to the College Board's *Science Standards for College Success*. That volume provides numerous examples in the life sciences, physical sciences, and earth sciences [4].

ONE ILLUSTRATION OF INTEGRATING THE DIMENSIONS INTO CURRICULUM AND INSTRUCTION

This section describes through example how the three dimensions might be brought together in designing curriculum and instruction. The particular example involves the development of the Structure and Properties of Matter (PS1.A)—a component of the physical sciences core idea Matter and Its Interactions—through the integration of practices and crosscutting concepts (see Box S-1). The example illustrates, however, only one of many paths that integrate the practices and cross-cutting concepts in developing this component idea, and thus it is not intended to be prescriptive. Rather, the committee emphasizes that there are many different ways to explore the disciplinary core ideas through the practices and crosscutting concepts but that such exploration is critical to aid student's development and support the deep conceptual change needed to move their understanding of the world closer to that of well-established scientific understandings.

The central question of PS1.A is "How do particles combine to form the variety of matter one observes?" In the design of curriculum and instruction regarding answers to this question, four of the crosscutting concepts (flagged in italics below) play important roles. First, across all grade levels, the relation-ship of *structure and function* is a key concept in studying how the structure of matter relates to the properties of matter. Second, the concept of *patterns* can be explored from the earliest grades as students investigate the various types of matter, discover their commonalities, and devise ways of characterizing their properties. Third, starting in grades 3-5 and continuing through grade 12, stu-dents work with the concept of *systems and system models* as they cultivate their understanding of the particle model of matter; students progress from the macroscopic idea of particles to imagine and model the effects of invisibly small particles (in grades 3-5) to the atomic scale (in grades 7-8) and finally to the subatomic scales (in grades 9-12). Fourth, as students encounter the notion that matter is conserved, critical to their understanding is the crosscutting concept of *energy and matter: flows, cycles, and conservation.*

The narrative for each grade band begins with a statement of the grade band endpoint ("By the end of . . ."), and the succeeding text elaborates on the grade band progression of learning that builds toward that endpoint; discussion shows how the progression involves both crosscutting concepts that students come to appreciate and practices in which they might engage as they develop and demonstrate their understanding. The discussion is followed by a boundary statement, which specifies things that do *not* need to be included in the grade band. Standards developers also should include such boundaries so as to delimit how far students, of whatever grade, are expected to progress.

Grades K-2: Endpoint and Progression

By the end of grade 2. Different kinds of matter exist (e.g., wood, metal, water), and many of them can be either solid or liquid, depending on temperature. Matter can be described and classified by its observable properties (e.g., visual, aural, textural), by its uses, and by whether it occurs naturally or is manufactured. Different properties are suited to different purposes. A great variety of objects can be built up from a small set of pieces. Objects or samples of a substance can be weighed and their size can be described and measured. (Boundary: Volume is introduced only for liquid measure.)

Students' investigations of matter begin with guided experiences, designed by the teacher, that introduce them to various kinds of matter (e.g., wood, metal, water, clay) in multiple contexts and engage them in discussion about the matter's observable characteristics and uses. These experiences begin to elicit students' questions about matter, which they answer by conducting their own investigations and by making observations; the path of the investigation is jointly designed by teacher and students. Observations here include not only how things look but also how they feel, how they sound when tapped, how they smell, and, in carefully structured situations such as a cooking project, how they taste (although students should be warned not to taste unknown substances).

In the course of these experiences the teacher engages and guides students in identifying multiple ways of characterizing matter—such as solid and liquid, natural and manufactured, hard and soft, edible or inedible—and that different types of materials are suited to different uses. Across grades K-2, the variety of properties of matter that students recognize and the specificity with which they can characterize materials and their uses develop through experiences with different kinds of matter.

The ability to make measurements of quantities, such as length, liquid volume, weight, and temperature, begins in kindergarten with qualitative observations of relative magnitude. An understanding both of the arbitrariness and the importance of measurement units is supported by allowing students to develop their own units for length before introducing them to standard units. After students observe and measure a variety of solids and liquids, classroom discussions help them focus on identifying and characterizing the materials that objects are made from and the reasons why particular materials are chosen for particular tasks. Students are then asked to present evidence to support their claims about different kinds of matter and their uses. Across the grade span, students progress in their ability to make and justify claims about different kinds of matter, to describe and quantify those claims, and to do so both with specificity and knowledge of the various properties of matter.

Starting in kindergarten (or before), students manipulate a variety of building toys, such as wooden blocks, interlocking objects, or other construction sets, leading them to recognize that although what one can build depends on the things one is building from, many different objects can be constructed with multiple copies of a small set of different components. Although such recognition occurs implicitly, it is supported at the higher end of the grade band by explicit discussion of this aspect of material objects. Students come to understand more deeply that most objects can be broken down into various component pieces and that any "chunk" of uniform matter (e.g., a sheet of paper, a block of wood, a wedge of cheese) can be subdivided into smaller pieces of the same material.

Students' building efforts progress from free play to solving design problems, and teachers facilitate this progression by asking appropriate questions about the objects that students build, by having them draw diagrams of what they have built, and by directing their attention to built objects outside the classroom (so as to discuss what these objects are built from or features of their design). By grade 2, a student should be able to follow a plan, preplan designs for simple projects, and recognize the common design elements of certain types of objects and the properties required—why axles are needed for wheels, for example, or why metal would be used for a frying pan and why rubber or plastic would be suitable for rain boots.

The awareness that some materials (not just water but also chocolate, wax, and ice cream, for example) can be either liquid or solid depending on the temperature and that there is a characteristic temperature for each material at which this transition occurs is another important concept about matter that should be developed in this grade band through teacher-guided student experiences and investigations. The transition from liquid to gas is not stressed in this grade band, however, because the concept of gases other than air, or even the fact that air is matter, cannot readily be developed on the basis of students' observations and experiences.

Boundary Statements. In this grade band, crosscutting concepts are referred to when they support development of the idea under study, but they are not stressed as separate ideas. For example, students may be asked to recognize patterns in the use of particular materials, but the idea that patterns are an important phenomenon to investigate is not stressed. Similarly, classroom discussion may focus on the components of a machine (e.g., a bicycle, a toaster) and on the roles they play, but the idea of a system is not stressed. The ideas of parts too small to see, gases other than air, evaporation, and condensation are not stressed either, and the conservation of matter when burning or evaporating is not introduced. Mass and weight are not distinguished when examining matter quantity, and volume is introduced only for liquids.

Grades 3-5: Endpoint and Progression

By the end of grade 5. Matter of any type can be subdivided into particles that are too small to see, but even then the matter still exists and can be detected by other means (e.g., by weighing, by its effects on other objects). For example, a model that gases are made from matter particles too small to see that are moving freely around in space can explain such observations as the impacts of gas particles on surfaces (e.g., of a balloon) and on larger particles or objects (e.g., wind, dust suspended in air) and the appearance of visible scale water droplets in condensation, fog, and, by extension, clouds or contrails of a jet. The amount (weight) of matter is conserved when it changes form, even in transitions in which it seems to vanish (e.g., sugar in solution, evaporation in a closed container). Measurements of a variety of properties (e.g., hardness, reflectivity) can be used to identify particular materials. (Boundary: At this grade level, mass and weight are not distinguished, and no attempt is made to define the unseen particles or explain the atomic-scale mechanism of evaporation and condensation.)

Exploration of matter continues in this grade band with greater emphasis on detailed measurement of objects and materials, and the idea that matter is conserved even in transitions when it changes form or seems to disappear (as in dissolving) begins to be developed. A critical step is to recognize from experience that weight is an additive property of matter—namely, that the weight of a set of objects is the sum of the weights of the component objects. Once students understand that weight is a measure of how much matter is present, their observations in that regard—such as the total weight of the water and sugar being the same before and after dissolving, or the weight of the water formed by melting ice being equal to the weight of the ice that melted—can be used to convey the idea that matter is conserved across transitions. (The distinction between mass and weight is not introduced at this grade band.)

Two important ideas—that gas is a form of matter and that it is modeled as a collection of particles (i.e., pieces of matter too small to see) moving around in space—are developed by the end of grade 5, with careful support from guided investigations and the use of simulations. Multiple learning experiences are needed for students to shift their concept of matter to include the gaseous state, and such experiences must accordingly be structured over time.

First, the idea that matter can be subdivided into ever-smaller pieces without changing the total amount of matter (regardless of how small the pieces are) is developed by carrying out a dividing and weighing activity with one or more substances. The students should engage in discussions of what would happen if one were to keep subdividing until the pieces were too small to see.

Next, the idea that matter is made of particles too small to see can be extended to encompass gases as a form of matter. Air is the first familiar-yet-

invisible material that students can learn to identify as a gas made of particles. This recognition is supported by the use of an appropriately designed simulation of particles moving around in a container, as well as by observations aimed at emphasizing the properties of air as a material (e.g., one can feel it, it affects other things, a balloon blown up weighs more than an empty balloon). Students should be helped to relate the observed properties of air to the characteristics of the simulation (e.g., the impacts of particles on surfaces) and also to their own experiences with visible particles, such as the movement of dust particles in air or the impacts of blowing sand on the skin.

Also by the end of grade 5, students' understanding of gases needs to progress a step beyond recognizing air as samples of materials. It should include recognition that the water remains the same kind of matter during evaporation and condensation, just as it does during melting and freezing. The fact that the amount of material remains the same as water is frozen and then melted again can be observed by weighing, and such continuity can be reaffirmed by freezing and melting a variety of other materials (e.g., various juices). Similarly, the amount of material remains the same as water is put through sequences of evaporation and condensation in a closed system (such as a plastic container with a lid)—a fact that can be confirmed with observation and measurement. The stress here is on qualitative comparative observations, not on precision measurements.

The additivity of volumes is a subtler concept than the addition of weights, and it must be developed with care so as not to introduce misconceptions. For like materials (e.g., water plus water, sand plus sand), volume is additive, but students should also be engaged in experiences in which volumes (as measured by a graduated container) do not combine additively, as when sand is added to a container of marbles, or rocks and pebbles are mixed together. With such examples, students can shift their perception of continuous matter to one that allows for a particle-based substructure.

In this grade band, however, definition of the particles involved is not stressed; rather, the objective is for students to begin developing and using models to explain observations. For example, they can build a model to explain why, when a volume of water is added to a volume of rubbing alcohol, the volume of the combined sample is less than the sum of the volumes of the starting samples. (Note that this experience requires careful measurement with appropriate measuring equipment—an ability that also is developed across this grade band.) The evolution of students' mental models of matter is facilitated by relating this experience to similar situations with macroscopic objects, such as the mixture of sand and marbles described above, and to simulations that provide an explicit visible model of the situation. In any case, this example is just one of the many ways in which students can begin to see that observed properties of matter are explainable in terms of a particle model.

Students' understanding of the categories of matter, properties of matter, and uses of matter is refined and expanded across this grade band. Categories of matter, such as metals and crystals, and the names of particular materials, such as iron or silicon, may be introduced in conjunction with experiences or investigations that help students identify the characteristics that distinguish one material from others, thereby allowing it to be categorized. However, no stress is placed on chemical formulas or symbols for substances. Based on studies of various kinds of matter and their properties (such as heat conduction, elasticity, or reflectivity), students can present evidence that measurements of a variety of properties are useful in identifying particular materials. Similarly, based on measurements that identify solid to liquid and liquid to gas transition temperatures for more than one substance, students generalize their understanding that substances change state at specific temperatures. Students also are encouraged to apply their understanding of matter in selecting materials for design purposes.

Throughout this grade band, all of the scientific and engineering practices begin to be developed explicitly, and the crosscutting concepts (flagged in italics below) are used to begin making linkages across disciplinary core ideas—for example, to connect students' understanding of *matter conservation* (e.g., in evaporation and condensation, as described above) to their understanding of the water cycle in earth science. Students also note *patterns* in their observations, recognizing that any pattern can be a clue that needs further investigation and explanation. By the end of grade 5, students should have developed both the ability and the habit of creating models, giving model-based explanations, and relating their models to evidence and inferences drawn from observations. Furthermore, building on their more general models of the substructure of matter, they recognize that it is useful to develop an explicit *system model* to understand any given system.

Boundary Statements. In this grade band, particles are introduced as pieces of matter too small to see, but their nature is not further specified; atoms and the distinction between atoms and molecules are not introduced. If particular pure substances, such as oxygen or iron, are named, the chemical formulas are not introduced; students' learning is confined to the familiar names of these substances, their important properties, and their roles in everyday experience. Mass and weight are not distinguished, and although solid volume can be introduced, students are not expected to be able to calculate volume, except for that of a rectangular solid. Evaporation and condensation are introduced as observable phenomena, but the processes by which they take place are not treated at this grade level. Nor is the calculation of density from measured weight and volume stressed, although a qualitative sense of density as a property of matter and of relative densities of different materials can be developed.

GRADES 6-8: ENDPOINT AND PROGRESSION

By the end of grade 8. All substances are made from some 100 different types of atoms, which combine with one another in various ways. Atoms form molecules that range in size from two to thousands of atoms. Pure substances are made from a single type of atom or molecule; each pure substance has characteristic physical and chemical properties (for any bulk quantity under given conditions) that can be used to identify it.

Gases and liquids are made of molecules or inert atoms that are moving about relative to each other. In a liquid, the molecules are constantly in contact with others; in a gas, they are widely spaced except when they happen to collide. In a solid, atoms are closely spaced and may vibrate in position but do not change relative locations. Solids may be formed from molecules, or they may be extended structures with repeating subunits (e.g., crystals). The changes of state that occur with variations in temperature or pressure can be described and predicted using these models of matter. (Boundary: Predictions here are qualitative, not quantitative.)

In this grade band, investigations are designed to enhance students' ability to create explicit models and to use them for developing explanations of observations, for building their conceptions of matter, and for analyzing new situations. In particular, students develop and apply their understanding of the particle model of matter. In grade 6 the particles are still not defined, but representations of the states of matter (solid, liquid, and gas) include the concept that, although the particles are in motion in all three states, the spacing and degree of relative motion differ substantially between them. The role of forces between particles also begins to be discussed in grade 6—topics include the recognition that particles in a solid are held together by the forces of mutual attraction and repulsion (which act like springs) and that there are forces between particles in a gas that cause them to change their paths when they collide. The core idea of energy developed across this grade band must similarly be applied in the context of models of matter—for example, to understand the temperature dependence of states of matter—and to develop consistent descriptions of such phenomena as convection and conduction, that is, heat transfer with and without fluid motion, respectively.

Across grades 6-8, investigations of matter continue to become more precise, and students' understanding of the particle model of matter continues to be refined through comparisons with empirical observations and suggested models that explain them. By grade 8, students should be able to distinguish between an atom and a molecule and the roles they play in the various states of matter. Students' own investigations and their experiences in examining data from external sources should be structured to help them examine their own understanding of the particle model and help them move toward a better understanding. Students continue to draw on and cultivate their skills in mathematics and language, in recognition of the need for precision in both the measurement and interpretation of data; precision is critical to supporting evidence-derived explanations of the behavior of matter. Students should be expected to apply their understanding of matter in the context of earth and life sciences, recognizing that matter conservation, energy conservation, and matter flows are critical concepts for understanding many large-scale phenomena.

Using evidence collected and analyzed from their own investigations, evidence from outside sources (e.g., atomic images), and the results of simulations, students confirm a model that matter consists of atoms in motion—with forces between the atoms—and that the motion of the particles is temperature dependent. Students can connect this particle model of matter to observations and present arguments based on it to defend the following claims: All substances are made from approximately 100 different types of atoms, which combine with one another in various ways; atoms form molecules that range in size from two to thousands of atoms; gases and liquids are made of molecules or inert atoms, which are moving about relative to each other; and in a solid, atoms may vibrate in position but do not change relative locations.

Students can select different materials as examples to support the claim that solids may be formed from molecules or may be extended structures with repeating subunits (e.g., crystals, metals). Recognizing that pure substances are made from a single type of atom or molecule, students present evidence to support the claim that each pure substance has characteristic physical and chemical properties that can be used to identify it.

Boundary Statement. In this grade band, the forces and structures within atoms and their role in the forces *between* atoms are not introduced—nor are the periodic table and the variety of types of chemical bonds.

Grades 9-12: Endpoint and Progression

By the end of grade 12. Each atom has a charged substructure consisting of a nucleus, which is made of protons and neutrons, surrounded by electrons. The periodic table orders elements horizontally by the number of protons in the atom's nucleus and places those with similar chemical properties in columns. The repeating patterns of this table reflect patterns of outer electron states. The structure and interactions of matter at the bulk scale are determined by electrical forces within and between atoms. Stable forms of matter are those in which the electric and magnetic field energy is minimized. A stable molecule has less energy, by an amount known as the binding energy, than the same set of atoms separated; one must provide at least this energy in order to take the molecule apart.

At this grade band, the structures within atoms and their relationships to the forces *between* atoms are introduced. Students' understanding of the particle model of matter is developed and refined through investigations and analysis of data, both their own and those from experiments that cannot be undertaken in the science classroom. Increased sophistication, both of their model-based explanations and the argumentation by which evidence and explanation are linked, is developed through mathematical and language skills appropriate to the grade level.

Students' conceptual models of matter are extended, based on evidence from their own and others' investigations, to include the following: atoms have a charged substructure of a nucleus (made from protons and neutrons) surrounded by electrons; the periodic table orders elements by the number of protons and places those with similar chemical properties in the same columns; and the repeating patterns of this table reflect patterns of outer electron states. Students can cite evidence that supports this model and relate it to the properties of matter, particularly to the variety of elements, isotopes, and chemical properties.

Students use their understanding of electrical interactions to support claims that the structure and interactions of matter at the bulk scale (link to PS2.A) are determined by electrical forces within and between atoms. Students also use their understanding of stability within systems (link to PS2.B) and the relationship between forces and energy (link to PS3.C) to support claims that stable forms of matter are those that minimize the energy in electric and magnetic fields within the system. Students can then argue that this model is consistent with the propositions that a stable molecule has less energy (by an amount known as the binding energy, which is the sum of all bond energies) than the same set of atoms separated and at rest, that one must provide at least this energy to break the molecule apart, and that it likewise takes energy to break apart stable solid matter.

Boundary Statement. The following topics are not required: the structures within protons and neutrons, the existence of quarks, and the relationship between (a) the strong forces between quarks and (b) the "strong nuclear" force between protons and neutrons.

REFERENCES

1. National Research Council. (2007). *Taking Science to School: Learning and Teaching Science in Grades K-8.* Committee on Science Learning, Kindergarten Through Eighth Grade. R.A. Duschl, H.A. Schweingruber, and A.W. Shouse (Eds.). Board on Science Education, Center for Education. Division of Behavioral and Social Sciences and Education. Washington, DC: The National Academies Press.
2. Krajcik, J., McNeill, K.L., and Reiser, B.J. (2008). Learning-goals-driven design model: Curriculum materials that align with national standards and incorporate project-based pedagogy. *Science Education, 92*(1), 1-32.
3. Berland, L.K., and McNeill, K.L. (2010). A learning progression for scientific argumentation: Understanding student work and designing supportive instructional contexts. *Science Education, 94*(1), 765-793.
4. College Board. (2009). *Science College Board Standards for College Success.* Available: http://professionals.collegeboard.com/profdownload/cbscs-science-standards-2009.pdf [March 2011].

IMPLEMENTATION
Curriculum, Instruction, Teacher Development, and Assessment

I n this chapter, we consider the changes needed across the K-12 science education system so that implementation of the framework and related standards can more readily occur. Standards provide a vision for teaching and learning, but the vision cannot be realized unless the standards permeate the education system and guide curriculum, instruction, teacher preparation and professional development, and student assessment.

By "system" we mean the institutions and mechanisms that shape and support science teaching and learning in the classroom. Thus the system includes organization and administration at state, district, and school levels as well as teacher education, certification requirements, curriculum and instructional resources, assessment policies and practices, and professional development programs. Our use of the term "system," however, does not necessarily imply that all the components of the science education system are well aligned and work together seamlessly. Rather, adopting the idea of a system (1) acknowledges the complex and interacting forces that shape learning and teaching at the classroom level and (2) provides an analytic tool for thinking about these various forces.

The next section is an overview of four major components of the K-12 science education system, and in succeeding sections we consider each of them in turn. For each component, we discuss what must be in place in order for it to align with the framework's vision.

These discussions do not include formal recommendations and are not framed as standards for each component, because the committee was not asked to undertake the kind of extensive review—of the research on teacher education, curriculum, instruction, professional development, and assessment—that would be required in order to make explicit recommendations for related sets of standards for each component. Indeed, the committee and the timeline for our work would have required considerable expansion in order to give such an endeavor adequate treatment.

The committee instead relied on a number of recent reports from the National Research Council (NRC) that did examine research related to each of the components discussed in this chapter. They include *Knowing What Students Know* [1], *Investigating the Influence of Standards* [2], *Systems for State Science Assessment* [3], *America's Lab Report* [4], *Taking Science to School* [5], and *Preparing Teachers* [6]. The discussions in the following sections are based primarily on these reports.

Explicit standards for teaching, professional development, education programs, and the education system were included in the original *National Science Education Standards* (*NSES*) published by the NRC in 1996 [7]. Although many of these standards are still relevant to K-12 science education today, the committee did not undertake a thorough review of these portions of the *NSES*. Instead, given our charge, we focused on the *NSES* standards that describe science content. For future efforts, we suggest that a review of the other *NSES* standards, in light of the research and development that has taken place since 1996, would be very valuable; such a review could serve as an important complement to the current effort.

KEY COMPONENTS OF K-12 SCIENCE EDUCATION

The key components of science education that we consider in this chapter are curriculum, instruction, teacher development, and assessment. It is difficult to focus on any particular component without considering how it is influenced by—and how it in turn influences—the other components. For example, what students learn is clearly related to what they are taught, which itself depends on many things: state science standards; the instructional materials available in the commercial market and from organizations (such as state and federal agencies) with science-related missions; the curriculum adopted by the local board of education; teachers' knowledge and practices for teaching; how teachers elect to use the curriculum; the kinds of resources, time, and space that teachers have for their instructional work; what the community values regarding student learning; and how local, state, and national standards and assessments influence instructional practice.

We are not attempting to provide a full discussion of all possible influences on science education; rather, we focus on four major components that have critical roles to play and how they will need to evolve in order to implement the kind of science education envisaged by this framework. Our discussion also does not include detailed consideration of the process of gaining support for adoption of standards—for example, developing public will and engaging with state and local policy makers. We also do not discuss informal settings for science education, which provide many opportunities for learning science that complement and extend students' experiences in school [8].

A Complex System

Much of the complexity of science education systems derives from the multiple levels of control—classroom, school, school district, state, and national—across which curriculum, instruction, teacher development, and assessment operate; thus what ultimately happens in a classroom is significantly affected by decision making distributed across the levels and multiple channels of influence.

Each teacher ultimately decides how and what to teach in his or her classroom, but this decision is influenced by decisions at higher levels of the system. First, there is the effect of decisions made at the school level, which include the setting of expectations and sequences in certain content areas as well as the principal's, department chairs', or team leaders' explicit and implicit signals about teaching and learning priorities [9]. Leaders at the school level may also make decisions about the time and resources [10] allocated to different subjects within guidelines and requirements set by the state, teacher hiring and assignments, the usage of science labs, and, in some cases, the presence of a school building's laboratory space in the first place. The school leaders' expectations, priorities, and decisions establish a climate that encourages or discourages particular pedagogical approaches, collegial interactions, or inservice programs [11, 12]. Furthermore, a school's degree of commitment to equity—to providing opportunities for all students to learn the same core content—can influence how students are scheduled into classes, which teachers are hired, how they are assigned to teach particular classes, and how instructional resources are identified and allocated [13, 14].

At the next level of the system, school districts are responsible for (1) ensuring implementation of state and federal education policies; (2) formulating additional local education policies; and (3) creating processes for selecting curricula, purchasing curriculum materials, and determining the availability of instructional resources. District leaders develop local school budgets, set instructional priorities, provide instructional guidance, create incentive structures, and influence the willingness and capacity of schools and teachers to explore and implement different instructional techniques. Teacher hiring and school assignment may also occur at the district level. Districts may provide support structures and professional development networks that enhance the capacity of schools and teachers to implement effective science curriculum, instruction, and formative assessments.

The state level is a particularly important one for schools. States, being constitutionally responsible for elementary and secondary education, play major roles in regulating and funding education—they provide nearly half of all public school revenues [15], with most of the remainder coming from local property taxes. Each state must develop and administer its own policies on standards, curriculum, materials selection and adoption, teacher licensure, student assessment, and educational accountability. Across states, the authority of schools and districts to formulate policy varies considerably. Some states have relatively high "local control," with more power residing at the district level; others states have more centralized control, with more influence exerted by the state.

Finally, although the federal government contributes less than 10 percent of all funds invested by states and local districts in education [16], it influences education at all levels through a combination of regulations, public advocacy, and monetary incentives. For example, the Elementary and Secondary Education Act (No Child Left Behind Act) requires the testing of students at specific grade levels.

There are also influences from the other stakeholders that have an interest in science education, such as parents, businesses, local communities, and professional societies. These stakeholders can become engaged at all levels—national, state, local—and often have a significant influence on what is taught and how it is taught.

Clearly, a science education system must be responsive to a variety of influences—some that emanate from the top down, some from the bottom up, and some laterally from outside formal channels. States and school districts generally exert considerable influence over science curricula, and they set policies for time

| A science education system must be responsive to a variety of influences—some that emanate from the top down, some from the bottom up, and some laterally from outside formal channels. |

spent on science. However, classroom teachers in the lower grades may have some latitude in how they use instructional time to meet district and state mandates. In high school, by contrast, district and state graduation requirements affect the types and numbers of science courses that all students are required to take. Beyond such minimum requirements, students and their parents determine the overall science course load that each student takes.

The Importance of Coherence in the System

The complexity of the system—with several components that are affected by or operate at different levels—presents a challenge to implementation of the framework and its related standards. Successful implementation requires that all of the components across the levels cohere or work together in a harmonious or logical way to support the new vision. This kind of system-wide coherence is difficult to achieve, yet it is essential to the success of standards-based science education.

In the literature on education policy, the term "coherence" is often used interchangeably with another term—"alignment" [17-19]—although others have suggested that alignment alone is not sufficient to make a system coherent [20]. For example, not only would a coherent curriculum be well aligned across the grades or across subjects, it would also be logically organized, integrated, and harmonious in its internal structure. Here we treat coherence as the broader concept and alignment as only one of its dimensions.

A standards-based system of science education should be coherent in a variety of ways [3]. It should be horizontally coherent, in the sense that the curriculum-, instruction-, and assessment-related policies and practices are all aligned with the standards, target the same goals for learning, and work together to support students' development of the knowledge and understanding of science. The system should be vertically coherent, in the sense that there is (a) a shared understanding at all levels of the system (classroom, school, school district, state, and national) of the goals for science education (and for the curriculum) that underlie the standards and (b) that there is a consensus about the purposes and uses of assessment. The system should also be developmentally coherent, in the sense that there is a shared understanding across grade levels of what ideas are important to teach and of how children's understanding of these ideas should develop across grade levels.

CURRICULUM AND INSTRUCTIONAL MATERIALS

Curriculum refers to the knowledge and practices in subject matter areas that teachers teach and that students are supposed to learn. A curriculum generally consists of a scope, or breadth of content, in a given subject area and of a sequence of concepts and activities for learning. While standards typically outline the goals of learning, curricula set forth the more specific means—materials, tasks, discussions, representations—to be used to achieve those goals.

Curriculum is collectively defined by teachers, curriculum coordinators (at both the school and the district levels), state agencies, curriculum development organizations, textbook publishers, and (in the case of science) curriculum kit publishers. Although standards do not prescribe specific curricula, they do provide some criteria for *designing* curricula. And in order to realize the vision of the framework and standards, it is necessary that aligned instructional materials, textbooks, and computer or other media-based materials be developed as well.

Curricula based on the framework and resulting standards should integrate the three dimensions—scientific and engineering practices, crosscutting concepts, and disciplinary core ideas—and follow the progressions articulated in this report. In order to support the vision of this framework, standards-based curricula in science need to be developed to provide clear guidance that helps teachers support students engaging in scientific practices to develop explanations and models [5, 21-24]. In addition, curriculum materials need to be developed as a multiyear sequence that helps students develop increasingly sophisticated ideas across grades K-12 [5, 25, 26]. Curriculum materials (including technology) themselves are developed by a multicomponent system that includes for-profit publishers as well as grant-funded work in the nonprofit sectors of the science education community. The adoption of standards based on this framework by multiple states may help drive publishers to align with it. Such alignment may at first be superficial, but schools, districts, and states can influence publishers if enough of them are asking for serious alignment with the framework and the standards it engenders.

> While standards typically outline the goals of learning, curricula set forth the more specific means—materials, tasks, discussions, representations—to be used to achieve those goals.

Integration of the Three Dimensions

The framework's vision is that students will acquire knowledge and skill in science and engineering through a carefully designed sequence of learning experiences. Each stage in the sequence will develop students' understanding of particular scientific and engineering practices, crosscutting concepts, and disciplinary core ideas while also deepening their insights into the ways in which people from all backgrounds engage in scientific and engineering work to satisfy their curiosity, seek explanations about the world, and improve the built world.

A major question confronting each curriculum developer will be which of the practices and crosscutting concepts to feature in lessons or units around a particular disciplinary core idea so that, across the curriculum, they all receive sufficient attention [27].

Every science unit or engineering design project must have as one of its goals the development of student understanding of at least one disciplinary core idea. In addition, explicit reference to each crosscutting concept will recur frequently and in varied contexts across disciplines and grades. These concepts need to become part of the language of science that students use when framing questions or developing ways to observe, describe, and explain the world.

Similarly, the science and engineering practices delineated in this framework should become familiar as well to students through increasingly sophisticated experiences with them across grades K-8 [28, 29]. Although not every such practice will occur in every context, the curriculum should provide repeated opportunities across various contexts for students to develop their facility with these practices and use them as a support for developing deep understanding of the concepts in question and of the nature of science and of engineering. This will require substantial redesign of current and future curricula [30, 31].

Important Aspects of Science Curriculum

In addition to alignment with the framework, there are many other aspects for curriculum designers to consider that are not addressed in the framework. This section highlights some that the committee considers important but decided would

█ Through discussion and reflection, students can come to realize that scientific inquiry embodies a set of values. These values include respect for the importance of logical thinking, precision, open-mindedness, objectivity, skepticism, and a requirement for transparent research procedures and honest reporting of findings. █

be better treated at the level of curriculum design than at the level of framework and standards. Considerations of the historical, social, cultural, and ethical aspects of science and its applications, as well as of engineering and the technologies it develops, need a place in the natural science curriculum and classroom [32, 33]. The framework is designed to help students develop an understanding not only that the various disciplines of science and engineering are interrelated but also that they are human endeavors. As such, they may raise issues that are not solved by scientific and engineering methods alone.

For example, because decisions about the use of a particular technology raise issues of costs, risks, and benefits, the associated societal and environmental impacts require a broader discussion. Perspectives from history and the social and behavioral sciences can enlighten the consideration of such issues; indeed, many of them are addressable either in the context of a social studies course, a science course, or both. In either case, the importance of argument from evidence is critical.

It is also important that curricula provide opportunities for discussions that help students recognize that some science- or engineering-related questions, such as ethical decisions or legal codes for what should or should not be done in a given situation, have moral and cultural underpinnings that vary across cultures. Similarly, through discussion and reflection, students can come to realize that scientific inquiry embodies a set of values. These values include respect for the importance of logical thinking, precision, open-mindedness, objectivity, skepticism, and a requirement for transparent research procedures and honest reporting of findings.

Students need opportunities, with increasing sophistication across the grade levels, to consider not only the applications and implications of science and engineering in society but also the nature of the human endeavor of science and engineering themselves. They likewise need to develop an awareness of the careers made possible through scientific and engineering capabilities.

Discussions involving the history of scientific and engineering ideas, of individual practitioners' contributions, and of the applications of these endeavors are important components of a science and engineering curriculum. For many students, these aspects are the pathways that capture their interest in these fields and build their identities as engaged and capable learners of science and engineering [34, 35]. Teaching science and engineering without reference to their rich variety of human stories, to the puzzles of the past and how they were solved, and to the issues of today that science and engineering must help address would be a major omission. It would isolate science and engineering from their human roots, undervalue their intellectual and creative contributions, and diminish many students' interest.

Finally, when considering how to integrate these aspects of learning into the science and engineering curriculum, curriculum developers, as well as classroom teachers, face many further important questions. For example, is a topic best addressed by invoking its historical development as a story of scientific discovery? Is it best addressed in the context of a current problem or issue? Or is it best conveyed through an investigation? What technology or simulation tools can aid student learning? In addition, how are diverse student backgrounds explicitly engaged as resources in structuring learning experiences [36, 37]? And does the curriculum offer sufficiently varied examples and opportunities so that all students may identify with scientific knowledge-building practices and participate fully [38, 39]? These choices occur both in the development of curriculum materials and, as we discuss in the following section, in decisions made by the teacher in planning instruction.

LEARNING AND INSTRUCTION

Instruction refers to methods of teaching and the learning activities used to help students master the content and objectives specified by a curriculum. Instruction encompasses the activities of both teachers and students. It can be carried out by a variety of pedagogical techniques, sequences of activities, and ordering of topics. Although the framework does not specify a particular pedagogy, integration of the three dimensions will require that students be actively involved in the kinds of learning opportunities that classroom research suggests are important for (1) their understanding of science concepts [5, 40-42], (2) their identities as learners of science [43, 44], and (3) their appreciation of scientific practices and crosscutting concepts [45, 46].

Several previous NRC committees working on topics related to science education have independently concluded that there is not sufficient evidence to make prescriptive recommendations about which approaches to science instruction are most effective for achieving particular learning goals [3-5]. However, the recent report *Preparing Teachers* noted that "there is a clear inferential link between the nature of what is in the standards and the nature of classroom instruction. Instruction throughout K-12 education is likely to develop science proficiency if it provides students with opportunities for a range of scientific activities and scientific thinking, including, but not limited to: inquiry and investigation, collection and analysis of evidence, logical reasoning, and communication and application of information" [6].

For example, researchers have studied classroom teaching interventions involving curriculum structures that support epistemic practices (i.e., articulation and evaluation of one's own knowledge, coordination of theory and evidence) [47]; instructional approaches for English language learners [48]; the effects of project-based curricula and teaching practices [49]; the effects of instruction on core ideas, such as the origin of species [50]; and the influence of multiple representations of learning [51]. Others have investigated curricular approaches and instructional practices that are matched to national standards [52] or are focused on model-based inquiry [24]. In some work, there is a particular interest in the role of students' learning of scientific discourses, especially argumentation [33, 53, 54]. Taken together, this work suggests teachers need to develop the capacity to use a variety of approaches in science education.

Much of this work has examined pedagogical issues related to the "strands" of scientific proficiency outlined in *Taking Science to School* [5], and we next turn to those strands.

What It Means to Learn Science

The NRC report *Taking Science to School* [5] concluded that proficiency in science is multifaceted and therefore requires a range of experiences to support students' learning. That report defined the following four strands of proficiency, which it maintained are interwoven in successful science learning:

1. Knowing, using, and interpreting scientific explanations of the natural world.
2. Generating and evaluating scientific evidence and explanations.
3. Understanding the nature and development of scientific knowledge.
4. Participating productively in scientific practices and discourse.

Strand 1 includes the acquisition of facts, laws, principles, theories, and models of science; the development of conceptual structures that incorporate them; and the productive use of these structures to understand the natural world. Students grow in their understanding of particular phenomena as well as in their appreciation of the ways in which the construction of models and refinement of arguments contribute to the improvement of explanations [29, 55].

Strand 2 encompasses the knowledge and practices needed to build and refine models and to provide explanations (conceptual, computational, and mechanistic) based on scientific evidence. This strand includes designing empirical investigations and measures for data collection, selecting representations and ways of analyzing the resulting data (or data available from other sources), and using empirical evidence to construct, critique, and defend scientific arguments [45, 56].

Strand 3 focuses on students' understanding of science as a way of knowing. Scientific knowledge is a particular kind of knowledge with its own sources, justifications, ways of dealing with uncertainties [40], and agreed-on levels of certainty. When students understand how scientific knowledge is developed over systematic observations across multiple investigations, how it is justified and critiqued on the basis of evidence, and how it is validated by the larger scientific community, the students then recognize that science entails the search for core explanatory constructs and the connections between them [57]. They come to appreciate that alternative interpretations of scientific evidence can occur, that such interpretations must be carefully scrutinized, and that the plausibility of the supporting evidence must be considered. Thus students ultimately understand, regarding both their own work and the historical record, that predictions or explanations can be revised on the basis of seeing new evidence or of developing a new model that accounts for the existing evidence better than previous models did.

Strand 4 includes students' effective engagement in science practices with an understanding of the norms for participating in science, such as norms for constructing and presenting scientific models and explanations, for critiquing and defending a claim while engaged in scientific debates, and for students' motivation and attitudes toward science. For example, over time, students develop more sophisticated uses of scientific talk—which includes making claims and using evidence—and of scientific representations, such as graphs [58], physical models [59], and written arguments [60, 61]. They come to see themselves as members of a scientific community in which they test ideas, develop shared representations and models, and reach consensus. Students who see science as valuable and interesting and themselves as capable science learners also tend to *be* capable learners as well as more effective participants in science [8]. They believe that steady effort in understanding science pays off—as opposed to erroneously thinking that some people understand science and other people never will. To engage productively in science, however, students need to understand how to participate in scientific discussions, how to adopt a critical stance while respecting the contributions of others, and how to ask questions and revise their own opinions [62].

The four strands imply that learning science involves learning a system of thought, discourse, and practice—all in an interconnected and social context—to accomplish the goal of working with and understanding scientific ideas. This perspective stresses how conceptual understanding is linked to the ability to develop explanations of phenomena and to carry out empirical investigations in order to develop or evaluate those knowledge claims. Furthermore, it recognizes the conceptual effort needed for students' naive conceptions of the world to be modified as they learn science, rather than maintained with little change even as they contradict the material being taught. These strands are not independent or separable in the practice of science, nor in the teaching and learning of science. Rather, they are mutually supportive—students' advances in one strand tend to leverage or promote advances in other strands. Furthermore, students use them together when engaging in scientific tasks.

The NRC report *Learning Science in Informal Environments* [8] built on these proficiencies by including two additional strands. The first highlighted the importance of personal interests related to science, and the second noted the importance of helping learners come to identify with science as an endeavor they want to seek out, engage in, and perhaps contribute to. Science-linked interests and identity are important aspects of the science proficiencies of all learners, and we have discussed them specifically in other parts of the framework (see Chapters 2 and 11).

Although the strands are useful for thinking about proficiencies that students need to develop, as framed they do not describe in any detail what it is that students need to learn and practice. Thus they cannot guide standards, curricula, or assessment without further specification of the knowledge and practices that students must learn. The three dimensions that are developed in this framework—practices, crosscutting concepts, and disciplinary core ideas—make that specification and attempt to realize the commitments to the strands of scientific literacy in the four strands. There is not a simple one-to-one mapping of strands to the dimensions, because the strands are interrelated aspects of how learners engage with scientific ideas. Table 10-1 summarizes how the strands of scientific literacy guided the design of the dimensions in the framework.

Implications for Instruction

As the report *Taking Science to School* concludes, "a range of instructional approaches is necessary as part of a full development of the four strands of proficiency. All students need to experience these different approaches" [5]. "Approaches" here refer to the wide range of instructional strategies—from those that are led exclusively by the teacher to those that are led primarily by the student—that teachers can employ in science classrooms. Instruction may involve teacher talk and questioning, or teacher-led activities, or collaborative small-group investigations [63], or student-led activities. The extent of each alternative varies, depending on the initial ideas that students bring to learning (and their consequent needs for scaffolding), the nature of the content involved, and the available curriculum support.

Current research in K-12 science classrooms reveals that earlier debates about such dichotomies as "direct instruction" and "inquiry" are simplistic, even mistaken, as a characterization of science pedagogy [5]. This research focuses on particular aspects of teaching methods, such

TABLE 10-1 Relationship of Strands and Dimensions

Strands from *Taking Science to School* [5]	Dimensions in Framework	How the Framework Is Designed to Deliver on the Commitment in the Strand
1. Knowing, using, and interpreting scientific explanations of the natural world	Disciplinary Core Ideas Crosscutting Concepts	*Specify big ideas, not lists of facts:* Core ideas in the framework are powerful explanatory ideas, not a simple list of facts, that help learners explain important aspects of the natural world. Many important ideas in science are crosscutting, and learners should recognize and use these explanatory ideas (e.g., systems) across multiple scientific contexts.
2. Generating and evaluating scientific evidence and explanations **4. Participating productively in scientific practices and discourse**	Practices	*Learning is defined as the combination of both knowledge and practice, not separate content and process learning goals:* Core ideas in the framework are specified not as explanations to be consumed by learners. The performances combine core ideas and practices. The practices include several methods for generating and using evidence to develop, refine, and apply scientific explanations to construct accounts of scientific phenomena. Students learn and demonstrate proficiency with core ideas by engaging in these knowledge-building practices to explain and make scientifically informed decisions about the world.
3. Understanding the nature and development of scientific knowledge	Practices Crosscutting Concepts	*Practices are defined as meaningful engagement with disciplinary practices, not rote procedures:* Practices are defined as meaningful practices in which learners are engaged in building, refining, and applying scientific knowledge, to understand the world, and not as rote procedures or a ritualized "scientific method." Engaging in the practices requires being guided by understandings about why scientific practices are done as they are—what counts as a good explanation, what counts as scientific evidence, how it differs from other forms of evidence, and so on. These understandings are represented in the nature of the practices and in crosscutting concepts about how scientific knowledge is developed that guide the practices.

as teachers' oral strategies in guided science inquiry [64] and how they influence students' progress in scientific practices, crosscutting concepts and core ideas. For example, McNeill and Krajcik [22] studied how teachers' instructional practices affected students' scientific explanations; Kanter and Konstantopoulos [32] reported on the effects of teachers' content knowledge and instructional practices on minority students' achievements, attitudes, and careers. Other research has tracked how students' learning of scientific argumentation related to their development of scientific knowledge [65, 66]. Technological resources for science learning offer another instructional option [67-69].

Engagement in the scientific and engineering practices and the undertaking of sustained investigations related to the core ideas and crosscutting concepts provide the strategies by which the four strands can be developed together in instruction. The expectation is that students generate and interpret evidence and develop explanations of the natural world through sustained investigations. However, such investigations must be carefully selected to link to important scientific ideas, and they must also be structured with attention to the kinds of support that students will need, given their level of proficiency. Without support, students may have difficulty finding meaning in their investigations, or they may fail to see how the investigations are relevant to their other work in the science classroom, or they may not understand how their investigations' outcomes connect to a given core idea or crosscutting concept [70]. Finally, sufficient time must be allocated to science so that sustained investigations can occur.

TEACHER DEVELOPMENT

Ultimately, the interactions between teachers and students in individual classrooms are the determining factor in whether students learn science successfully. Thus teachers are the linchpin in any effort to change K-12 science education. And it stands to reason that in order to support implementation of the new standards and the curricula designed to achieve them, the initial preparation and professional development of teachers of science will need to change.

Schools, districts, institutions of higher education, state agencies, and other entities recruit, prepare, license, and evaluate teachers and provide an array of opportunities for their continued professional learning. A coherent approach to implementing standards would require all of these entities to work toward common goals and to evaluate the effectiveness of their requirements, procedures, teaching experiences, and courses in supporting the desired

> Teachers are the linchpin in any effort to change K-12 science education. . . . In order to support implementation of the new standards and the curricula designed to achieve them, the initial preparation and professional development of teachers of science will need to change.

approaches. (A common response from state science supervisors who reviewed the framework's draft version was to recognize the professional development demands it would place on the education systems in which they operate.) Alignment of teacher preparation and professional development with the vision of science education advanced in this framework is essential for eventual widespread implementation of the type of instruction that will be needed for students to achieve the standards based on it.

Teaching science as envisioned by the framework requires that teachers have a strong understanding of the scientific ideas and practices they are expected to teach, including an appreciation of how scientists collaborate to develop new theories, models, and explanations of natural phenomena. Rarely are college-level science courses designed to offer would-be science teachers, even those who major in science, the opportunity to develop these understandings. Courses designed with this goal are needed.

Teachers also need to understand what initial ideas students bring to school and how they may best develop an understanding of scientific and engineering practices, crosscutting concepts, and disciplinary core ideas across multiple grades [71]. Furthermore, in order to move students along the developmental progression of practices, crosscutting concepts, and core ideas, teachers need science-specific pedagogical content knowledge [72-74]—such as the ability to recognize common prescientific notions that underlie a student's questions or models—in order to choose the pedagogical approaches that can build on those notions while moving students toward greater scientific understanding of the topics in question. In sum, teachers at all levels must understand the scientific and engineering practices, crosscutting concepts, and disciplinary core ideas; how students learn them; and the range of instructional strategies that can support their learning. Furthermore, teachers need to learn how to use student-developed models, classroom discourse, and other formative assessment approaches to gauge student thinking and design further instruction based on it. A single "science methods" course cannot develop this knowledge in any depth across all subjects for high school science teachers, nor across all grades for elementary school teachers. Furthermore, many teachers now enter the system through alternative paths that may not include coursework in science teaching.

The research base related to strategies for science teacher preparation has been growing in the past decades [75-77]. Recent research has focused on the kinds of teacher knowledge to be addressed [78-82], particular programs and courses for prospective teachers [83], and how induction programs (which provide early mentoring and evaluation experiences, for example) can support new teachers [84]. However, an NRC committee charged with reviewing teacher preparation programs concluded that there is virtually "no systematic information on the content or practices of preparation programs or requirements for science teachers across states" [6]. In other words, while there is some research on what might be effective in preservice education little is known about what is actually offered.

State licensure requirements and the content of state licensing exams suggest that the requirements in science are fairly weak for elementary teachers and probably inadequate for middle school teachers. Although there is some evidence about approaches to professional development for K-12 science teachers [85-93], the research base needs further evidence from studies across K-12 teachers at different grade levels and across different disciplines [94-96]. Given these circumstances, the discussion in the following subsections is based on the information available, the committee's professional judgments, and logical inferences about what knowledge and skills teachers need to have in order to provide the learning experiences implied by the framework.

Preservice Experiences

Prospective science teachers will need science courses and other experiences that provide a thorough grounding in all three of the framework's dimensions [97]. Thus science teacher preparation must develop teachers' focus on, and deepen their understanding of the crosscutting concepts, disciplinary core ideas [98, 99], and scientific and engineering practices [100] so as to better engage their students in these dimensions [101, 102]. The goal of building students' understanding of the core ideas over multiple grades means that teachers will need to appreciate both the current intellectual capabilities of their students and their developmental trajectories [103]. Toward this end, preservice teachers will need experiences that help them understand how students think, what they are capable of doing, and what they might reasonably be expected to do under supportive instructional conditions [81].

Preservice teachers will need experiences that help them understand how students think, what they are capable of doing, and what they might reasonably be expected to do under supportive instructional conditions.

Ensuring that teachers incorporate the full range of scientific and engineering practices described in the framework is likely to be a challenge, but science methods courses will need revision to support prospective teachers' eventual facility with that range in their classrooms. This means introducing prospective teachers to a spectrum of scientific investigations, including simple investigations in the classroom using everyday materials, field studies outside the classroom [6], formal experiments carried out in the laboratory [104], and student-designed investigations [54]. Teachers also need opportunities to develop the knowledge and practices to support these investigations, including how to prepare, organize, and maintain materials; implement safety protocols; organize student groups; and guide students as they collect, represent, analyze, discuss data, argue from evidence, and draw conclusions [80].

Given that prospective teachers often rely heavily on curricular materials to guide their preparation and teaching, they will also need experiences in analyzing and revising curricular materials using standards- and research-based criteria [105, 106]. In addition, in this age of accountability, new teachers will need support in developing their knowledge of forms of assessment [79].

Beyond investigations, the discourse practices also are an important component of the framework [82, 107]; teachers will need support to learn how to facilitate appropriate and effective discourse in their classrooms [108, 109]. The emphasis on modeling is also new and will need to be an explicit element of teacher preparation [75, 110].

Moreover, preservice experiences will need to help teachers develop explicit ways to bring the crosscutting concepts into focus as they teach disciplinary content ideas. In effect, the framework calls for using a common language across grade levels for both scientific and engineering practices and crosscutting concepts. Engaging teachers in using this language during their preparation experiences is one strategy for ensuring that they develop facility and comfort with using it in the classroom.

The practices of obtaining, representing, communicating, and presenting information pose a particular challenge. Although elementary science teachers are usually also teachers of reading and writing and have experience in that realm, this is not the case for most secondary science teachers. Even for elementary teachers, their experience as literacy teachers rarely stresses science-specific issues, such as developing understanding based on integrating text with pictures, diagrams, and mathematical representations of information. For science teachers to embrace their role as teachers of science communication and of practices of acquiring, evaluating, and integrating information from multiple sources and multiple forms of presentation, their preparation as teachers will need to be strong in these areas [111].

The committee recognizes that incorporating the elements identified above will place significant demands on existing teacher preparation programs and on science teaching in college-level science departments. This may be particularly the case for the preparation of elementary teachers, who are typically required to take only a limited number of science courses and a single science methods course. A variety of mechanisms for integrating these elements will probably need to be considered, including modification of courses, addition of courses, and changes in licensing requirements. Any such redesigns should be oriented to the framework's three dimensions while incorporating research-based knowledge of what is most effective in teacher preparation.

Inservice Professional Development

Preservice preparation alone cannot fully prepare science teachers to implement the three dimensions of the framework as an integrated and effective whole. Inservice professional development will also be necessary to support teachers as they move into classrooms and teach science education curricula based on the framework [19, 112] and to introduce current teachers to the elements of the framework and the teaching practices that are needed to support them. Science-specific induction, and mentoring, and ongoing professional development for teachers at all stages of their careers, are needed.

This professional development should not only be rich in scientific and engineering practices, crosscutting concepts, and disciplinary core ideas but also be closely linked to teachers' classroom practices and needs [113]. Such professional development will thus need to be closely tied to the standards and curricula specific to the school, district, and state in which a particular teacher is teaching [64]. This burden will fall at local and state levels, but the capacity to meet it could be improved by coordinated development of teacher inservice programs capable of serving multiple states that choose to adopt the same set of standards. The capacity of the informal science learning sector to support effective teacher development

will also need attention to ensure that the work that such institutions as science museums do in teacher professional development is likewise aligned to the framework's vision.

Because elementary teachers teach several subjects, it will be especially important to consider how best to meet their combined needs through teacher preparation, early-career induction support, and ongoing professional development [114]. Some exploration of alternate models of teacher assignment, particularly at the upper elementary and middle school grades, may be needed. Even for secondary science teachers, facility with conceptual understanding of the framework [115, 116] and with the practices described here [80, 117] will require continuing professional development.

It should be understood that effective implementation of the new standards may require ongoing professional development support and that this support may look different from earlier versions. For example, the use of technology-facilitated approaches—such as teachers' video clubs to study their practices collaboratively [118] or the use of geospatial or modeling technology—while rare today, may become commonplace [119].

ASSESSMENT

Assessment refers to the means used to measure the outcomes of curriculum and instruction—the achievements of students with regard to important competencies. Assessment may include formal methods, such as large-scale standardized state testing, or less formal classroom-based procedures, such as quizzes, class projects, and teacher questioning. In the brief subsections that follow, we discuss some of the more challenging issues related to assessment that are part of the landscape for implementing the framework and its resulting standards.

Purposes of Assessments

As discussed in *Knowing What Students Know* [1], there are at least three purposes for educational assessment:

1. *Formative assessment for use in the classroom to assist learning.* Such assessment is designed to provide diagnostic feedback to teachers and students during the course of instruction. Teachers need assessment information about their individual students to guide the instructional process.
2. *Summative assessment for use at the classroom, school, or district level* to determine student attainment levels. Such assessment includes tests, given at the end of a unit or a school year, that are designed to determine what individual students have achieved.
3. *Assessment for program evaluation*, used in making comparisons across classrooms, schools, districts, states, or nations. Such assessment often includes standardized tests designed to measure variation in the outcomes of different instructional programs.

Schools, districts, and states typically employ assessments for all three purposes and sometimes today for a fourth purpose—evaluation of teacher effectiveness. Often the multiple forms of assessment have been designed separately and may not be well aligned with each other [3]. But just as the education system as a whole needs to function coherently to support implementation of the framework and related standards, the multiple forms of assessment need to function coherently as well. That is, the various forms of assessment should all be linked to the shared goals outlined by the framework and related standards while at the same time be designed to achieve the specific purpose at hand.

In addition, designers of assessments need to consider the diverse backgrounds that students bring with them to science class. For example, from an analysis of the language demands faced by English language learners on science performance assessments, Shaw, Bunch, and Geaney [120] concluded that assessment developers need to eliminate barriers of language, gender-biased examples, and other forms of representation that preclude some students' useful participation.

More fundamentally, the education system currently lacks sophistication in understanding and addressing the different purposes of assessment and how they relate to each other and to the standards for a particular subject. For example, a glaring and frequent mistake is to assume that current standardized tests of the type used by most states to assess academic achievement for accountability purposes can also suffice to fulfill the other purposes of assessment. Such a "one-size-fits-all" notion of assessment is demonstrably inadequate. No single assessment, regardless of how well it might be designed, can possibly meet the range of information needs that operate from the classroom level on up [1, 3].

Assessment Contexts: Classroom and Large-Scale Uses

In addition to differences in purpose, there are differences among assessments (and similarities) in their contexts of use, which range from the classroom level to the national level. As discussed in the NRC report *Assessment in Support of Instruction and Learning: Bridging the Gap Between Large-Scale and Classroom Assessment* [121], there are many desirable design features that should be shared by assessments, whether intended for use at the classroom level (for formative or summative purposes) or intended for large-scale use by states and nations (typically for accountability purposes). There are also some unique design characteristics that apply separately to each context. Many of the desirable design characteristics, shared or unique (to each context of use) alike, are currently unmet by the current generation of science assessment tools and resources.

Most science assessments, whether intended for classroom or large-scale use, still employ paper-and-pencil presentation and response formats that are amenable only to limited forms of problem types. In fact, most large-scale tests are composed primarily of selected-response (multiple-choice) tasks, and the situation is often not much better at the classroom level. Assessments of this type can measure some kinds of conceptual knowledge, and they also can provide a snapshot of some science practices. But they do not adequately measure other kinds of achievements, such as the formulation of scientific explanations or communication of scientific understanding [122]. They also cannot assess students' ability to design and execute all of the steps involved in carrying out a scientific investigation [4] or engaging in scientific argumentation. A few states have developed standardized classroom assessments of science practices by providing uniform kits of materials that students use to carry out laboratory tasks; this approach has also been used in the National Assessment of Educational Progress (NAEP) science test. However, administering and scoring these hands-on tasks can be cumbersome and expensive [3].

Computer-based assessment offers a promising alternative [6, 123]. Simulations are being designed to measure not only deep conceptual understanding but also the science practices that are difficult to assess using paper-and-pencil tests or hands-on laboratory tasks [124]. In 2006 and 2009, the Programme for International Student Assessment (PISA) pilot-tested the Computer-Based Assessment of Science (CBAS), designed to measure science knowledge and inquiry processes. The 2009 NAEP science test included interactive computer tasks designed to test students' ability to engage in science inquiry practices. And the 2012 NAEP Technological Literacy Assessment will include simulations for assessing students' facility with information and communications technology tools and their ability to engage in the engineering design process. At the state level, Minnesota has an online science test with tasks that engage students in simulated laboratory experiments or in investigations of such phenomena as weather and the solar system. There is hope that some of these early developments in large-scale testing contexts can be used as a springboard for the design and deployment of assessments, ranging down to the classroom level, that support aspects of the framework.

Designing Assessments

Designing high-quality science assessments that are consistent with the framework, that satisfy the different purposes of assessment, and that function in the varying contexts of use is an important goal, which will require attention and investment to achieve. Such science assessments must target the full range of knowledge and practices described in this report. They must test students' understanding of science as a content domain and their understanding of science as an approach. And they must provide evidence that students can apply their knowledge appropriately and are building on their existing knowledge and skills in ways that lead to deeper understanding of the scientific and engineering practices, crosscutting concepts, and disciplinary core ideas. Science assessments must address all of these pedagogical goals while also meeting professional educators' standards for reliability, validity, and fairness.

Although we have distinguished three purposes of assessment and different contexts of use, quality instruments for each purpose and context depend on the same three basic components: (1) theories and data about content-based cognition that indicate the knowledge and practices that should be tested, (2) tasks and observations that can provide information on whether the student has mastered the knowledge and practices of interest, and (3) qualitative and quantitative techniques for scoring student performance that capture fairly the differences in knowledge and practice [1].

Every assessment has to be specifically designed to serve its intended purpose and context of use. An assessment designed to provide information about students' difficulties with a single concept so that it can be addressed with instruction would be designed differently from an assessment meant to provide information to policy makers for evaluating the effectiveness of the overall education system. Details about the design of assessments for any given purpose or context are beyond the scope of the framework, as are the principles for designing systems of assessments that operate across the classroom, district, and state levels. However, guidance to states for developing a coherent system of assessments can be found in the NRC report *Systems for State Science Assessment* [3].

SUMMARY

As this chapter's discussion suggests, the committee's work on the framework and resulting standards is only the beginning. In order for students to experience and engage in the opportunities needed for understanding the three dimensions of scientific and engineering practices, crosscutting concepts, and disciplinary core ideas described in the framework, many other players and components of the system will need to change, often in dramatic ways. And these changes will need to occur in parallel, driven by a common vision, as well as iteratively, because each affects the capacity of other components of the system to implement the framework and standards. It is the committee's vision that the framework and standards based on it can help drive ongoing evolutionary change in science instruction through parallel and interlocking developments across the multiple components of the system.

Curriculum developers will need to design K-12 science curricula based on research and on learning progressions across grade levels that incorporate the framework's three dimensions. Teacher preparation programs and professional development programs will need to provide learning opportunities for teachers themselves in order to deepen their conceptual understanding, engage in scientific and engineering practices, and develop an appreciation of science as a way of knowing in a community of knowledge builders. These programs will also need to enhance teachers' skills in investigating students' ideas, selecting effective teaching practices, assessing students' progress, and developing classroom communities and discourses in which all students and their ways of knowing are valued and respected. College science departments will need to attend to the needs of prospective science teachers. Assessment developers will need to develop creative, valid, and reliable ways of gathering evidence about students' progress across the domains and grade levels to satisfy different purposes at different levels of the science education system.

Furthermore, because these changes are needed across the entire science education system—involving not only the educators at the front lines but also those who make and implement policies—professional development for state-level science supervisors, school boards, district-level leaders, principals, and curriculum specialists will be necessary as well. In that way, all components and players in the science education system can mesh coherently with the framework's vision for a more inclusive, focused, and authentic science education experience for all students.

REFERENCES

1. National Research Council. (2001). *Knowing What Students Know: The Science and Design of Education Assessment.* Committee on the Foundations of Assessment. J.W. Pellegrino, N. Chudowsky, and R. Glaser (Eds.). Board on Testing and Assessment, Center for Education. Division of Behavioral and Social Sciences and Education. Washington, DC: National Academy Press.

2. National Research Council. (2002). *Investigating the Influence of Standards: A Framework for Research in Mathematics, Science, and Technology Education.* I.R. Weiss, M.S. Knapp, K.S. Hollweg, and G. Burrill (Eds.). Committee on Understanding the Influence of Standards in K-12 Science, Mathematics, and Technology Education, Center for Education, Division of Behavioral and Social Sciences and Education. Washington, DC: National Academy Press.

3. National Research Council. (2006). *Systems for State Science Assessment.* Committee on Test Design for K-12 Science Achievement. M.R. Wilson and M.W. Bertenthal (Eds.). Board on Testing and Assessment, Center for Education. Division of Behavioral and Social Sciences and Education. Washington, DC: The National Academies Press.

4. National Research Council. (2006). *America's Lab Report: Investigations in High School Science.* Committee on High School Science Laboratories: Role and Vision, S.R. Singer, M.L. Hilton, and H.A. Schweingruber (Eds.). Board on Science Education, Center for Education. Division of Behavioral and Social Sciences and Education. Washington, DC: The National Academies Press.

5. National Research Council. (2007). *Taking Science to School: Learning and Teaching Science in Grades K-8.* Committee on Science Learning, Kindergarten Through Eighth Grade. R.A. Duschl, H.A. Schweingruber, and A.W. Shouse (Eds.). Board on Science Education, Center for Education. Division of Behavioral and Social Sciences and Education. Washington, DC: The National Academies Press.

6. National Research Council. (2010). *Preparing Teachers: Building Evidence for Sound Policy.* Committee on the Study of Teacher Preparation Programs in the United States, Center for Education. Division of Behavioral and Social Sciences and Education. Washington, DC: The National Academies Press.

7. National Research Council. (1996). *National Science Education Standards.* National Committee for Science Education Standards and Assessment. Washington, DC: National Academy Press.

8. National Research Council. (2009). *Learning Science in Informal Environments: People, Places, and Pursuits.* Committee on Learning Science in Informal Environments. P. Bell, B. Lewenstein, A.W. Shouse, and M.A. Feder (Eds.). Board on Science Education, Center for Education. Division of Behavioral and Social Sciences and Education. Washington, DC: The National Academies Press.

9. Shen, J., Gerard, L., and Bowyer, J. (2010). Getting from here to there: The roles of policy makers and principals in increasing science teacher quality. *Journal of Science Teacher Education, 21*(3), 283-307.

10. Roth, W.-M., Tobin, K.G., and Ritchie, S. (2008) Time and temporality as mediators of science learning. *Science Education, 92*(1), 115-140.

11. McLaughlin, M.W., and Talbert, J.E. (1993). *Contexts That Matter for Teaching and Learning: Strategic Opportunities for Meeting the Nation's Educational Goals.* Stanford, CA: Stanford University, Center for Research on the Context of Secondary School Teaching.

12. Little, J.W. (1993). Teachers' professional development in a climate of educational reform. *Educational Evaluation and Policy Analysis, 15*(2), 129-151.

13. Tobin, K., Elmesky, R., and Seiler, G. (2005). *Improving Urban Science Education: New Roles for Teachers, Students, and Researchers.* New York: Rowman & Littlefield.

14. Lee, O., and Buxton, C. (2010). *Diversity and Equity in Science Education: Theory, Research, and Practice.* New York: Teachers College Press.

15. National Center for Education Statistics. (2000). *Highlights from the Third International Mathematics and Science Study-Repeat.* NCES 2001-027. Washington, DC: U.S. Department of Education.

16. U.S. Department of Education. (2000). *The Federal Role in Education.* Washington, DC: Author.

17. Smith, M.S., and O'Day, J. (1991). *Putting the Pieces Together: Systemic School Reform.* CPRE Policy Brief, RB-06-4/91. New Brunswick, NJ: Consortium for Policy Research in Education.

18. Fuhrman, S. (1993). *Designing Coherent Education Policy: Improving the System.* San Francisco, CA: Jossey-Bass.

19. Penuel, W.R., Fishman, B., Gallagher, L., Korbak, C., and Lopez-Prado, B. (2009). Is alignment enough? Investigating the effects of state policies and professional development on science curriculum implementation. *Science Education, 93*(4), 656-677.

20. Schmidt, W.H., Wang, H.C., and McKnight, C.C. (2005). Curriculum coherence: An examination of U.S. mathematics and science content standards from an international perspective. *Journal of Curriculum Studies, 37*(5), 525-559.

21. Osborne, J.F., Erduran, S., and Simon, S. (2004). Enhancing the quality of argument in school science. *Journal of Research in Science Teaching, 41*(10), 994-1,020.

22. McNeill, K.L., and Krajcik, J. (2008). Scientific explanations: Characterizing and evaluating the effects of teachers' instructional practices on student learning. *Journal of Research in Science Teaching, 45*(1), 53-78.

23. Schwarz, C.V., Reiser, B.J., Davis, E.A., Kenyon, L., Achér, A., Fortus, D., Shwartz, Y., Hug, B., and Krajcik, J.S. (2009). Developing a learning progression for scientific modeling: Making scientific modeling accessible and meaningful for learners. *Journal of Research in Science Teaching, 46*(6), 632-654.

24. Windschitl, M., Thompson, J., and Braaten, M. (2008). How novice science teachers appropriate epistemic discourses around model-based inquiry for use in classrooms. *Cognition and Instruction, 26*(3), 310-378.

25. Duncan, R.G., Rogat, A.D., and Yarden, A. (2009). A learning progression for deepening students' understandings of modern genetics across the 5th-10th grades. *Journal of Research in Science Teaching, 46*(6), 655-674.

26. Stevens, S.Y., Delgado, C., and Krajcik, J.S. (2010). Developing a hypothetical multi-dimensional learning progression for the nature of matter. *Journal of Research in Science Teaching, 47*(6), 687-715.

27. Bybee, R. (2009). *K-12 Engineering Education Standards: Opportunities and Barriers.* Paper presented at the National Academy of Engineering Workshop on Standards for K-12 Engineering Education, July 8, Washington, DC. Available: http://www.nae.edu/Programs/TechLit1/K12stds/WorkshoponStandardsforK-12EngineeringEducation/15165.aspx [January 2010].

28. Metz, K.E. (1997). On the complex relation between cognitive developmental research and children's science curricula. *Review of Educational Research, 67,* 151-163.

29. Metz, K.E. (2004). Children's understanding of scientific inquiry: Their conceptualization of uncertainty in investigations of their own design. *Cognition and Instruction, 22*(2), 219-290.

30. Kesidou, S., and Roseman, J.E. (2002). How well do middle schools science programs measure up? Findings from Project 2061's Curriculum Review. *Journal of Research in Science Teaching, 39*(6), 522-549.

31. Enfield, M., Smith, E.L., and Grueber, D.J. (2008). "A sketch is like a sentence": Curriculum structures that support teaching epistemic practices of science. *Science Education, 92*(4), 608-630.

32. Kanter, D., and Konstantopoulos, S. (2010). The impact of project-based science on minority student achievement, attitudes, and career plans: An examination of the effects of teacher content knowledge, pedagogical content knowledge, and inquiry-based practices. *Science Education, 94,* 855-887.

33. Varelas, M., Pappas, C.C., Kane, J.M., Arsenault, A., Hankes, J., and Cowan, B.M. (2008). Urban primary-grade children think and talk science: Curricular and instructional practices that nurture participation and argumentation. *Science Education, 92*(1), 65-95.

34. Archer, L., DeWitt, J., Osborne, J., Dillon, J., Willis, B., and Wong, B. (2010). "Doing" science versus "being" a scientist: Examining 10- and 11-year-old school-children's constructions of science through the lens of identity. *Science Education, 94*(4), 617-639.

35. Tan, E., and Barton, A.C. (2010). Transforming science learning and student participation in sixth grade science: A case study of a low-income, urban, racial minority classroom. *Equity and Excellence in Education, 43*(1), 38-55.

36. Banks, J.A., Au, K.H., Ball, A.F., Bell, P., Gordon, E.W., Gutiérrez, K., Heath, S.B., Lee, C.D., Lee, Y., Mahiri, J., Nasir, N.S., Valdes, G., and Zhou, M. (2007). *Learning In and Out of School in Diverse Environments: Lifelong, Life-wide, Life-deep.* Seattle: Center for Multicultural Education, University of Washington.

37. Santau, A.O., Secada, W., Maerten-Rivera, J., Cone, N., and Lee, O. (2010). U.S. urban elementary teachers' knowledge and practices in teaching science to English language learners: Results from the first year of a professional development intervention. *International Journal of Science Education, 32*(15), 2,007-2,032.

38. Calabrese Barton, A., and Brickhouse, N.W. (2006). Engaging girls in science. In C. Skelton, B. Francis, and L. Smulyan (Eds.), *Handbook of Gender and Education* (pp. 221-235). Thousand Oaks, CA: Sage.

39. Tan, E., and Barton, A. (2008). Unpacking science for all through the lens of identities-in-practice: The stories of Amelia and Ginny. *Cultural Studies of Science Education, 3*(1), 43-71.

40. Kirch, S. (2010). Identifying and resolving uncertainty as a mediated action in science: A comparative analysis of the cultural tools used by scientists and elementary science students at work. *Science Education, 94*(2), 308-335.

41. Lehrer, R., and Schauble, L. (2010). *Seeding Evolutionary Thinking by Engaging Children in Modeling Its Foundations.* Paper presented at the Annual Meeting of the National Association for Research in Science Teaching, Philadelphia, PA.

42. Metz, K. (2006). The knowledge-building enterprises in science and elementary school science classrooms. In L.B. Flick and N.G. Lederman (Eds.), *Scientific Inquiry and Nature of Science* (pp. 105-130). Dordrecht, the Netherlands: Kluwer Academic.

43. Olitsky, S., Flohr, L.L., Gardner, J., and Billups, M. (2010). Coherence, contradiction, and the development of school science identities. *Journal of Research in Science Teaching, 47*(10), 1,209-1,228.

44. Polman, J.L., and Miller, D. (2010). Changing stories: Trajectories of identification among African American youth in a science outreach apprenticeship. *American Educational Research Journal, 47*(4), 879-918.

45. Akerson, V., and Donnelly, L.A. (2010). Teaching nature of science to K-12 students: What understanding can they attain? *International Journal of Science Education, 32*(1), 97-124.

46. Berland, L.K., and McNeill, K.L. (2010). A learning progression for scientific argumentation: Understanding student work and designing supportive instructional contexts. *Science Education, 94*(1), 765-793.

47. Enfield, M., Smith, E.L., and Grueber, D. (2007). "A sketch is like a sentence": Curriculum structures that support teaching epistemic practices of science. *Science Education, 92*(4), 608-630.

48. Lee, O., Lewis, S., Adamson, K., Maerten-Rivera, J., and Secada, W. (2007). Urban elementary school teachers' knowledge and practices in teaching science to English language learners. *Science Education, 92*(4), 733-758.

49. Kanter, D.E. (2010). Doing the project and learning the content: Designing project-based science curricula for meaningful understanding. *Science Education, 94*(3), 525-551.

50. Berti, A.E., Toneatti, L., and Rosati, V. (2010). Children's conceptions about the origin of species: A study of Italian children's conceptions with and without instruction. *Journal of the Learning Sciences, 19*(4), 506-538.

51. Adadan, E., Irving, K.E., and Trundle, K.C. (2009). Impacts of multi-representational instruction on high school students' conceptual understandings of the particulate nature of matter. *International Journal of Science Education, 31*(13), 1,743-1,775.

52. Krajcik, J., McNeill, K.L., and Reiser, B.J. (2008). Learning-goals-driven design model: Developing curriculum materials that align with national standards and incorporate project-based pedagogy. *Science Education, 92*(1), 1-32.

53. Brown, B.A., and Spang, E. (2008). Double talk: Synthesizing everyday and science language in the classroom. *Science Education, 92*(4), 708-732.

54. Kuhn, D. (2010). Teaching and learning science as argument. *Science Education, 94*(5), 810-824.

55. Lehrer, R., Schauble, L., and Lucas, D. (2008). Supporting development of epistemology of inquiry. *Cognitive Development, 23*(4), 512-529.

56. Lehrer, R., and Schauble, L. (2002). Symbolic communication in mathematics and science: Co-constituting inscription and thought. In J. Byrnes and E. Amsel (Eds.), *Language, Literacy, and Cognitive Development: The Development and Consequences of Symbolic Communication* (pp. 167-192). Mahwah, NJ: Lawrence Erlbaum Associates.

57. Zhang, J., Scardamalia, M., Reeve, R., and Messina, R. (2009). Designs for collective cognitive responsibility in knowledge-building communities. *Journal of the Learning Sciences, 18*(1), 7-44.

58. Bowen, G., Roth, W-M, and McGinn, M. (1999). Interpretations of graphs by university biology students and practicing scientists: Toward a social practice view of scientific representation practices. *Journal of Research in Science Teaching, 36*(9), 1,020-1,043.

59. Margel, H., Eylon, B.-S., and Scherz, Z. (2008). A longitudinal study of junior high school students' conceptions of the structure of materials. *Journal of Research in Science Teaching, 45*(1), 132-152.

60. Furtak, E.M., and Ruiz-Primo, M.A. (2008). Making students' thinking explicit in writing and discussion: An analysis of formative assessment prompts. *Science Education, 92*(5), 798-824.

61. Zhang, M., Passalacqua, S., Lundeberg, M., Koehler, M.J., Eberhardt, J., Parker, J., Urban Lurain, M., Zhang, T., and Paik, S. (2010). "Science talks" in kindergarten classrooms: Improving classroom practice through collaborative action research. *Journal of Science Teacher Education, 21*(2), 161-179.

62. Chin, C., and Osborne, J. (2010). Supporting argumentation through students' questions: Case studies in science classrooms. *Journal of the Learning Sciences, 19*(2), 230-284.

63. Bennett, J., Hogarth, S., Lubben, F., Campbell, B., and Robinson, A. (2010). Talking science: The research evidence on the use of small group discussions in science teaching. *International Journal of Science Education, 32*(1), 69-95.

64. Oliveira, A. (2009). Improving teacher questioning in science inquiry discussions through professional development. *Journal of Research in Science Teaching, 47*(4), 422-453.

65. Simon, S., Erduran, S., and Osborne, J. (2006). Learning to teach argumentation: Research and development in the science classroom. *International Journal of Science Education, 28*(2-3), 235-260.

66. Cavagnetto, A. (2010). Argument to foster scientific literacy: A review of argument interventions in K-12 science contexts. *Review of Educational Research, 80*(3), 336-371.

67. Hsu, Y-S. (2008). Learning about seasons in a technologically enhanced environment: The impact of teacher-guided and student-centered instructional approaches on the process of students' conceptual change. *Science Education, 92*(2), 320-344.

68. McDonald, S., and Songer, N.B. (2008). Enacting classroom inquiry: Theorizing teachers' conceptions of science teaching. *Science Education, 92*(6), 973-993.

69. Urhahne, D., Schanze, S., Bell, T., Mansfield, A., and Holmes, J. (2010). Role of the teacher in computer-supported collaborative inquiry learning. *International Journal of Science Education, 32*(2), 221-243.

70. Schmidt, W.H., Wang, H.C., and McKnight, C.C. (2005). Curriculum coherence: An examination of U.S. mathematics and science content standards from an international perspective. *Journal of Curriculum Studies, 37*(5), 525-559.

71. Rivet, A.E., and Krajcik, J.S. (2008). Contextualizing instruction: Leveraging students' prior knowledge and experiences to foster understanding of middle school science. *Journal of Research in Science Teaching, 45*(1), 79-100.

72. Shulman, L.S. (1986). Those who understand: Knowledge growth in teaching. *Educational Researcher, 15*(2), 4-14.

73. Shulman, L.S. (1987). Knowledge and teaching: Foundations of the new reform. *Harvard Education Review, 57*, 1-22.

74. Wilson, S.M., Shulman, L.S., and Richert, A. (1987). 150 different ways of knowing: Representations of knowledge in teaching. In J. Calderhead (Ed.), *Exploring Teacher Thinking* (pp. 104-124). Sussex, England: Holt, Rinehart & Winston.

75. Schwarz, C.V. (2009). Developing preservice elementary teachers' knowledge and practices through modeling-centered scientific inquiry. *Science Education, 93*(4), 720-744.

76. National Science Teachers Association. (2008). *Science as Inquiry in the Secondary Setting*. J. Gess-Newsome, J. Luft, and R.L. Bell (Eds.). Washington, DC: Author.

77. Luft, J.A., Roehrig, G.H., and Patterson, N.C. (2003). Contrasting landscapes: A comparison of the impact of different induction programs on beginning secondary science teachers' practices, beliefs, and experiences. *Journal of Research in Science Teaching, 40*(1), 77-97.

78. Abell, S.K., and Lederman, N.G. (2007). *Handbook of Research on Science Education*. Mahwah, NJ: Lawrence Erlbaum Associates.

79. Buck, G.A., Trauth-Nare, A., and Kaftan, J. (2010). Making formative assessment discernable to preservice teachers of science. *Journal of Research in Science Teaching, 47*(4), 402-421.

80. Taylor, J.A., and Dana, T.M. (2003). Secondary school physics teachers' conceptions of scientific evidence: An exploratory case study. *Journal of Research in Science Teaching, 40*(8), 721-736.

81. De Jong, O., and van Driel, J.H. (2001). *Developing Preservice Teachers' Content Knowledge and PCK of Models and Modelling*. Paper presented at the Annual Meeting of the National Association for Research in Science Teaching, St. Louis, MO.

82. Kelly, G. (2007). Discourse in science classrooms. In S. Abell and N. Lederman (Eds.), *Handbook of Research on Science Teaching* (pp. 443-470). Mahwah, NJ: Lawrence Erlbaum Associates.

83. Davis, E.A., and Smithey, J. (2009). Beginning teachers moving toward effective elementary science teaching. *Science Education, 93*(4), 745-770.

84. Saka, Y., Southerland, S.A., and Brooks, J.S., (2009). Becoming a member of a school community while working toward science education reform: Teacher induction from a Cultural Historical Activity Theory (CHAT) perspective. *Science Education, 93*(6), 996-1,025.

85. Loucks-Horsley, S., Love, N., Stiles, K.E., Mundry, S., and Hewson, P.W. (2003). *Designing Professional Development for Teachers of Science and Mathematics*. Thousand Oaks, CA: Corwin Press.

86. Hewson, P.W. (2007). Teacher professional development in science. In S.K. Abell and N.G. Lederman (Eds.), *Handbook of Research on Science Education*. Mahwah, NJ: Lawrence Erlbaum Associates.

87. Metz, K. (2009). Elementary school teachers as "targets and agents of change": Teachers' learning in interaction with reform science curriculum. *Science Education, 93*(5), 915-954.

88. Penuell, W., Fishman, B., Gallagher, L., Korbak, C., and Lopez-Prado, B. (2009). Is alignment enough? Investigating the effects of state policies and professional development on science curriculum implementation. *Science Education, 93*(4), 656-677.

89. Rogers, M.A., Abell, S.K., Marra, R.M., Arbaugh, F., Hutchins, K.L., and Cole, J.S. (2010). Orientations to science teacher professional development: An exploratory study. *Journal of Science Teacher Education, 21*(3), 309-328.

90. Supovitz, J.M., and Turner, H.M. (2000). The effects of professional development on science teaching practices and classroom culture. *Journal of Research in Science Teaching, 37*(9), 963-980.

91. Weiss, I.R., Pasley, J.D., Smith, P.S., Banilower, E.R., and Heck, D.J. (2003). *Looking Inside the Classroom: A Study of K-12 Mathematics and Science Education in the United States*. Chapel Hill, NC: Horizon Research.

92. Garet, M., Birman, B.F., Porter, A.C., Desimone, L., Herman, R., and Yoon, K.S. (1999). *Does Professional Development Change Teaching Practice? Results from a Three-Year Study*. Prepared by American Institutes for Research for the U.S. Department of Education Office of the Under Secretary. Available: http://www.ed.gov/rschstat/eval/teaching/epdp/index.html [June 2011].

93. National Staff Development Council. (2001). *NSDC Standards for Staff Development*. Available: http://www.nsdc.org/standards/index.cfm [June 2011].

94. De Jong, O., and Taber, K.S. (2007). Teaching and learning the many faces of chemistry. In S.K. Abell and N.G. Lederman (Eds.), *Handbook of Research on Science Education* (pp. 631-652). Mahwah, NJ: Lawrence Erlbaum Associates.

95. Duit, R., Niedderer, H., and Schecker, H. (2007). Teaching physics. In S.K. Abell and N.G. Lederman (Eds.), *Handbook of Research on Science Education* (pp. 599-629). Mahwah, NJ: Lawrence Erlbaum Associates.

96. Lazarowitz, R. (2007). High school biology curricula development: Implementation, teaching, and evaluation from the 20th to the 21st century. In S.K. Abell and N.G. Lederman (Eds.), *Handbook of Research in Science Education* (Part III: Science Teaching). Mahwah, NJ: Lawrence Erlbaum Associates.

97. Akcay, H., and Yager R.E. (2010). The impact of a science/technology/society teaching approach on student learning in five domains. *Journal of Science Education and Technology, 19*(6), 602-611.

98. Arzi, H.J., and White R.T. (2008). Change in teachers' knowledge of subject matter: A 17-year longitudinal study. *Science Education, 92*(2), 221-251.

99. Mikeska, J.N., Anderson, C.W., and Schwarz, C.V. (2009). Principled reasoning about problems of practice. *Science Education, 93*(4), 678-686.

100. Van Rens, L., Pilot, A., and Van der Schee, J. (2010). A framework for teaching scientific inquiry in upper secondary school chemistry. *Journal of Research in Science Teaching, 47*(7), 788-806.

101. Luft, J.A. (2009). Beginning secondary science teachers in different induction programmes: The first year of teaching. *International Journal of Science Education, 31*(17), 2,355-2,384.

102. Zembal-Saul, C. (2009). Learning to teach elementary school science as argument. *Science Education, 93*(4), 687-719.

103. Plummer, J.D., and Krajcik, J.S. (2010). Building a learning progression for celestial motion: Elementary levels from an earth-based perspective. *Journal of Research in Science Teaching, 47*(7), 768-787.

104. Lunetta, V.N., Hofstein, A., and Clough, M.P. (2007). Learning and teaching in the school science laboratory: An analysis of research, theory, and practice. In S.K. Abell and N.G. Lederman (Eds.), *Handbook of Research on Science Education* (pp. 393-441). Mahwah, NJ: Lawrence Erlbaum Associates.

105. Duncan, R.G., Pilitsis, V., and Piegaro, M. (2010). Development of preservice teachers' ability to critique and adapt inquiry-based instructional materials. *Journal of Science Teacher Education, 21*(1), 81-102.

106. Schwarz, C.V., Gunckel, K.L., Smith, E.L., Covitt, B.A., Bae, M., Enfield, M., and Tsurusaki, B.K. (2008). Helping elementary preservice teachers learn to use curriculum materials for effective science teaching. *Science Education, 92*(2), 345-377.

107. Carlsen, W.S. (1991). Subject-matter knowledge and science teaching: A pragmatic perspective. In J. Brophy (Ed.), *Advances in Research on Teaching: Volume 2. Teachers' Knowledge of Subject Matter as It Relates to Their Teaching Practice* (pp. 115-143). Greenwich, CT: JAI Press.

108. Rosebery, A.S., Ogonowski, M., DiSchino, M., and Warren, B. (2010). "The coat traps all your body heat": Heterogeneity as fundamental to learning. *Journal of the Learning Sciences, 19*(3), 322-357.

109. Roychoudhury, A., and Rice, D. (2010). Discourse of making sense of data: Implications for elementary teachers' science education. *Journal of Science Teacher Education, 21*(2), 181-203.

110. Danusso, L., Testa, I., and Vicentini, M. (2010). Improving prospective teachers' knowledge about scientific models and modelling: Design and evaluation of a teacher education intervention. *International Journal of Science Education, 32*(7), 871-905.

111. Lee, V. (2010). How different variants of orbit diagrams influence student explanations of the seasons. *Science Education, 94*(6), 985-1,007.

112. Donnelly, L.A., and Sadler, T.D. (2009). High school science teachers' views of standards and accountability. *Science Education, 93*(6), 1,050-1,075.

113. Smith, D.C., and Neale, D.C. (1991). The construction of subject-matter knowledge in primary science teaching. In J. Brophy (Ed.), *Advances in Research on Teaching: Volume 2. Teachers Subject Matter Knowledge and Classroom Instruction*. New York: JAI Press.

114. Howes, E.V., Lim, M., and Campos, J. (2009). Journeys into inquiry-based elementary science: Literacy practices, questioning, and empirical study. *Science Education, 93*(2), 189-217.

115. Kokkotas, P., Vlachos, I., and Koulaidis V. (1998), Teaching the topic of the particulate nature of matter in prospective teachers' training courses. *International Journal of Science Education, 20*(3), 291-303.

116. Krall, R.M., Lott, K.H., and Wymer, C.L. (2009). Inservice elementary and middle school teachers' conceptions of photosynthesis and respiration. *Journal of Science Teacher Education, 20*(1), 41-55.

117. Wee, B., Shepardson, B., Fast, J., and Harbor, J. (2007). Teaching and learning about inquiry: Insights and challenges in professional development. *Journal of Science Teacher Education, 18*(1), 63-89.

118. van Es, E.A. (2009). Participants' roles in the context of a video club. *Journal of the Learning Sciences, 18*(1), 100-137.

119. Trautmann, N.M., and MaKinster, J.G. (2010). Flexibly adaptive professional development in support of teaching science with geospatial technology. *Journal of Science Teacher Education, 21*(3), 351-370.

120. Shaw, J.M., Bunch, G.C., and Geaney, E.R. (2010). Analyzing language demands facing English learners on science performance assessments: The SALD framework. *Journal of Research in Science Teaching, 47*, 909-928.

121. National Research Council. (2003). *Assessment in Support of Instruction and Learning: Bridging the Gap Between Large-Scale and Classroom Assessment*. Committee on Assessment in Support of Instruction and Learning. Board on Testing and Assessment, Committee on Science Education K-12, Mathematical Sciences Education Board. Center for Education. Division of Behavioral and Social Sciences and Education. Washington, DC: The National Academies Press.

122. Quellmalz, E., Timms, M., and Buckley, B. (2005). *Using Science Simulations to Support Powerful Formative Assessments of Complex Science Learning*. San Francisco, CA: WestEd.

123. Quellmalz, E., Timms, M.J., and Scheider, S. (2009). *Assessment of Student Learning in Science Simulations and Games*. Paper prepared for the National Research Council's Science Learning: Computer Games, Simulations, and Education Workshop, October, Washington, DC.

124. Quellmalz, E.S., and Pellegrino, J.W. (2009). Technology and testing. *Science, 323*, 75-79.

EQUITY AND DIVERSITY IN SCIENCE AND ENGINEERING EDUCATION

Communities expect many things from their K-12 schools, among them the development of students' disciplinary knowledge, upward social mobility, socialization into the local community and broader culture, and preparation for informed citizenship. Because schools face many constraints and persistent challenges in delivering this broad mandate for all students, one crucial role of a framework and its subject matter standards is to help ensure and evaluate educational equity. In the committee's judgment, concerns about equity should be at the forefront of any effort to improve the goals, structures, and practices that support learning and educational attainment for all students. See Box 11-1 for a discussion of different interpretations of equity.

In this chapter, we highlight equity issues that relate to students' educational experiences and outcomes in science and engineering. We argue that the conclusions and principles developed here should be used to inform any effort to define and promote standards for science and engineering education. Issues related to equity and diversity become even more important when standards are translated into curricular and instructional materials and assessments.

SCIENCE AND ENGINEERING LEARNING FOR ALL

Promoting scientific literacy among all of the nation's people is a democratic ideal worthy of focused attention, significant resources, and continuing effort. To help achieve that end, the committee thinks not only that standards should reflect high academic goals for all students' science and engineering learning—as

BOX 11-1

WHAT IS EQUITY?

The term "equity" has been used in different ways by different communities of researchers and educators. Equity as an expression of socially enlightened self-interest is reflected in calls to invest in the science and engineering education of underrepresented groups simply because American labor needs can no longer be met by recruiting among the traditional populations. Equity as an expression of social justice is manifested in calls to remedy the injustices visited on entire groups of American society that in the past have been underserved by their schools and have thereby suffered severely limited prospects of high-prestige careers in science and engineering. Other notions of equity are expressed throughout the education literature; all are based on the commonsense idea of fairness—what is inequitable is unfair. Fairness is sometimes considered to mean offering equal opportunity to all. The most commonly used definition of equity, as influenced by the U.S. Supreme Court's *Brown v. Board of Education* (1954, 1955) and *Lau v. Nichols* (1974), frames equity in terms of equal treatment of all.

outlined in this framework—but also that all students should have adequate opportunities to learn.

America's children face a complex world in which participation in the spheres of life—personal, social, civic, economic, and political—require deeper knowledge of science and engineering among all members of society. Such issues as human health, environmental conservation, transportation, food production and safety, and energy production and consumption require fluency with the core concepts and practices of science and engineering. As McDermott and Weber [1] point out, a major goal for science education should be to provide all students with the background to systematically investigate issues related to their personal and community priorities. They should be able to frame scientific questions pertinent to their interests, conduct investigations and seek out relevant scientific arguments and data, review and apply those arguments to the situation at hand, and communicate their scientific understanding and arguments to others.

Students could go yet further, because a growing number of important occupations in the 21st century—including those in expanding fields of science, technology, engineering, and mathematics as well as in many other segments of the workforce—will make use of the practices of scientific analyses, argumentation, communication, and engineering design. Providing more equitable access to the knowledge and practices associated with science- and engineering-related occupations requires a more equitable achievement of science and engineering literacy [2, 3]. All students should be able to learn about the broad set of possibilities that modern life offers and to pursue their aspirations, including their occupations of interest.

Considering Sources of Inequity

Today there are profound differences among specific demographic groups in their educational achievements and patterns of science learning, as in other subject matter areas. The reasons for these differences are complex, and researchers and educators have advanced a variety of explanations. We cannot address all of them in this chapter, so we focus instead on two key areas. The first links differences in achievement to differences in opportunities to learn because of inequities across schools, districts, and communities. The second considers how approaches to instruction can be made more inclusive and motivating for diverse student populations.

Other sources of inequity that are important but beyond the scope of this chapter are nevertheless important to keep in mind. For example, low learning expectations and biased stereotypical views about the interests or abilities of particular students or demographic groups also contribute, in both subtle and overt ways, to their curtailed educational experiences and inequitable learning supports [4-6]. Students' own motivation and interest in science and engineering can also play a role in their achievement and pursuit of these fields in secondary school and beyond. Thus attention to factors that may motivate or fail to motivate students from particular demographic groups is important to keep in mind when designing instruction.

Students' preparation in other subjects, especially literacy and mathematics, also affects their achievement in science. If some groups of students fail to become effective readers and writers by late elementary school, teachers have difficulty helping them to make progress—not only in science but also across all subject areas. These students fall further behind, and the problem for teachers grows more complex and challenging. Such dynamics can, in effect, reinforce the low-expectation tracking of students as they move through school, thereby significantly reducing their access to science and engineering pathways through K-12 and limiting the possibility of their going to college.

Students' Capacity to Learn Science

But can all students aspire to the science and engineering learning goals outlined in the framework? Psychological and anthropological studies of human learning broadly show that all individuals, with a small number of notable exceptions, can engage in and learn complex subject matter—especially if it connects to areas of personal interest and consequence—when supportive conditions and feedback mechanisms are in place and the learner makes a sustained effort [7, 8]. As we detail in the next section, a growing set of studies in science education show a similar consensus that students—from across social classes and other demographic groupings—can learn science when provided with supportive conditions to learn over an extended period [9-12]. Significant and persistent achievement gaps in science do exist on national and state assessments for low-income and minority students, but these outcomes should not be seen as stemming from an inability of some students to be capable of engaging in sophisticated learning.

Educational standards should therefore establish science and engineering learning goals that reflect common expectations for all students. Just as they are expected to learn how to read and write, they should also be expected to learn the core ideas and practices of science and engineering.

EQUALIZING OPPORTUNITIES TO LEARN

Science and engineering are growing in their societal importance, yet access to a high-quality education in science and engineering remains determined in large part by an individual's socioeconomic class, racial or ethnic group, gender, language background, disability designation, or national origin. As summarized by Banks et al.: "Being born into a racial majority group with high levels of economic and social resources—or into a group that has historically been marginalized with low levels of economic and social resources—results in very different lived experiences that include unequal learning opportunities, challenges, and potential risks for learning and development" [9]. Many students from lower socioeconomic strata enter formal schooling with smaller academic vocabularies [13], have less access to organized extracurricular activities and supplemental supports [14], and have less social capital mobilized on their behalf than their more economically advantaged peers [15]. Given the expectations of schooling, these differences pose numerous

> ▌All individuals, with a small number of notable exceptions, can engage in and learn complex subject matter . . . when supportive conditions and feedback mechanisms are in place and the learner makes a sustained effort. ▌

educational challenges that make positive learning outcomes difficult to attain. That said, students from lower socioeconomic strata often engage in more self-directed, creative play and receive support from a broader network of extended family members [14].

Achievement gaps are well documented, in science as well as in other subject areas, for black, Hispanic/Latino, and American Indian students. High school dropout rates are disproportionately high for these same groups. Girls' interest in science dramatically declines compared with boys' as students transition into middle school, and women continue to be underrepresented in a number of science and engineering fields and on the science and engineering faculties of many colleges and universities. The causes of these differences in educational achievement and professional attainment are multiple, explanations for them are somewhat contested, and in many ways they are the result of complex developmental processes that are difficult to study [15]. But one perspective on how these achievement differentials occur is to understand that they often result from "resource gaps" or gaps in "opportunities to learn" [16, 17].

Arguably, the most pressing challenge facing U.S. education is to provide all students with a fair opportunity to learn [17-19]. Many schools lack the material resources and instructional supports needed to provide exemplary science instruction

> Arguably, the most pressing challenge facing U.S. education is to provide all students with a fair opportunity to learn.

to all students on a regular basis. For example, in a survey of California teachers, 54 percent stated that they were indeed in that situation [20]. The study indicated that such shortages were more likely at schools that served high percentages of students at risk of low academic performance. These same schools were also more likely to have teachers who were uncredentialed or asked to teach outside their field of expertise. While science or engineering institutions can help nearby schools provide high-quality learning experiences for their students (e.g., with experts from industry who visit the classroom, student trips to science centers and aquariums, teacher participation in university programs), access to these assets cannot overcome the effects of inequitable in-school resources across the breadth of schools, and indeed they can reinforce those effects. The development of common and rigorous standards for use with all students rests on the assumption that all students are provided with similar learning opportunities.

Over the past decade, accountability pressures—generated by the focus on student achievement as measured by high-stakes assessments—have heightened the curricular emphasis on mathematics and English/language arts and lowered attention to (and investment in) science, art, and social studies—especially at the elementary school level. In another California study—this one involving elementary school teachers in nine San Francisco Bay area counties—participants indicated that science is the subject area in which they felt the most need of professional development [21]. They also reported that they taught science less than one hour per week on average across the elementary school grades—with science instruction being more prevalent in the upper elementary grades than in the K-2 grade band.

In schools serving the most academically at-risk students, there is today an almost total absence of science in the early elementary grades. This is particularly problematic, given the emerging consensus that opportunities for science learning and personal identification with science—as exemplified in this framework—are long-term developmental processes that need sustained cultivation. In other words, the lack of science instruction in early elementary school grades may mean that only students with sources of support for science learning outside school are being brought into that long-term developmental process; this gap initiates inequalities that are difficult to remediate in later schooling. This state of affairs is ironic in that students in the early elementary school grades are often deeply attracted to topics related to the natural and designed worlds—interests that provide a foundation for learning science [12]. Furthermore, for students with limited language skills, the absence of opportunities to engage in science learning deprives them of a rich opportunity for language development that goes beyond basic vocabulary.

To help resolve the problems noted above, standards should (a) highlight that rigorous learning goals are appropriate for all students and (b) make explicit the associated assumptions about instructional time, equipment and materials, and teacher knowledge needed for all students to achieve these goals. That information would help educators at the state, regional, and district levels make detailed plans and allocate resources in order to equalize students' opportunities to learn science and engineering in the ways described in the standards.

INCLUSIVE SCIENCE INSTRUCTION

Inclusive instructional strategies encompass a range of techniques and approaches that build on students' interests and backgrounds so as to engage them more meaningfully and support them in sustained learning. These strategies, which also have been shown to promote educational equity in learning science and engineering, must be attended to as standards are translated into curriculum, instruction, and assessment.

As we have discussed throughout this report, the framework reflects the fact that students learn science in large part through their active involvement in the practices of science. A classroom environment that provides opportunities for students to participate in scientific and engineering practices engages them in tasks that require social interaction, the use of scientific discourse (that leverages community discourse when possible), and the application of scientific representations and tools. Science and engineering practices can actually serve as productive entry points for students from diverse communities—including students from different social and linguistic traditions, particularly second-language learners. Tailored instructional perspectives and additional approaches, as we outline in the following sections, may be needed to engage these and other students in the full range of practices described in Chapter 4.

Approaching Science Learning as a Cultural Accomplishment

All science learning can be understood as a cultural accomplishment. Children and adults the world over explore their surroundings and converse about the seeming causes and consequences of the phenomena they observe, but they are raised in environments with varied exposures to activities (e.g., fishing, farming, computing) that relate to different science and engineering domains. What counts as learning and what types of knowledge are seen as important are closely tied to a community's values and what is useful in that community context [22-25].

Science has been described as being "heavily dependent on cultural contexts, power relationships, value systems, ideological dogma, and human emotional needs" [26]. Although this view is a contested one, seeing science as "a culturally mediated way of thinking and knowing suggests that learning can be defined as engagement with scientific practices" [27]. When people enter into the practices of science or engineering, they do not leave their cultural worldviews at the door. Instruction that fails to recognize this reality can adversely affect student engagement in science. Calabrese Barton therefore argues for allowing science and science understanding to grow out of lived experiences [28]. In doing so, people "remove the binary distinction from doing science or not doing science and being in science or being out of science, [thereby allowing] connections between [learners'] life worlds and science to be made more easily [and] providing space for multiple voices to be heard and explored" [28]. This view is very powerful when one considers how best to engage all youth in the learning of science. Everyday experience provides a rich base of knowledge and experience to support conceptual

changes in science. Students bring cultural funds of knowledge that can be leveraged, combined with other concepts, and transformed into scientific concepts over time.

Everyday contexts and situations that are important in children's lives not only influence their repertoires of practice but also are likely to support their development of complex cognitive skills. This is evident in the studies of activities described as meaningful by individuals from various American cultures [29-36]. Teachers pursuing a culturally responsive approach to instruction will need to understand the sense-making practices of particular communities, the science-related values that reside in them, and the historical relationship that exists between the community and local institutions of education. Instruction can then be crafted to reflect these cultural particulars and engage students in related disciplinary practices and associated learning, often in ways that link to their personal interests as well [12, 34, 37-39]. As one example, Tzou and Bell [40] describe a curriculum effort that redesigned an elementary science kit to focus on the local cultural practices that related to the central subject matter in the unit. This involved a shift in students inquiring into a range of microworlds to investigations of the microbiology of local community health practices [40]. Fifth-grade students helped to photo document the everyday connections to the science content and were then supported in investigating issues of personal interest. In another case, Luehmann engaged middle school girls in extended scientific investigations and sense-making on topics of their own choosing in an after-school science context [41]. Students were able to develop science-linked identities by realizing that science could be meaningfully related to circumstances of their own lives, which they could then investigate [41]. In many cases, a culturally responsive approach to science instruction involves the recognition of community practices and knowledge as being central to the scientific endeavor [42].

Relating Youth Discourses to Scientific Discourses

Many equity-focused interventions have leveraged the discourse (i.e., sense-making) practices of youth to productively engage them in the language and discourse styles of science and in the learning of science. While traditional classroom practices have been found to be successful for students whose discourse practices at home resemble those at school—mainly students from middle-class and upper-middle-class European/American homes [43]—this approach does not work very well for individuals from historically nondominant groups. For these students, traditional classroom practices function as a gatekeeper, barring them because their community's sense-making practices may not be acknowledged [38, 44-46].

Recognizing that language and discourse patterns vary across culturally diverse groups, researchers point to the importance of accepting, even encouraging, students' classroom use of informal or native language and familiar modes of interaction [47-49]. The research literature contains multiple examples. Lee and Fradd [47] noted distinct patterns of discourse (e.g., use of simultaneous or sequential speech) around science topics in groups of students from different backgrounds. Rosebery, Warren, and Conant [50] identified connections between Haitian Creole students' storytelling skills and their approaches to argumentation and science inquiry; they used those connections to support their learning of both the content and the practices of science. Hudicourt-Barnes demonstrated how *bay odyans*—the Haitian argumentative discussion style—could be a great resource for students as they practice science and scientific discourse [51].

As these studies indicate, diverse linguistic practices for making sense of natural phenomena can generate learning and be leveraged in instruction [9, 46, 50]. Brown has recently extended this line of work by developing an instructional model that helps students bridge the transition from using their vernacular language for scientific phenomena to using disciplinary terminology and forms of discourse; essentially, they describe and discuss the same phenomena in both modes in turn [46]. The challenge for teachers is to know enough about their students' relevant linguistic practices to be able to support this transition in the classroom.

A classroom rich in discourse is also a classroom that offers particular challenges for students still learning English. On the other side of the coin, engagement in the discourse and practices of science, built as it is around observations and evidence, also offers not only science learning but also a rich language-learning opportunity for such students. For both reasons, inclusion in classroom discourse and engagement in science practices can be particularly valuable for such students.

Building on Prior Interest and Identity

Research suggests that personal interest is an important factor in children's involvement in learning science [52, 53]. Educational experiences designed to leverage the personal interests of learners have been used to increase the participation of girls in middle school [41], of urban high school youth of color [28], and of elementary school children from immigrant families [40]. Tai and colleagues' nationally representative study of factors associated with science career choices suggested that an expressed interest in science during early adolescence is a strong predictor of science degree attainment [54]. But even though early interest in science does not guarantee extended learning in science, early engagement can trigger students' motivation to explore the broader educational landscape and pursue additional experiences that may persist throughout life.

Learning science depends not only on the accumulation of facts and concepts but also on the development of an identity as a competent learner of science with motivation and interest to learn more. As Lave and Wenger explain, "Learning involves the construction of identities. [It is] an evolving form of membership" [55]. Such identity formation is valuable not only for the small number of students who, over the course of a lifetime, will come to view themselves as scientists or engineers but also for the great majority of students who do not follow these professional paths. Science learning in school leads to citizens with the

> Learning science depends not only on the accumulation of facts and concepts but also on the development of an identity as a competent learner of science with motivation and interest to learn more.

confidence, ability, and inclination to continue learning about issues, scientific and otherwise, that affect their lives and communities.

For these reasons, instruction that builds on prior interest and identity is likely to be as important as instruction that builds on knowledge alone. All students can profit from this approach, but the benefits are particularly salient for those who would feel disenfranchised or disconnected from science should instruction neglect their personal inclinations.

Leveraging Students' Cultural Funds of Knowledge

Particular cultural groups frequently develop systematic knowledge of the natural world through their members' participation in informal learning experiences, which are influenced by the groups' history and values and the demands of specific settings [12]. Such culturally influenced ways of approaching nature reflect a diversity of perspectives that should be recognized in designing science learning experiences. Although some kinds of culturally valued knowledge and practices (including spiritual and mystical thought, folk narratives, and various accounts of creation) are at odds with science, a growing body of published research, briefly described below, shows that some of the knowledge derived from varied cultures and contexts provides valid and consistent scientific interpretations. This literature includes evidence from cultural psychology, anthropology, and education [12].

An emerging consensus in education scholarship is that the diverse knowledge and skills that members of different cultural groups bring to formal and informal science learning contexts are assets to build on [9, 12]. For example, researchers have documented that children reared in rural agricultural communities, who have regular and often intense interactions with plants and animals, develop a more sophisticated understanding of the natural world than do urban and suburban children of the same age [56]. Other researchers have identified connections between children's culturally based stories and the scientific arguments they are capable of making [50, 57]. Such research suggests that educators should accept, even enlist, diversity as a means of enhancing science learning [58].

MAKING DIVERSITY VISIBLE

Prior educational standards in science education [19] have been criticized because their well-intentioned equity goals were advanced in general terms and the specific circumstances, both historical and contemporary, of various cultural groups were not identified, which made them difficult to understand and act on [59]. Nor were acknowledgments made of the specific contributions of members from diverse cultures to scientific and technological enterprises.

We now know, as discussed in the previous section, that the pursuit of equity in education requires detailed attention to the circumstances of specific demographic groups [9, 60-62]. When appropriate and relevant to the science issue at hand, standards documents should explicitly represent the cultural particulars of diverse learning populations throughout the text (e.g., in referenced examples, sample vignettes, performance expectations). Similarly, an effort should be made to include significant contributions of women and of people from diverse cultures and ethnicities. We acknowledge the challenge of creating a set of standards that attempts to represent all salient cultural groups, but that should not be an excuse for excluding them all.

The goal of making diversity visible is also desirable at a more abstract theoretical level. Educational standards always embody one or more theoretical perspectives on how people learn, how educators should teach, and how equity should be pursued—some or all of which may not be made explicit in the standards' documents. Such documents in the future should instead be transparent about their underlying theoretical perspectives related to diversity, equity, and social justice. This will help the reader to understand the salience of these issues in the teaching of science and in standards-based efforts to improve science education for all students.

> The diverse knowledge and skills that members of different cultural groups bring to formal and informal science learning contexts are assets to build on.

VALUE MULTIPLE MODES OF EXPRESSION

How school systems evaluate the learning derived from educational standards—through high-stakes tests, formative classroom assessments, and informal evaluations of learning during instruction—has a driving influence on educational pathways and equity. Exemplary assessment practice recognizes that there are multiple ways in which students might express their developing understanding, although not all forms of assessment allow for such multiple modes of expression.

Indeed, an enduring concern is that tests may not accurately gauge what students have learned [63]. A core problem is that the tests often do not make use of contemporary views of learning and cognition and thereby fail to assess higher order skills or conceptual understanding. Another important problem is that tests can be culturally biased, especially for some of the most vulnerable populations. Students whose first language is not English can find it difficult to express what they know on assessment instruments written in English. And an extensive literature highlights how "stereotype threat" can negatively affect the cognitive performance of girls and students from particular demographic groups during high-stakes assessments [64]. In order to help ensure educational equity, specific strategies need to be employed to guard against such unintended and undesirable assessment-based underestimations of student understanding. The representation of performance expectations in the standards document provides an opportunity to address these issues.

Such concerns, however, go beyond standards and need to address the conditions under which assessments are given. For example, authentic assessments may allow students to edit their rough drafts in much the same way that scientists and engineers circulate initial findings to colleagues before submitting a final draft for public consumption. But open-ended or extended-response items on high-stakes state assessments often demand that students provide what is essentially a "first draft" of a performance. For students who need to take more time to express their understanding (e.g., if they learned English as their second language), opportunities to edit or to display their knowledge in less language-embedded tasks would help level the playing field. It is worth noting that current efforts in assessment for mathematics and language arts are moving in this direction by including embedded performance assessments in curricula and aggregating them with summative assessments to create broader assessments of student learning [65].

Performance on assessments is affected by context as well as content [6, 64], and this can also have cultural roots. For example, work by Deyhle suggests that many American Indian communities do not socialize their children to making the public displays of achievement that are required in schools [66]. As Delpit has argued, this suggests the importance of making explicit the norms not only of classroom participation but also of assessment [67]. When defining performance expectations in standards documents to be used for formative and high-stakes assessment, standards developers should highlight how students can demonstrate competence through multiple means of expression and in multiple contexts.

REFERENCES

1. McDermott, R., and Weber, V. (1998). When is math or science? In J.G. Greeno and S.V. Goldman (Eds.), *Thinking Practices in Mathematics and Science Learning* (pp. 321-339). Mahwah, NJ: Lawrence Erlbaum Associates.

2. Moses, R.P., and Cobb, C.E. (2001). *Radical Equations: Civil Rights from Mississippi to the Algebra Project*. Boston, MA: Beacon Press.

3. National Research Council. (2011). *Expanding Underrepresented Minority Participation: America's Science and Technology Talent at the Crossroads*. Committee on Underrepresented Groups and the Expansion of the Science and Engineering Workforce Pipeline. Washington, DC: The National Academies Press.

4. Malcom, S.M. (1994). Science for all: Easy to say, hard to do. In A. Pendergast (Ed.), *In Pursuit of Excellence: National Standards for Science Education: Proceedings of the 1992 AAAS Forum for School Science*. Washington, DC: American Association for Advancement of Science.

5. Brantlinger, E. (2003). *Dividing Classes: How the Middle Class Negotiates and Rationalizes School Advantage*. New York: Routledge Falmer.

6. Steele, C. (1997). A threat in the air: How stereotypes shape intellectual identity and performance. *American Psychologist, 52*, 613-629.

7. National Research Council. (1999). *How People Learn: Brain, Mind, Experience, and School*. Committee on Developments in the Science of Learning. J.D. Bransford, A.L. Brown, and R.R. Cocking (Eds.). Washington, DC: National Academy Press.

8. Nisbett, R.E. (2009). *Intelligence and How to Get It: Why Schools and Cultures Count*. New York: W.W. Norton.

9. Banks, J.A., Au, K.H., Ball, A.F., Bell, P., Gordon, E.W., Gutiérrez, K., Heath, S.B., Lee, C.D., Lee, Y., Mahiri, J., Nasir, N.S., Valdes, G., and Zhou, M. (2007). *Learning In and Out of School in Diverse Environments: Lifelong, Life-wide, Life-deep*. Seattle: Center for Multicultural Education, University of Washington.

10. Lee, O., and Buxton, C. (2010). Teaching science to English language learners. *NSTA Reports, 21*(8), 3-4.

11. National Research Council. (2007). *Taking Science to School: Learning and Teaching Science in Grades K-8*. Committee on Science Learning, Kindergarten Through Eighth Grade. R.A. Duschl, H.A. Schweingruber, and A.W. Shouse (Eds.). Board on Science Education, Center for Education. Division of Behavioral and Social Sciences and Education. Washington, DC: The National Academies Press.

12. National Research Council. (2009). *Learning Science in Informal Environments: People, Places, and Pursuits*. Committee on Learning Science in Informal Environments. P. Bell, B. Lewenstein, A.W. Shouse, and M.A. Feder (Eds.). Board on Science Education, Center for Education. Division of Behavioral and Social Sciences and Education. Washington, DC: The National Academies Press.

13. Hart, B., and Risley, T.R. (1995). *Meaningful Differences in the Everyday Experience of Young American Children*. Baltimore, MD: Paul H. Brookes.

14. Lareau, A. (2003). *Unequal Childhoods: Class, Race, and Family Life*. Berkeley: University of California Press.

15. Lee, K.S. (2009). The intersection of scholarship of teaching and learning with online course design in teacher education. *Insight: A Journal of Scholarly Teaching, 4*(1), 77-85.

16. Oakes, J. (1990). *Multiplying Inequalities: The Effects of Race, Social Class, and Tracking on Opportunities to Learn Mathematics and Science*. Santa Monica, CA: RAND.

17. Moss, P.A., Pullin, D., Haertel, E.H., Gee, J.P., and Young, L. (Eds.). (2008). *Assessment, Equity, and Opportunity to Learn*. New York: Cambridge University.

18. Porter, A. (1993). *State and District Leadership for the Implementation of Project 2061*. Background paper prepared for the American Association for the Advancement of Science, Project 2061, Washington, DC.

19. National Research Council. (1996). *National Science Education Standards*. National Committee for Science Education Standards and Assessment. Washington, DC: National Academy Press.

20. Harris, L. (2004). *Report on the Status of Public School Education in California: A Survey of a Cross-Section of Classroom Teachers in California Public Schools*. Menlo Park, CA: William and Flora Hewlett Foundation.

21. Dorph, R., Goldstein, D., Lee, S., Lepori, K., Schneider, S., and Venkatesan, S. (2007). *The Status of Science Education in the Bay Area: Research Brief*. Berkeley: Lawrence Hall of Science, University of California. Available: http://www.lawrence hallofscience.org/rea/bayareastudy/ [June 2011].

22. Heath, S. (2007). *Diverse Learning and Learner Diversity in "Informal" Science Learning Environments*. Background paper for the Committee on Science Education for Learning Science in Informal Environments. Available: http://www7.national academies.org/bose/Learning_Science_in_Informal_Environments_Commissioned_ Papers.html [June 2011].

23. Rogoff, B. (2003). *The Cultural Nature of Human Development*. New York: Oxford University Press.

24. Bruner, J. (1996). *The Culture of Education*. Cambridge, MA: Harvard University Press.

25. McDermott, R., and Varenne, H. (2006). Reconstructing culture in educational research. In G. Spindler and L. Hammond (Eds.), *Innovations in Educational Ethnography* (pp. 3-31). Mahwah, NJ: Lawrence Erlbaum Associates.

26. Harding, S. (1998). *Is Science Multicultural? Postcolonialisms, Feminisms, and Epistemologies*. Bloomington: Indiana University Press.

27.   Brickhouse, N.W., Lowery, P., and Schultz, K. (2000). What kind of a girl does science? The construction of school science identities. *Journal of Research in Science Teaching, 37*(5), 441-458.

28.   Calabrese Barton, A. (1998). Reframing "science for all" through the politics of poverty. *Educational Policy, 12*, 525-541.

29.   Bang, M., Medin, D., and Atran, S. (2007). Cultural mosaics and mental models of nature. *Proceedings of the National Academy of Sciences, 104*(35), 13,868-13,874.

30.   Nasir, N.S. (2000). "Points ain't everything": Emergent goals and average and percent understandings in the play of basketball among African American students. *Anthropology and Education Quarterly, 31*(3), 283-305.

31.   Nasir, N.S. (2002). Identity, goals, and learning: Mathematics in cultural practice. *Mathematics Thinking and Learning, 2*(2-3), 213-248.

32.   Nasir, N., and Saxe, G. (2003). Ethnic and academic identities: A cultural practice perspective on emerging tensions and their management in the lives of minority students. *Educational Researcher, 32*(5), 14-18.

33.   Rose, M. (2004). *Mind at Work: Valuing the Intelligence of the American Worker.* New York: Penguin Group.

34.   Rosebery, A., Warren, B., Ballenger, C., and Ogonowski, M. (2005). The generative potential of students' everyday knowledge in learning science. In T. Romberg, T. Carpenter, and F. Dremock (Eds.), *Understanding Mathematics and Science Matters* (pp. 55-80). Mahwah, NJ: Lawrence Erlbaum Associates.

35.   Warren, B., Ogonowski, M., and Pothier, S. (2005). "Everyday" and "scientific": Rethinking dichotomies in modes of thinking in science learning. In R. Nemirovsky, A. Rosebery, J. Solomon, and B. Warren (Eds.), *Everyday Matters in Mathematics and Science: Studies of Complex Classroom Events* (pp. 119-148). Mahwah, NJ: Lawrence Erlbaum Associates.

36.   Zimmerman, H.T., Reeve, S., and Bell, P. (2010). Family sense-making practices in science center conversations. *Science Education, 94*(3), 478-505.

37.   McIntyre, E., Rosebery, A., and Gonzalez, N. (Eds.). (2001). *Class Room Diversity: Connecting Curriculum to Students' Lives.* Portsmouth, NH: Heineman.

38.   Moje, E., Collazo, T., Carillo, R., and Marx, R. (2001). "Maestro, what is quality?": Language, literacy and discourse in project-based science. *Journal of Research in Science Teaching, 38*(4), 469-498.

39.   Warren, B., and Rosebery, A.S. (1996). This question is just too, too easy! Students' perspectives on accountability in science. In L. Schauble and R. Glaser (Eds.), *Innovations in Learning: New Environments for Education* (pp. 97-126). Mahwah, NJ: Lawrence Erlbaum Associates.

40. Tzou, C., and Bell, P. (2010). Micros and me: Leveraging home and community practices in formal science instruction. In K. Gomez, L. Lyons, and J. Radinsky (Eds.), *Learning in the Disciplines: Proceedings of the 9th International Conference of the Learning Sciences, Volume 1* (pp. 1,127-1,134). Chicago, IL: International Society of the Learning Sciences.

41. Luehmann, A. (2009). Accessing resources for identity development by urban students and teachers: Foregrounding context. *Cultural Studies of Science Education, 4*(1), 51-66.

42. Bang, M., and Medin, D. (2010). Cultural processes in science education: Supporting the navigation of multiple epistemologies. *Science Education, 94*(6), 1,008-1,026.

43. Kurth, L.A., Anderson, C., and Palincsar, A.S. (2002). The case of Carla: Dilemmas of helping all students to understand science. *Science Education, 86*(3), 287-313.

44. Lee, O., and Fradd, S.H. (1998). Science for all, including students from non-English language backgrounds. *Educational Researcher, 27*(4), 12-21.

45. Lemke, J.L. (1990). *Talking Science: Language, Learning, and Values.* Norwood, NJ: Ablex.

46. Brown, B.A. (2006). "It isn't no slang that can be said about this stuff": Language, identity, and appropriating science discourse. *Journal of Research in Science Teaching, 43*(1), 96-126.

47. Lee, O., and Fradd, S.H. (1996). Interactional patterns of linguistically diverse students and teachers: Insights for promoting science learning. *Linguistics and Education: An International Research Journal, 8*(3), 269-297.

48. Warren, B., Ballenger, C., Ogonowski, M., Rosebery, A.S., and Hudicourt-Barnes, J. (2001). Rethinking diversity in learning science: The logic of everyday sense-making. *Journal of Research in Science Teaching, 38*(5), 529-552.

49. Moschkovich, J.N. (2002). A situated and sociocultural perspective on bilingual mathematics learners. *Mathematical Thinking and Learning, 4*(2-3), 189-212.

50. Rosebery, A.S., Warren, B., and Conant, F. (1992). Appropriating scientific discourse: Findings from language minority classrooms. *Journal of the Learning Sciences, 2,* 61-94.

51. Hudicourt-Barnes, J. (2001). Bay odyans: Argumentation in Haitian Creole classrooms. *Hands On!, 24(*2), 7-9.

52. Hidi, S., and Renninger, A. (2006). A four-phase model of interest development. *Educational Psychologist, 41,* 111-127.

53. Jolly, E., Campbell, P. and Perlman, L. (2004). *Engagement, Capacity and Continuity: A Trilogy for Student Success.* Available: http://www.campbell-kibler.com/trilogy.pdf [June 2011].

54. Tai, R.H., Liu, C.Q., Maltese, A.V., and Fan, X. (2006). Planning early for careers in science. *Science, 312*(5,777), 1,143-1,144.

55. Lave, J., and Wenger, E. (1991). *Situated Learning: Legitimate Peripheral Participation*. New York: Cambridge University Press.

56. Coley, J.D., Vitkin, A.Z., Seaton, C.E., and Yopchick, J.E. (2005). Effects of experience on relational inferences in children: The case of folk biology. In B.G. Bara, L. Barsalou, and M. Bucciarelli (Eds.), *Proceedings of the 27th Annual Conference of the Cognitive Science Society* (pp. 471-475). Mahwah, NJ: Lawrence Erlbaum Associates.

57. Hudicourt-Barnes, J. (2003). The use of argumentation in Haitian Creole classrooms. *Harvard Educational Review, 73*, 73-93.

58. Nasir, N.S., Rosebery, A.S., Warren, B., and Lee, C.D. (2006). Learning as a cultural process: Achieving equity through diversity. In R.K. Sawyer (Ed.), *The Cambridge Handbook of the Learning Sciences* (pp. 489-504). New York: Cambridge University Press.

59. Rodriguez, A.J. (1997). The dangerous discourse of invisibility: A critique of the National Research Council's *National Science Education Standards*. *Journal of Research in Science Teaching, 34*(1), 19-37.

60. Lee, C.D. (2008). The centrality of culture to the scientific study of learning and development: How an ecological framework in education research facilitates civic responsibility. *Educational Researcher, 37*(5), 267-279.

61. Gutiérrez, K., and Rogoff, B. (2003). Cultural ways of learning: Individual traits or repertoires of practice. *Educational Researcher, 22*(5), 19-25.

62. Moll, L.C., and Gonzalez, N. (2004). Engaging life: A funds of knowledge approach to multicultural education. In J. Banks and C. McGee Banks (Eds.), *Handbook of Research on Multicultural Education* (2nd ed., pp. 699-715). New York: Jossey-Bass.

63. National Research Council. (2001). *Knowing What Students Know: The Science and Design of Educational Assessment*. Committee on the Foundations of Assessment. J. Pelligrino, N. Chudowsky, and R. Glaser (Eds.). Board on Testing and Assessment, Center for Education. Division of Behavioral and Social Sciences and Education. Washington, DC: National Academy Press.

64. Steele, C.M. (2010). *Whistling Vivaldi: And Other Clues to How Stereotypes Affect Us*. New York: W.W. Norton.

65. Smarter Balanced Assessment Consortium. (2011). *Smarter Balanced Assessment Consortium Home Page*. Available: http://www.k12.wa.us/SMARTER/ [June 2011].

66. Deyhle, D. (1987). Learning failure: Tests as gatekeepers and the culturally different child. In H.T. Trueba (Ed.), *Success or Failure? Learning and the Language Minority Student* (pp. 85-108). Cambridge, MA: Newbury House.

67. Delpit, L. (2006). *Other People's Children*. New York: New Press.

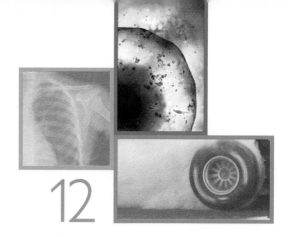

GUIDANCE FOR STANDARDS DEVELOPERS

The preceding chapters of this report describe the scientific and engineering practices, crosscutting concepts, and disciplinary core ideas—taken together, the framework—that should be the focus of K-12 science and engineering education. In this chapter, we offer guidance for developing standards based on that framework. The committee recognizes that several layers of interpretation occur between the outline articulated in the framework and actual instruction in the classroom, with the first layer being the translation of the framework into a set of standards. In this translation, it is important to keep in mind the possibilities and constraints of K-12 science education in the United States and to consider how standards can play a role in promoting *coherence* in science education—an element that is critical to ensuring an effective science education for all students, as discussed in Chapter 10 on implementation.

The emphasis on coherence includes consistency across standards for different subject areas. Given the large number of states that have adopted the Common Core Standards for mathematics and English/language arts, standards for K-12 science intended for multistate adoption need to parallel the expectations for development of mathematics and English/language arts competency reflected in corresponding standards [1].

The framework is designed to support coherence across the science and engineering education system by providing a template that incorporates what is known about how children learn these subjects. The committee's choice to organize the framework around the scientific and engineering practices, crosscutting concepts, and disciplinary core ideas is intended to facilitate this coherence. By consistently focusing on these practices, concepts, and ideas and by drawing on research to inform how they can be supported through instruction and developed over multiple grades, the framework promotes cumulative learning for students, coordinated learning experiences across years, more focused preparation and professional development for teachers, and more coherent systems of assessment.

The committee recognizes that simply articulating the critical practices, concepts, and core ideas for K-12 science education does not by itself provide sufficient guidance for developing standards. In that spirit, the recommendations outlined in this chapter are intended to offer more detailed guidance that will help ensure fidelity to the framework. These recommendations are based on previous research syntheses published by the National Research Council (NRC)—including *How People Learn* [2], *Systems for State Science Assessment* [3], *Taking Science to School* [4], and *Learning Science in Informal Environments* [5]—and they draw particularly on a list of characteristics for science content standards developed in *Systems for State Science Assessment* [3]. According to that report, science content standards should be clear, detailed, and complete; reasonable in scope; rigorously and scientifically correct; and based on sound models of student learning. These standards should also have a clear conceptual framework, describe performance expectations, and identify proficiency levels.

RECOMMENDATIONS

Recommendation 1: Standards should set rigorous learning goals that represent a common expectation for all students.

At a time when nearly every aspect of human life is shaped by science and engineering, the need for all citizens to understand these fields is greater than ever before. Although many reports have identified the urgent need for a stronger workforce in science and engineering so that the United States may remain economically competitive, the committee thinks that developing a scientifically literate citizenry is equally urgent. Thus the framework is designed to be a first step toward a K-12 science education that will provide *all* students with experiences in science that deepen their understanding and appreciation of scientific knowledge and give them the foundation to pursue scientific or engineering careers if they so choose. A growing evidence base demonstrates that students across economic, social, and other demographic groupings can and do learn science when provided with appropriate opportunities [4-7]. These opportunities include learning the requisite literacy and numeracy skills required for science.

Because the committee proceeded on the assumption that the framework and resulting standards identify those practices, crosscutting concepts, and disciplinary core ideas that are required for all students, some topics covered in advanced or specialized courses may not be fully represented. That is, the framework and resulting standards are not intended to represent all possible practices, concepts, and ideas covered in the full set of science courses offered through grade 12 (e.g., Advanced Placement or honors courses; technology courses; computer science courses; and social, behavioral, or economic science courses). Rather, the framework and standards represent the set of scientific and engineering practices, concepts, and ideas that all students should encounter as they move through required course sequences in the natural sciences.

Recommendation 2: Standards should be scientifically accurate yet also clear, concise, and comprehensible to science educators.

Standards for K-12 science education (a) provide guidance to education professionals about the priorities for science education and (b) articulate the learning goals that must be pursued in curricula, instruction, and assessments.

Scientific rigor and accuracy are paramount because standards serve as reference points for other elements of the system. Thus any errors in the standards are likely to be replicated in curricula, instruction, and assessments. Similarly, standards should clearly describe the scientific practices in which students will engage in classrooms [3]. Clarity is important because curriculum developers, textbook and materials selection committees, assessment designers, and others need to develop a shared understanding of the outcomes their efforts are intended to promote [3].

At the same time, standards related to the framework's concepts, ideas, and practices must be described in language that is comprehensible to individuals who are not scientists. Even though some of the professionals who play a role in interpreting standards do not have deep expertise in science, they nevertheless need to develop ways to support students' learning in science and to determine whether students have met the standards. Standards also provide a mechanism for communicating educational priorities to an even broader set of stakeholders, including parents, community members, business people, and policy leaders at the state and national levels. Thus, although standards need to communicate accurately important scientific ideas and practices, they must be written with these broader (nonscience) audiences in mind. Furthermore, the broad goals and major intent should be clear to any reader.

Recommendation 3: Standards should be limited in number.

The framework focuses on a limited set of scientific and engineering practices, crosscutting concepts, and disciplinary core ideas, which were selected by using the criteria developed by the framework committee (and outlined in Chapter 2) as a filter. We also drew on previous reports, which recommended structuring K-12 standards around core ideas as a means of focusing the K-12 science curriculum [3, 4]. These reports' recommendations emerged from analyses of existing national, state, and local standards as well as from a synthesis of current research on learning and teaching in science.

Standards developers should adhere to the framework by concentrating on the set of practices, concepts, and core ideas described here, although undoubtedly there will be pressure from stakeholder groups to expand that set. The above-mentioned criteria can be used in determining whether a proposed addition should be accepted. An overarching consideration is whether *all* students need to learn the proposed idea or practice and if there would be a significant deficiency in citizens' knowledge if it were not included. Another consideration should be recognition of the modest amount of time allotted to science in the K-12 grades. There is a limit to what can be attained in such time, and inclusion of additional elements of a discipline will always be at the expense of other elements, whether of that discipline or of another.

Recommendation 4: Standards should emphasize all three dimensions articulated in the framework—not only crosscutting concepts and disciplinary core ideas but also scientific and engineering practices.

The committee emphasized scientific and engineering practices for several reasons. First, as discussed in Chapter 2, competency in science involves more than knowing facts, and students learn key concepts in science more effectively when they engage in these practices. Second, there is a body of knowledge about science—for example, the nature of evidence, the role of models, the features of a sound scientific argument—that is best acquired through engagement in these practices. Third, emerging evidence suggests that offering opportunities for students to engage in scientific and engineering practices increases participation of underrepresented minorities in science [8-12].

The importance of addressing both knowledge and practice is not unique to this framework. In 1993, the *Benchmarks for Science Literacy* of the American Association for the Advancement of Science provided standards for students' engagement in scientific inquiry [13]. In 1996, the *National Science Education Standards* of the NRC emphasized five essential features of scientific inquiry [14]. Two more recent NRC reports also recommended that students' learning experiences in science should provide them with opportunities to engage in specific practices [4, 5]. The contribution of this framework is the provision of a set of scientific and engineering practices that are appropriate for K-12 students and moreover that reflect the practices routinely used by professional scientists.

Recommendation 5: Standards should include performance expectations that integrate the scientific and engineering practices with the crosscutting concepts and disciplinary core ideas. These expectations should include criteria for identifying successful performance and require that students demonstrate an ability to use and apply knowledge.

Chapter 9 further provides two examples of how performance expectations for particular life science and physical science component ideas could be integrated with core ideas, as well as with concepts and practices, across the grades (see Tables 9-1 and 9-2).

Developing performance expectations is a major task for standards developers, but it is an effort worth making; performance expectations and criteria for successful performance are essential in order for standards to fulfill their role of supporting assessment development and setting achievement standards [3]. An exhaustive description of every performance level for every standard is unrealistic, but at a minimum the performance expectations should describe the major criteria of successful performance [3].

Recommendation 6: Standards should incorporate boundary statements. That is, for a given core idea at a given grade level, standards developers should include guidance not only about what needs to be taught but also about what does *not* need to be taught in order for students to achieve the standard.

By delimiting what is included in a given topic in a particular grade band or grade level, boundary statements provide insights into the expected curriculum and thus aid in its development by others. Boundary statements should not add to the scope of the standards but rather should provide clear guidance regarding expectations for students. Such boundaries should be viewed as flexible and subject to modification over time, based on what is learned through implementation in the classroom and through research. However, it is important to begin with a set of statements that articulate the boundaries envisioned by standards developers.

Boundary statements can signal where material that traditionally has been included could instead be trimmed. For example, in the physical sciences, the progressions indicate that density is not stressed as a property of matter until the 6-8 grade band; at present, it is often introduced earlier and consumes considerable instructional time to little avail. Boundary statements may also help define which technical definitions or descriptions could be dispensed with in a particular grade band. Thus the boundary statements are a useful mechanism for narrowing the material to be covered, even within the core idea topics, in order to provide time for more meaningful development of ideas through engagement in practices. In other words, being explicit about what should *not* be taught helps clarify what *should* be taught.

Recommendation 7: Standards should be organized as sequences that support students' learning over multiple grades. They should take into account how students' command of the practices, concepts, and core ideas becomes more sophisticated over time with appropriate instructional experiences.

As noted in the introduction, the framework is designed to help students continually build on and revise their knowledge and abilities, starting from initial conceptions about how the world works and their curiosity about what they see around them. The framework's goal is thus to provide students with opportunities to learn about the practices, concepts, and core ideas, of science and engineering in successively more sophisticated ways over multiple years [4]. This perspective should prompt educators to decide how topics ought to be presented at each grade level so that they build on prior student learning and support continuing conceptual restructuring and refinement.

There is one overarching set of boundaries or constraints across the progressions for the disciplinary core ideas. Early work in science begins by exploring the visible and tangible macroscopic world. Then the domain of phenomena and systems considered is broadened to those that students cannot directly see but that still operate at the scales of human experience. Students then move to exploring or envisioning things that are too small to see or too large to readily imagine, and they are aided by models or specialized tools for measurement and imaging.

This overarching progression informs the grade band endpoints in the framework. Grades K-2 focus on visible phenomena with which students are likely to have some experience in their everyday lives or in the classroom. Grades 3-5 explore macroscopic phenomena more deeply, including modeling processes and systems that are not visible. Grades 6-8 move to microscopic phenomena and introduce atoms, molecules, and cells. Grades 9-12 move to the subatomic level and to the consideration of complex interactions within and among systems at all scales.

Recommendation 8: Whenever possible, the progressions in standards should be informed by existing research on learning and teaching. In cases in which insufficient research is available to inform a progression or in which there is a lack of consensus on the research findings, the progression should be developed on the basis of a reasoned argument about learning and teaching. The sequences described in the framework can be used as guidance.

Because research on these progressions is relatively recent, there is not a robust evidence base about appropriate sequencing for every concept, core idea, or practice identified in the framework. When evidence was available, the committee used it to guide the thinking about the progression in question. When evidence was not available, we made judgments based on the best knowledge available, as supported by existing documents such as the NAEP *2009 Science Framework* [15], the *College Board Standards for College Success* [16], and the AAAS *Atlas of Science Literacy* [17]. There is also a body of research on the intuitive understanding that children bring to school and on how that intuitive knowledge influences their learning of science [4]; this evidence base should be considered when developing standards.

Each progression described in the framework represents a particular vision of one possible pathway by which students could come to understand a specific core idea. The committee recognizes that there are many possible alternate paths and also that there are interplays among the ideas that here are subdivided into disciplines and component ideas within a discipline. In any case, progressions developed in the standards should be based on the available research on learning, an understanding of what is appropriate for students at a particular grade band based on research and on educators' professional experience, and logical inferences about how learning might occur.

Recommendation 9: The committee recommends that the diverse needs of students and of states be met by developing grade band standards as an overarching common set for adoption by multiple states. For those states that prefer or require grade-by-grade standards, a suggested elaboration on grade band standards could be provided as an example.

Given the incomplete nature of the evidence base, the committee could not specify grade-by-grade steps in the progressions. Indeed, for some ideas it was difficult just to develop research-based progressions at the grade band level; in those cases, we relied on expert judgment and previous standards documents. And even if grade-by-grade standards were feasible, research has shown that, within a particular grade, different students are often at different levels of achievement; thus expectations that every student will reach understanding of a core idea by the end of that grade may not be warranted. Across a grade band, however, students can continue to build on and develop core ideas over multiple school years; by the end of the grade band, they are more likely to have reached the levels of understanding intended.

In the committee's judgment, grade band standards are also more appropriate than grade-by-grade ones for systemic reasons, particularly for standards that may be adopted and implemented in numerous states. Because schools across the country vary both in their degree of organization, in their human and physical resources, and in the topics they have traditionally included at various grades, a national-level document's universal and homogeneous prescription for grade-by-grade standards may be too difficult for the schools in some states to meet, and it would perhaps be inappropriate for those localities to begin with. By contrast, specification by grade bands gives curriculum developers, states, districts, schools, and teachers the professional autonomy to ensure that content can be taught in a manner appropriate to the local context. This autonomy includes choosing from various possible strategies for course sequences and course organization at the middle and high school levels.

However, because it is recognized that many states require grade-by-grade standards for K-8 and course standards at the high school level, an example set of such standards may need to be provided. The intent of this recommendation is that states or districts wishing to offer alternative course sequences and organization at the high school level or alternative within grade band organization of content at the K-8 level can adopt the grade band standards.

This recommendation should not be interpreted as suggesting that students in some areas need not or cannot learn particular topics until later grade levels, but rather that the transition to a single common set of grade-by-grade standards is perhaps more onerous for schools and districts in term of curriculum materials, equipment, and teacher professional development needs than a transition to the somewhat more flexible definition of sequence given by grade band standards.

Recommendation 10: If grade-by-grade standards are written based on the grade band descriptions provided in the framework, these standards should be designed to provide a coherent progression within each grade band.

The content described in the framework is designed to be distributed over each grade band in a manner that builds on previous learning and is not repetitive. If standards developers choose to create grade-by-grade standards, it is necessary that these standards provide clear articulation of the content across grades within a band and attend to the progression of science learning from grade to grade within the band. At the middle and high school levels, course standards and suggested course sequences may be more appropriate than grade-level standards.

Recommendation 11: Any assumptions about the resources, time, and teacher expertise needed for students to achieve particular standards should be made explicit.

In designing the framework, the committee tried to set goals for science education that would not only improve its quality but also be attainable under current resources and other constraints. In addition, the committee intended for the framework's goals to act as levers for much-needed improvement in how schools are able to deliver high-quality science education to all students. For example, in order to meet the goals for science education in the elementary grades, more time may need to be devoted to science than is currently allocated. The committee recognizes as well that new curricula aligned to the framework will need to be developed and that professional development for teachers will need to be updated.

Standards developers should be cautious about limiting the rigor of standards in response to perceptions about the system's constraints. Research clearly demonstrates that all students have the capacity to learn science when motivated to do so and provided with adequate opportunities to acquire the requisite literacy and numeracy skills [4, 5]. Thus standards should catalyze change in the system when necessary, motivating states, school districts, and schools to ensure that all students have access to rich learning experiences.

Recommendation 12: The standards for the sciences and engineering should align coherently with those for other K-12 subjects. Alignment with the Common Core Standards in mathematics and English/language arts is especially important.

As noted earlier, achieving coherence within the system is critical for ensuring an effective science education for all students. An important aspect of coherence is continuity across different subjects within a grade or grade band. By this we mean "sensible connections and coordination [among] the topics that students study in each subject within a grade and as they advance through the grades" [3, p. 298]. The underlying argument is that coherence across subject areas contributes to increased student learning because it provides opportunities for reinforcement and additional uses of practices in each area.

For example, students' writing and reading, particularly nonfiction, can cut across science and literacy learning. Uses of mathematical concepts and tools are critical to scientific progress and understanding. Examples from history of how scientists developed and argued about evidence for different scientific theories could support students' understanding of how their own classroom scientific practices play a role in validating knowledge. Similarly, there should be coherence between science and social studies (as these terms are currently used in schools). Applications of natural sciences and engineering to address important global issues—such as climate change, the production and distribution of food, the supply of water, and population growth—require knowledge from the social sciences about social systems, cultures, and economics; societal decisions about the advancement of science also require a knowledge of ethics. Basically, a coherent set of science standards will not be sufficient to prepare citizens for the 21st century unless there is also coherence across all subject areas of the K-12 curriculum.

Greater coherence may also enhance students' motivation because their development of competence is better supported. And it could increase teacher effectiveness across subjects, as teachers could be mutually supportive of one another in weaving connections across the curriculum [3]. All in all, better alignment across the standards in the different subjects would contribute to the development of the knowledge and skills that students need in order to make progress in each of their subjects.

Recommendation 13: In designing standards and performance expectations, issues related to diversity and equity need to be taken into account. In particular, performance expectations should provide students with multiple ways of demonstrating competence in science.

As discussed in Chapter 11, the committee is convinced that, given appropriate opportunities to learn and sufficient motivation, students from all backgrounds can become competent in science. It is equally important that all students be provided with opportunities to demonstrate their competence in ways that do not create unnecessary barriers. Standards should promote broadening participation in science and engineering by focusing the education system on inclusive and meaningful learning as well as on assessment experiences that maintain high academic expectations for all students.

Previous standards for K-12 science education have been criticized for obscuring the educational histories and circumstances of specific cultural groups [18]. Diversity should be made visible in the new standards in ways that might, for example, involve (a) presenting some performance tasks in the context of historical scientific accomplishments, which include a broad variety of cultural examples and do not focus exclusively on scientific discoveries made by scientists in a limited set of countries; (b) addressing the educational issues encountered by English language learners when defining performance expectations; (c) attending to the funds of knowledge that specific communities possess with regard to specific core ideas and practices (e.g., knowledge of ecosystem dynamics in Native American communities, knowledge of living organisms in agricultural communities) and with regard to performance expectations; (d) drawing on examples that are not dominated by the interests of one gender, race, or culture; (e) ensuring that students with particular learning disabilities are not excluded from appropriate science learning; and (f) providing examples of performance tasks appropriate to the special needs of such students.

The variety of issues raised by the above list illustrates the challenges of providing learning opportunities and assessments that support all students in their development of competence and confidence as science learners. To ensure equity in a diverse student population, these challenges must be directly addressed not only by teachers in the classroom but also in the design and implementation of the standards, the curricula that fulfill them, the assessment system that evaluates student progress, and the accompanying research on learning and teaching in science.

REFERENCES

1. Common Core State Standards Initiative. (2011). *Common Core State Standards Initiative Home Page.* Available: http://www.corestandards.org/ [June 2011].

2. National Research Council. (1999). *How People Learn: Brain, Mind, Experience, and School.* J.D. Bransford, A.L. Brown, and R.R. Cocking (Eds.). Committee on Developments in the Science of Learning. Washington, DC: National Academy Press.

3. National Research Council. (2006). *Systems for State Science Assessment.* Committee on Test Design for K-12 Science Achievement. M.R. Wilson and M.W. Bertenthal (Eds.). Board on Testing and Assessment, Center for Education. Division of Behavioral and Social Sciences and Education. Washington, DC: The National Academies Press.

4. National Research Council. (2007). *Taking Science to School: Learning and Teaching Science in Grades K-8.* R.A. Duschl, H.A. Schweingruber, and A.W. Shouse (Eds.). Committee on Science Learning—Kindergarten Through Eighth Grade, Board on Science Education. Center for Education. Division of Behavioral and Social Sciences and Education. Washington, DC: The National Academies Press.

5. National Research Council. (2009). *Learning Science in Informal Environments: People, Places, and Pursuits.* P. Bell, B. Lewenstein, A.W. Shouse, and M.A. Feder (Eds.). Committee on Learning Science in Informal Environments, Board on Science Education, Center for Education. Division of Behavioral and Social Sciences and Education. Washington, DC: The National Academies Press.

6. Banks, J.A., Au, K.H., Ball, A.F., Bell, P., Gordon, E.W., Gutiérrez, K., Heath, S.B., Lee, C.D., Lee, Y., Mahiri, J., Nasir, N.S., Valdes, G., and Zhou, M. (2007). *Learning In and Out of School in Diverse Environments: Lifelong, Life-wide, Life-deep.* Seattle: Center for Multicultural Education, University of Washington.

7. Lee, O., and Buxton, C. (2010). *Diversity and Equity in Science Education: Theory, Research, and Practice.* New York: Teachers College Press.

8. Barton, A.C., Tan, E., and Rivet, A. (2008). Creating hybrid spaces for engaging school science among urban middle school girls. *American Educational Research Journal, 45*(1), 68-103.

9. Brotman, J.S., and Moore, F.M. (2008). Girls and science: A review of four themes in the science education literature. *Journal of Research in Science Teaching, 45*(9), 971-1,002.

10. Enfield, M., Smith, E.L., and Grueber, D.J. (2008). "A sketch is like a sentence": Curriculum structures that support teaching epistemic practices of science. *Science Education, 92*(4), 608-630.

11. Lee, O., Deaktor, R.A., Hart, J.E., Cuevars, P., and Enders, C. (2005). An instructional intervention's impact on the science and literacy achievement of culturally and linguistically diverse elementary students. *Journal of Research in Science Teaching, 42*(8), 857-887.

12. Page, S. (2007). *The Difference: How the Power of Diversity Creates Better Groups, Firms, Schools, and Societies.* Woodstock, England: Princeton University Press.

13. American Association for the Advancement of Science. (2009). *Benchmarks for Science Literacy.* Project 2061. Available: http://www.project2061.org/publications/bsl/online/index.php?txtRef=http%3A%2F%2Fwww%2Eproject2061%2Eorg%2Fpublications%2Fbsl%2Fdefault%2Ehtm%3FtxtRef%3D%26txtURIOld%3D%252Ftools%252Fbsl%252Fdefault%2Ehtm&txtURIOld=%2Fpublications%2Fbsl%2Fonline%2Fbolintro%2Ehtm [June 2011].

14. National Research Council. (1996). *National Science Education Standards.* National Committee for Science Education Standards and Assessment. Washington, DC: National Academy Press.

15. National Assessment of Educational Progress. (2009). *Science Framework.* National Assessment Governing Board. Washington, DC: U.S. Department of Education. Available: http://www.nagb.org/publications/frameworks/science-09.pdf [June 2011].

16. College Board. (2009). *Science College Board Standards for College Success.* Available: http://professionals.collegeboard.com/profdownload/cbscs-science-standards-2009.pdf [June 2011].

17. American Association for the Advancement of Science. (2007). *Atlas of Science Literacy*, *Volumes 1 and 2.* Project 2061. Washington, DC: Author.

18. Rodriguez, A.J. (1997). The dangerous discourse of invisibility: A critique of the National Research Council's *National Science Education Standards. Journal of Research in Science Teaching, 34*(1), 19-37.

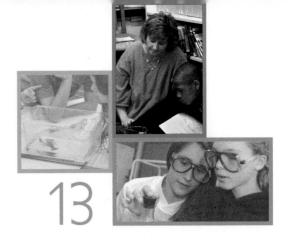

LOOKING TOWARD THE FUTURE
Research and Development to Inform K-12 Science Education Standards

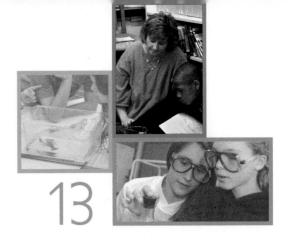

Throughout this report, the committee has acknowledged that the evidence base on which the framework rests is incomplete. In this final chapter, we lay out aspects of a research and development (R&D) agenda we think is needed to provide evidence-based guidance for future revisions to K-12 science education standards, which we expect will occur within the next 10-15 years. Three factors that have served to stimulate the current attempt are likely to be involved in the future effort: (1) changes in scientific knowledge and priorities; (2) changes in the understanding of science learning and teaching across the K-12 spectrum; and (3) changes in the understanding of how a given set of standards is interpreted, taken up, and used by a variety of players to influence K-12 educational practice and policy.

Given these factors, the R&D agenda proposed here is focused on the latter two areas, that is, on (1) enhancing understanding of how students learn the core ideas and practices of science and how best to support that learning through instruction and (2) developing a better understanding of how national- and state-level standards are translated and implemented throughout the K-12 science education system and how they eventually change classroom practice and affect student learning. It also addresses three additional elements related to understanding how standards are translated throughout the system: (1) research on K-12 teachers' knowledge of science and science practices and their teaching practices; (2) research on effective professional development for supporting teachers' understanding and uses of the standards; and (3) research on the resulting curricula, curriculum materials and technology-based tools, instructional approaches, and assessments. In addition, investments in the development of the associated curricula and curriculum support materials and technologies, professional development programs, and assessments must be ongoing, first to provide initial versions and then to improve them based on research results.

In each section below, we describe these broad issues for R&D. Finally, recognizing the importance of equity and diversity, we have woven questions related to these issues throughout both major sections of the chapter.

RESEARCH TO INFORM IMPLEMENTATION AND FUTURE REVISIONS OF THE FRAMEWORK

In the following subsections, we lay out a plan for programs of research to examine key elements of science learning and teaching that should serve to influence the future development of science education standards and implementation of the framework. To do so, we draw heavily from the prior National Research Council (NRC) report *Learning and Instruction: A SERP Research Agenda*, which described a framework for research and development on learning and instruction in the areas of mathematics, literacy, and science [1].

The research plan we develop here is centrally concerned with issues of teacher practice and curricular resources. The reason is that any set of standards is about expectations for students' knowledge and proficiency, which are necessarily mediated by (1) the knowledge, wisdom, and practices of teachers; (2) the tools provided to assist them in accomplishing their work; and (3) the contexts that support the intellectual efforts of both teachers and students.

Core Questions Behind an R&D Agenda on Learning and Teaching

The *Learning and Instruction* report laid out a set of core questions that focus on the normal course of development and learning, as well as on diagnosing and responding to students' problems in mastering new concepts and acquiring new knowledge and practices [1]. These questions, which provide a schema for examining teaching and learning, highlight the aspects of teachers' knowledge that must be supported through preservice experience and professional development. They are as follows:

1. What are the typical preconceptions that students hold about the practices, crosscutting concepts, and core ideas at the outset?

2. What is the expected progression of understanding, and what are the predictable points of difficulty that must be overcome?
3. What instructional interventions (e.g., curriculum materials, teaching practices, simulations or other technology tools, instructional activities) can move students along a path from their initial understanding to the desired outcome?
4. What general and discipline-specific norms and instructional practices best engage and support student learning?
5. How can students of both genders and of all cultural backgrounds, languages, and abilities become engaged in the instructional activities needed to move toward more sophisticated understanding?
6. How can the individual student's understanding and progress be monitored?

The paragraphs below summarize the committee's research recommendations corresponding to each of the above questions:

Questions 1 and 2. Insights into *typical student preconceptions* of a topic and *the expected progression of student understanding* require careful research on the typical trajectories of learning. This research aims (a) to identify how the nature and limits of children's cognitive abilities change with age and instruction and (b) to uncover common preconceptions that either support learning (e.g., the ability to halve or double relatively easily in mathematics) or undermine it (e.g., the belief that temperature measures the amount of heat present). Past findings have suggested that students' preconceptions are resilient, even after specific instruction to the contrary. That resilience highlights the importance of a carefully designed research program to inform and support teaching to achieve conceptual change from naive preconceptions toward a more sophisticated scientific understanding of a topic. Although research of this sort is often the domain of cognitive scientists and education researchers, their efforts can be enriched by the participation of experienced teachers and by detailed study of exemplary practice.

Question 3. *Educational experiences intended to move students along a learning path* constitute the core of what we consider to be "instruction." The work of curriculum developers, teachers, and researchers helps to enable these experiences, which may involve specific structured sequences of investigations or the use of simulations, or they may take place across individual units or longer segments of instruction. Regardless of the source, how each of these experiences contributes to students' development of more sophisticated understanding of crosscutting concepts, disciplinary core ideas, and scientific and engineering practices—and therefore to conceptual change—constitutes an important research agenda. Furthermore, the effectiveness of the instructional approach used—and for what groups of students it is effective—is a matter for empirical testing.

Question 4. *General and discipline-specific norms and instructional practices* define the expectations for students' and teachers' interactions in the classroom. "Classroom learning communities" and how they develop to support effective learning are currently a subject of considerable research in science education. Every such community is distinguished by norms for work and interactions, rang-

ing from when and how people collaborate to how they speak with one another. Some of those norms are general, rooted in the understanding of schools in a democratic society; others are discipline specific—that is, what it means to do mathematics differs from what it means to do chemistry or history. In all cases, the relationships between particular classroom norms and learning outcomes of interest for particular groups of students—for example, distin-

guished by ethnicity or gender—are a matter for empirical investigation. Another example is that the framework includes a number of discourse practices among the science practices; because such discourses are relatively rare in science classrooms at present, research that focuses on how teachers and students develop the related norms for them will be needed.

Question 5. *Assessing students' engagement in instructional activities* requires research on how young people of different backgrounds, cultures, races, genders, abilities, and languages can enter and become full participants in the scientific classroom community. Such research is especially needed if the framework's expectation that all students will have opportunities for accomplished scientific and engineering learning is to succeed. How best to develop and sustain students' interest in science is an important part of research in this area.

Question 6. *Assessing an individual student's understanding* is the task of research and development on methods and systems of assessment. This knowledge base can quite naturally be developed and tested in the context of curriculum R&D, but it may also draw on more fundamental research—for example, on the nature and measurement of text comprehension.

Key Areas of Research

Learning Progressions

In the context of the framework, an especially important line of inquiry should involve learning progressions that embed the core ideas and practices spelled out in this document. Such research may focus on a particular core idea and ask what sequence of learning experiences, including engagement in practices, around that idea best advance student understanding and address common misconceptions. Research should also focus on whether other ideas and practices, if found across multiple science topic learning progressions, ought to be specified as well. Such work would be pertinent to Questions 1-6 above, as it would, of necessity, include research on instructional approaches, sequences of curriculum, and students' progress using those approaches and curricula.

There now exists a set of R&D examples that include progressions for some of the life, physical, and earth sciences core ideas described in the current framework [2]. These examples also include student outcomes and instructional activities that connect very directly to elements of the practices described in the framework. Such work might be seen as constituting a set of downstream cases in which further investment in implementation and testing might prove very valuable, especially in terms of validating the hypothesized progressions and determining efficacy and effectiveness. Much of this work currently falls under the heading of design-based research, and with further investment it might be ready to travel farther via initial efficacy trials, which in turn move into large-scale replication, perhaps with randomized trials.

It is worth noting that, because R&D on learning progressions in science is at an early stage, many aspects of the core ideas and their progressions over time with instruction (as sketched out in the framework) remain unexplored territory. The work needed would probably start with design experiments situated in classrooms that explore (a) how to specify the knowledge to be acquired by students at particular grade bands and (b) what instructional approaches might best support the proposed progressions. One interesting challenge in such work is that the vast majority of what is known about the development of understanding across the full K-12 grade span is based on cross-sectional designs; available longitudinal work is of limited duration, given the sheer challenges of cost and practical management associated with instructional research of long duration. Thus very little is known about what can develop in later grades on the basis of successful implementation of solid learning progressions for a concept in the earlier grades [3].

Work on learning progressions will also need to explore how literacy, language skills, and mathematics intersect with learning in science across multiple years of school. This research is important for understanding how the practices develop over time and how learning experiences in other subjects might leverage or be leveraged by learning in science.

Scientific and Engineering Practices

Another key aspect of the current framework is its emphasis on scientific and engineering practices and their integration with the core concepts. Although research has been done on how well students are able to engage in aspects of some of the practices and how engagement in particular practices supports the development of both specific ideas in science and understanding of the nature of science, this work is fragmented. It does not yet provide insight into how students' proficiency with these practices can develop over multiple years, nor how the full set of practices interacts with understanding of the core ideas and crosscutting concepts. For example, people need to know a great deal more about the levels of sophistication in these practices that are possible as students move from the early grade bands to the later ones. In particular, the proficiencies that they can achieve and the types of instructional materials and methods that can support that learning should be explored. People also need to learn which scientific and engineering practices are likely to pose significant challenges in terms of teacher knowledge with regard both to content and pedagogy.

Development of Curricular and Instructional Materials

As discussed in Chapter 11, the framework and its resulting standards have a number of implications for implementation, one of which involves the need for curricular and instructional materials that embody all three dimensions: scientific and engineering practices, crosscutting concepts, and disciplinary core ideas. Some existing materials will be highly compatible with aspects of the framework, others will present implementation issues that bear further study, and there will also be a need to develop and test new materials and technological tools for learning that work across grades and are aligned with the framework's key ideas. In the case of new materials, studies of students and teachers will be needed as they interact with them over the short term (units) and long term (learning progressions). Furthermore, new ways of using technology in learning and teaching science and engineering (e.g., capturing data, analyzing and visualizing data, building models) will continue to change what children can learn and be able to do at particular grade bands [4] and provide new ways of assessing their learning. Thus, research on learning must include research on how technology can be used to support and enhance learning of specific topics.

R&D will also be needed on the intersections of science as described in the framework with literacy and mathematics and the implications for curriculum and instruction. This should include how science curriculum can be designed to best articulate with curriculum in English/language arts and mathematics.

Assessment

Assessment of the outcomes of learning and instruction—what students know and are able to do—merits special attention in R&D on science education. The high-quality evidence that derives from careful assessment allows practitioners, researchers, and policy makers to explore critical questions about the student's knowledge or a program's effectiveness and its possible need for revision

Designing Assessments. The first requirement for developing quality assessments is that the concepts and skills that signal progress toward mastery of a subject be understood and specified. In various areas of the curriculum, such as early reading, early mathematics, and high school physics, substantial work has already been done in this regard. In some cases, researchers have capitalized on such knowledge to develop the elements of an assessment strategy, although that work has generally concentrated on the development of materials for formative assessment [5-7]. But, in general, people have yet to fully capitalize on research and theory to develop valid assessment tools for other aspects of elementary and middle school science.

To design and implement assessments that are fair—that is, valid across different groups of students—it is crucial that patterns of learning for different student populations be studied. But much of the research on current theories of developing knowledge has been conducted with restricted groups of students (mostly middle-class whites). In many cases, it is not clear whether these theories apply equally well to diverse populations of students, including those who have been poorly served in the science and engineering education system—females, underrepresented minorities, English language learners, and students with disabilities.

Although there are typical learning pathways, often there is not a single pathway to competence. Furthermore, students will not necessarily respond in similar ways to assessment probes designed to diagnose knowledge and understanding. These kinds of natural variations among individuals need to be better understood through empirical study and incorporated into the cognitive models of learning that serve as a basis for assessment design.

Sophisticated models of learning do not by themselves produce high-quality assessment information. Also needed are methods and tools both for eliciting appropriate and relevant data from students and for interpreting the data collected about their performance. As described elsewhere [8], current measurement methods enable a much broader range of inferences to be drawn about student competence than many people realize. In particular, it is now possible to characterize student achievement in terms of multiple aspects of proficiency rather than in a single score; to chart students' progress over time instead of simply measuring performance at a particular point; to deal with multiple paths or alternative methods of valued performance; to model, monitor, and improve judgments based on informed evaluations; and to evaluate performance not only at the level of students but also at the levels of groups, classes, schools, and states.

However, further research is needed to (a) investigate the limits and relative usefulness of existing statistical models for capturing critical aspects of learning; (b) develop tools that make it easier for those who have professional interest but do not have the full range of psychometric expertise to apply new measurement approaches; and (c) develop cost-effective tools that allow education professionals, including teachers and policy makers, to use the results of these approaches.

Uses of Assessments. Important issues about assessment use also need to be pursued. Researchers should explore (a) how new forms of assessment can be made both accessible to teachers and practical for use in classrooms; (b) how assessments can be made efficient for use in large-scale testing contexts; (c) how assessments can be designed so that all students have equal opportunities to demonstrate their competencies; (d) how information from classroom-level assessments and large-scale assessments can be combined reliably for use in addressing educational problems; and (e) how various new forms of assessment affect student learning, teacher practice, and educational decision making [9].

It is particularly important that such work be done in close collaboration with practicing teachers who have diverse backgrounds and varying levels of teaching experience. Also to be studied are ways in which school structures (e.g., class time, class size, mechanisms for teachers to work together) affect the feasibility of new assessment types and their effectiveness.

Supporting Teachers' Learning

The research base on science teacher learning has been growing [10], often centered on Shulman's [11] framework of teacher knowledge [12]. For example, it is now known that preservice elementary school teachers have some of the same preconceptions of scientific concepts as their students [13] and that even experienced teachers have difficulty acquiring the kinds of science knowledge and teaching practices that support students' learning [14].

Preservice secondary school science teachers sometimes encounter problems with the conceptual content [15, 16] and in implementing aspects of scientific discourses and practices [17]. Similarly, these teachers often have an incomplete understanding of the nature of scientific evidence [18], and their knowledge about students' conceptions may be limited [19].

Thus continued research is needed to better understand the possible longitudinal trajectories that K-12 teachers may take in becoming knowledgeable and accomplished science teachers.

As noted in *Learning and Instruction* [1], the questions that frame student learning apply just as aptly to teacher learning. Teachers should understand students' naive ideas and learning processes well enough to assess and guide them, and they should understand the crosscutting concepts, disciplinary core ideas, and scientific and engineering practices well enough to select appropriate instructional materials and strategies and apply them effectively. Teachers should use assessments to plan for, revise, and adapt instruction; to evaluate teaching and learning;

to guide the pace and direction of instruction; and to select tasks, representations, and materials that engage students' interests and provide learning opportunities.

Teachers' knowledge of these things allows them to respond to students' questions and ideas, to probe and correct anomalies in classroom investigations, to understand the curriculum materials well enough to use or revise them flexibly as a means to an end rather than as ends in themselves, to apply norms and practices with sufficient skill to create a supportive and challenging learning environment in the classroom, and to comprehend the content and purposes of assessments with enough depth to interpret the outcomes and respond appropriately.

The typical learning trajectory for teachers and how it changes with learning opportunities also require empirical investigation. Questions for inquiry include: Under what conditions and in what contexts can teachers best learn particular scientific and engineering practices, crosscutting concepts, and disciplinary core ideas during their teacher preparation and with ongoing professional development? What knowledge and methods are most important for teachers to acquire at the beginning of their careers? What knowledge and methods are better acquired once they enter the profession? What organizational, material, and human resources are necessary to support and sustain teacher learning over time?

UNDERSTANDING THE IMPACT OF THE FRAMEWORK AND RELATED-STANDARDS

The R&D agenda for understanding the influence of standards is based heavily on the NRC report *Investigating the Influence of Standards: A Framework for Research in Mathematics, Science, and Technology Education* [20] and on a chapter in *The Impact of State and National Standards on K-12 Science Teaching* [21], which draws on the NRC report. Although much has changed since these reports were released, including substantial shifts in state and federal education policies, the analysis of the education systems and how standards may influence them is a valuable starting point.

In the subsections that follow, we focus on four components through which the framework and its resulting standards might ultimately influence student learning. These parallel components are also discussed in Chapter 10, which addresses implementation. The purpose of the research on implementation is both to determine whether the framework and standards are being implemented and, more importantly, to identify barriers to implementation and ways to overcome these barriers.

Curriculum and Instructional Materials

The framework intentionally does not prescribe a specific curriculum, but it does imply criteria for designing a curriculum and selecting instructional materials. If the framework were to influence what is taught to students, then curriculum policy, the design and development of instructional materials, including technology-based materials and tools, and the processes and criteria by which such materials were developed, selected, and implemented in classrooms would reflect the framework's practices, crosscutting concepts, and disciplinary core ideas.

Enrollment and achievement patterns in schools would reveal whether the vision expressed by the framework applied to all students. For example, if the framework were permeating the system, opportunities for taking challenging science courses would be open to every student, and resources needed to implement a robust standards-based curriculum would be allocated in equitable ways. Resources designed to accommodate diverse learners, including those learning English as a second language, would support the focus of the standards on all students having access to opportunities to learn important science and engineering concepts and practices.

Key questions related to tracing the influence of the framework and standards on the curriculum include

- What curriculum development efforts have been undertaken to provide materials that are well aligned to the framework and new standards? Who was engaged in these efforts? Were any incentives used to encourage these development efforts, and which of them were most effective?
- How do the new curricula differ from those used in the past, and are teachers prepared to address these differences?
- How has the funding from various federal and state agencies been allocated for curriculum development efforts that are aligned with the framework and standards?
- Is technology to support science learning being marshaled and used effectively to develop technology-based curriculum support materials and tools (e.g., simulations, data access)? [4, 22]
- What has been learned about the effectiveness of the new curriculum with various populations and under different implementation conditions?

Teacher and Administrator Development

As noted in Chapter 10 on implementation, the education system provides channels through which the framework might influence how teachers learn to teach science (and continue to improve their science teaching) and how school and district administrators offer instructional leadership in science education.

If the framework were to influence the preparation of new teachers, there would be an increased alignment of related policies and practices with those of the framework. States, districts, and postsecondary institutions, including lateral entry programs, would create mechanisms that enable prospective teachers to gain the knowledge and practices needed to help students meet the expectations outlined in the framework. Teacher preparation programs would prepare prospective teachers to teach in diverse classrooms, and the distribution across schools of teachers with the knowledge and practices for implementing effective science and engineering education would be such that all learners would have access to high-quality learning opportunities.

Policies and fiscal investments at the local, state, and federal levels would focus on recertification criteria, professional development opportunities, and system-wide support strategies aligned with the framework. States and localities would provide a rich framework-based infrastructure to support science and engineering teaching. Teachers would be motivated to enhance their understanding of core concepts and practices described in the framework, and recertification criteria and teacher evaluations would focus on evidence that verified teachers' knowledge, understanding, and practices were consistent with the framework.

Key questions related to tracing the influence of the framework and standards on teacher and administrator development include

- How have teacher educators used the framework and standards to improve their science teacher preparation programs? What changes have occurred in the science courses taken by preservice teachers? How widespread are these changes, and what policies or incentives were in place in those colleges or universities that successfully redesigned their programs?
- What professional development projects or programs have been enacted to support teachers in implementing instruction that is well matched to the framework and standards? Who was engaged in these efforts? With what results? What strategies or program structures are most successful, and what kinds of incentives or policies lead to teacher participation?

- What changes in teacher certification systems have been enacted to ensure that all students learn science from teachers who are well prepared to teach it? Who was responsible for such changes?

- What steps have been taken to ensure a more equitable distribution of qualified teachers so as to give all students access to learning opportunities consistent with the framework?
- What changes in administrator certification systems have been enacted to ensure that new administrators understand and can use the framework and standards in making decisions about science standards, the selection of science curricula, the design of professional development programs to support teachers, and the evaluation of teachers' and students' progress?
- What kinds of professional development programs have been offered to the administrators themselves so that their understanding, interpretation, and uses of the framework and standards support their decision making?

Assessment and Accountability

Consideration of assessment involves a careful study of how it interacts with accountability; how teachers conduct and use classroom and state assessments; how assessment influences teacher practices; and how it is used by schools, states, and districts. Key questions related to tracing the influence of the framework and standards on the assessment and accountability systems include

- What have assessment designers done in response to the framework and its resulting standards?
- Does the full complement of local and state assessments used for accountability cover all of the standards?
- What advances in assessment methodology have been pursued to ensure that assessments reflect the full range and intent of the framework and standards? Who was engaged in developing these advances?

- How can assessments be developed that are fair, both for different demographic groups and for students with disabilities? Have examples of these kinds of assessments for the practices, concepts, and core ideas in the framework been developed and implemented?

Organizational Issues

Institutional barriers can hamper widespread adoption of framework-based curricula and related approaches to instruction. These barriers include incentive structures, organizational culture, career patterns of teachers and administrators, and financial constraints [23]. This piece of the R&D agenda, which entails both short-term and long-term elements, necessitates uncovering obstacles to system reform and exploring innovative ways to overcome these obstacles. In other words, as emphasized in Chapter 11, the components of the system for science education must be coherent, and all of the players must be actively participating. Key questions include

- What is the process by which the framework is used to craft state-level science standards? Who is involved? How were they chosen?
- How does the capacity of the state and districts to fund education affect the writing of the standards and the development of assessments?
- What is the adoption process for the state science education standards? Is it voluntary or mandatory? What kinds of incentives or support are provided to districts to facilitate this adoption?
- To what extent does the state department of education provide funding for adopting new framework-aligned science curricula and professional development programs for teachers and administrators?
- What kinds of framework-related professional development are provided for state- and district-level science supervisors, superintendents, school boards, and other important policy makers (such as state legislators)? With what results?
- Are resources for science learning and qualified teachers equitably distributed across schools and districts of varying socioeconomic levels and differing populations? What efforts have been made to improve equity of opportunity to learn science?

CONCLUSION

In this final chapter, we have described the kinds of research that are needed so that, when the time comes to revise standards for K-12 science education, evidence-based decisions can be made about how to improve them. There is a need for ongoing research on science teaching and learning, and particularly on learning progressions for the core ideas detailed here. In addition there is need for research on the impacts and implementation of the next generation of standards, and of this framework, to identify both barriers and effective strategies. Such research needs to consider three levels—system, school, and classroom—in order to effectively inform future decisions about standards. Research on school-level factors—such as professional development targeted at administrators' and teachers' knowledge and practices, the design and testing of learning progressions across the framework's three dimensions—would support choices about where to place particular scientific and engineering practices, crosscutting concepts, and disciplinary core ideas in future K-12 science standards.

Perhaps most important, research is needed on classroom-level contexts, materials, and discourses that engage and support a wider range of students in high-quality teaching and learning experiences with the concepts, ideas, and practices. Action on this wide-ranging multilevel agenda would make it possible to advance the framework's vision and continue to improve access for all.

REFERENCES

1. National Research Council. (2004). *Learning and Instruction: A SERP Research Agenda*. Panel on Learning and Instruction. M.S. Donovan and J.W. Pellegrino (Eds.). Division of Behavioral and Social Sciences and Education. Washington, DC: The National Academies Press.

2. Consortium for Policy Research and Education. (2009). Learning progression in science: An evidence-based approach to reform. Prepared by T. Corcoran, F. Mosher, and A. Rogat. Center on Continuous Instructional Improvement. Teachers College-Columbia University. Available: http://www.cpre.org/images/stories/cpre_pdfs/lp_science_rr63.pdf.

3. National Research Council. (2007). *Taking Science to School: Learning and Teaching Science in Grades K-8*. Committee on Science Learning, Kindergarten Through Eighth Grade. R.A. Duschl, H.A. Schweingruber, and A.W. Shouse (Eds.). Board on Science Education, Center for Education. Division of Behavioral and Social Sciences and Education. Washington, DC: The National Academies Press.

4. National Science Foundation Task Force on Cyberlearning. (2008). *Fostering Learning in the Networked World: The Cyberlearning Opportunity and Challenge*. (Publication No. nsf08204). Arlington, VA: National Science Foundation. Available: http://www.nsf.gov/pubs/2008/nsf08204/nsf08204.pdf [June 2011].

5. Minstrell, J., and Kraus, P. (2005). Guided inquiry in the science classroom. In J. Bransford and S. Donovan (Eds.), *How Students Learn: History, Mathematics, and Science in the Classroom*. Washington DC: The National Academies Press.

6. Wiliam, D. (2007). Content then process: Teacher learning communities in the service of formative assessment. In D.B. Reeves (Ed.), *Ahead of the Curve: The Power of Assessment to Transform Teaching and Learning* (pp. 183-204). Bloomington, IN: Solution Tree.

7. Wilson, M., and Sloane, K. (2000). From principles to practice: An embedded assessment system. *Applied Measurement in Education, 12*(2), 181-208.

8. National Research Council. (2001). *Knowing What Students Know: The Science and Design of Education Assessment*. Committee on the Foundations of Assessment. J.W. Pellegrino, N. Chudowsky, and R. Glaser (Eds.). Board on Testing and Assessment, Center for Education. Division of Behavioral and Social Sciences and Education. Washington, DC: National Academy Press.

9. Black, P., Harrison, C., Lee, C., Marshall, B., and Wiliam, D. (2003). *Assessment for Learning: Putting It into Practice*. Buckingham, England: Open University Press.

10. Abell, S.K. (2007). Research on science teacher knowledge. In S.K. Abell and N.G. Lederman (Eds.), *Handbook of Research on Science Education* (pp. 1,105-1,149). Mahwah, NJ: Lawrence Erlbaum Associates.

11. Shulman, L.S. (1986). Those who understand: Knowledge growth in teaching. *Educational Researcher, 15*(2), 4-14.

12. Magnusson, S., Krajcik, J., and Borko, H. (1999). Nature, sources, and development of pedagogical content knowledge for science teaching. In J. Gess-Newsome and N.G. Lederman (Eds.), *PCK and Science Education* (pp. 95-132). Dodrecht, the Netherlands: Kluwer Academic.

13. Smith, D.C., and Anderson, C.W. (1999). Appropriating scientific practices and discourses with future elementary teachers. *Journal on Research in Science Teaching, 36*(7), 755-776.

14. Smith, D.C., and Neale, D.C. (1989). The construction of subject matter knowledge in primary science teaching. *Teaching and Teacher Education, 5*(1), 1-20.

15. Kokkotas, P., Vlachos, I., and Koulaidis, V. (1998). Teaching the topic of the particulate nature of matter in prospective teachers' training courses. *International Journal of Science Education, 20*(3), 291-303.

16. Lin, H.-S., Cheng, H.-J., and Lawrenz, F. (2000). The assessment of students and teachers' understanding of gas laws. *Journal of Chemical Education, 77*(2), 235-238.

17. Carlsen, W.S. (1991). The construction of subject matter knowledge in primary science teaching. In J.E. Brophy (Ed.), *Advances in Research on Teaching, Volume 2: Teachers' Subject Matter Knowledge and Classroom Instruction*. New York: JAI Press.

18. Taylor, J.A., and Dana, T.M. (2003). Secondary school physics teachers' conceptions of scientific evidence: An exploratory case study. *Journal of Research in Science Teaching, 40*(8), 721-736.

19. De Jong, O., and van Driel, J.H. (2001). *Developing Preservice Teachers' Content Knowledge and PCK of Models and Modelling*. Paper presented at the Annual Meeting of the National Association for Research in Science Teaching, St. Louis, MO.

20. National Research Council. (2002). *Investigating the Influence of Standards: A Framework for Research in Mathematics, Science, and Technology Education*. I.R. Weiss, M.S. Knapp, K.S. Hollweg, and G. Burrill (Eds.). Committee on Understanding the Influence of Standards in K-12 Science, Mathematics, and Technology Education, Center for Education. Division of Behavioral and Social Sciences and Education. Washington, DC: National Academy Press.

21. Weiss, I.R. (2006). A framework for investigating the influence of national science standards. In D.W. Sunal and E.L. Wright (Eds.), *The Impact of State and National Standards on K-12 Science Teaching* (pp. 51-82). Greenwich, CT: Information Age.

22. Linn, M., and Eylon, B.-S. (2011). *Science Learning and Instruction: Taking Advantage of Technology to Promote Knowledge Integration*. New York: Routledge.

23. Briars, D.J., and Resnick, L.B. (2000). *Standards, Assessments—and What Else? The Essential Elements of Standards-Based School Improvement*. CSE Technical Report 528. Available: http://www.cse.ucla.edu/products/Reports/TECH528.pdf [June 2011].

APPENDIXES

A

SUMMARY OF PUBLIC FEEDBACK AND SUBSEQUENT REVISIONS

The committee recognized early in the process that obtaining feedback from a broad range of stakeholders and experts would be crucial to the framework's success. For this reason, we secured permission from the National Research Council (NRC) to release a draft version of the framework for public comment. The draft underwent an expedited NRC review in early July 2010 and was posted online on July 12 for a 3-week period.

This draft did not include all of the chapters intended for the final volume, although it did thoroughly address all three dimensions of the framework: cross-cutting concepts, disciplinary core ideas, and scientific and engineering practices. Individuals could submit comments through an online survey. In addition, NRC staff contacted over 40 organizations in science, engineering, and education to notify them of the public comment period; they were asked to hold focus groups for gathering feedback from their members or to notify members of the opportunity to comment online. Notably, the NRC worked closely with the National Science Teachers Association, the American Association for the Advancement of Science, Achieve, Inc., and the Council of State Science Supervisors to facilitate the public input process. Finally, the committee asked a number of disciplinary experts to provide detailed feedback on the draft from their own particular perspectives.

During the 3-week public comment period, the committee received extensive input from both individuals and groups. Overall, more than 2,000 people responded to the online survey. Over 30 focus groups were held around the country by 24 organizations, with a total of over 400 participants. The committee also received letters from key individuals and organizations. Lists of the organizations that participated in the focus groups and those that submitted letters are provided at the end of this summary.

NRC staff and the committee chair reviewed this input, developed summaries identifying the major issues raised, and outlined possible revisions. Committee members then evaluated these summaries and potential revisions, and they had the opportunity to examine the public feedback in detail. After discussions at its fifth and sixth meetings, the committee made substantial revisions to the framework based on the feedback.

We summarize this feedback below and describe the revisions that were made in response. In cases in which the committee chose not to revise or to make only a limited revision, we explain why this choice was made. We organize the discussion into two sections: overarching issues, which pertain to the draft framework as a whole, and issues relating specifically to any of the framework's three dimensions or its learning progressions.

OVERARCHING ISSUES

In general, the feedback about the draft framework indicated support for the overall approach. In the online surveys, many individuals commented that they were impressed with the document and thought it provided a good next step toward refining standards for K-12 science education. At the same time, there were many critiques and suggestions for how to improve it. In looking across all of the modes of gathering feedback, some key overarching issues emerged:

- concerns about the purpose, audience, and voice;
- suggestions of additional fields or topics to include;
- how best to incorporate and describe ideas in engineering and technology;
- concerns that there was too much material;
- lack of guidance or examples about how to convey the integration of cross-cutting concepts, core ideas, and practices;
- insufficient indication of connections to other topics or issues, such as mathematics and literacy;
- need for a stronger statement about science for all and insufficient attention to diversity and equity;
- lack of "standards" for curriculum, programs, assessment, and professional development similar to those that were included in the *National Science Education Standards* [1]; and
- lack of attention to the challenges inherent in implementing the framework.

Purpose, Audience, and Voice

The feedback suggested some confusion about the purpose of the document and the intended audience. Several focus groups suggested that a coherent vision across the document was lacking. Some individuals thought Chapter 1 provided a good summary of key principles, and others thought the vision was too diffuse. Across all of the modes of response and across all kinds of individuals, people commented that the promise of the first chapter was not consistently delivered in the rest of the document. Some commenters said explicitly that the framework had gone too far toward standards. Others said that the document would be difficult for teachers to use.

Several comments from individuals and summaries from focus groups called for more discussion of the goals of science education and a stronger argument in the first chapter for why science education is important. There was confusion about whether the document was outlining goals for all students or only for college-bound students.

Commenters were divided on the tone of the document and its quality of writing. Some thought it was well written; others thought it needed to be entirely rewritten in more accessible language.

Response

The committee made several revisions aimed at giving the framework greater focus, clarifying its goals and audience(s), and eliminating differences in tone and writing style. We reframed the introductory chapter, incorporated an argument for the importance of science education, provided a concise discussion of the goals for science education for all students, and added an explicit vision statement. Also, we shifted material that described the theoretical and empirically based assumptions guiding the framework to a second chapter.

To enable readers to identify the major tasks for standards developers in translating the framework into standards, we added Chapter 12: Guidance for Standards Developers. In that chapter, the committee presents a set of 13 recommendations that lay out the steps that standards developers should take and the considerations they need to keep in mind as they translate the framework into standards. Finally, the report was edited extensively to achieve a more uniform style and voice for improved readability.

Suggestions of Fields or Topics to Be Included

Several stakeholder groups voiced strong concerns that content relevant to their disciplines was either underrepresented or left out entirely. The strongest concerns were voiced by organizations and individuals affiliated with the behavioral and social sciences, computer sciences, and ocean sciences. Each of these communities mounted some kind of formal response, including letters from professional societies and campaigns to encourage their membership to respond to the online survey. There also was mention of health, but this involved a less organized response.

Behavioral and Social Sciences. The behavioral and social sciences community made a very strong request for inclusion in the framework. Community members wanted to see these fields acknowledged throughout the document as legitimate elements of the overall scientific enterprise. They also wanted to see a separate set of core ideas developed for the behavioral and social sciences and included in the framework. They pointed out that courses related to the behavioral and social sciences are already included at the secondary level (e.g., Advanced Placement psychology). Acknowledging that developing a separate set of core ideas would take time, they asked that the framework's project time line be extended accordingly. They also noted many places where the social sciences could inform issues that were raised, particularly in discussions related to science, technology, and society.

Computer Science. We received a similar request for inclusion from the computer science community. Some of its members noted that computing and computational thinking are now an integral part of science and therefore constitute essential knowledge and practices for students who might pursue careers in science or engineering. They pointed out that computer science and programming courses are already part of the K-12 curriculum, although they are not usually identified as part of the science curriculum.

Ocean Science. This community pointed to the framework's lack of specific attention to the ocean, it suggested a greater focus on earth systems than was captured in the draft, and it offered very concrete and detailed suggestions for revisions. The community developed some standard wording for members to use in filling out the survey. For example, there was an argument for greater inclusion of ocean sciences in the earth and space sciences section.

Nature of Science. Many of those who provided comments thought that the "nature of science" needed to be made an explicit topic or idea. They noted that it would not emerge simply through engaging with practices.

Behavioral and Social Sciences. The committee considers the behavioral and social sciences to be part of science, but for a number of reasons we think it inappropriate at this time to include them as a separate disciplinary area with its own set of core ideas. The primary reason is that these subjects are not currently part of what is considered the K-12 science curriculum. To include them here would speak to a major reorganization of K-12 schooling, which would go far beyond the committee's charge and, indeed, the professional expertise of the committee. In grades K-8, topics related to the behavioral and social sciences are typically covered in social studies, although they are not necessarily taught from a scientific perspective. At the secondary level, there are courses that do teach behavioral and social sciences topics from a scientific perspective—for example, Advanced Placement psychology. However, the framework as currently structured does not prevent these courses from being taught. In fact, the committee considers them appropriate science courses for extending and enriching the foundational science education described in the framework.

The secondary reason is that the committee has a responsibility to meet its charge and to maintain as closely as possible the intended time line of its work in order to inform the science standards development efforts of Achieve, Inc. Undertaking the task of identifying and articulating the core ideas in the behavioral and social sciences would be impossible within the available time and budget constraints. In the committee's judgment, this is a task for another group.

Although the committee did not think it was appropriate to include the behavioral and social sciences as a separate discipline, we did make efforts to discuss them explicitly throughout the document and particularly to identify places where they intersect with the framework's three dimensions. More specifically, the following changes were made in response to this input:

- In the Introduction, we acknowledge that the behavioral and social sciences are part of science and that they are not broadly represented in this framework.
- We revised language throughout the report to note the role of behavioral and social sciences expertise for addressing such issues as the connections among science, technology, and society.
- We included some behavioral and social sciences examples in the descriptions of science and in the chapters on crosscutting concepts and scientific and engineering practices.

- We added more emphasis on behavior and psychology, especially cognitive science, in the life sciences chapter, including a component idea on information processing under LS1 and a component idea on social interactions and group behavior under LS2.

Computer Science. In considering whether and how to include topics related to computer science, the committee noted that such concepts are more typically included under mathematics; we acknowledge, however, that the mathematics common core does not include such topics as algorithms or algorithmic approaches to computation and includes very little about the use of computational tools.

Although the committee determined that it was not appropriate to include computer science in the framework as a separate discipline with its own set of core ideas, in the revisions of the draft we made an effort to stress the importance both of computational thinking and of the use of computers as scientific tools, particularly in Chapter 3: Scientific and Engineering Practices. One of the eight major practices is labeled "Using Mathematics, Information and Computer Technology, and Computational Thinking," and the chapter stresses the importance of the application of these skills throughout science learning. The chapter also includes more emphasis on computers as tools for modeling, data collection and recording, and data analysis.

Although the framework does not include material usually covered by courses under the title "computer science," we stress that this choice in no way diminishes the importance either of general computer literacy for all students or of options for advanced computer science courses at the high school level.

Ocean Science. The earth and space sciences core ideas and grade band endpoints were revised to include more attention to the ocean whenever possible and to shift to more of a focus on earth systems.

Nature of Science. The committee added a section to the end of Chapter 4 to emphasize the need to reflect on scientific and engineering practices as a means to deepen students' understanding of the nature of science.

Inclusion of Engineering and Technology

The inclusion of engineering and technology and their own set of core ideas generated a substantial amount of feedback. Many indicated that they were pleased to see engineering and technology given an explicit place in K-12 science education.

However, there were numerous concerns, including the amount of space devoted to engineering and technology, the kinds of core ideas included, and the capacity of the K-12 science education system to get these areas right. Some individuals commented that including engineering and technology could present a problem: given that a goal of the framework is to cut the amount of material to be covered in K-12 science, it would be ironic if such inclusion expanded the amount of material considerably.

One key issue that appeared frequently in the comments was whether engineering and technology were well defined in the framework. This suggested the need to be more explicit about how engineering and technology are related to each other and to the natural sciences. Thoughtful advice from the experts we consulted was that some of the engineering and technology ideas incorporated elements that would be more appropriately placed in practices.

A letter to the committee from the International Technology and Engineering Educators Association raised a number of issues related to including engineering and technology in the science framework. The association argued that science teachers might not have sufficient background to teach the new material and, moreover, that there is currently no agreement in the field about what the core ideas in engineering and technology should be. The letter also pointed out that a corps of technology teachers at the secondary level already exists.

A related issue among respondents was treatment of the applications of science (such as medicine, public health, and agriculture) and their links to engineering and technology. Some individuals suggested that this topic needed more attention in the draft framework. Experts we asked to review the draft also pointed out that discussion of applications of science was mostly absent there.

Response

The committee deliberated extensively on the best way to respond to these concerns and chose to make significant revisions. We trimmed the material included under engineering and technology and focused on design as one of the major elements of engineering. We did this because design is the one core idea of engineering around which there appears to be consensus [2]. There also is evidence that engaging in design activities can enhance students' understanding of science [3].

Elements of design are now represented in Chapter 3: Scientific and Engineering Practices and also under the first core idea in Chapter 8: Engineering, Technology, and Applications of Science. The second core idea, which stresses the connections among engineering, technology, science, and society, discusses applications of science as well. Definitions of engineering, technology, and applications of science and of the relationships among them are clearly stated. These definitions then inform how engineering and technology are treated throughout the framework.

Too Much Material

Many individuals and organizations indicated that the draft framework still contained too much material, and some thought that the committee had not succeeded in making any reduction compared with previous documents. There were particular concerns not only about the amount of the material but also about its difficulty for the earlier grades. People also expressed trepidation that the learning progressions in the draft contained too many discrete and disconnected notions and that some were not central to the core idea being developed.

Response

The committee was particularly concerned with this feedback and in response made significant revisions to the core ideas and progressions. We revised the structure and content of the core ideas in all of the disciplines and replaced detailed progressions with grade band endpoints for grades 2, 5, 8, and 12. When necessary we consulted experts in teaching and learning science to supplement the committee's expertise. For example, six experts on learning science in grades K-5 provided detailed input regarding what ideas were appropriate for those levels and in which grade. As a result, some core ideas or component ideas begin their progression only at the 3-5 grade band to allow necessary prior knowledge of other core ideas to be established.

Overall, the committee thinks that the framework's content is now contained in a more suitable structure—one that provides guidance to standards developers rather than extremely detailed sets of discrete content statements.

How to Integrate the Three Dimensions

There were many concerns that too little guidance was given about how to integrate the crosscutting concepts, disciplinary core ideas, and scientific and engineering practices. In particular it was deemed that the learning progressions in the draft framework did not integrate the three dimensions at all, focusing solely on the progression for the core ideas.

The presentation of the crosscutting concepts and the practices in separate chapters led some to ask whether there would be separate standards for the crosscutting concepts and for the practices. Some pointed out that, without guidance about integration, the crosscutting concepts might be omitted entirely or be taught as a set of separate ideas.

Response

The committee was charged with identifying the disciplinary core ideas and practices for K-12 science education and with providing examples of the integration of these ideas and practices. One of the major tasks of the standards developers will be to determine ways to integrate the dimensions at the level of standards and performance expectations; we anticipate that full integration of the dimensions will occur at the level of curriculum and instruction.

In attending to the framework itself, we expanded Chapter 9: Integrating the Three Dimensions, which in the draft included only examples of performance expectations; for example, we added an example of how the dimensions might be brought together in curriculum and instruction. We also created a chapter on implementation issues (Chapter 10) that spelled out the need for curricula and instruction that integrate the three dimensions. Finally, in Chapter 12: Guidance for Standards Developers, we explicitly recommended that standards should incorporate the three dimensions in both their content statements and performance expectations.

Strengthening Connections to Other Subjects

Many people wanted to see more connections made to mathematics and literacy, some asked for explicit connections to the Common Core Standards, and some wanted to see more indications of the links between the core ideas and other disciplines.

Response

We added explicit reference to other subject areas in multiple places. In the chapter on scientific and engineering practices, we included two practices that specifically link to mathematics and literacy: "Using Mathematics, Information and Computer Technology, and Computational Thinking" and "Obtaining, Communicating, and Presenting Information." In discussions of these practices, we called out the need to parallel the Common Core Standards. We also included a recommendation for standards developers that the science standards be consistent with the mathematics and English/language arts Common Core Standards. In

Chapter 8: Engineering, Technology, and Applications of Science, and elsewhere as appropriate, we have stressed linkages to social studies.

Science for All, Diversity, and Equity

Many readers thought it was unclear whether this document was intended to prepare future scientists or to acquaint all students with science. Many also commented on a lack of clear statements about diversity and equity.

Response

In the introductory chapter, we clarified the vision for the framework and its emphasis on science for all students. We added Chapter 11: Equity and Diversity in Science and Engineering Education. This chapter had already been planned, but it was not ready in time for the draft released in July 2010.

Implementation: Curriculum, Instruction, Teacher Development, and Assessment

Many educators raised concerns about the challenges to implementing the framework—especially the demands it would place on curriculum developers, providers of professional development, and others. In some cases, commenters suggested that it would be useful to include the kinds of standards related to curriculum, instruction, teacher development, and assessment that were presented in the *National Science Education Standards* [1].

Response

The committee already recognized the challenges that the framework will place on K-12 science education. But although we had planned a chapter related to implementation, it was not available for the 2010 draft release. We have since written this chapter, and it is included in the present document as Chapter 10.

ISSUES RELATED TO EACH DIMENSION

Chapter 3: Scientific and Engineering Practices

Overall, the majority of those who commented were pleased to see discussion of scientific and engineering practices. Some specifically mentioned that it was a positive step to discuss particular practices instead of referring broadly to inquiry. There were varying reactions to the chapter itself. Some felt that there was too much introductory material about the work of scientists and engineers generally and that this discussion could be cut. Others thought that too many discrete practices with no uniform "grain size" were specified. Some had difficulty understanding how the tables in the chapter that described progressions were to be used in conjunction with the tables outlining the learning progressions for the disciplinary core ideas. Feedback from the individual experts indicated that in several cases the detailed progressions for the practices did not have supporting empirical evidence.

Response

We revised the introductory material in the chapter to make it more focused. We collapsed the practices into a shorter top-level list. We discussed developmental trajectories for each practice but cut the tables and the "levels" of practice that they had introduced. We refined the parallel treatment of scientific and engineering practices and clarified how the goals of work in the two areas differ.

Chapter 4: Crosscutting Concepts

Most of those who provided comments liked the framework's inclusion of crosscutting concepts. There were some suggestions of particular concepts to cut and of others to add. Many suggested that the section titled "Topics in Science, Engineering, Technology, and Society" did not fit in this dimension and should be integrated elsewhere.

Response

We chose not to delete or add to the crosscutting concepts. We did remove "Topics in Science, Engineering, Technology, and Society" from this chapter and placed the important elements of that material elsewhere (in practices; in the engineering, technology, and applications of science chapter; and in the chapter on implementation under the discussion of curriculum).

Chapters 5-8: Disciplinary Core Ideas

Many commenters provided detailed feedback on the core ideas and component ideas in each discipline. Their comments ranged from whether the inclusion of a core or component idea was appropriate, to suggestions for additions, to word-level editorial changes. Expert feedback from individuals and focus groups was particularly helpful in guiding the revisions of these four chapters.

Overall, readers tended to assume that each core idea would be given equal time in curriculum and instruction, leading to the impression, for example, that we were advocating that 25 percent of time be devoted to engineering. Although we have reduced the number of core ideas in Chapter 8: Engineering, Technology, and Applications of Science, we also noted that different core ideas will take different amounts of instructional time, both within and across grade levels; thus, the above-cited accounting was not a correct interpretation of the document. We have made appropriate clarifications in the introductory chapter and in the guidance for standards developers.

Physical Sciences. Physicists expressed concern that the content in physics was not articulated clearly, and chemists had a similar concern about the chemistry ideas. These responses suggested confusion about whether the framework is intended to define a full chemistry and physics course at the high school level. The committee's actual intent is for the framework to outline a foundational set of core ideas and for individual courses in physics or chemistry to deepen or extend the study of these ideas. Input from a group convened by the American Association of Physics Teachers, the American Physical Society, the American Institute of Physics, and the American Chemical Society was particularly useful.

There were some specific critiques of the core ideas on waves and communication technology, with some individuals suggesting that they were inappropriate to include in the physical sciences.

Life Sciences. Aside from a small subset of responders who wanted to eliminate evolution, overall the response to the life sciences core ideas was positive. Critique focused on (a) elements perceived as missing or underemphasized, particularly regarding psychology and behavior, and (b) elements perceived as misplaced in terms of grade-level appropriateness. Our disciplinary experts, who gave thoughtful input based on research on learning, suggested greater stress on the physical, chemical, and molecular bases of biological processes, at least in the higher grades.

Earth and Space Sciences. Several responders indicated that there were too many component ideas in this domain, and they offered concrete suggestions for reducing or streamlining the number of topics. Some individuals thought that the organization of the core and component ideas in the earth and space sciences was less conceptually coherent than in the other disciplines. They expressed concern that the ideas were more like a table of contents for a textbook than a coherent learning progression. Some noted that the level of detail was uneven, both within the earth and space sciences chapter and in comparison to the other science disciplines. Responders offered specific examples of ideas in the learning progressions that seemed developmentally inappropriate—that would require understanding of concepts from other disciplines or that were actually introduced in later grades. A number of reviewers suggested placing more emphasis on an "earth systems" approach; this suggestion was particularly emphasized by the ocean science community.

Engineering and Technology. The feedback related to these core ideas, together with the committee's response, is summarized in the previous section (Chapter 3: Scientific and Engineering Practices).

Response

The committee undertook significant revisions of the core and component ideas for all of the disciplines. For the physical sciences and the earth and space sciences, the revisions included reorganization and relabeling of the core and component ideas.

Learning Progressions

Many concerns were expressed about the draft learning progressions—the sections in Chapters 5-8 now labeled "Grade Band Endpoints." Several people, including some of the individual experts we asked to comment, objected to the term "learning progressions" for these sequences. They offered a number of reasons for why this term should not be used and made strong cases for changing it.

There was also concern about the level of detail included in the progressions; some felt that they went too far toward becoming standards. There was concern that the progressions were presented as many discrete bits of knowledge, which seemed to promote memorization of facts. Some thought that, for certain component ideas, the connections from grade band to grade band were unclear. And there was concern that the progressions were not clearly based on research; a couple of the experts pointed out places for which research suggests realignment of the content.

A number of criticisms stated that the progressions were not always grade appropriate; some pointed out that material included in the K-5 bands in particular was often too difficult. Others thought that the progressions underestimated what younger students can do. There was general concern that the expectations for the 3-5 and 6-8 grade bands were quite high, given the number of very important, but challenging, ideas that were covered. Finally, there was concern that the progressions focused on the disciplinary core ideas and did not attempt to integrate the crosscutting concepts and scientific and engineering practices in any way.

Response

The committee was especially attentive to the feedback on the learning progressions. The detailed progressions were changed to grade band endpoints, with the number of details significantly reduced. Meanwhile, the introductory discussion of each core idea was expanded into a single coherent statement that reflected the idea's overall knowledge content.

To address the concerns about grade-level appropriateness, the committee solicited additional comments from six experts in science learning in grades K-5. Based on this feedback and review of the document by committee members with expertise in elementary school science, some core ideas or component ideas were excluded at the K-2 level, with development of these ideas beginning instead in the 3-5 grade band.

ORGANIZATIONS THAT CONVENED DISCUSSION/FOCUS GROUPS

Achieve, Inc.
American Association of Physics Teachers, American Physical Society,
    American Institute of Physics
American Astronomical Society Astronomy Education Board
American Chemical Society
American Geological Institute
American Geophysical Union
American Society of Plant Biologists
Association for Computing Machinery
Association for Science Teacher Education
Biotechnology Institute
Climate Literacy Network
Computer Science Teachers Association
Council of Elementary Science International
Council of State Science Supervisors (45 state representatives in 8 groups)
Einstein Fellows
Hands-On Science Partnership
International Technology and Engineering Education Association
Massachusetts Department of Education
Minnesota Department of Education
NASA Science Education and Public Outreach

NASA Science Mission Directorate Education Community
National Association of Biology Teachers
National Association of Geoscience Teachers
National Association of Research in Science Teaching
National Earth Science Teachers Association
National Middle Level Science Teachers Association
National Science Education Leaders Association
National Science Teachers Association (100 people in 4 groups across the country)
New Hampshire Department of Education
North American Association for Environmental Education
Rhode Island Department of Elementary and Secondary Education
Triangle Coalition
University of Colorado at Boulder Biology Educators Group
University of Washington, Seattle
Vermont Department of Education
Wisconsin Department of Public Instruction

REFERENCES

1. National Research Council. (1996). *National Science Education Standards.* National Committee for Science Education Standards and Assessment. Washington, DC: National Academy Press.
2. National Academy of Engineering. (2010). *Standards for K-12 Engineering Education?* Committee on Standards for K–12 Engineering Education. Washington, DC: The National Academies Press.
3. National Academy of Engineering and National Research Council. (2009). *Engineering in K-12 Education: Understanding the Status and Improving the Prospects.* Committee on K-12 Engineering Education. Washington, DC: The National Academies Press.

B

BIBLIOGRAPHY OF REFERENCES CONSULTED ON TEACHING AND LEARNING

The committee consulted a variety of references throughout the development of the framework, not all of which are cited explicitly in the report itself. This appendix lists some of the additional references the committee used to develop the practices, crosscutting concepts, and core ideas and to construct the grade band endpoints. This is certainly not an exhaustive list of all of the references relevant to teaching and learning in science. Rather, it is intended to provide a sense of the range of research literature the committee considered.

REFERENCES FOR PRACTICES

In addition to those references cited in Chapter 3, the following references were consulted to inform the committee's selection of practices, the definitions for what the practices can look like in the classroom, and the committee's arguments about the feasibility of young learners engaging in scientific practices.

Berland, L.K., and McNeill, K.L. (2010). A learning progression for scientific argumentation: Understanding student work and designing supportive instructional contexts. *Science Education, 94*(5), 765-793.

Berland, L.K., and Reiser, B.J. (2009). Making sense of argumentation and explanation. *Science Education, 93*(1), 26-55.

Berland, L.K., and Reiser, B.J. (2011). Classroom communities' adaptations of the practice of scientific argumentation. *Science Education, 95*(2), 191-216.

Lehrer, R., and Schauble, L. (2006). Scientific thinking and science literacy: Supporting development in learning in contexts. In W. Damon, R.M. Lerner, K.A. Renninger, and I.E. Sigel (Eds.), *Handbook of Child Psychology, Sixth Edition* (vol. 4). Hoboken, NJ: John Wiley and Sons.

Lehrer, R., Schauble, L., and Lucas, D. (2008). Supporting development of the epistemology of inquiry. *Cognitive Development, 23*(4), 512-529.

Metz, K.E. (2004). Children's understanding of scientific inquiry: Their conceptualization of uncertainty in investigations of their own design. *Cognition and Instruction, 22*(2), 219-290.

Metz, K.E. (2008). Narrowing the gulf between the practices of science and the elementary school science classroom. *Elementary School Journal, 109*(2), 138-161.

Osborne, J., Erduran, S., and Simon, S. (2004). Enhancing the quality of argumentation in school science. *Journal of Research in Science Teaching, 41*(10), 994-1,020.

Sampson, V., and Clark, D. (2008). Assessment of the ways students generate arguments in science education: Current perspectives and recommendations for future directions. *Science Education, 92*, 447-472.

Schwarz, C.V., Reiser, B.J., Davis, E.A., Kenyon, L., Acher, A., Fortus, D., Shwartz, Y., Hug, B., and Krajcik, J. (2009). Developing a learning progression for scientific modeling: Making scientific modeling accessible and meaningful for learners. *Journal of Research in Science Teaching, 46*(6), 632-654.

Schwarz, C.V., Reiser, B.J., Kenyon, L.O., Acher, A., and Fortus, D. (in press). Issues and challenges in defining a learning progression for scientific modeling. In A. Alonzo and A.W. Gotwals (Eds.), *Learning Progressions for Science.* Boston, MA: Sense.

Simon, S., Erduran, S., and Osborne, J. (2006). Learning to teach argumentation: Research and development in the science classroom. *International Journal of Science Education, 28*(2-3), 235-260.

Windschitl, M., Thompson, J., and Braaten, M. (2008). Beyond the scientific method: Model-based inquiry as a new paradigm of preference for school science investigations. *Science Education, 92*(5), 941-967.

REFERENCES FOR DISCIPLINARY CORE IDEAS

The committee consulted the references below to inform the development of the core ideas and their components and to develop the grade band endpoints. The research evidence was considered to determine which ideas students might be able to engage with at a given grade band given appropriate instructional support, as well as where they might have difficulty or hold preconceptions that conflict with scientific explanations. The committee also reviewed draft documents from the Massachusetts Department of Education compiled to support science standards that are informed by research on learning progressions.

Physical Sciences

Ashbrook, P. (2008). Air is a substance. *Science and Children, 46*(4), 12-13.

Feher, E., and Rice, K. (2006). Shadows and anti-images: Children's conceptions of light and vision II. *Science Education, 72*(5), 637-649.

Haupt, G.W. (2006). Concepts of magnetism held by elementary school children. *Science Education, 36*(3), 162-168.

Lehrer, R., Schauble, L., Strom, D., and Pligge, M. (2001). Similarity of form and substance: From inscriptions to models. In D. Klahr and S. Carver (Eds.), *Cognition and Instruction: 25 Years of Progress* (pp. 39-74). Mahwah, NJ: Lawrence Erlbaum Associates.

Palmeri, A., Cole, A., DeLisle, S., Erickson, S., and Janes, J. (2008). What's the matter with teaching children about matter? *Science and Children, 46*(4), 20-23.

Smith, C.L., Solomon, G.E.A., and Carey, S. (2005). Never getting to zero: Elementary school students' understanding of the infinite divisibility of number and matter. *Cognitive Psychology, 51*, 101-140.

Smith, C.L., Wiser, M., Anderson, C.W., and Krajcik, J. (2006). Implications of research on children's learning for standards and assessment: A proposed learning progression for matter and the atomic molecular theory. *Measurement: Interdisciplinary Research and Perspectives, 4*, 1-98.

Stevens, S.Y., Delgado, C., and Krajcik, J.S. (2009). Developing a hypothetical multidimensional learning progression for the nature of matter. *Journal of Research in Science Teaching, 47*, 687-715.

Life Sciences

Barrett, J.E., and Clements, D.H. (2003). Quantifying path length: Fourth-grade children's developing abstractions for linear measurement. *Cognition and Instruction, 21*(4), 475-520.

Carey, S. (1986). *Conceptual Change in Childhood.* Cambridge, MA: MIT Press.

Carpenter, T.P., Fennema, E., Franke, M.L., Levi, L., and Empson, S.B. (1999). *Children's Mathematics.* Portsmouth, NH: Heinemann.

Catley, K., Lehrer, R., and Reiser, B. (2005). *Tracing a Prospective Learning Progression for Developing Understanding of Evolution.* Paper commissioned by the National Academies Committee on Test Design for K-12 Science Achievement. Available: http://www7.nationalacademies.org/BOTA/Evolution.pdf [June 2011].

Cobb, P., McClain, K., and Gravemeijer, K. (2003). Learning about statistical covariation. *Cognition and Instruction, 21*(1), 1-78.

Demastes, S.S., Good, R.G., and Peebles, P. (1995). Students' conceptual ecologies and the process of conceptual change in evolution. *Science Education, 79*(6), 637-666.

Evans, E.M. (2001). Cognitive and contextual factors in the emergence of diverse belief systems: Creation versus evolution. *Cognitive Psychology, 42,* 217-266.

Freyberg, P., and Osborne, R. (1985). *Learning in Science: The Implications of Children's Science.* Portsmouth, NH: Heinemann.

Gelman, S.A., Coley, J.D., and Gottfried, G.M. (1994). Essentialist beliefs in children: The acquisition of concepts and theories. In L.A. Hirschfield and S.A. Gelman (Eds.), *Mapping the Mind: Domain Specificity in Cognition and Psychology Reader* (pp. 222-244). New York: New York University Press.

Golan Duncan, R., Rogat, A., and Yarden, A. (2009). A learning progression for deepening students' understandings of modern genetics across the 5th-10th grades. *Journal of Research in Science Teaching, 46,* 655-674.

Kanter, D.E. (2010). Doing the project and learning the content: Designing project-based science curricula for meaningful understanding. *Science Education, 94*(3), 525-551.

Kelemen, D., Widdowson, D., Posner, T., Brown, A.L., and Casler, K. (2003). Teleo-functional constraints on preschool children's reasoning about living things. *Developmental Science, 6*(3), 329-345.

Kyza, E.A. (2009). Middle-school students' reasoning about alternative hypotheses in a scaffolded, software-based inquiry investigation. *Cognition and Instruction, 27*(4), 277-311.

Leach, J., Driver, R., Scott, P., and Wood-Robinson, C. (1995). Children's ideas about ecology 1: Theoretical background, design, and methodology. *International Journal of Science Education, 17*(6), 721-732.

Leach, J., Driver, R., Scott, P., and Wood-Robinson, C. (1996). Children's ideas about ecology 2: Ideas found in children aged 5-16 about the cycling of matter. *International Journal of Science Education, 18*(1), 19-34.

Lehrer, R., and Schauble, L. (2000). Inventing data structures for representational purposes: Elementary grade students' classification models. *Mathematical Thinking and Learning, 2*(1&2), 51-74.

Lehrer, R., and Schauble, L. (2004). Modeling natural variation through distribution. *American Educational Research Journal, 41*(3), 635-679.

Lehrer, R., and Schauble, L. (2010a). *Seeding Evolutionary Thinking by Engaging Children in Modeling Its Foundations.* Paper presented at the Annual Conference of the National Association for Research on Science Teaching.

Lehrer, R., and Schauble, L. (2010b). What kind of explanation is a model? In M.K. Stein and L. Kucan (Eds.), *Instructional Explanations in the Disciplines* (pp. 9-22). New York: Springer.

Lehrer, R., Carpenter, S., Schauble, L., and Putz, A. (2000). The inter-related development of inscriptions and conceptual understanding. In P. Cobb, E. Yackel, and K. McClain (Eds.), *Symbolizing and Communicating in Mathematics Classrooms: Perspectives on Discourse, Tools, and Instructional Design* (pp. 325-360). Mahwah, NJ: Lawrence Erlbaum Associates.

Lehrer, R., Jaslow, L., and Curtis, C. (2003). Developing an understanding of measurement in the elementary grades. In D.H. Clements and G. Bright (Eds.), *Learning and Teaching Measurement: 2003 Yearbook* (pp. 100-121). Reston, VA: National Council of Teachers of Mathematics.

Manz, E. (2010, March). *Representational Work in Classrooms: Negotiating Material Redescription, Amplification, and Explanation.* Poster presented at the Annual Meeting of the National Association for Research in Science Teaching, Philadelphia.

Metz, K.E. (2000). Young children's inquiry in biology: Building the knowledge bases to empower independent inquiry. In J. Minstrell and E.H. van Zee (Eds.), *Inquiring into Inquiry Learning and Teaching in Science.* Washington, DC: American Association for the Advancement of Science.

Metz, K.E., Sisk-Hilton, S., Berson, E., and Ly, U. (2010). *Scaffolding Children's Understanding of the Fit Between Organisms and Their Environment in the Context of the Practices of Science.* Paper presented at the 9th International Conference of the Learning Sciences, June 29-July 2, Chicago.

Mohan, L., Chen, J., and Anderson, C.W. (2009). Developing a multi-year learning progression for carbon cycling in socioecological systems. *Journal of Research in Science Teaching, 46*(6), 675-698. (This reference also informed the earth and space sciences ideas.)

Passmore, C., and Stewart, J. (2002). A modeling approach to teaching evolutionary biology in high schools. *Journal of Research in Science Teaching, 39*(3), 185-204.

Sandoval, W.A., and Reiser, B.J. (2004). Explanation-driven inquiry: Integrating conceptual and epistemic scaffolds for scientific inquiry. *Science Education, 88*(3), 345-372.

Shtulman, A. (2006). Qualitative differences between naïve and scientific theories of evolution. *Cognitive Psychology, 52*, 170-194.

Smith, C.L., Wiser, M., Anderson, C.W., and Krajcik, J. (2006). Implications of research on children's learning for standards and assessment: A proposed learning progression for matter and atomic-molecular theory. *Measurement, 14*(1&2), 1-98.

Tabak, I., and Reiser, B.J. (2008). Software-realized inquiry support for cultivating a disciplinary stance. *Pragmatics and Cognition, 16*(2), 307-355.

Zuckerman, G.A., Chudinova, E.V., and Khavkin, E.E. (1998). Inquiry as a pivotal element of knowledge acquisition within the Vygotskian paradigm: Building a science curriculum for the elementary school. *Cognition and Instruction, 16*(2), 201-233.

Earth and Space Sciences

Anderson, C.W. (March, 2010). *Learning Progressions for Environmental Science Literacy.* Paper prepared for the National Research Council Committee to Develop a Conceptual Framework to Guide K-12 Science Education Standards. Available: http://www7.nationalacademies.org/bose/Anderson_Framework_Paper.pdf [June 2011].

Harris, P. (2000). On not falling down to Earth: Children's metaphysical questions. In K. Rosengren, C. Johnson, and P. Harris (Eds.), *Imagining the Impossible: The Development of Scientific and Religious Thinking in Contemporary Society* (pp. 157-178). New York: Cambridge University Press.

Hogan, K., and Fisherkeller, J. (1996). Representing students' thinking about nutrient cycling in ecosystems: Bio-dimensional coding of a complex topic. *Journal of Research in Science Teaching, 33,* 941-970.

Leach, J., Driver, R., Scott, P., and Wood-Robinson, C. (1996). Children's ideas about ecology 2: Ideas found in children aged 5-16 about the cycling of matter. *International Journal of Science Education, 18,* 19-34.

Lehrer, R., and Pritchard, C. (2003). Symbolizing space into being. In K. Gravemeijer, R. Lehrer, L. Verschaffel, and B. Van Oers (Eds.), *Symbolizing, Modeling, and Tool Use in Mathematics Education* (pp. 59-86). Dordrecht, the Netherlands: Kluwer.

Lehrer, R., and Romberg, T. (1996). Exploring children's data modeling. *Cognition and Instruction, 14,* 69-108.

Lehrer, R., Schauble, L., and Lucas, D. (2008). Supporting development of the epistemology of inquiry. *Cognitive Development, 23*(4), 512-529.

Liben, L.S. (2009). The road to understanding maps. *Current Directions in Psychological Science, 18*(6), 310-315.

Panagiotaki, G., Nobes, G., and Banerjee, R. (2006). Is the world round or flat? Children's understanding of the Earth. *European Journal of Developmental Psychology, 3,* 124-141.

Rapp, D., and Uttal, D.H. (2006). Understanding and enhancing visualizations: Two modes of collaboration between earth science and cognitive science. In C. Manduca and D. Mogk (Eds.), *Earth and Mind: How Geologists Think and Learn about the Earth.* Denver, CO: Geological Society of America.

Schauble, L., Glaser, R., Duschl, R., Schulze, S., and John, J. (1995). Students' understanding of the objectives and procedures of experimentation in the science classroom. *Journal of the Learning Sciences, 4*(2), 131-166.

Uttal, D.H. (2005). Spatial symbols and spatial thought: Cross-cultural, developmental, and historical perspectives on the relation between map use and spatial cognition. In L. Namy (Ed.), *Symbol Use and Symbolic Representation: Developmental and Comparative Perspectives* (pp. 3-23). Mahwah, NJ: Lawrence Erlbaum Associates.

Uttal, D.H., Fisher, J.A., and Taylor, H.A. (2006). Words and maps: Children's mental models of spatial information acquired from maps and from descriptions. *Developmental Science, 9*(2), 221-235.

Vosniadou, S., and Brewer, W. (1994). Mental models of the day and night cycle. *Cognitive Science, 18*, 123-183.

Vosniadou, S., Skopeliti, I., and Ikospentaki, K. (2004). Modes of knowing and ways of reasoning in elementary astronomy. *Cognitive Development, 19*, 203-222.

Vosniadou, S., Skopeliti, I., and Ikospentaki, K. (2005). Reconsidering the role of artifacts in reasoning: Children's understanding of the globe as a model of the Earth. *Learning and Instruction, 15*, 333-351.

Windschitl, M., and Thompson, J. (2006). Transcending simple forms of school science investigation: Can pre-service instruction foster teachers' understandings of model-based inquiry? *American Educational Research Journal, 43*(4), 783-835.

Wiser, M. (1988). The differentiation of heat and temperature: History of science and novice-expert shift. In S. Strauss (Ed.), *Ontogeny, Phylogeny, and Historical Development* (pp. 28-48). Norwood, NJ: Ablex.

Wiser, M., and Amin, T.G. (2001). Is heat hot? Inducing conceptual change by integrating everyday and scientific perspectives on thermal phenomena. *Learning and Instruction, 11*(4&5), 331-355.

Engineering, Technology, and Applications of Science

Bolger, M., Kobiela, M., Weinberg, P., and Lehrer, R. (2009). *Analysis of Children's Mechanistic Reasoning about Linkages and Levers in the Context of Engineering Design.* Paper presented at the American Society for Engineering Education (ASEE) Annual Conference and Exposition, June, Austin, TX.

Kolodner, J.L. (2009). *Learning by Design's Framework for Promoting Learning of 21st Century Skills.* Presentation to the National Research Council Workshop on Exploring the Intersection of Science Education and the Development of 21st Century Skills. Available: http://www7.nationalacademies.org/bose/Kolodner_21st_Century_Presentation.pdf [June 2011].

Kolodner, J.L., Camp, P.J., Crismond, D., Fasse, B.B., Gray, J., Holbrook, J., and Ra, M. (2003). Promoting deep science learning through case-based reasoning: Rituals and practices in Learning by Design classrooms. In N.M. Seel (Ed.), *Instructional Design: International Perspectives.* Mahwah, NJ: Lawrence Erlbaum Associates.

Lehrer, R., and Schauble, L. (1998). Reasoning about structure and function: Children's conceptions of gears. *Journal of Research in Science Teaching, 35*(1), 3-25.

Lehrer, R., and Schauble, L. (2000). Inventing data structures for representational purposes: Elementary grade students' classification models. *Mathematical Thinking and Learning, 2*(1&2), 51-74.

Penner, D., Giles, N.D., Lehrer, R., and Schauble, L. (1997). Building functional models: Designing an elbow. *Journal of Research in Science Teaching, 34*(2), 125-143.

Penner, D.E., Lehrer, R., and Schauble, L. (1998). From physical models to biomechanical systems: A design-based modeling approach. *Journal of the Learning Sciences, 7*(3&4), 429-449.

Petrosino, A.J. (2004). Integrating curriculum, instruction, and assessment in project-based instruction: A case study of an experienced teacher. *Journal of Science Education and Technology, 13(*4), 447-460.

Schauble, L. (1990). Belief revision in children: The role of prior knowledge and strategies for generating evidence. *Journal of Experimental Child Psychology, 49*(1), 31-57.

Schauble, L., Klopfer, L.E., and Raghavan, K. (1991). Students' transition from an engineering to a science model of experimentation. *Journal of Research in Science Teaching, 28(*9), 859-882.

C

BIOGRAPHICAL SKETCHES OF COMMITTEE MEMBERS AND STAFF

Helen R. Quinn (*Chair*) is professor emerita of physics at SLAC National Accelerator Laboratory. A theoretical physicist, she was elected to the National Academy of Sciences in 2003 and was president of the American Physical Society in 2004. In addition to her scholarship in physics, she has had long-term involvement in science education and in the continuing education of science teachers. She was an active contributor to the California State Science Standards development process. She is a former president and founder of the nonprofit Contemporary Physics Education Project. She served as chair of the Review and Evaluation of the Pre-College Education Program Committee of the National Aeronautics and Space Administration. At the National Research Council, she was a member of the Committee on Science Learning, K-8; the Federal Coordinating Committee on Science, Mathematics, and Technology Education; and the Center for Education Advisory Board. She has a Ph.D. in physics from Stanford University (1967).

Wyatt W. Anderson is the alumni foundation distinguished professor in the Genetics Department at the University of Georgia. He is a member of the National Academy of Sciences. His research interests include evolutionary genetics of mating behavior and chromosomal polymorphisms of the *Drosophila* species, evolutionary genomics of *Drosophila*, and science education and minority participation in college science curricula. At the National Research Council, he has served on a number of committees, including the Committee to Review Northeast Fishery Stock Assessments and the Committee on the Release of Genetically Engineered Organisms into the Environment. He has a B.S. in molecular evolution and an M.S. in population genetics and population biology from the University of Georgia and a Ph.D. in science literacy and education from Rockefeller University.

Tanya Atwater is professor of tectonics at the University of California, Santa Barbara. She was elected to the National Academy of Sciences in 1997. Her research has concerned various aspects of tectonics, ranging from the fine details of sea floor spreading processes to global aspects of plate tectonics. She has participated in or led numerous oceanographic expeditions in the Pacific and Atlantic Oceans, including 12 dives to the deep sea floor in the tiny submersible, Alvin. She is especially well known for her works on the plate tectonic history of western North America, in general, and of the San Andreas fault system, in particular. She is devoted to science communication, teaching students at all levels in the university, presenting numerous workshops and field trips for K-12 teachers, and consulting for the written media, museums, television, and video producers. She is a fellow of the American Geophysical Union and the Geological Society of America and was a co-winner of the Newcomb Cleveland Prize of the American Association for the Advancement of Science. She received her education at the Massachusetts Institute of Technology; the University of California, Berkeley; and Scripps Institution of Oceanography, completing a Ph.D. in 1972.

Philip Bell is associate professor of the learning sciences and the Geda and Phil Condit professor of science and mathematics education at the University of Washington. He pursues a cognitive and cultural program of research across diverse environments focused on how people learn in ways that are personally consequential to them. He directs the ethnographic and design-based research of the Everyday Science and Technology Group as well as the University of Washington Institute for Science and Mathematics Education, which cultivates innovative projects in P-20 education in science, technology, engineering, and mathematics between university groups and community partners. He has studied everyday expertise and cognition in science and health, the design and use of emerging learning technologies in science classrooms, children's argumentation and conceptual change in science, culturally responsive science instruction, the use of emerging digital technologies in youth culture, and new approaches to inquiry instruction in science. He is a co-leader of the Learning in Informal and Formal Environments Science of Learning Center (http://life-slc.org/) and is a co-principal investigator of COSEE-Ocean Learning Communities (http://cosee-olc.org/). At the National Research Council, he is a member of the Board on Science Education and co-chaired the Committee on Learning Science in Informal Environments. He has a Ph.D. in education in human cognition and development from the University of California, Berkeley.

Thomas B. Corcoran is co-director of the Consortium for Policy Research and Education (CPRE) at Teachers College of Columbia University. He has been a state policy maker, a designer of programs to improve teaching, a researcher, an evaluator, and an adviser to governors, state legislatures, foundations, and reform organizations. His research interests focus on the linkages between research and practice, the use of evidence-based instructional practices, the design of knowledge transfer systems for public education, the effectiveness of professional development, and the impact of changes in work environments on the productivity of teachers and students. He heads the Center on Continuous Instructional Improvement and Teachers College projects in Jordan and Thailand. At the National Research Council, he served on the Committee on Science Learning, K-8. Since 1998 he has taught policy analysis at the Woodrow Wilson School of International and Public Affairs at Princeton University. He has an M.Ed. from the University of London.

Rodolfo Dirzo is professor of biology at Stanford University. A tropical forest ecologist and conservation biologist, he has performed seminal work on evolutionary ecology. He carried out classical experimental studies on the ecosystem significance of biodiversity loss, fragmentation, and deforestation. He is a foreign associate of the National Academy of Sciences as well as a member of the Mexican Academy of Sciences and of the California Academy of Sciences. He has been awarded the Presidential Award in Ecology from the secretary of environment of Mexico. He was a Pew Scholar in Conservation and received its Outstanding Service Award: Teaching, Organization for Tropical Studies. He has M.Sc. and Ph.D. degrees from the University of Wales.

Phillip A. Griffiths is director emeritus and professor of mathematics at the Institute for Advanced Study, which he led from 1991 to 2003. He was formerly provost and James B. Duke professor of mathematics at Duke University and professor of mathematics at Harvard University. Over the last four decades, he has made crucial contributions in several fields, including complex analysis, algebraic geometry, and differential systems. He chaired the committee that produced the Carnegie Corporation report *The Opportunity Equation*. He served on the

National Science Board from 1991 to 1996. He is a member of the National Academy of Sciences and a foreign associate of the Third World Academy of Sciences. At the National Research Council, he has served as a member, ex officio member, or chair of the Mathematical Sciences Education Board; the Committee on Science, Engineering, and Public Policy; the Center for Science, Mathematics, and Engineering Education Advisory Board; and the U.S. National Committee for Mathematics; and he is currently a member of the Board on African Science Academy Development. He has an M.S. in mathematics from Wake Forest University and a Ph.D. in mathematics from Princeton University.

Dudley R. Herschbach is emeritus professor in the Department of Chemistry and Chemical Biology at Harvard University and professor of physics at Texas A&M University during the fall term. He is a member of the National Academy of Sciences. He won the 1986 Nobel Prize in chemistry jointly with Yuan T. Lee and John C. Polanyi for their contributions concerning the dynamics of chemical elementary processes. He has been a strong proponent of science education and science among the public and frequently gives lectures to students of all ages, sharing his enthusiasm for science and his playful spirit of discovery. He is engaged in several efforts to improve K-12 science education and public understanding of science. He is a board member of the Center for Arms Control and Non-Proliferation and is the chairman of the board for Society for Science & the Public. At the National Research Council, he has served on the Committee on Education and Employment of Women in Science and Engineering; the Panel for National Science Education Standards and Television Project; the Board of Overseers; and the Communications Advisory Committee. He has a B.S. in mathematics and an M.S. in chemistry from Stanford University. He has an A.M. in physics and a Ph.D. in chemical physics from Harvard University.

Linda P.B. Katehi is chancellor of the University of California, Davis. Previously, she served as provost and vice chancellor for academic affairs at the University of Illinois at Urbana-Champaign, the John Edwardson dean of engineering and professor of electrical and computer engineering at Purdue University, and associate dean for academic affairs and graduate education in the College of Engineering and professor of electrical engineering and computer science at the University of Michigan. She led the effort to establish the Purdue School of Engineering Education, the first department at a U.S. university focused explicitly on engineering education, particularly on K-12 engineering curricula, standards, and teacher education. She is a member of the National Academy of Engineering, a fellow and board member of the American Association for the Advancement of Science, chair of the nominations committees for the National Medal of Science and National Medal of Technology and Innovation, and a member of the Kauffman National Panel for Entrepreneurship. She is currently a member of a number of National Academies committees, the Advisory Committee for Harvard Radcliffe College, and the Engineering Advisory Committees for Caltech, the University of Washington, and the University of California, Los Angeles. She has an M.S. and a Ph.D. in electrical engineering from the University of California, Los Angeles.

Thomas E. Keller is a senior program officer with the National Research Council's (NRC's) Board on Science Education. In his current role, Keller is co-director of an NRC study committee that is developing a conceptual framework to guide new science education standards. In 2010, he was the vice president for education at the Biotechnology Institute in Arlington, Virginia. At the Institute, he was responsible for planning and implementing state leadership programs and teacher professional development programs, including the National Biotechnology Teacher Leader Program. In 2007, while a program officer at the National Research Council, he directed the development of the award-winning *Surrounded by Science: Learning Science in Informal Environments*. From 1986 to 2007, he held several positions in K-12 education, including director of secondary instruction and state science supervisor for the Maine Department of Education. He served a term as president of the Council of State Science Supervisors and of the Maine Curriculum Leaders Association. He was a member of the NRC's Committee on Science Education K-12 and the National Committee on Science Education Standards and Assessment, which produced the *National Science Education Standards*. Keller has also served on the National Science Teachers Association board of directors. He has an Ed.D. in science education from the University of Massachusetts and has experience teaching high school science.

John C. Mather is a senior astrophysicist at the U.S. space agency's (National Aeronautics and Space Administration) Goddard Space Flight Center in Maryland and is an adjunct professor of physics at the University of Maryland, College Park. He won the Nobel Prize in physics jointly with George Smoot for their work on the Cosmic Background Explorer Satellite (COBE). COBE was the first experiment to precisely measure the black body form and anisotropy of cosmic microwave background radiation, helping cement the Big Bang theory of the universe. He is also the senior project scientist for the James Webb Space Telescope. At the National Research Council, he was a member of the Board on Physics and Astronomy and the Committee on Physics of the Universe. He has a B.A. in physics from Swarthmore College and a Ph.D. in physics from the University of California, Berkeley.

Brett D. Moulding is director of the Utah Partnership for Effective Science Teaching and Learning, a five-district professional development collaborative. He was the director of curriculum and instruction at the Utah State Office of Education before retiring in 2008. He was the state science education specialist and coordinator of curriculum from 1993 to 2004. He taught chemistry for 20 years at Roy High School in the Weber school district and served as the district science teacher leader for 8 years. Moulding received the Governor's Teacher Recognition Award, the Presidential Award for Excellence in Mathematics and Science Teaching, and the Award of Excellence in Government Service from the Governor's Science and Technology Commission. He served on the Triangle Coalitional Board and the National Assessment of Educational Progress 2009 Framework Planning Committee and was the president of the Council of State Science Supervisors from 2003 to 2006. He has an administrative supervisory certificate from Utah State University; a B.S. in chemistry from the University of Utah, Salt Lake City; and an M.Ed. from Weber State University.

Jonathan Osborne holds the Shriram family professorship in science education at Stanford University. Previously, he was a professor of science education at King's College, University of London. His research focus is a mix of work on policy and pedagogy in the teaching and learning of science. In the policy domain, he is interested in exploring students' attitudes toward science and how school science can be made more worthwhile and engaging, particularly for those who will not continue with the study of science. In pedagogy, his focus has been on making the case for the role of argumentation in science education, both as a means of improving the use of a more dialogic approach to teaching science and improving student understanding of the nature of scientific inquiry. He led the project on Enhancing the Quality of Argument in School Science Education, from which IDEAS (Ideas, Evidence and Argument in Science Education) materials to support teacher professional learning were developed. He was one of the partners in the Centre for Informal Learning and Schools. He has a Ph.D. in education from King's College, University of London.

James W. Pellegrino is liberal arts and sciences distinguished professor and distinguished professor of education at the University of Illinois at Chicago (UIC). He is co-director of UIC's interdisciplinary Learning Sciences Research Institute. His current work is focused on analyses of complex learning and instructional environments, including those incorporating powerful information technology tools, with the goal of better understanding the nature of student learning and the conditions that enhance deep understanding. A special concern of his research is the incorporation of effective formative assessment practices, assisted by technology, to maximize student learning and understanding. At the National Research Council, he has served on the Board on Testing and Assessment and co-chaired the Committee on the Cognitive Science Foundations for Assessment, which issued the report *Knowing What Students Know: The Science and Design of Educational Assessment*. He recently helped the College Board build new frameworks for curriculum, instruction, assessment, and professional development in Advanced Placement biology, chemistry, physics, and environmental science. He has a B.A. in psychology from Colgate University and M.A. and Ph.D. degrees from the University of Colorado.

Stephen L. Pruitt is the chief of staff for the Office of the State Superintendent of Schools in the Georgia Department of Education. He is the current president of the Council of State Science Supervisors. Previously, he taught high school science for 12 years. He supervised the revision and implementation of Georgia's new science curriculum. The Georgia Performance Standards have taken the state in a new direction in education with an emphasis on conceptual learning and inquiry. In the position of director of the Division of Academic Standards, he supervised the implementation of all content areas' new curriculum. Currently, as the chief of staff for assessment and accountability, he supervises the development and operation of all state testing and adequate yearly progress determinations. He has a B.S. in chemistry from North Georgia College and an M.Ed. from the State University of West Georgia. He is currently completing a Ph.D. in chemistry education from Auburn University.

Brian Reiser is professor of learning sciences in the School of Education and Social Policy at Northwestern University. His research examines how to make scientific practices, such as argumentation, explanation, and modeling, meaningful and effective for classroom teachers and students. Reiser leads the MoDeLS project (Modeling Designs for Learning Science), to develop an empirically based learning progression for the practice of scientific modeling, and BGuILE (Biology Guided Inquiry Learning Environments), developing software tools for supporting students in analyzing biological data and constructing explanations. Reiser is also on the leadership team for IQWST (Investigating and Questioning our World through Science and Technology), a collaboration with the University of Michigan developing a middle school project-based science curriculum. He was a founding member of the first graduate program in learning sciences, created at Northwestern, and chaired the program from 1993 to 2001. He was co-principal investigator in the Center for Curriculum Materials in Science, exploring the design and enactment of science curriculum materials. At the National Research Council, he served on the panel authoring the report *Taking Science to School*. He also served on the editorial boards of *Science Education* and the *Journal of the Learning Sciences*. He has a Ph.D. in cognitive science from Yale University (1983).

Rebecca R. Richards-Kortum is the Stanley C. Moore professor of bioengineering at Rice University. She is a member of the National Academy of Engineering. Her work has focused on translating research that integrates advances in nanotechnology and molecular imaging with microfabrication technologies to develop optical imaging systems that are inexpensive and portable and provide point-of-care diagnosis. This basic and translational research is highly collaborative and has led to new technologies to improve the early detection of cancers and other diseases, especially in impoverished settings. Over the past few years, Richards-Kortum and collaborators have translated these technologies from North America to both low- and medium-resource developing countries (Botswana, Brazil, India, Mexico, and Taiwan). She served on the inaugural National Advisory Council for Biomedical Imaging and Bioengineering for the National Institutes of Health (2002-2007) and was elected fellow of the American Association for the Advancement of Science and Biomedical Engineering Society (2008). At the National Research Council, she served on the Committee on Being a Scientist: Responsible Conduct in Research. She has a Ph.D. in medical physics and an M.S. in physics from the Massachusetts Institute of Technology.

Heidi A. Schweingruber is the deputy director of the Board on Science Education at the National Research Council (NRC). She has worked in some capacity on most of the major projects of the board since it was formed in 2004. She served as study director for a review of the National Aeronautics and Space Administration's pre-college education programs in 2007 and co-directed the study that produced the 2007 report *Taking Science to School: Learning and Teaching Science in Grades K-8*. She co-authored two award-winning books for practitioners that translate findings of NRC reports for a broader audience: *Ready, Set, Science!: Putting Research to Work in K-8 Science Classrooms* (2008) and *Surrounded by Science* (2010). Prior to joining the NRC, Schweingruber worked as a senior research associate at the Institute of Education Sciences in the U.S. Department of Education where she administered the preschool curriculum evaluation program and a grant program in mathematics education. Previously, she was the director of research for the Rice University School Mathematics Project. She holds a Ph.D. in psychology (developmental) and anthropology and a certificate in culture and cognition from the University of Michigan.

Walter G. Secada is senior associate dean of the School of Education and chair of the Department of Teaching and Learning at the University of Miami (UM). Previously, he was professor of curriculum and instruction at the University of Wisconsin–Madison and the director of diversity in mathematics education. His research interests have included equity in education, mathematics education, bilingual education, school restructuring, professional development of teachers, student engagement, and reform. He was associate director and co-principal investigator of Promoting Science among English Language Learners (P-SELL) with a High-Stakes Testing Environment, associate director and co-principal investigator of Science Made Sensible, and a member of the university's social sciences institutional review board. He has worked on the development of a secondary school mathematics and science academy at UM. As director of the U.S. Department of Education's Hispanic Dropout Project, he was senior author of its final report, *No More Excuses*. He has a B.A. in philosophy from the University of Notre Dame and an M.S. in mathematics and a Ph.D. in education, both from Northwestern University.

Deborah C. Smith is assistant professor in the Department of Curriculum and Instruction at Pennsylvania State University. She teaches elementary science methods and graduate courses in science curriculum; the history, philosophy, and sociology of science; and science teacher knowledge. She is a former preschool and elementary school teacher, with a background in biology. Her research focuses on how teachers and young children build communities of scientific discourses and practices in the early years of schooling. She was the author and co-principal investigator on a 5-year grant to the Lansing (Michigan) School District and Michigan State University, in which grade-level groups of K-8 teachers studied scientific content, standards-based and inquiry-oriented curriculum design, research-based teaching practices, and their students' science learning. At the National Research Council, she served on the Teacher Advisory Council and was a consultant for the popular publication, *Ready, Set, Science!* She has a B.S. in biology from Boston University, an M.A.T. in science education from the Harvard Graduate School of Education, and a Ph.D. in curriculum and instruction from the University of Delaware.

D

DESIGN TEAM MEMBERS

PHYSICAL SCIENCES

Lead

Joseph Krajcik, University of Michigan, Ann Arbor

Joseph Krajcik is professor of science education and associate dean for research in the School of Education at the University of Michigan. He co-directs the Center for Highly Interactive Classrooms, Curriculum, and Computing in Education at the University of Michigan and is a co-principal investigator in the Center for Curriculum Materials in Science and the National Center for Learning and Teaching Nanoscale Science and Engineering. He has authored or co-authored many manuscripts and makes frequent presentations at international, national, and regional conferences. He is a fellow of the American Association for the Advancement of Science and served as president of the National Association for Research in Science Teaching in 1999. Krajcik taught high school chemistry before obtaining a Ph.D. in science education from the University of Iowa and has been a guest professor at the Beijing Normal University in China as well as the Weston visiting professor of science education at the Weizmann Institute of Science in Israel.

Members

Shawn Stevens, University of Michigan, Ann Arbor

Sophia Gershman, Princeton Plasma Physics Lab, Princeton, NJ, and Watchung Hills Regional High School, Warren, NJ

Arthur Eisenkraft, University of Massachusetts, Boston
Angelica Stacy, University of California, Berkeley

LIFE SCIENCES

Lead

Rodger Bybee, Biological Sciences Curriculum Study, Colorado Springs
Roger Bybee served as executive director of Biological Sciences Curriculum Study (BSCS) from 1999 to 2007. He also served as chair of both the science forum and the science expert group for the 2006 Programme for International Student Assessment (PISA). In addition, he worked on the 1999 *Trends in International Mathematics and Science Study* science lesson video study. His major areas of work have included scientific literacy, scientific inquiry, the design and development of school science curricula, the role of policy in science education, and work on international assessments, in particular PISA. He recently retired from BSCS but continues consulting and publishing on policies, programs, and practices for science education at local, national, and international levels. He has a Ph.D. from New York University and M.A. and B.A. degrees from the University of Northern Colorado.

Members

Bruce Fuchs, National Institutes of Health, Bethesda, MD
Kathy Comfort, WestEd, San Francisco
Danine Ezell, San Diego County Office of Education

EARTH AND SPACE SCIENCES

Lead

Michael Wysession, Washington University, St. Louis
Michael Wysession is associate professor of earth and planetary sciences at Washington University in St. Louis. An established leader in seismology and geophysical education, he is noted for his development of a new way to create three-dimensional images of Earth's interior from seismic waves. These images have provided scientists with insights into the makeup of Earth and its evolution throughout history. Wysession is co-author of *An Introduction to Seismology, Earthquakes, and Earth Structure*; the lead author of *Physical Science: Concepts in Action*; and co-author of the K-6 *Integrated Science* textbook program. He received a science and engineering fellowship from the David and Lucille Packard Foundation, a National Science Foundation presidential faculty fellowship, and

fellowships from the Kemper and Lily Foundations. He received the Innovation Award of the St. Louis Science Academy and the Distinguished Faculty Award of Washington University. In 2005, he had a distinguished lectureship with the Incorporated Research Institutions for Seismology and the Seismological Society of America. He has an Sc.B. in geophysics from Brown University and a Ph.D. from Northwestern University.

Members
Scott Linneman, Western Washington University, Bellingham
Eric Pyle, James Madison University
Dennis Schatz, Pacific Science Center, Seattle
Don Duggan-Haas, Paleontological Research Institution, Ithaca, NY

ENGINEERING, TECHNOLOGY, AND APPLICATIONS OF SCIENCE

Lead
Cary Sneider, Portland State University, Oregon
Cary Sneider is associate research professor at Portland State University in Portland, Oregon, where he teaches courses in research methodology for teachers in master's degree programs and consults for a number of organizations, including Achieve, Inc., the Noyce Foundation, and the state of Washington's Office of Public Instruction. He is currently co-chair of the planning committee to develop the National Assessment of Educational Progress's technology framework. He has taught science at the middle and high school levels in California, Maine, Costa Rica, and Micronesia. During the past 10 years, Sneider was vice president for educator programs at the Museum of Science in Boston and previously served as director of astronomy and physics education at the Lawrence Hall of Science, University of California, Berkeley. His curriculum development and research interests have focused on helping students unravel their misconceptions in science and on new ways to link science centers and schools to promote student inquiry.

Members
Rodney L. Custer, Illinois State University, Normal
Jacob Foster, Massachusetts Department of Elementary and Secondary Education, Malden
Yvonne Spicer, National Center for Technological Literacy, Museum of Science, Boston
Maurice Frazier, Chesapeake Public School System, Chesapeake, VA

INDEX

asking questions and, 54, 75, 76

assessment of skills in, 262

data analysis and interpretation and, 63

in engineering, 53, 54, 57, 75, 77, 206, 207, 208

goals, 75-76

graphical and pictorial representations, 51, 58, 61, 62, 63, 65, 66, 74, 76, 77, 93, 206

importance of skills in, 43, 208, 250

learning progressions, 76-77

mathematics and, 64, 74, 206

with models and computer simulations, 34, 45-46, 56, 57, 58, 63, 66, 77, 90, 92, 198, 206, 207, 208, 210, 252

oral, 75, 76, 77, 93

and pattern recognition, 65, 66, 86, 133, 183

in science, 53, 54, 57, 74-75, 77

statistical analysis, 14, 15, 51, 61, 63, 65, 66

tables, 61, 62, 63, 76, 77

teacher proficiency, 256-259

technology and, 75

venues for, 75

written, 74-75, 76, 77

Communication systems and devices, 136, 137, 202, 210, 214, 263, 342

Computer-Based Assessment of Science (CBAS), 263

Computer science, 10, 14-15, 299, 334, 336

Computer Science Teachers Association, 344

Computer simulations, 45-46, 56, 57, 58, 66, 92, 198, 210

Concepts of evidence (*see* Procedural knowledge)

Conservation of matter and energy, 84, 86, 94-96, 106, 108, 109, 110-111, 112, 120-121, 123, 124-126, 128, 148, 153, 154, 175, 222, 223, 226, 228, 230, 233-234, 236, 238

Constructing explanations

and argument from evidence, 68, 73, 251

cause-and-effect mechanisms, 67, 69-70, 86

data analysis and interpretation, 68

goals, 69

hypothesis formulation and testing, 43, 44, 45, 59, 60, 61, 62, 67, 76, 78, 79, 84, 87, 139

learning progressions, 69-70

modeling theories, 67, 68, 70, 79

Content knowledge, practices integrated with, 11, 78

Context for improving science education, 1, 7

Convection, 123, 124, 126, 179, 181, 182, 237

Core ideas (*see* Disciplinary core ideas)

Council of Chief State School Officers, 19

Council of Elementary Science International, 344

Council of State Science Supervisors, 18, 331, 344

Course structure, 12

Crosscutting concepts, 3 (*see also* Cause-and-effect mechanisms; Energy; Matter and energy; Patterns and pattern recognition; Scale, proportion, or quantity; Stability and change; Structure and function; Systems and system models)

importance, 83

interconnections with core disciplinary ideas, 30, 101

public feedback on, 341

research base, 30, 84

Cultural issues, 28 (*see also* Equity in education)

ecosystem knowledge, 307

storytelling and arguments from evidence, 29, 285-286, 287

Curriculum and instructional materials

framework impact on, 2, 321

implementation of framework, 246-249

important aspects, 247-249

integrating dimensions into, 2, 219, 230-240, 247, 338-339

research and development agenda, 316-317

standards and, 2, 321

D

Data analysis and interpretation

communicating findings, 63

constructing explanations, 68

engineering design, 51, 53, 62

goals, 62-63

learning progressions, 63

mathematical representation, 65-66, 91

organizing data, 61, 62

pattern recognition and, 51, 61, 62, 63, 65, 66, 94, 131, 197

science, 61

tools, 62

Databases and data sets, 62, 66

Designing solutions, 49 (*see also* Engineering design)

Development of framework (*see also* Public feedback on report; Vision for K-12 science and engineering education)

approach, 15-18

grade band endpoints, 151-152, 153-154, 155-157

human (anthropogenic) impacts on, 141, 155, 156-157, 166, 167, 184, 195

interdependent relationships in, 86, 140, 143, 150-152

introduced species, 152, 155, 167

matter and energy flows, 140, 147, 148, 150, 152-154, 189, 223

modeling/models, 93, 101, 153-154

patterns in, 86, 101, 152, 155

services, 166, 167

social interactions and group behavior, 140, 156-157

stability, 100, 152

structure and function, 150

Einstein, Albert, 64

Einstein Fellows, 344

Electric power generation, 128, 130

Electrical energy, 123, 125, 128

Electromagnetic force, 88, 109, 111, 113, 116, 117-118, 121, 123, 126, 127, 239

Electromagnetic radiation, 64, 112, 121, 122, 130, 133-136, 149, 188

Energy (*see also* Forces and motion)

binding energy in molecules, 109, 110, 111, 112, 239-240

cause-and-effect mechanisms, 125-126, 237

chemical energy, 111, 122, 123, 148, 223

in chemical processes and everyday life, 128-130

conservation of, 110, 120-121, 123, 124-126, 128, 148, 153, 154, 175, 223, 238

crosscutting concepts, 84

definitions of, 120-124

electric and magnetic fields, 64, 109, 121, 122, 133, 135, 239

electrical energy, 123, 125, 128

and forces, 126-127

grade band endpoints, 122-124, 125-126, 127, 129-130

kinetic (motion) energy, 110, 111, 121, 122, 123, 124, 126

mechanical energy, 122-123

modeling and mathematical expressions, 123-124, 126

patterns, 121

photosynthesis, 104, 128, 129, 130, 146, 147, 148, 153, 154, 180, 187, 189, 223

"producing" or "using" in everyday life, 128-130

scale of manifestations and, 121, 122, 123-124, 127, 238

in systems, 120-121, 123, 124-126, 128

terminology, 96, 122

thermal energy, 121, 122, 123, 125, 130, 136, 180, 181 (*see also* Heat)

transfer between objects or systems, 93, 110, 120, 121-122, 124-126

stored (potential) energy, 96, 121-122, 123, 124, 126, 127, 128, 129, 130, 221

Energy efficiency, 128-129, 130

Engineering and technology

defined, in K-12 context, 11-12, 202

distinguishing science from, 50-53, 62

goals, 55, 68-69

public feedback on, 336-338, 343

rationale for inclusion, 2

standards, 204

Engineering in K-12 Education, 23

Engineering design

argumentation and analysis, 48, 52, 72

cause-and-effect mechanisms, 87, 88, 98-99, 169-170

communicating information, 53, 54, 57, 75, 77, 206, 207, 208

creative process, 46-47, 49, 52, 68-69, 70-71, 206-208

data analysis and interpretation, 51, 53, 62, 207

defining and delimiting problems, 50, 54-56, 204-206

grade band endpoints, 205-206, 207-208, 209-210

investigations, 50, 59-61

learning progressions, 56, 70-71, 93

mathematics and computational thinking, 51, 65

matter and energy flows and, 95

models and simulations, 45-46, 50, 51, 57-58, 62, 65, 77, 93, 94, 206-207, 208, 210, 212

optimizing solutions, 208-210

and pattern recognition, 51, 70, 86

practices, 45-47, 49, 52, 58, 65, 68-69, 70-71

scale in, 89, 90-91, 206

systems and system models, 12, 30, 46, 50, 57, 86, 88, 94, 98-99, 128-129, 130, 133, 202, 204, 205, 206, 208, 214

Engineering–technology–science links, 32, 203

grade band endpoints, 211-212, 213-214

influences on society and natural world, 212-214

interdependence, 210-212

Epistemic knowledge and practices, 78, 79, 250

Equity in education, 28-29 (*see also* Cultural issues)

in assessments, 289-290

capacity to learn, 279-280

I

Ideal gas law, 57

Implementation of framework
  assessing individual student's understanding, 315
  assessing student engagement, 314
  assessment, 260-265
  coherence in the system and, 2, 244-245
  complexity of science education system and, 243-245
  core questions about, 312-315
  curriculum and instructional materials, 246-249
  key components of science education, 242-245
  learning and instruction, 250-255
  norms and practices, 314
  organizational barriers, 324
  preconceptions of students and, 313
  progression of student understanding, 313
  public feedback on, 340
  research and development agenda, 312-320
  teacher development, 255-260

Information acquisition and evaluation (*see* Reading science texts)

Instruction (*see also* Curriculum and instructional materials)
  building on prior interest and knowledge, 25, 26, 28, 59, 60-61, 83-84, 286-287, 302, 338
  inclusive, 283-287
  strands of proficiency and, 253-255
  on systems and system models, 94

Integrating dimensions
  in curriculum and instruction, 2, 219, 230-240, 247, 338-339
  grades K-2 endpoint and progression, 231-233
  grades 3-5 endpoint and progression, 233-236
  grades 6-8 endpoint and progression, 236-238
  grades 9-12 endpoint and progression, 239-240
  life sciences example, 220-223
  performance expectations, 218-230
  physical sciences example, 224-229, 230-240
  public feedback on, 338-339
  in standards development, 2, 218

International Technology and Engineering Education Association, 344

Investigations
  controls, 59, 61
  correlations, 61
  engineering design projects, 50, 59-61

goals, 59-60
hypothesis or model testing, 59, 61
kinds of, 61
learning progressions, 60-61
measurements and instrumentation, 59-60, 61
planning and implementation, 59-61

K

Kinetic (motion) energy, 110, 111, 121, 122, 123, 124, 126

L

Language (*see* Terminology and language of science)

Learning
  argumentation and, 250, 251, 255
  instruction approaches and, 250-255
  strands of proficiency, 251-255

Learning progressions
  argumentation and analysis, 34, 56, 73-74, 89, 220, 222, 223, 228, 229, 238, 239
  asking questions and defining problems, 56
  boundary statements, 34
  cause-and-effect mechanisms, 88-89, 223
  constructing explanations, 69-70
  data analysis and interpretation, 63
  designing solutions, 70-71
  for disciplinary core ideas, 33-34
  engineering design, 56, 70-71, 93
  evaluation and communication of information, 76-77
  framework vision, 10-11
  grade band endpoints, 33-34
  investigation planning and implementation, 60-61
  mathematics and computational thinking, 66-67
  model development and use, 58-59
  pattern recognition, 60, 66, 70, 86-87, 88, 101, 233
  for practices, 34, 56, 58-59
  prior conceptions and, 25, 26
  public feedback on, 343-344
  research and development agenda, 315-316
  scale, proportion, or quantity, 36, 90-91, 233, 238, 239
  systems and system models, 93-94, 230, 233, 235
  and understanding of science, 26

Learning Science in Informal Environments, 23, 252, 298

Life sciences
  cause-and-effect mechanisms, 140, 145, 157-158, 160, 161, 167

chemical reactions, 110, 111, 148
core ideas, 140-141 (*see also* Biological evolution;
    Ecosystems; Heredity; Organisms, living)
information resources for framework, 141, 349-351
patterns in, 139, 152, 155
public feedback on, 342
scale, proportion, or quantity in, 100, 139, 140, 143,
    144
Light, 70, 89-90, 104, 106, 112, 113, 114, 115, 116, 121,
    122, 123, 125, 128, 130, 131, 133-135, 136, 137,
    147, 148, 149, 151, 153, 174, 189, 222, 223 (*see
    also* Electromagnetic radiation; Photons; Waves)
Literacy, science (*see* Communicating information; Reading
    science texts; Terminology and language of science)

M

Magnets and magnetic fields, 116, 117-118, 121, 123, 127,
    181, 182 (*see also* Electromagnetic radiation)
Mass, 64, 90, 96, 107, 108, 109, 111, 114, 115, 116, 118,
    121, 123, 126, 174, 180, 227, 233, 234, 236
Massachusetts Department of Education, 344
Mathematical representations, 56, 57, 65-66, 86, 91
Mathematics and computational thinking, 49
    applications, 64-65
    communicating information through, 64, 74, 206
    data analysis and evaluation, 61, 62, 63, 65, 66
    engineering, 51, 65
    goals, 65-66
    learning progression, 66-67
    modeling, 51, 65, 66-67, 90, 94, 114, 116, 118
    and pattern recognition, 51, 64, 65, 66, 86, 94
    scale and, 91
    scientific investigation, 51, 64-65
    statistics and statistical analysis, 14, 15, 51, 61, 63, 65,
      66, 91
    systems and system models, 51, 57, 64-65, 67, 94, 126
    tools, 64-65
Mathematization, 16
Matter and energy (*see also* Energy)
    atoms and atomic theory, 34, 57, 64, 79, 86, 87-88, 89,
      92, 94, 96, 97-98, 100, 101, 103, 106-107, 108-109,
      110, 111, 112, 113, 114, 117, 118, 121, 122, 123,
      124, 125, 134, 135-136, 140, 143, 153-154, 173,
      225, 227, 229, 230, 233, 236-237, 238, 239-240,
      303

chemical reactions, 106, 109-111, 148
collision theory, 110
conservation of, 84, 86, 94-96, 106, 108, 109, 110-111,
    112, 120-121, 123, 124-126, 128, 148, 153, 154,
    175, 222, 223, 226, 228, 230, 233-234, 236, 238
crosscutting concepts, 84, 93, 94-96
cyclic, 96, 110
ecosystem transfers of, 140, 147, 148, 150, 152-154,
    189, 223
electrical attractions and repulsions, 107
engineering design and, 95
grade band endpoints, 108-109, 110-111, 113, 147-148,
    230-240
incorrect beliefs and misconceptions, 96
learning progression, 95-96, 230-240
models, 58, 95, 97-98, 106, 108, 109, 110, 153
molecules, 58, 86, 92, 94, 96-98, 106, 107, 108, 109,
    110, 111, 119, 120, 121, 123, 124, 125, 128, 129,
    130, 139, 140, 144, 145, 147, 148, 153, 154, 158,
    161, 223, 225, 227, 236-237, 238, 239-240, 303
nuclear processes, 88, 96, 106, 111-113, 116, 117, 118,
    128, 130, 134, 136, 173, 240
pattern recognition, 86-87, 106, 109, 223, 227, 228,
    230
performance expectations example, 224-229
periodic table of elements, 106, 109, 227, 239
stability and change, 109
state changes, 70, 107, 108, 109, 110, 226, 227, 231,
    232, 235-236, 237, 238
structure and properties, 106-109, 224-240
in systems and system models, 84, 92, 93, 94-95, 96,
    106, 110, 119, 120-122, 123, 124-126, 128-129,
    147, 148, 150, 152-154, 169, 179, 223, 239
terminology, 96
water cycle, 95
Maxwell's equations, 64
Measurement and units, 90-91, 205, 231
Measurement error, 63
Mechanical energy, 122-123
Milky Way galaxy, 174
Minnesota Department of Education, 344
Mitosis, 145, 146
Model-It, 59
Modeling/models (*see also* Systems and system models)
    assumptions and approximations in, 93, 94
    cause-and-effect mechanisms, 79, 86, 88, 93, 221, 229

communicating information, 34, 45-46, 56, 57, 58, 63, 66, 77, 90, 92, 94, 198, 206, 207, 208, 210, 252

computer simulations, 45-46, 56, 57, 58, 66, 92, 198, 210

conceptual, 56-57

constructing explanations, 67, 68, 70, 79

ecosystems, 93, 101, 153-154

energy, 123-124, 126

engineering applications, 45-46, 50, 51, 57-58, 62, 65, 77, 93, 94, 206-207

evaluation and refinement, 57, 59, 62

forces and motion, 93, 116, 117, 118, 127

goals, 58

heat transfer, 124

learning progressions, 58-59, 93-94

limitations, 56, 58

mathematics and, 51, 65, 66-67, 90, 94, 114, 118

matter and energy flows, 58, 95, 97-98, 106, 108, 109, 110, 153

mental, 56, 100

organisms, 93

purposes of, 94

reflecting on applications of, 78

reliability and precision, 93

scale and, 90, 100, 101, 122, 123-124, 127, 206

science applications, 57, 67

space science, 176

specifications, 93

theories, 67, 68, 70, 79

tools, 59

Molecules, 58, 86, 92, 94, 96-98, 106, 107, 108, 109, 110, 111, 119, 120, 121, 123, 124, 125, 128, 129, 130, 139, 140, 144, 145, 147, 148, 153, 154, 158, 161, 223, 225, 227, 236-237, 238, 239-240, 303

Momentum, 115, 116

Motion and stability (*see also* Forces and motion)
  grade band endpoints, 115-116, 117-118, 119-120
  interaction types, 116-118
  stability/instability in physical systems, 118-120

Mutations, 140, 143, 157-158, 159, 160, 161, 165

N

National Aeronautics and Space Administration
  Science Education and Public Outreach, 344
  Science Mission Directorate Education Community, 345

National Assessment of Educational Progress (NAEP), 141, 262, 263 (see also *Science Framework for the 2009 National Assessment of Educational Progress*)
  Technological Literacy Assessment, 263

National Association of Biology Teachers, 345

National Association of Geoscience Teachers, 345

National Association of Research in Science Teaching, 345

National Council for the Social Studies, 13-14

National Curriculum Standards for Social Studies, 13

National Earth Science Teachers Association, 345

National Governors Association, 19

National Middle Level Science Teachers Association, 345

National Research Council (NRC), 14, 23, 96, 242, 298, 312

National Science Education Leaders Association, 345

National Science Education Standards, 13, 16, 17, 23, 30, 91-92, 103, 141, 242, 301, 332, 340

National Science Teachers Association (NSTA), 18, 23, 30, 331, 345

Natural hazards, 170, 172, 191, 192-194

Natural resources, 161, 170, 171, 191-192, 195, 196, 197, 212, 213
  consumption, 195, 196

Natural selection, 141, 143, 161, 162, 163-164, 165, 166

NetLogo, 59

Neurobiology, 13, 143

New Hampshire Department of Education, 345

Newton's laws, 114, 115, 116, 118, 175

Nitrogen cycle, 180

North American Association for Environmental Education, 345

Nuclear processes, 87-88, 96, 106, 111-113, 116, 117, 118, 128, 130, 134, 136, 173, 240
  fission, 111, 112, 113, 128
  fusion, 111, 112, 113, 130, 173
  radioactive decay, 87-88, 111, 112, 113, 117, 118, 125, 178, 182, 183, 186

O

Ocean science, 334, 336

Orders of magnitude, 90

Organisms, living
  grade band endpoints, 144-145, 146-148, 149-150
  growth and development, 140, 145-147
  information processing, 149-150

matter and energy flows in, 130, 147-148, 220-223

models and representations, 93

performance expectations example, 220-223

structure and function, 96, 139, 140, 143-145, 147

system pespective, 92, 99, 107, 140, 143, 144-145, 147, 148

P

Parsimony, 48

Patterns and pattern recognition, 3

    analyzing and interpreting data, 51, 61, 62, 63, 65, 66, 94, 131, 197

    argumentation from evidence of, 71

    and asking questions, 55, 84, 85, 86, 236

    and cause-and-effect relationships, 86, 88-89

    in classification, 85, 86-87, 222

    cyclical, 98, 119, 176

    definition of concept, 84

    in earth and space sciences, 173, 174, 175, 176, 178, 182-183, 186, 187, 188, 191-192, 193, 195, 197

    energy, 121

    in engineering design, 51, 70, 86

    in forces and motion, 115, 116-117, 118, 119, 121, 127, 130, 173, 174, 175, 178, 181, 185

    of interactions, 115, 116-117, 118, 119, 121, 127, 130, 152

    learning progressions, 60, 66, 70, 86-87, 88, 101, 233

    in life sciences, 139, 152, 155

    mathematics and computational thinking and, 51, 64, 65, 66, 86, 94

    matter structure and properties, 106, 109, 223, 227, 228, 230

    natural resource use, 191-192

    in physical sciences, 106, 109, 115, 116-117, 118, 119, 121, 127, 130, 131, 132-133, 223, 227, 228, 230, 239

    representation of data and, 65, 66, 86, 133, 183

    scale and, 86-87

    in science, 47-48, 51, 78, 84-85, 86

    and stability/instability, 98, 99, 101, 118, 120

    systems and system models, 182-183, 188, 195, 229

Peer review, 71, 73, 74, 75, 78

Periodic table, 106, 109, 227, 239

Photoelectric effect, 122

Photons, 112, 122, 135

Photosynthesis, 104, 128, 129, 130, 146, 147, 148, 153, 154, 180, 187, 189, 223

Photovoltaic materials, 133, 136

Physical scale models and prototypes, 34, 46, 58, 63, 77, 90, 206, 207, 208, 252

Physical sciences (*see also* Energy; Forces and motion; Matter and energy; Motion and stability; Waves)

    cause-and-effect mechanisms in, 100, 103, 107, 112, 113, 114, 115-116, 125-126, 127, 132, 223, 229, 237

    core ideas, 103-105

    information resources for framework, 103, 349

    mathematics and computational thinking, 64

    patterns in, 106, 109, 115, 116-117, 118, 119, 121, 127, 130, 131, 132-133, 223, 227, 228, 230, 239

    public feedback on, 342

    scale, proportion, or quantity in, 103, 108, 109, 110, 111, 112, 114, 116-117, 118, 119, 121, 122, 238

    systems and system models, 103, 107, 110, 113, 114, 115, 116, 118-120

Plate tectonics, 97, 177, 178-179, 180, 181, 182-183

Political science, 13, 14

Practices of science and engineering (*see also* Modeling/ models)

    argumentation and analysis, 27, 44, 46, 48, 49, 52, 71-74

    asking questions (science) and defining problems (engineering), 49, 50, 54-56

    for classrooms, 49-77

    collaboration, 27, 53

    communicating findings, 53, 56, 57, 61, 62, 63, 65, 66, 74-77

    constructing scientific explanations, 49, 51, 67-68, 69-70

    content integrated with, 11, 25, 26-28, 43, 78-79

    crosscutting concepts and, 42

    data organization, analysis, and interpretation, 49, 51, 61-63, 65, 66, 68

    defined, 30

    design development (engineering), 45-47, 49, 52, 58, 65, 68-69, 70-71

    distinguishing science from engineering, 50-53, 62

    evaluation-based approach, 46, 53, 74-77

    goals, 55, 58, 60, 62-63, 65-66, 69, 72-73, 75-76

    inquiry-based approach, 30, 41, 44-45, 63

investigation planning and implementation, 45, 49, 50, 55, 59-61

learning progressions, 26, 34, 56, 58-59, 60-61, 63, 66-67, 69-71, 73-74, 76-77

mathematics and computational thinking, 49, 51, 61, 62, 63, 64-67

public feedback on, 340-341

rationale for, 41, 42-46

references consulted for, 347-348

reflecting on, 78-79

research and development agenda, 316

"scientific method" myth, 44, 78

spheres of activity, 44-46

standards and, 10

understanding how scientists work, 43-44

Pressure

and rock formation, 180

temperature and, 96-97, 107, 109, 112, 113, 180, 227, 237

waves, 131

Principles of the framework

building on prior interests and experience, 28

capacity of children to learn, 24-25

core ideas and practices, 25-26

equity in education, 28-29

knowledge and practice, 26-28

learning progressions, 26

Prior conceptions, 25

Prisms, 135

Procedural knowledge, 78-79

Programme for International Student Assessment (PISA), 141, 262-263

Proportionality, 90, 91, 110, 121, 123, 166

Psychology, 10, 13-14, 143, 212, 301, 334, 335, 336, 342

Public feedback on report, 18

audience, 333

connections to math and literacy, 339-340

content suggestions, 334-336

crosscutting concepts, 341

disciplinary core ideas, 341-343

diversity and equity issues, 340

earth and space sciences, 342-343

engineering and technology, 336-338, 343

implementation, 340

integration of three dimensions, 338-339

learning progressions, 343-344

life sciences, 342

organizations involved in, 344-345

overarching issues, 332-340

physical sciences, 342

purpose of document, 333

quality of writing, 333

quantity of material, 338

scientific and engineering practices, 340-341

Q

Quantities and quantitative relationships, 51, 65, 88, 89, 90, 91, 98, 106, 107, 115, 124, 126

Quantum physics, 64, 116, 122, 133, 135, 137

R

Radioactive decay, 87-88, 111, 112, 113, 117, 118, 125, 178, 182, 183, 186

Radiometric dating, 112, 113

Reading science texts, 53, 74, 75, 76-77, 258-259

Reasoning ability of young children, 24-25

Relativity, 64, 116

Reproduction, 140, 144, 145-146, 147, 151, 152, 157, 158, 159, 160, 161, 163-164, 165-166

Research and development agenda

accountability, 323-324

assessment, 314-315, 317-319, 323-324

core questions behind, 312-315

curricular and instructional materials, 316-317, 321

educational experiences, 313-314

implementation of framework, 212-220

key areas, 315-320

learning progressions, 315-316

norms and practices, 314

organizational issues, 324

practices, scientific and engineering, 316

preconceptions of student, 313

progression of student understanding, 313

standards influence, 320-324

teacher and administrator development, 319-320, 322-323

Rhode Island Department of Elementary and Secondary Education, 345

S

Scale, proportion, or quantity
  and cause-and-effect mechanisms, 88, 111, 113
  definition of concept, 84, 85
  in earth and space sciences, 169, 170, 173, 175, 178,
      179, 180, 181, 182-183, 186, 188, 238
  in engineering, 89, 90-91, 206
  and force and motion, 114, 116-117, 118, 175
  learning progression, 36, 90-91, 233, 238, 239
  in life sciences, 100, 139, 140, 143, 144
  and mathematics and computational thinking, 91
  measurement and units, 90-91, 205, 231
  and modeling, 90, 100, 101, 122, 123-124, 127, 206
  orders of magnitude, 90
  and pattern recognition, 85, 86-87, 186
  in physical sciences, 103, 108, 109, 110, 111, 112, 114,
      116-117, 118, 119, 121, 122, 238
  proportionality, 90, 91, 110, 121, 123, 166
  quantities and quantitative relationships, 51, 65, 88, 89,
      90, 91, 98, 106, 107, 115, 124, 126
  in scientific studies, 89
  spatial, 170, 179, 180
  and stability changes, 99, 100, 101, 114, 119
  and structure and properties, 86, 96-97, 103, 107, 109,
      110, 117, 143, 238, 239
  in systems and system models, 92, 182-183, 186, 188,
      230, 303
  temporal, 89-90, 99, 100, 112, 139, 169, 178, 180,
      182, 186, 188
Science (see also specific disciplines and practices)
  defined, in K-12 context, 11
  goals, 55, 69
  nature of, 334, 336
Science Anchors project, 23, 30
Science College Board Standards for College Success, 13,
      17, 23, 30, 141
Science education system
  coherence, 244-245
  complexity, 243-245
Science Framework for the 2009 National Assessment of
      Educational Progress (NAEP), 13, 16, 17, 23, 303
Skills (see Practices)
Social interactions and group behavior, 140, 156-157
Sociology, 13, 14, 212
Solar cells/energy, 50, 130, 134, 143, 211

Solar system, 117, 118, 169, 170, 173, 174, 175-176, 177,
      179, 180, 263
Sound, 104, 121, 122, 123, 124, 125, 130, 131, 132, 135,
      136-137, 231
Space sciences (see also Earth and space sciences)
  cause-and-effect mechanisms, 175, 176
  Earth's place in universe, 170, 173-174
  grade band endpoints, 174, 176, 177-179
  gravity/gravitational forces, 64, 88, 92, 100, 113, 116,
      117-118, 121-122, 123, 126, 127, 169, 173, 175,
      176, 179, 180, 181-182, 184, 185
  Kepler's laws, 175
  models/modeling, 176
  nuclear processes, 112, 113, 173
  planetary history of Earth, 100, 170, 176-178, 181-182
  rotation and tilt of Earth, 175-176
  scale in, 100, 173, 175, 178
  seasonal variations, 175-176
  solar system, 117, 118, 169, 170, 173, 174, 175-176,
      177, 179, 180, 263
  systems and system models, 118
  universe and stars, 67, 112, 113, 173-174
Speciation, 154, 155, 161, 165, 166, 167
Speed of light, 114, 115, 116, 134, 135, 136, 137
Spreadsheets, 59, 62, 63, 66
Stability and change
  cause-and-effect mechanisms, 98, 100
  dynamic equilibrium, 99-100
  in ecosystems, 100, 152
  feedback loops, 98-99, 101
  homeostasis, 119, 143
  patterns in, 98, 99, 101, 118, 120
  progression, 100-101
  scale and, 99, 100, 101, 114, 119
  in systems, 84, 98-99, 100, 101, 113, 114, 118-120,
      125, 126, 150, 152, 154-155, 169, 180, 239
Standards (see also National Science Education Standards)
  alignment with other K-12 subjects, 306-307
  and assessment and accountability, 2, 218, 323-324
  boundary statements, 301-302
  and curriculum and instructional materials, 2, 218, 321
  development, 2, 8, 19-20
  equity and diversity in, 280, 307-308
  and fragmentation of education, 10
  grade band progressions, 304-305
  grade-by-grade progressions, 305

T

Technology (*see* Communications systems and devices; Engineering and technology)

Temperature
  body, 145, 148, 149, 220, 223
  and chemical reactions, 110-111
  data sets, 62
  ecosystem impacts, 99, 151, 155
  and electromagnetic radiation, 134
  energy transfer and, 112, 113, 121, 123, 124, 126
  feedback loops, 99
  mean surface, of Earth, 68, 100, 188, 189, 198
  misunderstandings about, 313
  and motion of particles, 120, 121, 123, 124, 229, 238
  ocean, 185
  and pressure, 96-97, 107, 109, 112, 113, 180, 227, 237
  and stability in systems, 119
  and state changes in matter, 70, 107, 108, 109, 110, 226, 227, 231, 232, 235-236, 237, 238
  units and measurement, 91, 231, 313
  and weather and climate, 185, 186, 188

Terminology and language of science, 67, 74, 76-77, 95-96, 100, 101, 115, 122, 123, 128, 247, 258, 285, 286

Theory
  application of, 52, 79
  defined, 67
  modeling, 67

Thermal energy, 121, 122, 123, 125, 130, 136, 180, 181

Torricelli, Evangelista, 54

Trends in International Mathematics and Science Study (TIMSS), 141

Triangle Coalition, 345

U

University of Colorado at Boulder Biology Educators Group, 345
University of Washington, Seattle, 345

V

Vermont Department of Education, 345
Vision for K-12 science and engineering education
  core ideas, 2, 11
  goals, 8-10
  learning progressions, 10-11

limitations of framework, 11-15
practices integrated with knowledge, 11

Volume, 90, 97, 107, 108, 231, 233, 235

W

Water
  abundance, 185-186
  evaporation and condensation, 98, 104, 108, 184, 185, 233, 234, 235, 236
  cycle, 180, 184, 185
  grade band endpoints, 184-186
  matter and energy transfers, 96
  pattern recognition in, 185
  and surface processes, 179, 184-186

Waves
  amplitude, 132, 133
  cause-and-effect mechanisms, 132
  color reflection and absorption, 135
  electromagnetic radiation, 64, 112, 121, 122, 130, 133-136, 149, 188
  energy transfer/conversion, 131, 133, 136
  frequency, 132
  grade band endpoints, 132-133, 134-136, 137
  information technologies and instrumentation, 104, 130, 131, 132-133, 136-137, 342
  light, 70, 89-90, 104, 106, 112, 113, 114, 115, 116, 121, 122, 123, 125, 128, 130, 131, 133-135, 136, 137, 147, 148, 149, 151, 153, 174, 189, 222, 223
  modeling, 122, 132, 133, 135
  patterns, 130, 131, 132, 132-133
  photons, 112, 122, 135 (*see also* Light)
  properties, 131-133
  refraction, 132
  resonance, 131, 133
  seismic, 132, 181
  sound, 104, 121, 122, 131
  and structure and function, 131, 133
  in water, 132, 184
  wavelength, 125, 131-132, 134

Weak nuclear force, 88, 111, 112, 113, 116, 117, 118

Weather and climate
  Earth systems interactions and, 179, 180, 186-189
  El Niño Southern Oscillation conditions, 197
  feedback loops, 187

X

PHOTO CREDITS

Special thanks to the students and teachers of the following schools and school districts for inviting photographers and videographers into their science classrooms and for allowing the images of students' investigations to be included in this volume. We also acknowledge the diligent efforts of the schools' partner organizations as they seek to improve the quality of K-12 science education, both locally and nationally.

School/School District	Partner Organization	Pages
Hillside Public Schools (NJ) Linden Public Schools (NJ) North Penn School District (PA)	Merck Institute for Science Education (photos by Merck Photography Services)	32, 61, 126, 146, 238, 314, 323
Parkview School (IL)	Northwestern University's School of Education and Social Policy (photos by Jim Ziv)	133, 134, 249

Front cover (clockwise from top left): Sun and Earth, ©1999 PhotoDisc Inc., InterNetwork Media, Inc.; students of Japan's Osaka University operate spider shaped robots "Asterisk" © AFP/Stringer/Getty Images; young explorers, © iStockphoto; female scientist working with lasers while doing research in a quantum optics lab © Bigstock photo; herbal remedies ©1996 PhotoDisc, Inc. All rights reserved. Images provided by ©1996 PhotoDisc, Inc./Keith Brofsky; test tubes holding colored liquid, ©2003 Comstock Inc.

Pages: 1 (bottom right) iStockphoto; **9** TERC (all TERC images are video stills from the Talk Science Project); **24** Bigstock; **29** American Images Inc.; **47** Bigstock; **57** Science Museum of Minnesota; **64** iStockphoto; **68** TERC; **72** TERC; **85** Getty Images, photo by Fred Widall; **92** Fotosearch; **97** iStockphoto; **107** Bigstock; **114** iStockphoto; **117** iStockphoto; **122** NASA Goddard Space Flight Center Solar Dynamics Observatory, image AIA 304; **129** iStockphoto; **131** Fotosearch; **136** iStockphoto; **143** iStockphoto; **151** iStockphoto; **156** iStockphoto; **159** Fotosearch; **163** iStockphoto; **167** PhotoAlto; **172** NASA/JPL-Caltech; **174** NASA; **177** Tom Keller; **181** iStockphoto; **185** iStockphoto; **187** PhotoDisc; **189** iStockphoto; **194** iStockphoto; **206** iStockphoto; **208** iStockphoto; **213** Fotosearch; **229** TERC; **234** iStockphoto; **244** TERC; **253** TERC; **260** TERC; **263** TERC; **281** TERC; **284** Getty Images, photo by Susan Woog-Wagner; **288** Getty Images; **318** TERC.